FAMILY SYSTEMS THINKING

FAMILY SYSTEMS THINKING

Stephen J. Schultz, M.D.

Jason Aronson Inc.
Northvale, New Jersey
London

THE MASTER WORK SERIES

Copyright © 1984 by Jason Aronson Inc.

First softcover edition 1993

Library of Congress Cataloging-in-Publication Data *pending*

ISBN: 1-56821-145-7 (softcover)

Manufactured in the United States of America. Jason Aronson Inc. offers books and cassettes. For information and catalog write to Jason Aronson Inc., 230 Livingston Street, Northvale, New Jersey 07647.

To my teachers, with appreciation

About the Author

Dr. Schultz received his Ph.D. in clinical psychology from the University of California, Berkeley, in 1977, and then worked as a staff psychologist at the Veterans Administration Medical Center in San Francisco where he directed its Family Therapy Program. Since 1980 he has practiced psychology and family therapy in San Leandro, California. For the past 10 years Dr. Schultz has been on the adjunct faculty of the California School of Professional Psychology, Berkeley/Alameda, where he currently teaches courses on Principles of Psychotherapy and Modern Character Analysis and conducts an Advanced Clinical Seminar. His clinical and academic interests include the understanding and treatment of character disorders and psychosomatic problems from both systemic and psychodynamic points of view.

Contents

PART II
APPLICATIONS OF FAMILY SYSTEMS THERAPY

Preface

To learn systems thinking, one must initially be a systems purist. Learning family systems thinking is indeed like learning a new language. Those of us whose native tongue is English do not learn conversational French by switching to English to do our thinking in a familiar language and then translating back again into French. We learn to speak (and think) French by jumping in and speaking it.

For most of us, nonsystemic thinking is still our native tongue, despite the significant impact of family therapy since 1955. As with learning any foreign language, one learns family systems thinking by putting aside the old ways of conceptualizing and doing therapy, and instead, thinking and acting using this new language.

The task of integrating family systems thinking with the individual approaches upon which most of us still cut our teeth as therapists is a project best saved for later, after we learn to think systemically.

This two-step approach to learning family systems thinking is consistent with the biologically based principles for human development articulated by Heinz Werner (1948). Werner describes how, in the growth of organisms, differentiation precedes integration. This is certainly how the field of family therapy developed. The early polarizing emphasis on the distinctiveness and differentness of family therapy (perhaps most clearly expressed in some of the early writing of Jay Haley, e.g., 1962) was a necessary stage in successfully differentiating family therapy from the individual intra-psychic thinking that has dominated the mental health field since early in this century. Only now, some 25 years later, are we seriously ready to begin the task of integrating what family therapy has learned with older ways of viewing human problems.

A phrase I recall from an undergraduate psychology course expresses this parallel between the historical development of family therapy and how one should go about learning family systems thinking today. It is, "ontogeny recapitulates phylogeny," and it means that the growth of a particular individual organism retraces the evolutionary development of the species itself.

In this book, I initially concentrate on the first task, learning family systems thinking, and then (Chapter 9) describe a promising approach to the important task of integration.

This book is not a theoretical treatise. Although I emphasize the importance of systems thinking, my main goal is clinical train-ing: Teaching people how to do family systems therapy. My model for clinical learning is perhaps closer to that of medical education than of graduate school training. Clinical learning is essentially case-focused. The motto is: See one, do one, teach one. Students learn by observing senior students and teachers and through the close, live supervision of their own work by more experienced clinicians. The purpose is always to apply general principles and knowledge to the case at hand.

The heart of this book is its many case examples, ranging from brief narrative vignettes to extensive case studies supplemented by annotated transcripts of family therapy sessions in which theo-retical principles and clinical models are being applied to clinical data. The reader will, I think, be rewarded by investing the time and effort needed to follow the case narratives and transcripts closely.

Two caveats are in order here. First, this book is by no means a substitute for supervision. No one learns to do competent therapy of any kind only from reading books. Corrective feedback on one's own work is essential. Obtain good supervision, preferably live (i.e., with the supervisor actually watching the session live). Neither is this book a substitute for reading the masters. I have included an annotated list of additional readings at the end of the book, and you are urged to consult these sources.

The book begins with an overview of the field of family therapy today and, specifically, of family systems therapy. Chapter 2 ex-amines the roots of family therapy in the psychotherapeutic treatment of schizophrenics during the 1940s. By the middle 1950s, these early clinical efforts had produced four pioneering research programs focusing on schizophrenics and their families, thus launching the family therapy field.

The next seven chapters focus on family systems thinking and comprise Part I of the book. Chapter 3 introduces the reader to the basic theoretical principles underlying systemic thinking. Although the theoretical ideas presented in this chapter are crucial for learning family systems therapy, by themselves they are too general and abstract to be immediately applicable to clinical work. Riskin and Faunce (1972) made this point several years ago, when they exhaustively reviewed the related family interaction research literature and found the field "seriously handicapped by a lack of intermediate-level concepts" (p. 399).

The necessary middle-level thinking is supplied by the *clinical models* of the next five chapters. By the term model I mean a useful simplification. Both words are important. As a clinician I am not interested in a model unless it is useful in clinical work. To be useful clinically, a model must simplify the world, showing the therapist where to look and what to pay attention to. There is so much happening in a family therapy session (or an individual interview, for that matter) that without a model (explicit or implicit) the clinician can easily become overwhelmed, even paralyzed. Four family systems models developed by leading family therapists are described. Chapters 4 and 5 discuss Minuchin's structural model, applied to families and to couples, respectively. In Chapter 6, the developmental model described by Haley in his writings on Milton Erickson is presented. The strategic model articulated by Haley and by Watzlawick and his colleagues at the Mental Research Institute is outlined in Chapter 7. And Singer and Wynne's work is discussed in Chapter 8, on the transactional model.

In each of these chapters, a single basic concept underlying the model is presented, followed by a case example. Treatment techniques are discussed in the context of the models that guide their use.

A word about the transcripts of family therapy sessions is in order here. I have selected portions of the sessions which illustrate the concepts of each chapter. Each excerpt is presented as it happened, without further editing. Some of the therapy was done by trainees under my supervision, and in other cases I was the therapist. I have made no attempt to hide our bungled interventions, believing that one can learn as much from errors as from flawless performance. To provide maximum information for the reader, transcripts are as literal as posible, including hestitations and disruptions in speech and ungrammatical forms. Passages marked "unintelligible" in the transcript are due to poor audio quality or to the soft voice of the speaker. When necessary for the reader to follow the interaction, nonverbal behavior is noted.

The last chapter in Part I presents what I call *systemic psychopathology,* a new view of the psychopathology of the individual from a systems perspective. Using systemic psychopathology as a framework, I develop a second-order model to integrate the four (first-order) models of the previous chapters, and I describe its use in guiding the therapist's selection of the clinical models appropriate for a given family and phase of treatment.

Part II extends and applies the material of Part I. Chapter 10 is a practical nuts-and-bolts guide to implementing family systems thinking and the clinical models presented earlier. There the notion of the treatment frame, the overall context within which therapy is conducted, is introduced, and I examine how the therapist entices the family to join in the treatment process. The initial interview and the use of a treatment contract are also discussed, along with the place of cotherapy in family systems work. Finally, frames for training and for the practicing family therapist are presented. Chapter 11, a full-length case example of psychogenic vomiting in the adolescent daughter of a cancer patient, illustrates the application of all four first-order models, as well as the second-order model. Chapter 12 extends the application of systemic psychopathology to the task of integrating biological, psychological, and social explanations of an individual's disturbed behavior. Here the clinical problem is post-traumatic stress disorder in a Vietnam combat veteran. The clinical material provides an additional application of the strategic model of Chapter 7 and is used to generate a cybernetic model for post-traumatic disorder that is truly "biopsychosocial."

The book concludes with some comments on the process of systemic change in view of changes currently underway in the family therapy field, and with an outline for a new systemic psychology to guide future work.

This text is the end product of a lecture course on family systems therapy that I developed over the past six years. I hope the book conveys some of the freshness and enthusiasm I felt while lecturing on the material. I have tried to write in direct, spoken language, rather than in the prose of more formal texts, in order to recapture the spirit of those times.

Acknowledgments

This text was inspired by the great teachers I have had over the years, many of whom I knew long before ever hearing of family therapy. As an impressionable college freshman in an honors calculus course I was exhilarated the first day of class when Professor Pollak began by announcing that "mathematics is pure and naked beauty." In Dr. Giannone, my first-year English professor, I got my first glimpse of the teacher as a charismatic figure. And I will never forget Dr. Goerner who delivered beautifully composed lectures on comparative government dressed in an impeccable suit, white shirt, and black engineer boots. Later, as a graduate student in physics struggling to learn enough psychology to be admitted to a graduate program in clinical psychology, Phil Cowan's fine course on Piaget stimulated my interest in the field. Experiences such as these were, I think, the roots of my aspirations to become a teacher.

Four teachers have particularly influenced this book. The first two I have never met, but they inspired me nonetheless through their textbooks. As a college sophomore majoring in physics, I was thrilled to find that the author of our textbook, Richard Feynman, had just won the Nobel Prize in physics. Over the course of that year Feynman's wonderful *Lectures on Physics* (Feynman et al., 1963) continued to amaze me. Here was a great teacher as well as a brilliant physicist, one who could make his subject both clear and alive.

In my final year of graduate study in psychology, I read Irvin Yalom's (1975) *The Theory and Practice of Group Psychotherapy*. Yalom made his pages come alive, skillfully interweaving an original conceptual frame, which organized the entire field of group therapy, with the richness of his clinical experience.

Margaret Singer was my first great family therapy teacher. She taught me respect for my patients (the "customers," as she called them). Watching Margaret, I realized that clinical thinking occurs at a middle level of abstraction, somewhere between abstract theoretical notions and concrete clinical data. Her concepts (e.g., "shared focus of attention") were immediately sensible and easily grasped. Margaret insisted on focusing on the observable transactions between persons rather than on making inferences about internal psychological processes. And I saw that she was not only able to do clinical magic herself, but could also teach the rest of us some of her wizardry through her detailed analysis of transactional behavior.

Neil Scott gave me my first job after graduate school. He became the mentor who guided me through the at-times difficult transition from student to teacher and tutored me in the intricacies of life in a medical setting. As colleagues, we taught together, frequently observed each other's work, occasionally did cotherapy, and continually talked about family therapy. Throughout the book I attempt to credit Neil specifically where appropriate, but beyond that, I owe him two special debts of gratitude. First, he encouraged me to think and talk in purely systems terms, eschewing the more prevalent tendency to combine terms from all sorts of therapy vocabularies. And second, the idea of writing a family therapy textbook was Neil's. It was a project we had planned to do together until he left the San Francisco Bay Area for the mountains of Colorado.

The families I have treated and my colleagues and students have continually stimulated my thinking about family therapy and helped me develop and refine my ideas. To all of them, I am grateful.

I especially wish to thank colleagues who have read and commented upon all or parts of the manuscript: Phil Cowan, Shelly Korchin, Jim Kurkjian, and Ken Perlmutter. And I am grateful to Paul Mussen who tutored me in the fine art of finding a publisher and encouraged me when I needed it most.

1

The Current State of Family Therapy

Family therapy today is undergoing an important developmental transition. The field has handily survived its childhood and has emerged on the mental health scene as an important and viable treatment modality. But it suffers from a kind of adolescent identity diffusion. The growth of family therapy has been quite different from that of psychoanalysis, for example. That field began with a single, orthodox approach (Freud's) and developed as others (initially Jung and Adler, most recently analysts such as Kohut) abandoned the orthodox way. In contrast, from the very beginning a wide variety of approaches or "schools" of family therapy grew up, typically around a charismatic innovative figure. Perhaps in reaction to the psychoanalytic orthodoxy of the day, early family therapists prized the diversity of thinking in their field. For example, *Family Process*, under Haley's editorship, published an editorial (Haley, 1968) signed by 60 leading family therapists and arguing against a move then afoot to establish a national organization of family therapists:

> Until this time there have been no organizational restrictions upon what kind of theory should be allowed in the field. A family therapist was free to make use of whatever body of ideas seemed relevant to him with no fear of accusations of heresy from an organized group. . . . Rather than create a national organization at this time, we recommend that there be a delay of a few more years. Such a delay will allow the family field to continue an unrestricted development. (pp. 4–5)

Although the field has undoubtedly benefited from this early period of unregulated growth, the variety of approaches is bewildering to anyone attempting to learn family therapy. Particularly as a family therapy teacher and supervisor, I have felt the need for a more integrated view. And pedagogy aside, no field can remain in adolescent disarray forever. It is time for a mature integration.

Family Systems Thinking

This book does not include a survey of all family therapy approaches in use today, for several reasons. First, it has already been done (see, e.g., Bell, 1975; Erickson and Hogan, 1980). Second, such surveys tend, of necessity, to be too broad and general to be of much help in teaching people to actually do family therapy. And finally, as the reader will see below, I think that there is no "field" there. What is called "family therapy" does not really hang together.

Instead, I focus here on family *systems* therapy, that is, on those family therapies based upon systems theory. Here my thinking received a boost from Mara Selvini Palazzoli, an Italian psychoanalyst turned family therapist.

At its 1979 Don Jackson Memorial Conference, the Mental Research Institute (MRI) gathered together in San Francisco six of today's leading family therapists. In addition to Selvini Palazzoli, there were Murray Bowen, Jay Haley, Virginia Satir, Margaret Singer, and Carl Whitaker. On the last afternoon of the conference, all six were assembled into a panel moderated by Paul Watzlawick and John Weakland of MRI. During a particularly confusing debate on the question of individual versus family therapy, the audience was treated to a rare glimpse of the interactions among these famous family therapists. For example, Haley sat with his chair a few feet back from the table like the "bad boy" of the field he is reputed to be. Virginia Satir, seated next to him, tried to draw Haley in with a hug, insisting that her views were not really that different from his, after all. And Margaret Singer, in her usual clear manner, attempted to make some sense of the confusion.

Finally Mara Selvini Palazzoli, who up to this point had watched the spectacle, brought the house down by stating in her wonderful Italian-accented English: "Family systems is a way of thinking, not a garage for repairing families." Just as preachers use a biblical text around which they weave their sermons, Selvini Palazzoli's words are the text for this book.

In her inimitable way, Selvini Palazzoli expressed what I too had come to believe: Family systems therapy is first of all a way of thinking about human problems and only second a method of treatment.

Family systems thinking truly lies at the heart of family therapy. It was the new point of view introduced by the family therapy movement beginning in the middle 1950s. And systems thinking continues to have a pervasive influence on the entire field.

However, there is a lot of muddled thinking about systems. Some assume that because the therapist gathers the family members together in the same room it is necessarily systems therapy. Others mix and match family therapy approaches without regard to the compatibility of their underlying theoretical premises. The resulting conceptual muddle both hinders the further development of the field and complicates the learning and teaching of family therapy.

I regularly recommend that clinicians learning family systems therapy consult Haley's (1975) article, "Why a Mental Health Clinic Should Avoid Family Therapy." Written in the outrageous style that over the years has become his trademark, Haley nonetheless emphasizes the crucial point I have struggled to make here: Family systems thinking is a view of the world profoundly different from traditional individual approaches, and the failure to appreciate this difference leads both to conceptual quagmires and to practical problems.

The stress on clear systems *thinking* has a corollary in my belief that the field of family therapy has become too technique oriented. Family therapy training often overemphasizes techniques at the expense of helping therapists learn to think about their cases, assess them using appropriate models, devise a treatment plan that follows rationally from this assessment, and *then* decide which intervention techniques are appropriate. In other words, there is a lot of work to do with a given family *before* deciding which techniques to try.

It was gratifying to hear Minuchin make this point at a workshop (Minuchin, 1980) where he did a very humorous three-minute monologue about how one could take a workshop from therapist A and learn technique X, go to therapist B to learn technique Y, etc., and then come back and confuse the hell out of the families one is working with. The concluding chapter of Minuchin's latest book *Family Therapy Techniques* (Minuchin and Fishman, 1981) also discusses this issue.

Charting the Field of Family Therapy

If you were to ask a group of family therapists to name the practitioners they have heard of or read about, you would likely end up with a list like that shown in Figure 1. Particularly for a novice learning about the field, this is indeed a rather formidable array of names, representing a wide range of approaches to family work.

To bring some order to this diversity the therapists listed in Figure 1 have been grouped into what could be termed "schools" of family therapy. Most of these leading practitioners can be more or less adequately identified as psychodynamic, experiential, structural, strategic, or behavioral family therapists. Murray Bowen has his own school, with people now referring (e.g., Hoffman, 1981) to

Structural:	Salvador Minuchin, Ronald Liebman, Harry Aponte, Braulio Montalvo
Strategic:	Jay Haley, Richard Rabkin, Paul Watzlawick, Richard Fisch, John Weakland, Mara Selvini Palazzoli
Behavioral:	Gerald Patterson, Neil Jacobson, Robert Weiss
Experiential:	Virginia Satir, Carl Whitaker, Shirley Luthman
Psychodynamic:	Nathan Ackerman, Helm Stierlin, Ivan Boszormenyi-Nagy, James Framo
Bowen:	Murray Bowen
Network:	Carolyn Attneave, Ross Speck
(Pioneers):	Gregory Bateson, Don Jackson, Milton Erickson, Theodore Lidz, Margaret Singer, Lyman Wynne, John Bell

Figure 1. Schools of family therapy, with their well-known practitioners. Those listed as "pioneers" are the early leading figures in the field who are not closely identified with any particular current school.

"Bowenian family therapy." An additional group of "network" therapists is also identifiable—the therapists who routinely involve 30 to 50 persons in a session, including family members, neighbors, teachers, and the clergy. Madanes and Haley (1977) classify both Bowen and the network therapists as the "extended family systems" school. A final group of family therapists does not fit well into any of the current schools. I have parenthetically labeled these therapists "pioneers" because they are the early figures in the field whose work continues to be influential but who tend not to have a group of followers forming what we usually think of as a school of therapy.

Is it possible to further organize the complexity of the current family therapy scene? Madanes and Haley (1977) list seven dimensions along which family therapy schools can be classified: past versus present; interpretation versus action; growth versus presenting problem; method versus specific plan for each problem; unit of one, two, or three people; equality versus hierarchy; and analogical versus digital. In a recent, expanded version of this paper, Madanes (1981) adds an eighth dimension: straightforward versus deliberately paradoxical.

I have found it useful to select two of these dimensions, past–present and growth–presenting problem, to organize the schools of family therapy listed in Figure 1 into a two-dimensional map of the field (Figure 2). There the vertical dimension has to do with whether the therapy's main focus is on the present or on the past. Structural, strategic, and behavioral schools are all particularly present focused, while the psychodynamic approach is very much interested in the past. The horizontal dimension indicates whether the therapy is interested mainly in solving the presenting problem or in growth, defined more broadly (though often vaguely). At one extreme are the behavioral and strategic family therapists whose chief goal is solving the presenting problem. At the other are the experiential and psychodynamic schools, interested in growth in a broader sense. The pioneers of the field are symbolically located at the intersection of the axes, not because they necessarily fall at the center of each dimension, but rather because the midpoint suggests their place at the origin of the whole field and their influence across schools of family therapy.

Of course one could pick other dimensions as identified by Madanes and Haley and arrive at a slightly different map. And one might certainly quibble about the exact placement on the map of certain schools or particular therapists. What I wish to demonstrate

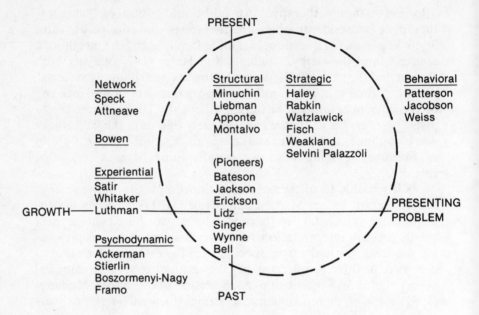

Figure 2. The field of family therapy today. The area within the circle indicates the position of family systems therapy within the field as a whole.

first is that it is possible to bring a bit of order to the current complexity of the field.

This map notwithstanding, the current family therapy field is anything but neat and simple. In fact, the real lesson of this whole exercise is that *there is no such thing as family therapy*. The field is so diverse and hangs together so precariously that we fool ourselves by pretending that it is a single field. We would more accurately reflect the reality of the current state of affairs by talking instead about family therapies. This way it is more difficult to fall into the erroneous belief that all family therapists speak the same language and would recognize each other's work as "family therapy."

I wish to make one more point using the map discussed above. The circled area in Figure 2 identifies the territory comprising family systems therapy, the subject of this text, and places family systems therapy among the various family therapies. Schools falling outside the area enclosed by the dashes have likely been influenced by systems concepts but are not pure applications of systems thinking.

2

Historical Roots of Family Therapy

This chapter explores the roots of family therapy and, especially, family systems thinking. Here the principal focus is on the four schizophrenia research projects that appeared simultaneously and independently around the country in the early 1950s: Theodore Lidz and his group at Yale; Lyman Wynne and his associates at the National Institute of Mental Health (NIMH) in Washington, D.C.; Murray Bowen, also at NIMH; and Gregory Bateson, Don Jackson, and their colleagues in Palo Alto.

However, before examining the origins of the field in these pioneering studies of schizophrenics and their families, the time clock will be pushed back a decade further to take a look at the climate within which this seminal work grew. The first section below explores the developments within psychiatry under the influence of Harry Stack Sullivan, particularly as expressed in the work of Frieda Fromm-Reichmann in the 1940s. Following this, the writings of Nathan Ackerman are examined, allowing a glimpse of the mental health field at just the time family therapy appeared on the scene. Then, each of the four schizophrenia research projects is examined, in turn.

I do not undertake here an exhaustive historical account of the development of family. That has already been done, most recently and comprehensively by Broderick and Schrader (1981) in the *Handbook of Family Therapy*. Some important early family therapists are mentioned only in passing in this chapter or are left out entirely. For example, in her chapter entitled "Family Therapy and The Great Originals" Lynn Hoffman (1981) portrays Virginia Satir, Carl Whitaker, and Milton Erickson as well as Nathan Ackerman and Don Jackson discussed here. And, to cite another important omission, John Bell is credited by many (including Broderick and Schrader) as having been the first to interview a family together and thus entitled to the accolade "father of family therapy." My neglect of these and other early workers in the field reflects no lack of respect for their contributions. Rather, through the representative selection of work examined here, this chapter explores the intellectual roots of the field.

According to Piaget (1971), new knowledge is created from the interaction of observational data and ideas in the mind of the observer (see, e.g., Cowan, 1978). This chapter explores the notion that family therapy developed through the confluence of both crucial clinical observations and ideas that were "in the air" around 1950. The following two questions guide this excursion into the past: First, what clinical observations launched the field of family therapy? And second, what new ideas emerged on the mental health scene, and where did these notions come from?

Later chapters make extensive use of transcripts of family therapy sessions to illustrate the clinical models presented. Here the data are the writings of the pioneering family therapists. I quote liberally from these works to allow these early workers in the field to speak for themselves and, I hope, interest the reader in exploring the classic papers further (see readings listed at the end of the book).

Frieda Fromm-Reichmann and the Sullivanians

Just as Freud's study of the clinical phenomenon of hysteria contributed to the development of new knowledge about the mind and its relationship to behavior as well as to a new treatment (psychoanalysis), the investigation of schizophrenia facilitated new understanding of the link between behavior and the social environment and led to the development of family therapy.

The work of Harry Stack Sullivan and his followers during the 1940s, principally with schizophrenics, set the stage for the emergence of family therapy a decade later. Influenced by sociologists and anthropologists, Sullivan's work emphasized social factors and came to be known as *The Interpersonal Theory of Psychiatry*, the title of his book published posthumously in 1953.

Jackson (1960) notes that prior to the investigations of Sullivan and his student and colleague Frieda Fromm-Reichmann in the 1940s, analysts had shown little interest in schizophrenia. Beginning in 1935, Fromm-Reichmann worked at Chestnut Lodge near Washington, D.C., a private, long-term psychiatric hospital for schizophrenic and other seriously disturbed patients. In a short paper in 1941 she summarized some recent advances in psychoanalytic therapy, emphasizing a shift from the mental realm, with a focus on unconscious wishes and fantasies, to the social sphere and a concern with the patient's real relationships. Along with this trend, Fromm-Reichmann noted a corresponding change in the patient population from classical conversion hysteria to psychosomatic disorders, "neurotic characters," and psychotics.

HOPE

Scott (1979) has argued that a crucial contribution of Fromm-Reichmann and the other Sullivanians was the hope they brought to psychiatry that schizophrenics could be treated using psychoanalytic psychotherapy. This is nowhere more evident than in a 1946 article, "Remarks on the Philosophy of Mental Disorder." The paper begins with an account of one of Fromm-Reichmann's own cases, a young South American woman who recovered from an 8-year schizophrenic process to become a published poet. Fromm-Reichmann (1946) uses this case to illustrate her conviction that "a person can emerge from a severe mental disorder as an artist of rank. His previous liabilities . . . can be converted into assets" (p. 294). She goes on to cite biographical material on the philosopher Arthur Schopenhauer, Robert Schumann, the composer, the painter Vincent Van Gogh, "the inarticulate, at times practically mute schizophrenic dancer Nijinsky . . . [who] used bodily movement instead of spoken words" (p. 301), and Clifford Beers, the founder of the mental hygiene movement, all to support her optimistic position.

A related point emphasized by Fromm-Reichmann in this paper (as well as by Sullivan) is that behaviors of mental patients differ in degree rather than kind from behaviors of healthy, "normal" individuals. She insisted that all psychiatric as well as physical symptoms not only express the patient's illness, but also function as moves toward health. Fromm-Reichmann noted in passing ["if one is given to teleological thinking" (p. 297)] that to think in terms of the *function* of some behavior was not quite scientifically acceptable in 1946. As will be seen in Chapter 3, teleological explanation is central to family systems thinking.

MODIFYING TECHNIQUE

In the final point of her 1946 paper, Fromm-Reichmann argued that by modifying analytic technique appropriately, psychotics can be successfully treated with psychotherapy. Here she noted the formidable opposition to her point of view, citing the fact that the classical German psychiatrists Kraepelin and Bleuler, as well as such analysts as Fenichel and Schilder, insisted that psychotherapy with psychotics was impossible. Fromm-Reichmann then quoted no less an authority than Freud himself, who expressed the hope, in 1904, that psychoanalytic technique might be adapted to the needs of schizophrenics and other seriously disturbed patients.

The issue of modifying technique is elaborated in the well-known 1948 paper in which Fromm-Reichmann incidentally introduced the term "schizophrenogenic mother." Although the emphasis of the paper is on technical modifications, Fromm-Reichmann (1948) began by summarizing the Sullivanian view of schizophrenic dynamics:

> The schizophrenic is painfully distrustful and resentful of other people, due to the severe early warp and rejection he encountered in important people of his infancy and childhood, as a rule, mainly in a schizophrenogenic mother. (p. 265)

As a result of these early experiences, Fromm-Reichmann suggested, the potential schizophrenic develops a great interpersonal sensitivity and subsequently experiences a succession of similar rejections, either actual or interpreted as such by this extremely sensitive individual. The schizophrenic's eventual regression and emotional withdrawal from the social world was seen as motivated by the fear of further rejection and by the anxiety generated by his retaliative hostility.

If Freud seemed to give his blessing in 1904 to attempts to modify psychoanalysis to treat schizophrenics, Fromm-Reichmann (1948) also noted how another of the master's papers, "On Narcissism" (Freud, 1914), written just 10 years later, formed the basis for the psychotherapeutic pessimism regarding schizophrenia, which is shared by later generations of analysts. The heart of the matter here is Freud's notion that "the narcissistic origins and the regressive character of schizophrenic disorders excluded . . . the possibility of establishing a workable relationship between the schizophrenic and the psychoanalyst" (p. 264).

At this point in her argument, Fromm-Reichmann (1948) turned to Sullivan (1947), who "teaches that there is no developmental period when the human exists outside of the realm of interpersonal relatedness" (p. 264). The regressive withdrawal in schizophrenia is, she argued, only partial, and one is always able to find traces of the patient's prepsychotic interpersonal development that form a basis, however tenuous, for the establishment of a new relationship between analyst and patient.

The specific technical modifications advocated by Fromm-Reichmann (1943) include abandoning the couch in favor of face-to-face interaction that better equips the analyst to serve as a "bridge to external reality" (p. 277); giving up the "classical 'victrola record'" (p. 277) analytic attitude for the therapist's alertness, spontaneity, and genuine concern for the patient; replacing free association (which, unlike the case of the inhibited neurotic, is already the schizophrenic's strength) with "utterly unconventional direct, and precise questioning" (p. 278) of the patient by the analyst in order to facilitate reality-oriented thinking; a thriftiness in the use of interpretation; attention to the nonsexual as well as the sexual causes for repression; a willingness to tolerate and to therapeutically utilize nondestructive acting out in patients who are unable to communicate verbally; and replacing adaptation to society's or the therapist's values with the patient's "freedom, growth, and maturation" (p. 279) as the legitimate goals of treatment. Fromm-Reichmann (1948) also emphasized the necessity of "clear directness" (p. 268) and "active therapeutic moves" (p. 269) in working with schizophrenics, approaches to the patient remarkably consistent with modern family systems therapy.

In addition to nurturing hope that technical modifications might render schizophrenia treatable using psychotherapy, Fromm-Reichmann's enduring legacy for family therapy lies perhaps in the boldness with which she undertook these changes in technique, revealing a willingness to sacrifice psychoanalytic convention to the needs of her patients. It is this spirit that, a few years later, led such psychiatrists as Ackerman, Lidz, Wynne, Bowen, and Jackson to begin an even bigger "modification in analytic technique"—family therapy.

Nathan Ackerman and Mental Health circa 1950

Schooled in the psychoanalytic milieu of his day, Nathan Ackerman was always both an analytic insider and a "pesky gadfly" (Bloch and Simon, 1982, p. xvi). Ackerman's first paper on the family, "The Family as a Social and Emotional Unit," was written in 1937 when he was a 29-year-old psychiatrist at the Menninger Clinic, just out of residency training there. From then until his death in 1971, Ackerman questioned traditional views in the mental health field and championed family therapy in countless papers, lectures, and films.

NO ONE SEES FAMILIES

For those of us who entered the mental health field after 1960, perhaps the biggest surprise in Ackerman's early papers is how difficult it is to tell from his writings whether or not he was actually interviewing families conjointly. For example, in a 1954 paper published in *Psychiatry*, Ackerman (1954a) opened with the question "Is there a possible psychotherapeutic approach to the family as a family?" He noted that concomitant individual therapy of several family members was sometimes supplemented with an attempt to integrate these several therapies for the good of the mental health of the family as a whole. Ackerman then patiently documented the limitations of this separate, individual treatment approach and the difficulties encountered in attempting to integrate these separate therapies. But he never directly advocated treating the whole family together. At most, Ackerman (1954a) suggested preceding the individual treatment of a mother–child dyad or a marital pair with a "short series of interviews with both patients" (p. 363). Similarly, in a 1958 paper that appeared in the *American Journal of Psychiatry*, whenever Ackerman suggested an interview with several family members at the same time he qualified it in some way. For example, in discussing a strategy for combining individual and family group interviews, Ackerman (1958) stated: "*At certain stages* [italics added] it may be appropriate to work concentratedly with mother and child together, husband and wife together, *or even* [italics added] mother, father, and child together" (p. 732). He also talked of interviewing "salient family pairs, *occasionally threesomes* [italics added]" (p. 732).

Given that we now take family treatment for granted, how can we understand Ackerman's reticence in discussing conjoint interviewing? A family therapist once described his early days in the field as "in the closet." Although clinicians were beginning to do family therapy, they were at first reluctant to admit to colleagues that they were actually gathering family members together in the same room for therapeutic purposes. Gradually, whispered reports of such unorthodox practices began circulating in the corridors at meetings of such groups as the American Orthopsychiatric Association. Still later, symposia and panels were organized as part of the official proceedings of these meetings, and the new family therapists began talking openly and publicly about what they were doing.

Haley (1962) referred to such "furtive conversations" in "quiet hotel rooms" (p. 69) at psychiatric meetings and cited two reasons for the early secrecy. First, the original workers in the field were uncertain of their techniques and results and were initially reluctant to commit themselves in print. And second, they feared charges of heresy by psychiatrists, who considered the influence of family members to be largely irrelevant.

It is difficult now to imagine the power of the notion that treatment *must* be a private affair between a therapist and an individual patient. Ackerman captured this perfectly in an anecdote he delighted in telling [included in at least two articles (1959 and 1962)]. He (1962) asked an analyst if she treated the mothers of her child patients. She replied: "Oh, heavens no!" (p. 40).

Just a few years later, however, writing in the first issue of *Family Process*, Ackerman (1962) abandoned his earlier schemes for elaborate combinations of individual, dyadic, and family interviews and stated simply and boldly: "The basis of family treatment is the therapeutic interview with . . . all those who live together as family under a single roof and any additional relatives who fulfill a significant family role . . ." (p. 32). It is likely that this shift reflects a change more in what Ackerman was willing to *write* about than in what he actually *did*. This is particularly evident when we recall that the two papers cited earlier were published in important established psychiatric journals, whereas the 1962 article appeared in the family therapy movement's own fledgling publication.

CRITIQUE OF EARLY-1950s PSYCHIATRY

Like Fromm-Reichmann and the Sullivanians, Ackerman was a part of the movement within psychiatry that took the social world into account. He (1954a) looked back to the earlier part of this century, before psychoanalysis took over the American mental health scene, and recalled that interventions in families then took the form of social therapy rather than psychotherapy. Social workers, in particular, were trained to help mobilize the economic, educational, and religious resources of the community to support families. When psychoanalysis, with its emphasis on the inner life of the individual person, arrived on the scene, psychiatry and social work alike embraced this "deeper" view of human experience, and the earlier interest in the impact of social and economic factors on family life was dismissed as "superficial." Social workers who continued to focus on welfare and unemployment had less prestige than those who graduated to more glamorous psychiatric casework with its concern with the individual psyche and its unconscious conflicts.

Although Ackerman acknowledged the advances made by psychoanalysis in understanding the individual personality and admitted that he was exaggerating things a bit to make his point, he (1954a) strongly believed that "social workers and psychiatrists seemed often to lose contact with social reality" (p. 360) and set for himself the goal of integrating social therapy with psychotherapy.

Ackerman (1960) cited, in particular, the changing pathology confronting the psychiatrist, a challenge he believed individual psychoanalytic treatment could not meet. Rather than the "neatly packaged symptomatic neuroses with fully contained conflicts" (p. 37), ubiquitous in Freud's day, character disorder with acting-out as a central feature had become common in the patients Ackerman encountered in the 1950s. Ackerman argued that character disorder is a social as well as an individual phenomenon, requiring the complicity of others in the social environment. Treatment of such persons, he went on to say, is based upon the ability "to evaluate the individual within a network of family relationships, in which the maladaptive forms of behavior are patterned and maintained" (p. 38).

Ackerman singled out the child guidance clinic, a setting with which he was very familiar, as a noble but incomplete attempt to view the individual within the family group. He described (Ackerman and Sobel, 1950) the thoroughness of one such effort aimed at studying and treating preschool children in the context of their families, including, in this case, individual child analytic treatment, a therapeutic nursery school program, group therapy for parents, individual psychotherapy for mothers and fathers, and educational sessions conducted by nursery school teachers and pediatricians. Periodic "integration conferences" were held in an effort to relate the work with the child to that being done with the rest of the family. Although Ackerman appeared to find this approach promising in 1950, in a chapter in a 1968 child psychiatry text he was sharply critical of the limitations of the traditional child guidance approach to diagnostic assessment based, as it is, on observation of pieces of the family undertaken by different persons at different times and under different conditions. Instead, Ackerman argued, understanding the relationship of child to family requires *direct observation* of family behavior.

CRUCIAL CLINICAL OBSERVATIONS

Ackerman (1954a) presented a number of clinical observations that convinced him and some of his colleagues of the importance of expanding the unit of evaluation and treatment to include the family. For example, he noted that there is usually a second family member involved in the patient's pathology and cites the truism among psychiatrists that the person who accompanies the patient to the first psychiatric interview is somehow a part of the patient's problems. The person initially referred for psychiatric treatment may, in fact, be the sickest family member or the healthiest (Ackerman, 1958).

Ackerman (1954a) also emphasized that although the individual patient's symptoms may improve as a result of therapy, his social relationships may not. In fact, in some cases, as the patient improves another family member becomes symptomatic. Ackerman came close at this point to viewing the individual's symptoms as a means of maintaining family homeostasis, a point emphasized a few years later by Jackson (1957a). For example, Ackerman (1954a) discussed the question of whether or not to involve family members in simultaneous individual therapy, stressing that in certain precariously balanced families poor timing can lead to "disorganization of the family equilibrium" (p. 362). Elsewhere (Ackerman and Sobel, 1950), he described the homeostatic function of the patient's symptoms more clearly when he talked of looking at "the child's present-day problems in terms of adjustive behavior required to maintain equilibrium within the disturbed family constellation" (pp. 744–745).

THE NEED FOR FAMILY DIAGNOSIS

Throughout his career Ackerman retained his physician's belief in the necessity for making a careful and accurate diagnosis of the problem before attempting to correct it. For example, Ackerman (1958) took child psychiatrists to task for emphasizing treatment over diagnosis, insisting that "therapy cannot be primary; it must always be secondary to the precise assessment of pathology" (p. 727). In this respect he departed from perhaps the majority of family therapists who rejected a concern with diagnosis as one of the trappings of the medical model they were struggling to leave behind.

Unlike most of his psychiatric colleagues around 1950, however, Ackerman was not satisfied with a diagnosis of individual intrapsychic functioning alone. Instead, he began to call (Ackerman, 1958) for the development of a "social psychopathology." Such an undertaking, Ackerman noted, requires

> an expansion of the dimensions of diagnostic thinking so as to make the unit of evaluation the individual within his family group, rather than the individual assessed in isolation. (p. 728)

This notion of a social psychopathology continued to occupy Ackerman's interest until the time of his death in 1971 and appeared in his writings in several places (e.g., 1960, 1968) as he developed and reworked his ideas. After discussing some of this thinking, Ackerman's social psychopathology will be examined further.

TOWARD SYSTEMS THINKING

An early paper on family diagnosis that focuses on the preschool child contains a remarkably clear statement of systems thinking. Noting the inadequacies of traditional psychiatric diagnostic categories for preschool children and the necessity of understanding the "incomplete" personalities of children within the context of their families, Ackerman (Ackerman and Sobel, 1950) wrote: "Accordingly, we undertook to define such child personalities not as separate individuals, but rather as functional parts of the family group" (p. 744). In a later article (1954a), he argued that one must "view the disturbed person both as an individual and as a member of an integrated family group" (p. 368), a position consistent with the "holon" concept introduced many years later by Minuchin (Minuchin and Fishman, 1981). This willingness to view the individual as *both* part and whole characterizes Ackerman's thinking over the years and distinguishes him from those in the mental health field who emphasized one point of view only.

Ackerman struggled not only with viewing the person as both individual and group member, part and whole, but he also sought to conceptualize, simultaneously, biological, psychological, and social levels of analysis and relate them over the course of development. In a 1956 paper on family diagnosis he noted (Ackerman and Behrens, 1956) "physically, a child is a separate and distinct organism; but socially and psychically, the child is an incomplete entity" (p. 67). He went on to state that "the progressive stages of personality organization of the child are viewed as advancing levels of biosocial integration with, and differentiation from, the environment" (p. 69) and "the emerging identity of the child is molded by a continuous process of emotional union with and differentiation from the significant parent" (p. 70). Ackerman also suggested that adults as well as children should be viewed within this framework, the difference being one of degree (of completeness of individual personality) rather than of kind.

Ackerman (Ackerman and Behrens, 1956) also displayed an early awareness of circular and reciprocal causal influences, emphasizing his concern not only with the impact of family interaction processes on the child, but also with the effect of the child's problems on the family as a whole, on parental and marital functioning, and on the behavior of siblings.

PERSONALITY AND ROLE

Ackerman's (1954a) goal of viewing "individual personality in the context of the dynamics of family role" (p. 367) reveals two central concepts in his thinking: personality and social role. The concept of personality has, of course, long been prominent in the field of psychology and refers to those enduring features of an individual's behavior and psychological functioning. It fits easily with the traditional view of the person as "whole." Within the mental health field, the concept of social role is a much newer way of thinking about human behavior, and emphasizes that the individual is "part" of a larger social organism. Here Ackerman was influenced by the work of such sociologists and social psychologists as Talcott Parsons (e.g., Parsons and Bales, 1955) whose ideas figured prominently in the social science thinking of the early 1950s.

Ackerman (Ackerman and Behrens, 1956) employed the concept of family role "as a bridge between the internal processes of personality and those of family participation" (p. 174) and struggled with the task of interrelating individual personality and family role. For example, in discussing the child guidance treatment of the early 1950s, Ackerman complained that the prevailing model too often focused exclusively on the child and mother as individuals, ignoring their relationship. He (1954a) noted that treating the mother of a disturbed child involves treating a family role: "It is not identical with the therapy of a whole woman, but rather of the personality of that woman integrated into a special social function, that of mothering" (p. 367). Ackerman (Ackerman and Behrens, 1956) was particularly concerned with how well an individual's personality allowed him to fulfill family roles and with the reciprocity of roles within the family necessary for effective family functioning.

Despite his intuitive conceptual grasp of systemic thinking, Ackerman's attempt to formalize his ideas using the concepts of personality and role reflects the static quality of these notions and fails to do justice to the innovative, dynamic, and even provocative quality of his actual clinical work with families, some of which is preserved on film. Based upon her study of these films, Hoffman (1981) argues that Ackerman was struggling toward what has come to be called the structural school of family therapy (see Chapters 4 and 5), which was subsequently developed by Salvador Minuchin (1974).

Glimpses of the thinking behind Ackerman's innovative way of working can also be found in his writing over the years. A 1956 (Ackerman and Behrens) paper offered a theoretical typology of disturbed families with a decidedly structural quality. Families are divided into a number of overlapping types, including: Externally isolated from community; externally integrated compensatory to lack of internal unity and satisfaction; internally unintegrated, with failure in internal unity, marital conflict, internal splits, and mutual isolation; the unintended family in which the parents' needs predominate at the expense of the child; the immature family in which parents fail to accept adult roles and lean on the extended family; and the deviant family in rebellion against the community, with or without internal rebellion. Minuchin's structural concept of *boundary* (see Chapter 4) elegantly describes the clinical phenomena Ackerman portrays in this typology.

TOWARD A SOCIAL PSYCHOPATHOLOGY

Beginning in the 1960s, Ackerman focused on interpersonal conflict as a social process that was, in some sense, parallel to the notions of intrapsychic conflict and defense against anxiety so successfully used by Freud and subsequent generations of analysts to account for certain psychopathological conditions. Some of these new ideas were set down in a 1964 paper, "Prejudicial Scapegoating and Neutralizing Forces in the Family Group." Ackerman listed mechanisms for coping with conflict and anxiety, including "repeopling" the group—adding or subtracting members, shifting alignments and splits within the group, and the scapegoating of one part of the group by another. Elsewhere Ackerman (1962) described other defensive maneuvers for handling conflict, including reversal of parent-child roles, tightening or loosening of family organization, and a "thinning of the border between family and community" (p. 37), all suggestive of what has come to be known as structural thinking. Where such conflict is not successfully contained, Ackerman noted (1964), it spills over into acting-out behavior and, eventually, into the progressive disorganization of the family. In discussing ways the therapist can assist the family in managing conflict, Ackerman (1962) included activating complementarity in role relationships, a form of "unbalancing" perfected by Minuchin (see Chapter 5).

In analyzing scapegoating as a specific family defensive maneuver for dealing with conflict, Ackerman (1964) significantly viewed the phenomenon as a *three-person* affair: A destroyer or *persecutor* uses a special prejudice to attack a *victim*, who sustains an emotional injury making him susceptible to breakdown. Such attack is neutralized by a *family helper* or doctor who rescues the victim. Ackerman saw scapegoating as a dynamic process: Various family and extended family members fulfill the three roles at different times, and patterns of attack and defense are met with reciprocal counterattack in a circular fashion as the scapegoat aligns himself with first one and then another family faction. He noted that the scapegoating process typically has the temporary effect of binding the family closer together, but as the prejudice becomes more irrational, the process may, in fact, divide the family and progressively distort role relationships and impair family functioning.

A few years later, Ackerman (1968) commented on the triangular relationship pattern central to the structural approach later developed by Minuchin, referring in particular to the mother–father–child triad: "Does the need and anxiety of one member of the threesome invade and impair the emotional complementarity of the other two?" (p. 210). Later in the same paper, Ackerman noted how "the breakup of the family into warring factions distorts the execution and balance of family functions" (p. 211). Both these comments suggest that although Ackerman was keenly aware of the negative potential of family splits and alliances, he apparently failed to appreciate the positive aspects of the family's subsystem organization that permit it to carry out its tasks effectively. Ackerman did not ignore the phenomenon of status differences and division of labor within the family, but he saw this as "role behavior" and "complementarity in role functioning" and did not appear to have conceptually linked these aspects of normal family functioning with his observations about family pathology. Minuchin (1974) subsequently called attention to the necessity of organizing the family appropriately into executive and sibling subsystems and created, in the structural model, a unified way of viewing both the constructive and destructive effects of family subsystem organization.

What Ackerman appears to be struggling toward is a typology of family pathology—his social psychopathology—based on the family's defensive strategies for managing conflict. This line of thinking is clearest in his chapter in a 1968 child psychiatry text.

Ackerman believed that in families who produce psychotic offspring, the price of family membership for the child is that the child must *not be*, a total sacrifice of the child in order to maintain family integration. At the other end of the spectrum of pathology, families in which children develop neurotic disorders demand that the child *not be different* and require that the child surrender a part of his individual self in order to successfully contain conflict and anxiety within the family. Here anxiety is encapsulated and internalized as specific neurotic conflicts. Finally, Ackerman identified an intermediate category between the neurotic and psychotic in which conflict is only partially contained. Among the symptoms of this group, Ackerman listed alienation, with each family member going his own way; sociopathic rebellion and abuse of drugs or alcohol; and psychosomatic disorders. These conditions are characterized by excessive anxiety and defective emotional control or by either aggressive attack on the family or defensive withdrawal from it and preoccupation with self. He noted that these disorders, in some cases, prevent a complete breakdown of defenses and consequent psychotic decompensation. Ackerman also suggested that cases of mixed symptoms may arise from different defensive solutions being utilized by the family at different stages of family development.

Chapter 9 develops a "systemic psychopathology" consistent with Ackerman's typological thinking, as outlined here, and I think, true to the spirit of this pioneer of the field.

For the reader who wishes to review Ackerman's important work, his collected papers are now available (Bloch and Simon, 1982).

Lidz and the Yale Group

Theodore Lidz's interest in the families of schizophrenics dates back to the early 1940s at Johns Hopkins when he and his wife (Ruth Lidz and Theodore Lidz, 1949) made the following critical observation:

> It was noted during the treatment of a small series of schizophrenic patients that they had frequently been deprived of at least one parental figure early in life; and also that the parental home was usually markedly unstable, torn by family schisms and constant emotional turmoil, and frequently patterned according to the whims of grossly eccentric and abnormal personalities. (p. 332)

THE SCHIZOPHRENIA STUDIES

A retrospective analysis of the case files of 50 consecutive admissions to the Henry Phipps Psychiatric Clinic was undertaken (Lidz and Lidz, 1949) to determine the frequency of broken homes or seriously disturbed family environments in the histories of schizophrenics whose first psychotic break occurred before age 21. Although the study was largely completed by 1941, World War II delayed the published report until 1949. During the intervening years, Lidz published a few papers on war-related psychiatric problems and also began writing on psychosomatics, an interest that continued well into the 1950s.

Forty percent of the young adults in the sample had lost a parent by death or divorce before the age of 19. The authors reported comparable rates in two other studies of schizophrenic patients and compared these to figures of 17 to 20 percent in control samples of medical students, manic-depressive patients, and psychotically depressed individuals.

The Lidzes were impressed by the high incidence of loss of parental figures from their schizophrenic patients' homes, yet doubted that such deprivation in itself could produce schizophrenia. Further scrutiny of their data revealed that in one-half of the cases suffering loss of a parent, the parent was either psychotic and committed suicide or one parent divorced the other because of psychotic or grossly unstable behavior. In addition, they noted that over 60 percent of the homes had been marked by the parents' serious incompatibility and strife.

These data set the course for Theodore Lidz's pioneering study of the families of schizophrenics conducted after he moved to Yale in 1951. There Lidz and the group which included Stephen Fleck, Alice Cornelison, and Dorothy Terry, began examining what he (Lidz and Lidz, 1949) had earlier termed the "heaping up of deleterious factors" (p. 343) found in these families, observing the subtle, but chronically present pervasive factors shaping the development of the child who becomes schizophrenic in adolescence or young adulthood. This work was reported in a series of papers, "The Intrafamilial Environment of Schizophrenic Patients." Scattered through various journals, these papers had subtitles that included "I. The Father" (Lidz et al., 1957a); "II. Marital Schism and Marital Skew" (Lidz et al., 1957b); "IV. Parental Personalities and Family Interaction" (Lidz et al., 1958a); and "VI. The Transmission of Irrationality" (Lidz et al., 1958b). Ten articles from the series were collected and published in German as a single volume in 1959.

These papers report on 14 cases studied intensively while the late adolescent or young adult schizophrenic patient was hospitalized at Yale Psychiatric Institute. Lidz noted that his sample was biased toward intact upper-class families who could afford to keep their offspring in an expensive private psychiatric hospital for periods ranging from 6 months to over 2 years. Family members were repeatedly interviewed individually, were given projective tests, and were observed interacting with each other and with the hospital staff. Home visits were made and often teachers, nurse-maids, and family friends were interviewed as well. It does not appear from the published reports that family interviews were used systematically to gather data. Instead, the observations of family interaction were unsystematic and anecdotal. By today's standards this seems surprising, but, as discussed above in the case of Acker-man, it is necessary to recall psychiatry's reverence at the time for the individual interview. A later and more obscure paper in the series (Lidz et al., 1958b) does mention a conjoint meeting that included a patient, her parents, and two psychiatrists. The rationale for and approach to the session is revealing:

> As the patient could not be kept in the hospital for a long period and as the psychiatrist who was interviewing the parents found it impossi-ble to get them to focus upon any meaningful problems that might be upsetting, *a therapeutic experiment was undertaken, with great trepi-dation* [italics added]. (p. 312)

Unfortunately, the therapists' worries about the session appear to have been justified: the day after the session in which the mother totally disqualified her daughter's moving description of her di-lemma in the family, the patient relapsed into the silly, incoherent behavior that had characterized her condition at admission.

AWAY FROM A TRAUMATIC ETIOLOGY

Impressed by earlier findings of *chronically* disturbed home en-vironments in the families of schizophrenics, Lidz focused "on the entire period of maturation" (Lidz et al., 1957a) of the schizo-phrenics studied rather than upon a single traumatic experience or relationship at a particular stage of development. Here he departed from the dominant analytic wisdom of the day that emphasized early infantile deprivation and a serious fixation at the early oral stage, to which the adolescent or young adult schizophrenic later regresses. Lidz (Lidz and Lidz, 1949) took issue with Fromm-Reichmann, in particular:

> There has been an increasing tendency of late, more so than appears in the literature, for those interested in the psychotherapy of schizo-phrenic patients to lay stress upon the pernicious influence of the mothers, the severely rejecting mother, the so-called schizophreno-genic mother [here Lidz cites Fromm-Reichmann (1948)]. (p. 344)

Lidz (Lidz et al., 1957a) rather cleverly exploited Freud's (1943) methaphor for schizophrenia to make his point. Freud had compared the massive regression of the schizophrenic patient to a migrant people who construct fortified points to which they can retreat from the dangers of a hostile environment, but in the panic of a battle gone against them, run past these shelters and back to the ships from whence they came. Lidz pointed out that there are many other reasons for losing a war, including differing objectives, overwhelming opposition, dissension among the forces, poor training of the troops, and lack of grasp of reality by the generals. The latter, he noted is pertinent in both military matters and in child rearing. Lidz concluded that "one cannot focus prematurely on a single explanation for all of the catastrophic defects in living that are termed schizophrenia" (p. 332).

In raising the question of the etiology of schizophrenia, Lidz was moving away from the notion that a single traumatic event in the past causes the disorder and toward the idea that multiple chronic or recurrent factors throughout the child's growth distort personality development and create an environment favorable to the appearance of schizophrenia. He uses the biological notion of "anlage" here to refer not to causes, but rather to the recognizable foundations of subsequent development. Lidz does not appear to have made the next step, taken later by others in the field, of eschewing etiological questions to focus, instead, upon current factors maintaining the disordered behavior.

DISCOVERING FATHERS

Lidz next cited (Lidz et al., 1957a) another objection to the then-fashionable emphasis on the "schizophrenogenic" mother: "We would like to make room—theoretical room—for the consideration of the potentiality that the father requires scrutiny in the effort to understand schizophrenia and the schizophrenic patient" (p. 333). In addition to the theoretical reasons for focusing on the mother and her early interactions with the schizophrenic patient, Lidz noted another reason for the past emphasis on the mother: Psychiatrists have been unable to avoid harassment by some of these mothers who, with their disordered thinking and eccentric behavior, make a lasting impression that is then generalized to all mothers of schizophrenic patients.

In defense of the notion that the father is important in the family milieu of the patient who becomes schizophrenic, Lidz cited Parsons and Bales' (1955) notion that the father is the adaptive-instrumental leader of the family, whereas the mother's task is integrative-expressive. Lidz went on to note also that the mother's ability to carry out her role cannot be evaluated without taking into account the father's support of her role.

Lidz (Lidz et al., 1957a) found that none of the 14 fathers in his study fulfilled a paternal role, and most demonstrated serious psychopathology. He presents a typology of deviant role behavior: (1) fathers in constant, severe conflict with their wives who seek to ally themselves with their daughters; (2) fathers of sons who turn their hostility toward their sons rather than their wives; (3) fathers whose grandiose and paranoid thinking and self-concepts create a paralogical atmosphere within the family that diverges from the larger culture; (4) fathers who have failed in life, becoming non-entities in their homes; and (5) passive fathers who demand little for themselves and act like lesser siblings in the family.

MARITAL SCHISM AND MARITAL SKEW

In turning from the fathers of schizophrenics to the marital relationship in these families, Lidz (Lidz et al., 1957b) was again careful to note that he was not attempting to establish a direct etiological link between the parents' marital difficulties and schizophrenia in the child. Rather, he suggested that the marital relationship is another important part of the family environment in which the schizophrenic-to-be develops.

Like Ackerman, Lidz noted the inadequacy of describing a family or a couple in terms of the individual personalities of each member and he, too, turned to the sociologists and social psychologists, citing the work of people like Parsons and Bales (1955), Spiegel (1957), Hill et al. (1953), and Ackerman himself (1954b). He emphasized, in particular, the necessity of role reciprocity if the marital relationship is to function effectively.

Again like Ackerman, Lidz's work gives glimpses of the structural approach later developed by Minuchin. Lidz (Lidz et al., 1957b) stated: "We have been particularly impressed by the need to maintain lines between generations" (p. 242) and listed a number of ways the generational lines became blurred in the families he studied: Parents remain dependent upon their own parents, interfering with the marital relationship; one parent becomes a child to the other; a parent becomes a rival with his children for the other parent's attention; or the parental role is completely rejected.

Lidz and his colleagues (1957b) are perhaps best remembered for coining the terms *marital schism* and *marital skew* to describe the couple relationships in the families of schizophrenics they studied. Marital schism refers to a "state of severe chronic disequilibrium and discord" (p. 243). In the eight (of the sample of fourteen) families thus characterized, Lidz noted the virtual absence of complementarity, instead finding demanding and defiant behavior that produced a schism between the parents—dividing the family and creating loyalty conflicts for their children. In over one-half of these families, one or both parents retained a primary loyalty to their family of origin.

In skewed marriages, on the other hand, "serious strife was avoided because the dominant parent's seriously distorted ideas were accepted by a more normal but very dependent spouse, giving rise to a deviant and paralogical family environment" (Lidz et al., 1958a, p. 767). Six of the families in Lidz's sample showed this pattern. None of these parents retained a close tie to their families of origin, and instead, one partner was extremely dependent upon the other, who appeared to be strong, but was, in fact, seriously disturbed. The pathology permeating the home was seen as normal within the family, which effectively isolated it from the larger community.

The words "schism" and "skew" are themselves structurally oriented terms describing family groups rather than individual members. They label the patterns of unresolved conflict and rigid complementarity discussed in Chapter 5 on the structural model.

A later paper in the series (Lidz et al., 1958b) discussed those irrational aspects of communication in the families of schizophrenics that appear to contribute to the development of the disorder. In over one-half of the cases studied, at least one parent could be diagnosed as essentially psychotic or markedly paranoid. In the other cases, the psychic integration of a parent demanded serious distortion of reality by the entire family. Lidz states:

> our patients were not raised in families that adhered to culturally accepted ideas of causality and meanings, or respected the instrumental utility of their ideas and communications, because one or both parents were forced to abandon rationality to defend their own precarious ego structure. (p. 315)

The next section describes the work of Wynne and his colleagues who emphasized the disordered thinking found in the families of schizophrenics.

Lyman Wynne at the National Institute of Mental Health

Ackerman's and Lidz's work reveal the influence of the sociologists of the 1950s, particularly Talcott Parsons, and this trend is even clearer in the case of Lyman Wynne. Upon completing his medical internship in 1948, Wynne enrolled as a graduate student in Harvard's Department of Social Relations where he studied psychology, sociology, and anthropology and earned a Ph.D. At Harvard, Wynne was influenced by physiological psychology as well as social psychology. His major work there included the experimental study of conditioned fear reactions in dogs, resulting in a series of publications during the years 1950-1955, with Richard Solomon as first author. This work reveals Wynne's thorough grounding in physiological approaches to behavior, including the cybernetic feedback processes common in biological thinking.

In 1952, Wynne moved to the National Institute of Mental Health (NIMH) in Washington, D.C., where he began studying schizophrenics and their families. His interest in schizophrenia continued long after others from the early days of the family field had abandoned the topic to concentrate on easier and more hopeful clinical problems. For the past 10 years or so, Wynne has been at the University of Rochester where he and his colleagues have undertaken a prospective study of children at risk for the development of schizophrenia. Here, I examine Wynne's work during the 1950s. Chapter 8 picks up the story around 1960, when he was joined by Margaret Singer.

THE NATURE OF THE STUDY

Wynne (Wynne et al., 1958) presented his early work on schizophrenia in the classic paper "Pseudo-Mutuality in the Family Relations of Schizophrenics." He began that article with a description of its purpose: "to develop a psychodynamic interpretation of schizophrenia that takes into conceptual account the social organization of the family as a whole" (p. 205).

Wynne (Wynne et al., 1958) notes that for the purposes of the study begun in 1954, "a case is regarded as consisting of the entire family unit" (p. 205). Index patients all had their first psychotic breaks as late adolescents or as young adults. The hospitalized patient received intensive individual psychotherapy, and parents were seen individually as outpatients twice a week by a different therapist. Data from these therapeutic interviews, as well as information from other family members and from nursing staff and ward administrators, were used to "reconstruct" family patterns. As with the Lidz work, it is not clear from this paper that any systematic observations of family interaction were made. Wynne does not mention conjoint family treatment interviews. The 1958 paper was based primarily on the group's intensive study of four families.

PSEUDOMUTUALITY

Wynne (Wynne et al., 1958) focused on two basic human needs or problems: To develop *relationships* with others while at the same time maintaining a sense of personal *identity*. He stated:

> the universal necessity for dealing with *both* the problems of relation and identity leads to three main "solutions." These three resultant forms of relatedness, or complementarity, are mutuality, nonmutuality, and pseudo-mutuality. (p. 206)

Nonmutual complementarity is generally role-limited behavior (e.g., the transactions between customer and shoe clerk). *Pseudo-mutuality* is characterized by "a predominant absorption in fitting together, at the expense of the differentiation of the identities of the persons in the relation" (p. 207). There is a tremendous investment in maintaining a sense of relatedness, even where this is illusory. This is contrasted with *mutuality*, in which each person brings to the relationship a sense of his or her own identity as a separate and valuable person.

In pseudomutual relationships, the open acknowledgment of any differences, including those required to establish a separate identity, is perceived as a threat to the relationship itself. In mutual forms of relatedness, on the other hand, the exploration of difference may lead to growth in the form of altered, but deeper relatedness. Wynne (Wynne et al., 1958) summarized:

> In short, the pseudo-mutual relation involves a characteristic dilemma: divergence is perceived as leading to disruption of the relation and

therefore must be avoided; but if divergence is avoided, growth of the relation is impossible. (p. 207)

Pseudomutual relationships were seen by Wynne as consistent with a homeostatic model. However, in a long footnote he questioned

whether the physiologic model of homeostasis can be transposed to human relations and still leave room for the imaginative, selective, nonautomatic details of fully mutual complementarity. It is only in the simpler situation of nonmutuality and in the pathological situation of pseudo-mutuality that the automaticity of homeostatic equilibration seems an appropriate analogy. (p. 208)

Here Wynne is registering a cautious note regarding the generalizability of the notion of homeostasis at a time when others, particularly Jackson (see below), had begun to emphasize the concept.

Wynne contended in the first hypothesis of the 1958 paper that intense and enduring pseudomutuality characterizes the family relationships of individuals who develop acute schizophrenic episodes. He was careful, however, to *disclaim* that pseudomutuality is a *cause* of schizophrenia; instead he asserted that "it is a major feature of the kind of setting in which reactive schizophrenia develops when other factors are also present" (p. 208).

Wynne's focus in this paper helps answer a question central to the intellectual history undertaken in this chapter: Why did family therapy develop from the study of schizophrenics rather than from the investigation of other pathological or normal populations? Family therapy focuses on the interface between the individual and the larger society and is concerned with how much the individual should be seen as a separate person and how much as a member of a group, such as the family. This, following Wynne, is the essential dilemma of the schizophrenic. Accordingly, study of schizophrenics and their families highlights the individual–group boundary, making crucial processes easier to identify in the schizophrenic population than in other groups and raising issues that had been ignored before family therapy developed.

FAMILY ROLE BEHAVIOR

Unlike Ackerman and Lidz, who observed how well various family members perform *specific* role functions (e.g., mothering), Wynne's (Wynne et al., 1958) use of role concepts was global. He saw the prepsychotic picture of the family as "a fixed organization of a limited number of engulfing roles" (p. 208), noting that the overall role structure remains rigidly fixed while the persons filling the roles may vary. The emphasis here was on an undifferentiated, monolithic family structure with no room for the articulation of individual differences or for change consistent with individual growth. In less pathological families, Wynne noted, early expectations and role assignments also occur, but they are less rigid and are continually modified to reflect changing circumstances and individual needs. In the case of families of schizophrenics, however, the pseudomutual emphasis on fitting together at all costs prevents the recognition of difference and change, and the family role structure is instead rigidly maintained.

In a later paper (Ryckoff et al., 1959), Wynne and his colleagues described in more detail the maintenance of stereotyped family roles. They introduced the concept of *family legend or myth* to describe the family's shared conception of itself, which, in turn, feeds back to reinforce and fix role behaviors. In the case of serious pathology, such as schizophrenia, this "family identity" becomes a self-perpetuating force that constricts the development of and even entirely displaces an individual identity.

DISORDERED THINKING IN SCHIZOPHRENIA

In a second hypothesis, Wynne et al. (1958) examined the mechanisms that maintain pseudomutuality:

> In the families of potential schizophrenics, the intensity and duration of pseudo-mutuality has led to the development of a particular variety of shared family mechanisms by which deviations from the family role structure are excluded from recognition or are delusionally reinterpreted. These shared mechanisms act at a primitive level in preventing the articulation and selection of any meanings that might enable the individual family member to differentiate his personal identity either within or outside of the family role structure. Those dawning perceptions and incipient communications which might lead to an articulation of divergent expectations, interests, or individuality are, instead, diffused, doubled [doubted?], blurred, or distorted. (p. 210)

This hypothesis is the basis of Wynne's subsequent program of research, carried out with Margaret Singer (see Chapter 8), into the ways that the learning environment of the potential schizophrenic fails to support the development of a sense of reality that can be consensually validated. Wynne noted here (Wynne et al., 1958) that he is not talking about "normal" or "neurotic" attempts to conceal information or coerce the beliefs of another, but rather the way in which "in characteristic schizophrenic relations perceptual and communicative capacity is involved in an *earlier and more primitive* [italics added] way" (p. 210). These mechanisms in the families of schizophrenics do not simply mask differences, but rather alter the perception of reality in such a way that differences cannot be recognized.

Wynne coined the term "rubber fence" to summarize the effects of pseudomutuality and the shared family mechanisms that maintain it. He saw the family of the schizophrenic as surrounded by an elastic boundary with no identifiable openings. The rubber fence continually shifts and changes form so that no matter what a family member says and does in an attempt to differentiate, the boundary moves to blur differences and still includes him within the family's all-encompassing role structure. Similarly, the rubber fence contracts to exclude all threats of difference from outside the family.

In a third hypothesis, Wynne (Wynne et al., 1958) connected the schizophrenic's disordered thinking to the family environment:

> The fragmentation of experience, the identity diffusion, the disturbed modes of perception and communication, and certain other characteristics of the acute reactive schizophrenic's personality structure are to a significant extent derived, by *processes of internalization* [italics added], from characteristics of the family social organization. (p. 215)

Individuals growing up in such families develop ways of perceiving, thinking, and communicating that make it impossible for them to articulate and attach clear meanings to both external events and to their own internal states. Rather than being able to label such feelings as anger and disappointment, Wynne (Wynne et al., 1958) speculates that the schizophrenic may instead experience a vague distress and, at times, panic:

> Under these conditions, the person becomes flooded with anxiety *at precisely those moments* [italics added] when he is starting to articulate a meaningful indication of his individuality, in the same way that pseudo-mutual family relations become flooded with anxiety when noncomplementarity threatened to emerge into shared recognition. (p. 216)

Wynne and his colleagues (1958) saw the panic and disorganization of the acute schizophrenic break as a kind of identity crisis, with overwhelming anxiety and guilt associated with the attempt to move outside the family's role structure. In fact, the violence and disruption of the psychotic break was viewed as the only possible way for the schizophrenic to differentiate himself from the family. The psychotic episode is, in effect, "a miscarried attempt at attaining individuation" (p. 219). Here Wynne echoed Fromm-Reichmann's conviction that the patient's symptom is both an expression of pathology as well as a move toward health.

Wynne and his colleagues saw the chronic schizophrenic state as a reestablishment of the old pseudomutual relationships within the family, this time at a greater distance and often characterized by the schizophrenic's withdrawal. In some cases, this takes the form of scapegoating, with all the family noncomplementarity focused on the schizophrenic, allowing the pseudomutual relationships within the rest of the family to remain undisturbed.

Along with Margaret Singer, Wynne's schizophrenia studies continued through the 1960s and the 1970s to the present, with papers scattered through many journals and books. (See the Annotated Suggested Readings for Chapter 8.)

Murray Bowen

Bowen's early writings impress with their vivid and compelling clinical observations. This is particularly true of a paper presented at the 1957 meeting of the American Orthopsychiatric Association, which appeared (1978b) as the first chapter of Bowen's collected papers *Family Therapy in Clinical Practice* (1978a). In it he described the evolution of his approach from the individual to the family in the study and treatment of schizophrenia.

INITIAL APPROACH TO SCHIZOPHRENIA

Bowen's NIMH research project was conducted during the years 1954 to 1958. He initially conceptualized schizophrenia as a disorder within the patient. The eventual psychotic symptoms in the adolescent or young adult patient were seen by him (Bowen, 1978b) as "superimposed upon an unresolved attachment to the mother" (p. 4). This attachment, according to Bowen's early view, is due to the mother's own emotional immaturity and, in turn, causes a developmental arrest in the child. The child is used to satisfy the mother's needs and is kept dependent, while the mother continues to urge the child to achieve and to grow up.

Based upon this hypothesis, three chronic schizophrenic young women and their mothers were invited to participate in the NIMH research project. Bowen chose dyads in which the symbiotic attachment appeared to be particularly intense, with the hope that the accompanying processes would be easier to observe. The patients were hospitalized and the mothers were given the choice of rooming with their daughters on the ward or of living at home. The most symbiotically attached mother chose to live in the hospital. Bowen's initial treatment program rested upon the belief that given a supportive individual psychotherapeutic relationship, these mothers' own psychological deficits would be remedied, and the patient would thus be freed to mature developmentally. Ward milieu was designed to interfere minimally with the mother–daughter relationship.

During the initial phase of the study, Bowen made a number of striking observations, which lead eventually to his reconceptualization of schizophrenia and to the reorganization of the research and treatment program. In the unstructured ward milieu, Bowen was able to observe relationship patterns more clearly than had been possible in other clinical settings. One of these he labeled the "closeness–distance cycle." Here as elsewhere in his work, Bowen reported his observations in simple, descriptive language. In describing his shift from an individual to a family point of view, Bowen (1961) suggested that such habits of description helped him avoid falling back upon familiar psychiatric jargon with its implicit individual thinking.

What Bowen saw was that over time spans ranging from several hours to many weeks, the mother–daughter pairs would alternately become extremely close, fight and separate, maintain distance, reunite, etc. The dyad often attempted to induce staff members to structure their relationship (via rules, advice, etc.), and when they were successful, the outsiders' involvement reduced the clarity of the cyclic closeness–distance pattern.

Bowen's original conceptualization of the symbiotic mother–child relationship led him to expect a rather "fixed fusion" characterized by consistently poor definition of individual boundaries. Instead of this rather fixed state of affairs, he was struck instead by the variability and fluidity of the dyadic relationship, which he (Bowen, 1978b) began to conceptualize as a "transfer of anxiety, of weakness, of sickness, or of psychosis from one member to another" (p. 6). For example, when the mother herself became anxious she would focus her attention on the patient's sickness. Soon, the daughter's psychotic symptoms would increase and the mother's anxiety would decrease. Here Bowen spoke of "almost a quantitative transfer of anxiety" (p. 7), using a rather mechanistic, hydraulic model to refer to a phenomenon that family thinkers such as Jackson and Bateson would come to describe in cybernetic terms. Bowen emphasized that in situations such as those he described, the mother's behavior appeared to be triggered by her own anxiety rather than by anything connected with the reality of the patient's functioning.

Bowen observed that when the intense dyadic closeness was disrupted, either member often attempted to duplicate that relationship in an overly close tie with an outside person, such as another relative or a staff member. When this did occur, despite the staff's efforts to remain detached from this process, the family members' anxiety inevitably decreased, and the anxiety and problematic relationships shifted to the outside figures now involved. In fact, Bowen (1961) suggested, the mother and daughter pairs used individual therapy to re-equilibrate their symbiotic relationship rather than to differentiate from each other as had been hypothesized and hoped for.

SCHIZOPHRENIA RECONCEPTUALIZED

These observations, particularly the dyad's ability to reduce its own level of anxiety by involving a third person, led Bowen to reconceptualize his entire project. Rather than seeing the dyad as a separate unit, he (Bowen, 1978b) began to see it more as a fragment of a larger family group: "the symbiotic pair . . . [is] a weak undifferentiated fragment of a larger group . . . lack[ing] within itself the strength to differentiate into two autonomous people" (p. 10).

Bowen (1978b) continued his earlier interest in symbiotic relations in schizophrenia, but subsequently described the "extension of the [research] hypothesis to consider the schizophrenic symptoms in the patient member to be part of an active dynamic process that involves the entire family" (p. 10). He decided to admit family units to his inpatient program, requiring parents to live on the ward with the schizophrenic patient. Well siblings who were in school joined the rest of the family in the hospital on weekends.

Bowen also began to reconceptualize the treatment program based upon his new notion of schizophrenia as a family-wide process. Individual therapy was discontinued, as were routine staff meetings. Initially, a daily group meeting attended by the members of all hospitalized families (the unit could accommodate three families at a time) as well as the entire project staff was instituted instead. Bowen (1978b) described the function of this meeting as follows:

> The meeting plan was designed to encourage family participation in the problems of each other, to discourage practices which had been found to encourage fragmentation of the family, and to encourage free relationships between staff and families. (p. 12)

He particularly advocated such sessions for avoiding secrets, both within families and between family members and staff.

SCHIZOPHRENIA AS A FAMILY PROCESS

By the time the schizophrenia project ended, Bowen had reformulated his notion of schizophrenia in family terms. His new view was described in a workshop presented at the American Orthopsychiatric Association meeting in 1959 and later published (Bowen, 1961) and in a chapter (Bowen, 1960) of the volume *The Etiology of Schizophrenia*, edited by Don Jackson.

Bowen's view of the family of the schizophrenic rests upon the observation that its members are not really distinct individuals at all, but instead form a single psychological unit. In 1957, Bowen (1978b) spoke of an undifferentiated "family ego mass" (p. 13), a term he said he (Bowen, 1961) discarded, two years later, because it contains "certain inaccuracies" (p. 45). In later writings (Bowen, 1961) tended to emphasize instead the remedial process of "differentiation of self" (p. 57) from other family members. This notion is central to Bowen's well-known paper, originally published anonymously, describing his work with his own family of origin (Anonymous, 1972).

In speculating on how this "emotional oneness" develops, Bowen (1960) came to regard schizophrenia as a process requiring at least three generations to develop, an idea he attributes to Lewis Hill (1955), a consultant to the Bowen project. The notion of psychological "maturity" figures prominently in this line of thinking. Bowen suggested that two reasonably mature members of the grandparental generation marry and have children whose maturities fall within a certain range. The most immature child of this second generation, the one most symbiotically attached to the mother, will seek out and marry another of similar immaturity, and they will also have children (the third generation) with a still lower range of maturity levels. The most immature of these children, Bowen suggests, will have a level of immaturity roughly equal to that of the parents' combined levels of immaturity and is at risk for developing clinical schizophrenia.

In later writings, Bowen (e.g., Anonymous, 1972) made this notion more explicit and concrete, suggesting that a person's level of maturity could be measured along a scale ranging from zero to one hundred and ascribing a descending set of maturity scores to individuals across the three generations. He subsequently (Bowen, 1979) indicated that his specification of such a scale had been a terrible mistake because, although he had meant it metaphorically, most readers took him literally and then criticized the scale as scientifically inadequate.

In addition to choosing a mate of similar immaturity, Bowen also suggested that such individuals select a partner with a complementary defensive style for dealing with their immaturity. Here Bowen introduced the notion of "overadequate" and "inadequate" functioning. The individual using the former style denies his immaturity and operates from behind a facade of overadequacy; the latter accentuates inadequacy. He noted that these styles are functional states rather than fixed characteristics of the two persons involved, with both persons capable of operating in either mode. This fluidity makes decision-making difficult and conflict likely and renders the couple relationship unstable.

The child is seen as the vehicle for stabilizing the marital dyad. The arrival of a realistically helpless baby puts the mother securely in the overadequate position. Bowen (1960) wrote:

> She could now control her own immaturity by caring for the immaturity of another. With her emotional functioning more stabilized in the relationship with the child, the mother becomes a more stable figure for the father. He could better control his relationship to her when her functioning did not fluctuate so rapidly. He tended to establish a more fixed position of aloof distance from the mother. . . . (pp. 357–358)

Although this "interdependent triad" succeeds in maintaining stability in the family, the child is placed in a position that becomes more untenable as the years go by. Bowen saw the mother as placing two contradictory demands upon the child. The overt, often verbal message is: Grow up, become an independent, mature person. The more forceful covert message is, however: Remain helpless. He noted (1960) that this view of the schizophrenic's dilemma is consistent with the double bind notion arrived at independently by Bateson et al. (1956). Within this arrangement, the mother can function adequately by projecting her own inadequacy onto the child, an example of the "family projection process" (Bowen, 1978b, p. 12), a notion that has become central in Bowen's thinking.

Bowen (1960) stressed that schizophrenia is a "functional helplessness" in the child rather than a constitutional helplessness, designed to stabilize the mother emotionally and permit the father to relate to her with less anxiety. He insisted that the patient participates so actively in this process that it is impossible to regard the schizophrenic as a "victim."

During the later years of the NIMH project, Bowen apparently abandoned the initial family–staff group treatment approach in favor of conjoint family sessions conducted by a single therapist. He (1961) described the therapist as operating from a position of "unbiased detachment," avoiding individual relationships in an effort to get the family to "work together" (p. 49) to define and solve their own problems. Considerable attention is paid to the task of getting the family to find a leader among its own members.

Early in the family treatment of schizophrenics, Bowen suggested, the conflict between the mother and the patient is prominent. As the father becomes less peripheral, conflict shifts instead to the mother–father dyad. Bowen (1960) notes that the patient improves to the extent that the parents can become "emotionally close, more invested in each other than either was in the patient" (p. 370).

Subsequent refinements in Bowen's thinking are presented systematically in a 1966 paper. A recent chapter by Kerr (1981) is among the most up-to-date discussions of Bowen's work. And Bowen's own collected papers (1978a) includes many of the articles discussed here.

Bateson, Jackson, and their Palo Alto Colleagues

Of the four pioneering groups discussed here, Bateson and Jackson and their colleagues in Palo Alto during the early 1950s, particularly Jay Haley, John Weakland, and Virginia Satir, are the most heterogeneous and difficult to characterize. These investigators are often lumped together as the MRI group, but this is somewhat inaccurate, since Bateson himself was never formally connected with MRI. Their association began with Gregory Bateson's research projects at the Veterans Administration Hospital (VA) in Palo Alto. Bateson, an anthropologist, received a Rockefeller Foundation grant in 1952 to study paradox in human and animal communication (Malcolm, 1978). He hired Jay Haley, a Stanford graduate student studying communication, and John Weakland, a former chemical engineer turned anthropologist, as research assistants. Haley notes (Simon, 1982b) that in those days the group was studying all kinds of communication and one day a psychiatry resident at the VA suggested that Haley might be interested in talking to one of his schizophrenic patients. Haley was interested, found himself particularly impressed with the patient's use of metaphor, and managed to interest Bateson as well. When the original Bateson project was not funded again in 1954, the group turned to investigating communication in the families of schizophrenics, apparently a more salable research enterprise. Don Jackson was hired at this point as a consultant to supervise the project's study and treatment of the schizophrenic patients and their families.

Beginning with this crossing of paths in the middle 1950s, the Palo Alto group provided a fertile environment for the development of family thinking before its members eventually went their own separate ways. Bateson finally became disenchanted with his brush with psychiatry and, in 1963, moved to the Oceanic Institute in Hawaii (Malcolm, 1978). At the end of 1958, Jackson (1968) established MRI (p. v) and invited Virginia Satir to join him as training director. There he focused his energies on promoting the development of family therapy. Through his writings and influence as cofounder (with Ackerman) of the journal *Family Process*, Jackson was an important figure in the field until his death in 1968. Satir's (1964) influential book, *Conjoint Family Therapy*, written during these years, popularized some of the ideas generated in Palo Alto during this period. Later she herself left Palo Alto, becoming involved at Esalen with the human potential movement, and spearheading what was described in Chapter 1 as the experiential school of family therapy. Haley became interested in the power aspects of communication, a line of thinking described in his *Strategies of Psychotherapy* (1963). This direction proved unpalatable to Bateson, who found it epistemologically, if not personally distasteful (Malcolm, 1978). Haley subsequently left Palo Alto to join Minuchin in Philadelphia, his interest in power tactics leading eventually to his strategic approach to family therapy. Weakland stayed behind at MRI and was joined by Paul Watzlawick and Richard Fisch. Together, they developed MRI's brief therapy approach, the West Coast branch of strategic therapy.

This section examines the roots of the Palo Alto group's thinking in the work of Jackson and Bateson, culminating in their classic double bind paper.

DON JACKSON

Jackson was a psychoanalytically schooled psychiatrist influenced by the Sullivanians during his residency training at Chestnut Lodge. He (Jackson, 1957b) traced his own interest in schizophrenia to 1943, the year he graduated from medical school, and the influence of Kasanin (1944) who investigated language and thought in schizophrenia.

Like the other early schizophrenia researchers discussed in this chapter, Jackson too felt the need to comment on his departure from the dominant analytic position that emphasized the importance of early traumatic events in determining later development. He (Jackson, 1957b) cited a current study by Johnson and her colleagues (1956) at the Mayo Clinic purporting to establish discrete physically or psychologically traumatic events as etiological agents in schizophrenia, and caustically complained "this, to me, has a flavor that renders schizophrenia perilously close to a kind of psychological subdural hematoma" (p. 181). Rather, Jackson saw the contribution of the family to the development of schizophrenia as "nondiscrete and continuing" (p. 182), a position consistent with the view of his contemporaries, Lidz and Wynne.

Jackson's earliest papers reveal both his psychoanalytic orthodoxy at the time as well as his struggle to include data and ideas outside the range of usual analytic thinking. For example, in a 1954 paper, "Some Factors Influencing the Oedipus Complex," published in the *Psychoanalytic Quarterly*, Jackson used psychoanalytic terms exclusively, yet he urged his colleagues to examine "the additive effect on the child of the parents' mutual adaptation" (p. 566) to each other, focusing on the interaction between the parents as well as on the separate relationships of the child to each parent. In this paper he observed that "as long as the girl was in difficulty, the parents functioned as a team" (p. 568) and described how, as the patient changed in therapy, her parents became upset, quarreled openly for the first time, and drastically altered their behavior toward their daughter. A footnote applied the term "family homeostasis" to such phenomena, an idea discussed further below.

It is not at all evident from this paper that when Jackson wrote in 1954 of the importance of considering the *interaction* between the parents as influencing the child's development he had already imagined observing this interactional behavior directly. In that article it is clear that the data on parental interaction come from the patients' reports during individual therapy, in some cases verified by interviews with one or both parents or an outside source, such as a family physician. As Jackson and Weakland (1959) noted a few years later:

> Before the intensive study of the families of schizophrenic patients was begun, relatively few years ago, only the patient's statements and the hunches of the therapist were available as data, because it was not considered proper for the therapist to see the family and the hospital was usually happier when they did not come around. (p. 618)

Jackson (1957b) traced the beginning of his understanding of schizophrenia to 1955, when he and his colleagues on the Bateson project began conducting conjoint family therapy sessions and recording and studying what actually transpired within these families: "By participating in the interaction of the families of schizophrenics, I have gotten a feel for what the patient has been up against" (p. 181). Jackson contrasted his new understanding with the limited meanings for such concepts as "rejection" and "flooding of the ego by the id" he had heretofore been able to glean from seeing schizophrenic patients in intensive individual therapy and group therapy and through the collaborative individual treatment of their parents.

Of Jackson's early papers, perhaps the best known is "The Question of Family Homeostasis," published in 1957, but written four years earlier (Jackson, 1957a). Loosely organized and impressionistic, the paper reveals Jackson's struggles to conceptualize the crucial phenomenon he had observed in his clinical work: Sometimes when the patient gets better, another family member gets worse. For example, Jackson cited the case of a young woman plagued with recurrent depressions who began to become more self-assured as a result of individual psychotherapy. As the wife improved, her husband became increasingly alarmed, but refused to enter treatment himself, complaining instead to her psychiatrist about his wife's "worsening" condition. After reporting to the psychiatrist one evening that he feared his wife would commit suicide, the husband shot himself the next morning.

Jackson implied by the paper's title, and a reference in the first few paragraphs to the work of Bernard and Cannon on physiological homeostasis, that he believed that similar homeostatic mechanisms are responsible for the clinical phenomena he presented, although he never quite got around to stating this directly or to discussing it in any depth. This rather surprising inarticulateness notwithstanding, the concept of family homeostasis has had a profound impact upon the family therapy field, as will be evident later in this book (see Chapter 13).

Greenberg (1977) reviews Jackson's entire body of work, including the papers written in the 1960s, which fall outside the scope of this chapter.

GREGORY BATESON

Among the pioneering thinkers discussed in this chapter, Bateson is like a breath of fresh air blowing through the somewhat musty confines of psychiatric thinking of the 1940s and 1950s. For struggle as they might against the restrictions of their psychoanalytic training, Fromm-Reichmann, Ackerman, Lidz, Wynne, and Bowen were still psychiatrists socialized within a particular view of the world. Bateson, an anthropologist by training and at heart a philosopher, was a true outsider who, during family therapy's formative years, worked in medical settings just as earlier in his career he had done field work in the far-flung cultures of New Guinea and Bali. Bateson (1958) noted, for example, that "*Naven* was written almost without benefit of Freud" (p. 282), a "fortunate circumstance" (p. 282), he thought, which allowed him to avoid indulging in "an orgy of interpreting symbols" (p. 282) and instead, to view other cultures in new ways.

In part because he was an outsider speaking a different language, Bateson is difficult to understand. He provides, in the words of my colleague Neil Scott, a kind of litmus test for family therapists: You are making progress in the field if you understand a bit more of Bateson each time you read him. Other factors contribute to this difficulty. Malcolm (1978) likens Bateson's work more to poetry than the usual scientific exposition and suggests that, within the British intellectual system of Bateson's training, "a serious thinker should sound as if he were mumbling to himself" (p. 56).

Bateson himself sheds light on this issue in an autobiographical account of the development of his ideas. He (Bateson, 1941) refers to his "mystical view of phenomena" and regards loose, analogical thinking as essential to the development of fresh ideas and necessary alongside the stricter, operational thinking long seen as the epitome of scientific thought. "As I see it, the advances in scientific thought come from a *combination of loose and strict thinking*, and this combination is the most precious tool of science" (p. 75).

Bateson's early anthropological contributions, along with his descriptions of the thought processes leading to these notions, illustrate the point of view of this chapter: New knowledge is created from the intersection of crucial observations and ideas. In turn, this early work forms the basis for Bateson's important contributions to family therapy.

Bateson self-consciously reflects on the process of his own learning about foreign cultures, using his intellectual struggles as data about the development of knowledge. For example, in the epilogue to the 1958 edition of *Naven* he stated:

> *Naven* was a study of the nature of explanation. The book contains of course details about Iatmul life and culture, but it is not primarily an ethnographic study, a retailing of data for later synthesis by other scientists. Rather, it is an attempt at synthesis, a study of the ways in which data can be fitted together, and the fitting together of data is what I mean by "explanation." (pp. 280–281)

In the 1930s, Bateson was doing anthropological field work among the Iatmul, a headhunting tribe in New Guinea. This research was described in *Naven* (1958), first published in 1936 and recently reviewed by Hoffman (1981). Bateson (1941) reports being struck by an essential difference between the Iatmul culture and our own: They have no chiefs and lack any sort of hierarchical organization within clans to settle differences between clan members or punish members' behavior. In searching for an analogy to understand this difference between the two cultures, Bateson seized upon the difference between two methods of segmentation in animals: Radially symmetric animals, such as jellyfish, where the parts are similar to each other versus transversely segmented animals, such as earthworms and man, where successive parts differ from one another. Bateson wrote that this analogy provided him with an idea in the form of a visual diagram that he could use to describe more precisely the contrast between the Iatmul culture and our own: Fission in our own hierarchical society tends to be heretical, as when a group secedes from the larger society because of differences in beliefs; among the Iatmul, in contrast, fission was schismatic, resulting in a new, separate group with more or less identical beliefs.

Impressed with this striking contrast with our own culture, Bateson began to look more intently at the rivalrous, warring behavior among males that seemed to dominate the Iatmul society: One aggressive display led to another even more intense, often resulting in homicide or the splitting of the group. Bateson's attention was also soon captured by the naven ceremony, which he eventually saw as a means of reducing the group's tendency to split.

The naven ceremony celebrated the acts or achievements of a *laua*—who could be a boy or girl or man or woman—by the laua's mother's brother, termed *wau*. Although it also marked the accomplishments of females, the naven ceremony was more frequently performed for males. Bateson (1958) describes several classes of events that could serve as the occasion for the naven, including major achievements, such as homicide and acts related to the killing of animals as well as of humans; the first performance of any culturally prescribed act (e.g., making a spear or a digging stick); changes of status; and boasting by *laua* to *wau*. The outstanding characteristic of the naven ceremony is exaggerated crossdressing by both men and women. The *wau* dresses himself in filthy widow's clothing, adopts a totally decrepit posture, and is addressed as "mother" as he walks feebly about the village looking for his "child" (the *laua*). In the case of a boy, if the *wau* finds his *laua*, he further demeans himself by rubbing the cleft of his buttocks along the *laua's* shin in a gesture of sexual submission. The *laua*, in turn, presents valuables to the *wau* to "make him all right" and end the display. The more elaborate navens involve the women as well. The *laua's* sisters, paternal aunts, and sisters-in-law dress in the finest of male attire and walk proudly about the village in caricature of the males' typical aggressive and exhibitionistic behavior.

Bateson thus directed his attention to two central processes that appeared to characterize the Iatmul: the escalating rivalry among the men, resulting frequently in killing and the splitting of the group; and the clear role differentiation between the sexes, which was fantastically exaggerated in the naven ceremony. To conceptualize these phenomena he invented the term "schismogenesis," referring to those "vicious circles" in human behavior in which the actions of A stimulate B's behavior, leading in turn to more intense action by A, etc. Furthermore, he distinguished between symmetrical schismogenesis in which the actions of A and B are similar (e.g., competition, rivalry) and complementary schismogenesis in which they are dissimilar, but reciprocal (e.g., dominance–submission or exhibitionism–admiration). Schismogenesis corresponds to what cybernetics calls deviation-amplifying feedback (see Chapter 3).

Bateson (1958) then discussed certain psychiatric phenomena in terms of his notion of schismogenesis. For example, he saw the paranoid's delusions about his wife's unfaithfulness as part of an escalating complementary schismogenic process in which her attempts to convince him of her utter devotion make him more suspicious. Drawing on these observations, Bateson proposed a psychotherapeutic approach that departs from Freudian psychoanalysis. He noted that analysis promotes a "diachronic" view of the individual, which sees present misery as a result of past events. Contrasting this with a "synchronic" approach, which focuses instead upon the current behavior in the individual's social environment, Bateson (1958) proposed a therapy aimed at making "the patient see his reactions to those around him in synchronic terms, so that he would realise and be able to control the schismogenesis between himself and his friends" (p. 181). Here Bateson clearly foreshadowed the emphasis in modern family systems thinking on explanatory factors in the present rather than the past (see Chapter 3).

Bateson (1958) also recognized that the inevitable outcome of schismogenic processes as he described them (whether of the complementary or the symmetrical type) was the eventual collapse of the system and concluded:

> We must therefore think of schismogenesis, not as a process which goes inevitably forward, but rather as a process of change which is in some cases either controlled or continually counteracted by inverse processes. (p. 190)

Here he invoked the term "dynamic equilibrium," borrowed from chemistry where it refers to apparently stationary states that involve simultaneous opposed chemical reactions. Bateson admitted that he had no systematically collected data to demonstrate the existence of such processes, but he expressed confidence that some such phenomena must occur to limit schismogenesis.

In struggling with this issue, Bateson considered two classes of possibilities: (1) An additional factor might limit the progress of schismogenesis. For example, although the Iatmul boy is trained to admire and to imitate harsh behavior (thus creating the danger of escalating harshness), he also learns that certain extremes of harshness are dangerous and will not be tolerated by the group; (2) there may be a counterbalancing schismogenesis that, by itself, would also escalate out of control. Here Bateson (1958) suggested that

> actually no healthy equilibrated relationship . . . is either purely symmetrical or purely complementary, but that every such relationship contains elements of the other type . . . it is possible that a very small admixture of complementary behaviour in a symmetrical relationship, or a very small admixture of symmetrical behaviour in a complementary relationship, may go a long way towards stabilising the position. (p. 193)

He cited the example of the squire who mitigates the tension of his essentially complementary relationship with the villagers by once a year engaging in the symmetrical rivalry of cricket.

Bateson (1949) wrote that immediately after finishing the manuscript of *Naven* he went to Bali, prepared to apply his new idea of schismogenesis to the study of another culture. There, however, he found no schismogenic sequences. In contrast to the Iatmul, Balinese society discouraged competitive displays, had definite methods for resolving quarrels, and was structured according to a very rigid caste system. In attempting to understand these new observations, Bateson borrowed the game theory of von Neumann (von Neumann and Morgenstern, 1953). Although Iatmul men appear to be striving to maximize such things as prestige or self-esteem, the Balinese, Bateson concluded, seem to be attempting to maximize "stability." In describing the "steady state" arrived at by the Balinese, Bateson (1949) clearly saw this as a dynamic rather than a static equilibrium, where "motion is essential to balance" and the "steady state is maintained by continual nonprogressive change" (p. 51).

In contrasting cultures such as the Balinese, which is organized to maintain a steady state, with those dominated by schismogenesis, Bateson added what cyberneticists came to call deviation-reducing feedback (Chapter 3) to the picture he had developed earlier from his work among the Iatmul.

In the 1940s, Bateson's own acquaintance with cybernetic thinking appears to have been in its infancy as he groped for more precise ways to describe the observations of schismogenic and steady-state processes. He was intrigued (Bateson, 1949) to find in Richardson's (1939) analysis of international armaments races a mathematical equation to describe the escalating process he had termed symmetrical schismogenesis. And Bateson noted that Richardson's equations for "submission" described a process that differed from his own definition of progressive complementary relationships; he does not, however, seem to have connected Richardson's formulation with his own description of the steady-state processes among the Balinese reported later in the same essay.

It is clear that by 1949, Bateson was becoming familiar with the work of the cyberneticists. For example, he cited (Bateson, 1949) Ashby's (1945) discussion of control mechanisms in steady-state systems. And in the same year he coauthored a *Psychiatry* article with Jurgen Ruesch (Ruesch and Bateson, 1949), which described an ambitious program for the study of social interaction. Ruesch and Bateson noted that interpersonal events had traditionally been described either in terms of individual personalities or of social structure. Breaking new ground, they outlined a conceptual framework for the observational description of social interaction itself. They cited Weiner's (1948) concept of information, discussed self-regulatory, reversible processes as well as irreversible change in systems, and described circular causal processes (see Chapter 3).

In the epilogue to the revised edition of *Naven*, Bateson (1958) credited the Macy Conferences that met during the years following World War II with having introduced him to cybernetic thinking. He noted that in these meetings the importance of the idea of negative feedback was emphasized. This notion had been exploited previously by Maxwell in describing the mechanics of steam engines and by Bernard and Cannon in formulating the principle of physiological homeostasis, but the power of this idea had previously gone unrecognized in the social sciences.

According to Jackson (1968) it was, in fact, the notion of homeostasis that sparked his own acquaintance with Bateson:

> On a bleak January day in 1954, I gave the Frieda Fromm-Reichmann lecture at the Palo Alto Veterans Administration Hospital. In the audience was Gregory Bateson, and he approached me after the lecture. My topic was the question of family homeostasis, and Bateson felt the subject matter related to interests that he shared on a project with Jay Haley and John Weakland. (p. v)

Armed later with a clearer understanding of negative feedback and self-correcting causal circuits, in a new epilogue to *Naven*, Bateson (1958) again took up the problem of the Iatmul culture that, he admitted, he had not solved to his satisfaction in the original 1936 edition:

Schismogenesis appeared to promote progressive change, and the problem was why this progressive change did not lead to a destruction of the culture as such. With self-corrective causal circuits as a conceptual model, it was now natural to ask whether there might exist, in this culture, functional connections such that appropriate controlling factors would be brought into play by increased schismogenic tension. It was not good enough to say [as Bateson had to be content with saying in 1936] that symmetrical schismogenesis happened by coincidence to balance the complementary. It was now necessary to ask, is there any communicational pathway such that an increase in symmetrical schismogenesis will bring about an increase in the corrective complementary phenomena? Could the system be circular and self-corrective? The answer was immediately evident [Bateson refers here to his initial description of one of the occasions for the naven ceremony: the boasting of *laua* to *wau*]. The *naven* ceremonial, which is an exaggerated caricature of a complementary sexual relationship between *wau* and *laua*, is in fact set off by overweening symmetrical behavior. When *laua* boasts in the presence of *wau*, the latter has recourse to *naven* behavior. Perhaps in the initial description of the contexts for *naven* it would have been better to describe this as the primary context, and to see *laua's* achievements in headhunting, fishing, etc., as particular examples of achieved ambition or vertical mobility in *laua* which place him in some sort of symmetrical relationship with *wau* . . . *wau* uses *naven* to control that breach of good manners of which *laua* is guilty when he presumes to be in a symmetrical relationship with *wau*. (pp. 289–290)

The nature of the relationship between positive and negative feedback, between symmetry and complementarity, with which Bateson struggled continues to be a live issue in the field to the present day (See Chapters 3 and 13).

Some of Bateson's most important papers have been collected and published as his *Steps to an Ecology of Mind* (1972). For the serious family systems thinker and therapist, there is no substitute for wrestling with Bateson in the original.

THE DOUBLE BIND PAPER

From Frieda Fromm-Reichmann's 1948 notion of the schizophrenogenic mother to Bateson's developing interest in cybernetics, the stage was set for what was perhaps the single most important catalytic event in the formation of the family therapy movement:

the 1956 publication of the famous double bind paper by Bateson, Jackson, Haley, and Weakland.

Bateson and his colleagues based their approach to schizophrenia on the part of communications theory that Whitehead and Russell (1910) had labeled the Theory of Logical Types. According to this notion, introduced by Whitehead and Russell to avoid certain paradoxes in formal logic, a class and its members are of different levels of abstraction (logical type). Unlike the mathematician's and philosopher's ability to prohibit certain occurrences by decree, in human interaction differences of logical type are often not maintained, resulting in extreme cases, Bateson et al. argued, in the symptoms of schizophrenia. They cited the schizophrenic's use of unlabeled metaphor as a particular example of the failure to discriminate logical type. That is, the schizophrenic uses metaphor either without knowing himself that his statements are metaphoric rather than literal or else without letting the listener know that his utterances are to be taken metaphorically. Such use of metaphor is a particular instance of a more general inability to discriminate the logical type of communication.

Assuming that the schizophrenic's difficulty with logical typing of his own and others' messages is a product of his particular family learning environment, Bateson and his colleagues hypothesized that in this learning context, which they term the "double bind," it is adaptive to fail to learn to discriminate logical types.

The double bind situation has the following necessary ingredients:

1. Two or more persons, one of whom is the "victim" of the bind perpetrated by the other(s). Apparently following the thinking of Fromm-Reichmann, Bateson and his colleagues pictured the mother of the schizophrenic as binding the child, although they noted that the mother may be joined in inflicting the bind by the father or siblings and also that the father may contribute by failing to protect the child from the pathological influence of the mother. The authors' causal thinking appears to be essentially linear here: The double bind is something the mother does to the child. However, later in the paper, when discussing the double bind vis-à-vis the therapeutic situation, they allow that the patient may at times impose a double bind on the therapist.

2. Repeated experience rather than a single traumatic event.

3. A primary message. This may take the form of an injunction that threatens punishment if it is not obeyed. For example, "If you do X I will punish you."

4. A secondary message that conflicts with the first, but is at a more abstract level. This higher-order secondary message is often communicated nonverbally and may, for example, take the form "Do not see me as punishing."

5. A tertiary injunction that prohibits the victim from either leaving the field or from commenting upon the discrepancy between the primary and the secondary injunction. Ultimately, the child's dependence upon the relationship to the parent enforces this tertiary injunction.

The authors assert that a breakdown will occur in an individual's ability to discriminate between logical types when (1) the person believes that it is vitally important that he accurately discriminate the message being received in order to make an appropriate response; (2) the other person is sending two orders of message, one of which disconfirms the other; and (3) the individual cannot metacommunicate, i.e., comment on the messages, in order to find out which message should be responded to.

In describing the application of the double bind situation to clinical work with schizophrenics, the authors made it clear that their data included observations made in the course of conjoint family therapy with schizophrenics and their families as well as information gathered using the traditional methods of scrutinizing therapists' reports about their patients, individual interviews of family and patient, etc.

The authors' clinical example of the double bind situation focused on the mother of the schizophrenic who becomes anxious and withdraws as the child approaches her, but who cannot accept her anxiety and hostility and instead simulates closeness and affection. Two orders of message are involved here. First, as the child approaches, the mother withdraws, telling the child "I don't want to get close to you." However, since this message is unacceptable to the mother, it must be qualified in some way by a second message. If the mother explains her withdrawal with an overtly loving statement such as "You're tired. Go to bed and get some sleep," her second message indicates that the first is not to be taken as hostility at all and that she is really a loving mother who puts the child's needs first. Unable to metacommunicate on the conflicting messages or clarify whether approach to or avoidance of the mother is indeed appropriate, Bateson et al. suggested that the child may learn to adapt to this double bind in a variety of ways. The child may become suspicious, searching all communications for hidden meanings, a paranoid adaptation. Or the child may adapt in a hebephrenic way, giving up on the attempt to discriminate messages at all, and instead laughing them off or responding literally. Alternatively, the child might employ catatonic withdrawal to detach from a world seemingly without sense.

Bateson and his colleagues also suggested that the child's failure to learn to accurately discriminate levels of message is the price paid to maintain the mother's security and, by extension, assure the family's homeostasis.

THE DOUBLE BIND, REVISITED

Evaluating the double bind more than 25 years after its original statement is no easy matter. Two generalizations appear to be warranted. First, as a specific hypothesis about the etiology of schizophrenia, the double bind has turned out to be rather disappointing. Olson (1972) reviewed the first 15 years of research stimulated by the 1956 paper and found that most studies failed to provide an adequate test of the double bind hypothesis, either due to methodological problems or to the failure to operationalize the double bind notion adequately. He concluded: "So while the results are generally negative, the double bind still has not been rigorously tested" (p. 79). Olson noted further that "the predominant difficulty with the double bind is that it remains so abstract that it is elusive" (p. 80) and suggested a reformulation of the notion and some guidelines for future research.

In his own retrospective on the double bind, Bateson (1969) pointed to an error of reification contained in the 1956 paper that suggested that the double bind was some *thing* that could be counted. Subsequent research, much of which was interpreted as disproving the double bind hypothesis, has rested upon the idea that one should simply count up the double binds and thus confirm or disconfirm the theory.

A review of the double bind by John Weakland (1974) suggests a second and perhaps more important view of its significance. He believes that the original paper was important because it "developed and utilized a new general view of communication" (p. 274). The 1956 article can be seen as a step toward fulfilling the promise contained in Ruesch and Bateson's (1949) call for an observation-based study of interpersonal relationships. Weakland (1974) cleverly used the view of communication implicit in the original article to demonstrate its significance. Communication, he noted, involves both reports—observations—and commands—proposals for a view-point. To judge it [the 1956 paper] on the basis of its reports alone—inquiry as to "the truth of the theory" being a specific instance of this—is to take a limited standpoint and one which is at odds with the main thrust of the article itself. Man does not live by truth alone, but by ideas and influences. . . . "Toward a Theory" is more an opening wedge, proposing a new way of conceptualizing and observing old problems. (pp. 275–276)

Setting aside both the intrapsychic descriptions of schizophrenic pathology and sociological notions concerned with social structure, "Toward a Theory of Schizophrenia" focused the nascent family therapy movement on the observable communication processes occurring within the family. Thus it "commanded" a new view not only of schizophrenia, but also of the human condition and signaled the arrival of family systems thinking on the mental health scene.

Part I
Family Systems Thinking

3

The Family Systems Paradigm

Family systems is a way of thinking,
not a garage for repairing families.
Selvini Palazzoli, 1979

This chapter outlines the set of theoretical principles underlying family systems thinking. Taken together, these principles define the boundaries of family systems therapy, although they fall short of a well-worked-out theory. Those approaches not consistent with these principles are some other kind of family therapy, not part of family systems therapy.

General Systems Theory

General systems theory has its roots in the 1920s work of von Bertalanffy (Bertalanffy, 1974) in the field of organismic biology. The central notion is that an organism is an open system, that is, a system that maintains its integrity while interacting (exchanging information) with its environment. Similar developments in other fields, including communication engineering, eventually led to the realization that these ideas could be generalized to nonliving and even to nonmaterial systems.

General systems theory concerns the relationship of some *whole* consisting of interacting *parts* and interacting with its *environment*.

It is much easier to state this abstract definition than to understand what it means. In fact, it was not until I heard Minuchin speak at a workshop about general systems theory that I really began to grasp the essence of the definition.

THE BASIC CONCEPT

Minuchin (1980) said that "the individual is a part, not a whole." This innocuous statement implies a huge step away from conventional philosophical and scientific thinking, a step I will now explore.

The individual person is the subject matter of psychology. Following Western scientific thinking, traditional, nonsystemic psychology looks at the individual as *a whole consisting of parts* (Figure 3A) and explains the behavior of the whole (the person) in terms of its constituent parts. For example, in psychodynamic psychology, the parts might be ego, id, and superego, whereas in biological psychology the parts would include various organ systems.

Systemic thinking, on the other hand, sees the individual person as *a part of a larger whole* rather than as a whole in itself (Figure 3B). The behavior of the part (the person) is explained in terms of its relationship with other parts and its function for the whole. For example, to understand the behavior of a symptomatic child, the general systems thinker would not look within the child, but may look at the child as part of the family system and wonder about the child's role in maintaining the parents' marriage.

CONSEQUENCES OF ADOPTING SYSTEMIC THINKING

As a consequence of the apparently small shift to viewing the individual as a part rather than as a whole, we must revise cherished philosophical and scientific points of view as well as a common belief about what family therapy is about.

The primacy and responsibility of the individual is so much a part of Western philosophical thinking that it is very difficult to begin to think another way. And if we are adventurous enough to attempt to think in this new way, it means modifying our notions of personal autonomy, internal motivation, "being the captain of one's soul," etc.

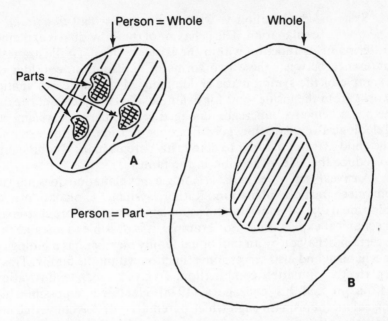

Figure 3. Nonsystemic versus systemic thinking. (**A**) Nonsystemic psychology sees the individual person as a whole consisting of parts. (**B**) According to systemic thinking, the individual person is part of a larger whole.

Systemic thinking also means a departure from traditional Western scientific explanation. Since at least the time of Aristotle, philosophers have debated the nature of scientific explanation. In his *Physics* (Hope, 1961), for example, Aristotle identified four different types of explanation. With the rise of classical physics, however, one type of explanation supplanted the rest and became established as the preeminent form of scientific understanding. Often termed *mechanical* explanation, this is the nonsystemic explanation of the whole in terms of its constituent parts, as discussed above. Mechanistic explanation has dominated Western scientific thinking since the time of Isaac Newton and was in full flower in nineteenth-century Europe when Freud developed psychoanalysis. Until the introduction of family therapy in the middle of this century, most of psychology was mechanistic, looking to intrapsychic or biological phenomena to explain human behavior. The major exception was the work of the Gestalt psychologists (e.g., Kohler, 1929; Lewin, 1935).

Systemic explanation is what philosophers call *functional* or *teleological* explanation. The behavior of the individual is explained in terms of its function within the larger system. To illustrate the difference between these two forms of explanation, consider the example of the symptomatic child again. Mechanistic explanation works from the inside, out: for example, the child acts out because he has a defective superego, damaged central nervous system, etc. Teleological explanation goes from the outside, in: for example, the child acts out in order to detour his parents marital conflict and to reduce the level of tension in the family.

A caveat is in order here. Teleological explanation does not rule out mechanistic explanation. Rather, systemic explanation is an additional type of understanding supplementing the more customary mechanical explanation. For example, it is possible to imagine that a certain behavior by an individual family member has a biological mechanism and also serves some function within the family. This is a perfectly compatible combination. To give a concrete illustration, Minuchin and his colleagues (1978) identified a possible biological mechanism through which parental conflict is converted into diabetic acidosis in the psychosomatically ill child and have documented how the occurrence of symptoms in the child serves the useful systemic function of reducing the parents' emotional arousal.

In fact, the relationship between mechanistic ("part explains whole") and systemic ("whole explains part") understanding is complementary rather than contradictory. The difficulty arises because we are so used to thinking mechanistically that we forget that there are other ways to understand and explain, assuming instead that our habits and conventions define reality. Learning systemic thinking requires that we break old habits and free ourselves to think in a different way.

Now, for a consequence of the shift to systemic thinking that hits family therapists much closer to home than this excursion into the philosophy of man and science: Contrary to popular belief, *family therapy systems is not about families at all, but rather about individual persons.* One way to see this is to go back to the history of family therapy. As outlined in Chapter 2, family therapy grew out of an attempt to better understand (and more successfully change) the behavior of individuals, in particular those persons labeled schizophrenic. It did not arise from an attempt to understand families as such.

Careful attention to the nature of systemic explanation reveals that this individual focus is more than an historical accident. To understand families using general systems theory, the family is the "part" and is explained in terms of some larger "whole," for example, the society or culture. But then one is a sociologist or an anthropologist, not a family therapist. I am not suggesting here that family therapy has nothing in common with sociology and anthropology or has learned nothing from these disciplines. What I am saying is that family systems thinking applies general systems theory to individuals, not to families.

Family therapies that are about families rather than about individuals seen in the context of their families tend to slip from systemic thinking into traditional mechanistic explanation. The (whole) family is explained in terms of its members (parts) and, in the process, teleological explanation falls by the wayside, reducing the whole to the sum of its parts.

ELEMENTARY GENERAL SYSTEMS THEORY

In the most elementary application of general systems theory, the world is divided into three kinds of objects: the whole, its parts, and the rest of the world. The whole is called the *system*, the parts the *subsystems*, and everything outside the system the *environment*. This is represented graphically in Figure 4.

Besides showing the relationship among the system, its subsystems, and the environment, Figure 4 illustrates two additional features of the elementary general systems paradigm. First, the subsystems interact (exchange information) with each other (represented in the diagram by the interconnecting arrows). The system is, in fact, comprised not only of the subsystems themselves, but of the subsystems together with their mutual interactions. Second, the system interacts with its environment, depicted in Figure 4 by the arrows crossing the system–environment boundary. Systems that exchange information with their environments are termed *open* systems.

In most of the applications in this book, the subsystems consist of individual persons, family dyads, triads, etc.; the system is the family; and our interest will be focused on the subsystem–system interface. At times it will be necessary (see, for example, the concluding sections of Chapters 4 and 6) to explicitly consider the system–environment interface as well. This might be termed an "ecological" perspective (see Auerswald, 1968), which emphasizes that the system (e.g., the family) is itself part of a still larger context (i.e., the society or culture).

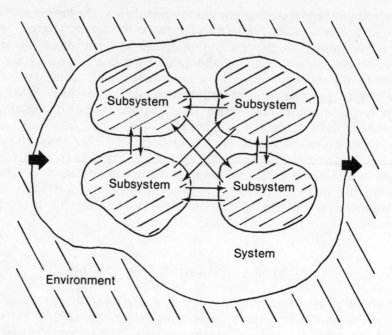

Figure 4. Elementary general systems theory.

ADVANCED GENERAL SYSTEMS THEORY

Of course, "whole" and "part" are relative terms. Any part can be further divided into subparts, just as each whole can be seen as part of a superwhole. General systems theory is indeed so general and grand that the whole universe of phenomena can be conceptualized as a hierarchically organized set of systemic levels. Each higher level includes all lower-order levels. And each level exchanges information with higher- and lower-order levels. I call this the *systemic scale.*

For a psychologist interested in explaining individual human behavior, the relevant portion of the systemic scale looks something like the diagram of Figure 5. Physicists, on the other hand, are interested in quite different regions of the systemic scale: The elementary particle physicist focuses on the extreme left end of this scale, whereas the astrophysicist concentrates on the extreme right.

Arranging natural phenomena along the systemic scale permits yet another way to contrast systemic and nonsystemic approaches to explanation and understanding. Systemic understanding always looks *up* the systemic scale to higher-order systems in order to explain the phenomena of a given level. Nonsystemic understanding, on the other hand, looks *down* the systemic scale to lower-order phenomena.

The systemic scale, as diagrammed in Figure 5, emphasizes that the family system is not the only context within which the behavior of the individual person can be understood, but is simply the most intimate context. Social and cultural contexts are important as well, and in particular cases, they may be more useful than the family context for understanding and changing behavior.

For example, to understand the behavior of a certain patient it might be much more productive to look at that behavior within the context of the hospital or work setting than within the family system. In particular, in the Veterans Administration hospital where I worked for several years I learned to pay very close attention to the way the disability compensation system at times maintains the patient's dysfunctional behavior.

Family systems therapists learn to think about the behavior of the individual in the context of the larger system. *Any* larger system. It is this way of thinking that is central, no matter which larger system is crucial in a particular case.

Cybernetics

There is some confusion about the difference between cybernetics and general systems theory. Some authors use the terms interchangeably. Others suggest that the two are different languages that apply to distinct but overlapping domains. One thing that is

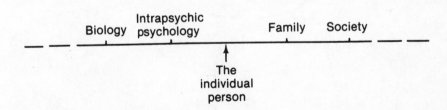

Figure 5. The portion of the systemic scale of interest in psychology.

clear is that cybernetics has its roots in communication engineering, computer science, and information theory (Bertalanffy, 1974), fields that differ greatly from organismic biology that gave rise to general systems theory.

THE BASIC IDEA

Cybernetics has essentially to do with how systems are *regulated*, that is, how they stay the same or change. In the cybernetic paradigm, part and whole are linked (see Figure 6) by a closed informational loop or circuit. The part performs some *action* (e.g., the person engages in some behavior) that has an impact upon the whole. This is the *feedforward* part of the loop. The whole then has some *reaction* back upon the part. This is called the *feedback* portion of the loop.

The relationship between the action and reaction portions of the cybernetic loop classify cybernetic paradigms into two important types: negative or deviation-reducing feedback and positive or deviation-amplifying feedback.

In the case of *deviation-reducing* feedback, the reaction to the original action results in *less* of that original action. For example, if

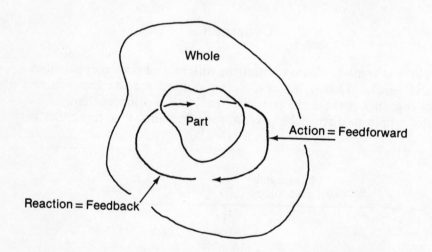

Figure 6. The basic cybernetic paradigm. A closed informational loop consists of some action of part on whole (feedforward portion of loop) plus a reaction of whole on part (feedback portion).

I shout at you (action) and you become quiet and give in to or placate me (reaction) and I then quiet down (less of my original action), deviation-reducing feedback has restored our system to its original tranquil state.

Note that "deviation reduction" is a property of the feedback loop as a whole, not of any part of it alone. It is not possible to say, for example, that your becoming quiet in reaction to my shouting involves deviation-reduction until we know that I indeed do stop shouting. This defies our usual way of describing behavior in which attributions are made about behaviors apart from the contexts in which they occur.

Deviation-reducing feedback is a model for how things stay the same in systems. The counterbalancing effects of action and reaction that reduce deviation from some standard or base-line condition are an example of a *homeostatic* mechanism. As described in Chapter 2, this cybernetic term was introduced into the family therapy literature in an early paper by Don Jackson (1957a), "The Question of Family Homeostasis." It is consistent with the experience of many therapists who have been impressed (and frustrated) by the family's ability to stay the same no matter what the therapist tries to do to change things.

In *deviation-amplifying feedback*, on the other hand, the reaction to the original action results in more of that original action. For example, if I hit you (action) and you hit me back (reaction) and I hit you again, harder (more action), deviation-amplifying feedback is occurring.

Deviation-amplifying feedback is a model for *continuous change* in systems. What are originally small deviations from some initial condition can quickly be amplified into large ones that may result in a reorganization of the system or, in some cases, threaten its integrity.

Another language is often used to describe related phenomena, but sometimes generates confusion as well. Behaviors that are similar to each other are referred to as *symmetrical* (e.g., exchanging blows in a fight) whereas those that are different, but fit together, are *complementary* (e.g., placating someone who begins shouting).

It is tempting to identify symmetry with deviation-amplification and complementarity with deviation-reduction, but this is incorrect. The terms symmetry and complementarity compare the *nature* of two behaviors A and B, whereas the concepts of deviation-amplifying and deviation-reducing feedback refer to the relationship between *a change in A and a change in B*. The latter is a second, higher-order description.

To avoid confusion and meaningless abstraction, it is necessary to be precise and tie the terms symmetrical and complementary to specific behaviors and orders of description. For example, it is possible for two persons to compete with each other to see who can be the most one-down (e.g., dependent or incompetent) in a relationship. Here, the behaviors exchanged are complementary (e.g., caretaker versus being taken care of). Yet at a higher order of analysis, the two are engaged in a symmetrical, competitive process that spirals down to lower and lower levels of competence on the part of the persons involved. In other words, deviation-amplification is occurring. This is an example of Bateson's complementary schismogenesis (see Chapter 2). One sometimes sees in couples such symmetrical struggles over who will be the most dependent upon the other.

CYBERNETICS AND CAUSALITY

Just as general systems theory bends out of shape our usual Western notions of scientific explanation, so cybernetics asks us to change the way we think about causality. Ordinary causal models are *linear*: Event A causes or leads to event B, but B does not cause A. In a *circular* or *mutual* causal process, A leads to B and B leads (eventually) back to A in a circular way.

Mutual causal processes are ubiquitous in family therapy. For example, wife nags, husband drinks, wife nags, husband drinks, wife nags, etc. Watzlawick et al. (1974) say that husband and wife are likely to punctuate this stream of events in two entirely different ways: (1) Husband says that he drinks because his wife nags; and (2) wife says that she nags because her husband drinks. From the cybernetic viewpoint, both husband and wife err in inferring linear causality in what is really a mutual causal process.

ELEMENTARY CYBERNETICS

Figure 7 represents an elementary application of cybernetic thinking and permits us to take a closer look at deviation-reduction and deviation-amplification in simple systems. It consists of a closed informational loop with three components—a receptor that receives information from the environment, an analyzer that processes this input and arrives at a decision, and an effector that translates

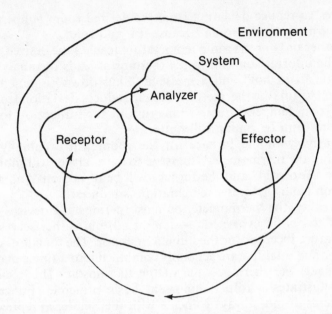

Figure 7. A cybernetic prototype. Here the system consists of three subsystems (receptor, analyzer, and effector) connected by a closed informational loop.

the analyzer's decision into an operation upon the environment. The arrows to the right represent the feedforward loop that translates input data from the environment into an output action upon the environment. The feedback loop (arrow to left, from effector through the environment and back to the receptor) provides the receptor with information about the effect of the system's action upon the environment.

The ubiquitous thermostatic system for controlling room temperature is the most familiar example of a deviation-reducing cybernetic system. Here the system includes a thermometer (the receptor), the thermostat (the analyzer), and the furnace (the effector of the system). The environment in this case is the rest of the world, in particular, a room or a house. In this simplest of models, the analyzer is preset for a certain value, the desired room temperature, by a human operator who is outside the system we are considering.

As long as the room temperature is below the desired value, the information sent to the analyzer by the thermometer leads the thermostat to conclude "Too cold" and a message is sent to the furnace requesting "More heat." The thermostatic system always operates to reduce deviation from the desired room temperature, here warming up the room because it is too cold.

Sooner or later the room temperature reaches the desired value. Now the information sent to the thermostat leads the analyzer to conclude "Too hot" and a message "Shut down" is sent to the furnace. Again, the thermostatic system reduces deviation from the preset room temperature, this time turning the furnace off to keep the room from becoming still hotter.

Clearly, with the furnace off the room will eventually cool down and the thermometer's message to the analyzer will sooner or later be "Too cold" and the furnace will be turned on. And again, deviation from the preset temperature is reduced.

In reality, the thermometer on most thermostatic devices is not part of the basic cybernetic system at all, but rather serves as a temperature receptor for the human operator. The functions of the receptor and analyzer are generally combined into a single material component, the thermocouple of the thermostat. This technical detail illustrates a rather important basic principle: Functional subsystems do not always coincide with their material representations. We twentieth-century Western thinkers take for granted that the individual human being is the functional unit whose boundaries are the skin. Family systems therapists must learn to think differently. More about this below.

Lest the reader erroneously conclude that cybernetic paradigms are appropriate for describing the operation of nonhuman machines only, a quick human example is in order. When performing many overlearned functions, such as driving a car, we act like cybernetic systems governed by deviation-reducing feedback. We have all had the experience of driving our car along a well-defined and familiar route, performing in a thoroughly competent and appropriate manner only to realize that for the past several minutes we have been paying no attention to our driving.

In this case, our eyes, as well as our auditory and kinesthetic senses, function as the receptors of the cybernetic system regulating our driving behavior. The analyzer includes many regions of the brain's cortex. And the effector, in this case, consists of the brain's motor strip and the muscles of the arms and legs plus the automobile itself. The present condition is one in which the car is traveling nicely down the middle of the proper lane at an appropriate speed. The car is maintained on course because this cybernetic machine is "error-activated." Information (primarily visual) on deviations from the appropriate course is provided to the areas of the brain that integrate sensory input and organize coordinated chains of motor behavior. Activated by such errors, adjustments are made automatically, keeping the car on course entirely without conscious attention.

A plausible, though luckily uncommon example of a deviation-amplifying cybernetic system is the couple who get the dual controls of their electric blanket crossed. If the husband is too hot, he turns down "his" control. Since this actually turns down his wife's side of the blanket, he remains too hot and turns down "his" control some more. Sooner or later, his wife becomes uncomfortably cold and turns up "her" control, heating up her husband's side of the blanket even more, leading him to turn "his" control down further, etc.

This situation can be made to fit the basic cybernetic paradigm as shown in Figure 8. (Here the husband is arbitrarily made part of the "system" while his wife is part of the "environment.")

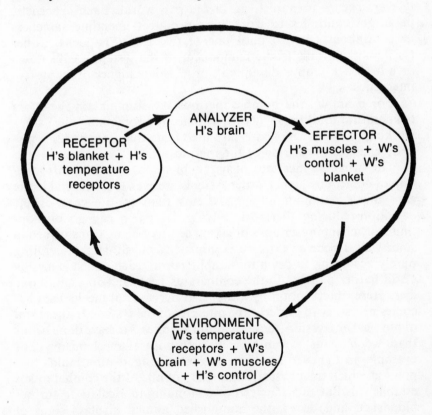

Figure 8. An example of deviation-amplifying feedback. The couple (husband, H; wife, W) get the dual controls of their electric blanket crossed.

This example illustrates even more clearly than does that of the thermostat the important idea that functional subsystems do not necessarily coincide with their material realizations. Here, for instance, the system's analyzer includes the husband's muscles and the wife's control and blanket. To apply cybernetic thinking to even fairly simple human systems, one can no longer define an individual as bounded by skin. This is the kind of thinking that led Bateson (1971) to conclude that the mind is not contained within the body.

MORE COMPLEX CYBERNETIC SYSTEMS

Although it is absolutely essential to understand these two basic cybernetic paradigms, each by itself is rather dull and rarely, if ever, occurs in pure form in the real world. Each cybernetic paradigm continues to work (i.e., produces unending sameness or continuous change) until one of two things happens. Either (1) the system fails (some component of the system breaks down or a feedback loop is disrupted); or (2) some higher-order system intervenes.

For example, the humble thermostat will maintain the room temperature until either (1) the furnace (or something else) stops working or the thermostat is insulated from the room or (2) somebody changes the setting of the thermostat.

The twin complications of system breakdown and the introduction of control by higher-order systems are even more crucial in the case of deviation-amplifying systems than in the case of the deviation-reducing thermostat. No real system can go on continuously changing without breaking down or being transformed in some way. To cite an extreme example, in a physical fight operating purely according to deviation-amplification, each punch is met by a still harder punch and the combatants beat each other until one dies. Here, intervention by a higher-order control mechanism becomes necessary to preserve the integrity of the system. In the realm of physical aggression, the animal world appears to have done better than we humans at building in such control mechanisms. For example, in fights to establish dominance, aggression builds to a point at which the physical superiority of one of the combatants is established. But then, instead of continuing to escalate to further bloodshed and death, the vanquished animal displays signs of submission, switching the system from deviation-amplification to deviation-reduction, and the fight is over. Animal behaviorists refer to such submissive displays as "cut-off" behavior (Chance, 1962).

It is easy to see how, in extreme cases, pathology occurs when deviation-amplifying and deviation-reducing processes are imbalanced. Consider, for example, the "runaway" system in a crisis of physical violence between family members, on one hand, and the "stuck" family unable to change to meet new demands from within or outside the family, on the other.

But this should not lead to the belief that either deviation-amplifying or deviation-reducing processes are "bad." It is obvious that all living systems maintain stability and are also able to change. Clearly, deviation-reducing mechanisms are needed to ensure the system's integrity, but without deviation-amplifying processes, growth is impossible.

Cybernetics is general enough so that, theoretically at least, all natural phenomena can be described as complex combinations of deviation-amplifying and deviation-reducing processes. As with general systems theory, however, this generality quickly becomes more curse than blessing as the complexity of several levels of interacting cybernetic systems quickly boggles the mind. Family therapists have barely scratched the surface in applying cybernetic thinking beyond pure deviation-amplifying or deviation-reducing types.

In particular, the task of integrating deviation-amplifying and deviation-reducing processes in a single descriptive paradigm is one Bateson struggled with as early as the 1930s (see Chapter 2) and with which the family therapy field still wrestles today (see Chapter 13).

The Principle of Equifinality

Open systems in which deviation-reducing feedback operates reach a *steady state* that is independent of the initial conditions of the system and depends only on the system parameters, that is, on the characteristics of the system itself. This observation goes by the impressive name of the *principle of equifinality* (Bertalanffy, 1974).

For example, the steady-state room temperature maintained by the thermostat depends solely upon the preset temperature (a system parameter), independent of the temperature of the room at the time the thermostat was set. (This is strictly true only if the effector includes an air conditioner as well as a furnace so that if the room is initially too hot it will be cooled to the desired temperature.)

The equifinality of open systems is to be contrasted with the state of affairs in closed systems in which initial conditions determine the system's equilibrium.

The principle of equifinality has important implications for family systems thinking. A given organismic state may have evolved from any of several different initial states along multiple paths. There is no one-to-one correspondence between past and present states of the system.

As a consequence of the principle of equifinality, family systems therapists are not interested in the kind of *etiological* explanations (in which current conditions depend on past causes) that characterize most medical and psychological thinking. Instead they are primarily interested in the here-and-now, in observing ongoing sequences of current behavior rather than in learning family history. From the systemic point of view, the *current* functioning of the system is maintaining the dysfunctional behavior, and so it is the current behavior patterns that need changing.

The Developmental Principle

Having just explained the principle of equifinality and dismissed the past as being of no interest to family systems thinkers, I am immediately forced to qualify this statement. This is a very muddled issue within the field, one with which I have struggled in my own thinking and teaching for the past several years.

Family systems thinking must include some form of *developmental principle* that recognizes the evolutionary change in system membership across time. Cybernetics explains the mutual regulation of behavior among a given set of system members, but has no way to account for the addition and subtraction of the members themselves. Families begin, reproduce themselves and change in certain predictable ways, and end. Individuals are born into families and eventually leave or die and family life unfolds from within, as it were, according to a pattern that has both biological and sociocultural elements. The biological givens are birth and death.

The cultural contribution is chiefly society's expectation that the individual eventually becomes independent of the family.

The developmental principle implies that the family's current organization (the interest of cybernetic thinking) must be seen in the context of its past and, perhaps more important, its future. Developmental thinking leads family systems therapists to ask such questions as: Is the family's current way of operating inappropriate for its present family membership (e.g., the important case of unresolved grief when the family is unable to let go of one who died)? Is the family having difficulty shifting from one life stage to another (e.g., the equally important and often related case of emancipation problems in families)? These questions are explored more concretely and in greater detail in Chapter 6.

Given all of this, what really is the role of the past in family systems therapy? The family systems therapist always tries to change the current family organization so that the family functions better in the present and future. When there are significant developmental issues in a particular family, the past provides part of the relevant and necessary context for viewing and changing the present.

A New General Systems Theory

Exciting recent developments in physics are stimulating a re-evaluation of the "classical" family systems thinking outlined in the first three sections of this chapter. Jantsch (1975) sees these advances as leading to a new, dynamic general systems theory. This section briefly sketches some of these new developments and links them to the theoretical principles already discussed.

More than ten years ago, Hoffman (1971) called attention to deviation-amplifying processes in families that have often been neglected by family therapists. More recently, Dell (1982a) sharply criticized the field for its overemphasis on deviation-reducing feedback and homeostasis in family systems. This tension between the change-negating branch of cybernetics (sometimes called the first cybernetics) and its change-promoting side [the second cybernetics (Maruyama, 1968)] may eventually be transcended through the work of Prigogine, a European physicist who specializes in thermodynamics.

Classical thermodynamics was developed to explain what happens in any physical system at conditions close to equilibrium. Here deviations or "fluctuations" from the average equilibrium state continually occur, but die out through the action of "entropic effects" (deviation-reduction), leaving the overall conditions of the system unchanged. In the realm of equilibrium or near-equilibrium conditions, the Second Law of Thermodynamics applies, which requires that if the system is closed it inevitably must approach a state of maximum disorder or randomness (maximum entropy). This is a boring state of affairs, possibly of interest to physicists, but hardly applicable to social systems phenomena.

Prigogine's (1976) work extends classical thermodynamics to conditions far from equilibrium. There, very different phenomena occur and the classical view does not hold. If large enough fluctuations push the system far from equilibrium, these deviations are amplified and trigger an instability and the system undergoes transformation to an entirely new organization. Unlike the classical situation in which the fluctuations tend to be seen uninteresting "random noise," and the focus is on the steady-state conditions, in the nonequilibrium range, the fluctuations themselves generate a new organization of the system. This gives rise to a new ordering principle, which Prigogine calls "order through fluctuation." Or, to put it another way, "Creation feeds on the random" (Aranovich, 1982).

For such transformations in system organization to occur, three conditions must be met. First, the fluctuation must be "large enough." Fluctuations large enough to trigger deviation-amplification are termed "nucleons" (Aranovich, 1982). Second, there is an optimal speed or system temperature which favors transformation of the system. Third, the system must be open to the transfer of energy from the outside to feed the transformation process.

Prigogine's ideas (which can be described precisely in the form of differential equations) have been successfully applied to phenomena as diverse as chemical reactions, aggregation in slime molds, the collective movement of ants, the construction of a termite nest, and patterns of traffic flow (Prigogine, 1976).

Although this new work so far is hardly a theory of family therapy, much less a clinically useful model (nonetheless family therapists are already beginning to talk about "promoting fluctuations" in the family system large enough to produce a transformation), its implications are significant and far-ranging.

Prigogine's principle of order through fluctuation provides a framework for understanding the place of deviation-amplification in the growth of a system through the transformation of its structure. Despite the lip service often paid to this notion, it is frequently difficult to see how escalating conflict can be growth-enhancing, particularly when sitting with a family torn apart by chronic, unresolved strife. A homeostasis-oriented approach to such conflict sees successful therapy in terms of tension reduction, a return to an equilibrium state without conflict. Prigogine's work suggests a nonequilibrium approach in which conflict is amplified to drive the system to an entirely different (and, it is hoped, more adaptive) state. Minuchin's structural model appears to fit this paradigm. See, in particular, the discussion in Chapter 5 of modes of conflict management.

This new general systems theory apparently can also include the developmental principle I found necessary to add to the discussion of classical cybernetics earlier in this chapter. The addition of a new family member, for example, can be thought of as producing a "nucleon" in the system, a gigantic fluctuation that immediately changes the system's previous feedback patterns. In this way, a single theory can account for both the radical reorganizations that periodically mark family development as well as the regulation processes maintaining the family between such shifts.

These issues are discussed further in Chapter 13.

Change versus Understanding

For family systems therapists, the work of therapy is to produce change in behavior. Insight or understanding by family members is not seen as necessary for change to occur. The therapist, not the family, must understand the family. Some families change without understanding why things were the way they were or how change occurred. For a family systems therapist, this is a satisfactory outcome.

Family systems therapy alters the relationship between change and understanding. Traditionally, insight has been seen as a prerequisite to change in psychotherapy. Family systems therapists think that change comes first, and then understanding—sometimes. Whitaker has described insight as a by-product of change (Malcolm, 1978).

For some families, understanding may be useful for consolidating change that is already occurring or in generalizing these

changes to other contexts. In other cases, the attempt to understand can make change more difficult. This may be so because
when we stand back and look at a process in order to understand it,
we stop the process itself. This tends to reify it, to turn it into a
"thing" to be observed and scrutinized instead of lived and transformed.

Affect

The role of affect in family systems therapy is somewhat controversial. I have heard Minuchin tell an annoying questioner who
was taking him to task for not paying attention to a family member's feelings in a session: "I'm not interested in affect." Yet it is
very clear from watching Minuchin work (rather than listening to
him respond provocatively to questions) that he uses affect very
effectively. In another context, Minuchin (1980) explained that he
is not at all interested in asking people to say how they feel about
something, which is the approach many psychotherapists take in
working with affect. Such a question stops the process of which the
affect is a part and instead asks the individual to distance himself
and report about what has occurred. Instead, Minuchin prefers to
allow the family interaction to continue to unfold, which often
intensifies the accompanying affect and may eventually reshape the
entire process.

For family systems therapists, affect is the by-product of action
rather than the driving force of behavior. This follows from general
systems theory. Systemic thinking does not look inside the individual, whether to affects, instincts, or other types of intrapsychic
apparatus, to explain behavior. Rather, internal feeling states are
seen as the individual's response to his or her own behavior and to
the behavior of others in the social environment.

Family systems therapists are, however, often interested in
increasing the emotional temperature in a family session, not because of an interest in affect itself, but rather because crucial family
patterns are often revealed more clearly when the level of affect is
high. And certain patterns are seen only when particular, intense
affects are experienced by the family (or when their expression is
imminent). For example, the therapist may notice one family member struggling to hold back tears. If the therapist then intervenes to
get more tears, the family's protective mechanisms designed to

prevent the expression of sadness are often activated. There may be a great flurry of activity aimed at distracting the therapist's attention from the tears or at changing the topic entirely. Or the rest of the family may gang up and attack the therapist for making that family member cry.

Prigogine's (1976) work offers a theoretical perspective for this view of the role of affect in family systems therapy. We often speak, as I just did, of "increasing the emotional temperature" in a family session. This metaphor suggests that the intensity of affect in human systems may be an analog of the characteristic speed or temperature of physical systems. Perhaps at higher (or optimal) levels of affect, systems can be more readily transformed through the amplification of fluctuations.

The Unit of Intervention

The size of the unit with which family therapists choose to work can vary tremendously. Especially in the early days, some therapists [e.g., Bell (1970)] rather dogmatically insisted that they would meet with nothing short of the "whole" family (variously, but typically vaguely defined as all persons living in the household, all important persons, etc.). Others [e.g., Framo (1981), Whitaker (1976)] routinely attempt to involve three generations in treatment. Still others [Speck and Attneave (1974)] assemble "networks" of 30 to 50 relatives, friends, neighbors, etc. And some [e.g., Haley (1976)] insist that every intervention with an individual is an intervention in a family system, whether intended or not.

Here again, Selvini Palazzoli's pronouncement adopted as the text for this book is useful in conceptualizing the issue: It is family systems therapy if what the therapist says and does is based upon family systems thinking.

As a practical guide to the formation of treatment unit, I offer the following. It is generally advisable to include as many family members as possible in the initial evaluation sessions. Based upon this evaluation of the family, the therapist may then decide that it is useful, expedient, or even necessary to include certain family members in the treatment.

But it is always the therapist's way of thinking and not the number of people in the room that makes it family systems therapy.

The Treatment System

Along with post-Heisenberg physicists, family systems therapists assume that it is impossible to make an observation without affecting the thing observed. The treatment unit is, in fact, a new system that includes the therapist and the family. The therapist is a participant in the treatment system as well as an observer of the family system. This statement, which goes beyond seeing the therapist as a "participant-observer," emphasizes that two different systems are involved here. All the principles that apply to the family system operate in the treatment system as well.

The therapist's participation in the therapy is more than just lip service to the impossibility of noninvolvement. The therapist is an active participant in the treatment system, one who assumes much responsibility for the direction of the therapy. This differs greatly from the role of the traditional therapist who adopts the stance of a relatively passive observer.

Here too Prigogine's (1976) work offers a new perspective: Just as the addition of a new family member provides a "nucleon" for transformation of the family system, the presence of the therapist in the treatment system is also a source of fluctuations that may transform the system.

Finally, a supervisor, or an observer, of the therapy is part of the treatment system as well. Haley has noted (1979) that supervised family therapy with the prototypic nuclear family is at least a five-person affair: mother, father, child, therapist, and supervisor. To conduct treatment successfully in such a setting, it is at times necessary to be able to see the therapy in terms of a system of this complexity.

4

The Structural Model
Applied to Families

In presenting the clinical models in Chapters 4 through 8, a single basic concept underlying each model is introduced. If this idea is understood, so is the model. After that, additional features of the model are discussed, and the model is then illustrated with a clinical example.

The next five chapters present four clinical models that apply the theoretical principles of Chapter 3 to actual therapeutic work with families. A word about the difference between these "models" and the "schools" of Chapter 1 is in order. In that chapter, I discussed the family therapy field in terms of a somewhat confusing array of overlapping and competing schools of family therapy. A school is simply a collection of more or less integrated ways of functioning as a therapist that typically developed around a charismatic figure (e.g., Minuchin's structural school, Haley's strategic school). The models of this and subsequent chapters represent purer therapeutic methods abstracted from the mixture of approaches used by a school.

I have found that chopping up the field in terms of these models, rather than using the more common division by schools, facilitates clinical teaching and learning. Chapter 9 puts things back together again with a framework for integrating the clinical models and a discussion of the relationship between these models and various schools of family systems therapy.

Here, and in Chapter 5, I present the important work of Salvador Minuchin and his colleagues at the Philadelphia Child Guidance Clinic. This chapter focuses on the applications of the structural model to families of two or three generations. In Chapter 5, the concepts are extended for work with couples, that is, family units of one generation.

The Basic Idea

The basic structural idea is the concept of *boundary*. The term is first of all a spatial metaphor. To apply this geographical notion to social systems, a working definition of "social system" is needed. For our purposes, a social system can be defined simply as a collection of members (persons), together with their behavior with each other. Schematically,

$$\text{Social system} = \text{persons} + \text{behavior}$$

Both terms on the right side of this equation are important. Identifying only the persons involved in the social system is not sufficient. Neither is it enough to define just their behavior. To specify a social system, we need to know both who is involved and what these people are doing.

With this definition, a "boundary" in a social system can now be defined as follows:

A boundary exists in a social system if some persons in the system perform a particular behavior which others in the social system do not perform.

For example, in a lecture hall, the behavior "talking" defines the speaker–audience boundary: the teacher talks and the students (in theory, at least) do not.

Typically, a number of behaviors go together to define social system boundaries. Again in the lecture hall, the teacher typically stands while the students sit. And the students are generally closer to their nearest neighbors than the teacher is to his or hers. So the behaviors "talking/standing/spatially separate" together define the speaker–audience boundary in a lecture hall.

Another Language

The idea of boundary can be expressed in another language as well, that of *subsystems*. A boundary separates a subsystem from the rest of the system. With respect to the boundary-defining behavior, all subsystem members resemble each other and differ from the rest of the system.

Family subsystems of interest to us may be an individual (sometimes referred to as a monad), a dyad (i.e., a two-person subsystem), a triad, etc. Note, however, that this is only a shorthand way of referring to the subsystem. To be complete, the behaviors involved must be specified along with the subsystem membership.

Figure 9 shows two different graphical representations of the complementary notions of boundary and subsystem. Figure 9A emphasizes that a subsystem is a subset of the persons constituting the system. Figure 9B focuses on the boundary-defining behavior,

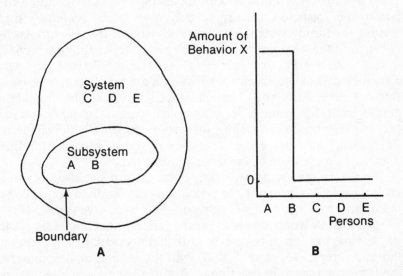

Figure 9. Graphical representation of boundaries and subsystems. The system consists of persons A, B, C, D, and E performing a set of behaviors that include behavior X, the boundary-defining behavior in the system. (A) The part–whole relationship, among subsystem-system members. (B) The boundary-defining behavior.

showing that subsystem members all perform the boundary-defining behavior, whereas other system members do not.

Figure 9B helps make the important point that boundaries in all real social systems are *relative* rather than absolute. That is, subsystem members engage in "a lot of" the boundary-defining behavior, while other system members engage in only "a little." Rarely would the graph be all or none as shown in Figure 9B. Instead, the step function would only approach zero for non-subsystem members. To return to the lecture hall example, it is not true in most real classrooms that only the teacher talks. Students ask questions and discuss the lesson, as well as whisper asides to each other. But, and this is what defines the boundary, the teacher does much more of the talking than do any of the students.

Example: The Generational Boundary

To illustrate these notions with an example closer to home for family therapists, let us turn to the *generational boundary* that divides the family system into two subsystems: the *executive subsystem* and the *sibling subsystem*. The boundary-defining behavior, in this case, is executive, parenting, leadership behavior. The persons included in the executive subsystem are typically the parents. But not necessarily so: The executive subsystem may include a grandparent, for example, or a so-called "parental child." And the persons making up the sibling subsystem are usually the children. But again, there are exceptions: For example, in some families a parent is a member of the sibling subsystem.

To determine the composition of the executive subsystem in a given family it is necessary to watch how the family works, asking the question: Who in this family performs executive functions?

Minuchin's work suggests that the generational boundary is the single most important boundary in the family system. In general, if things are right (see next section) with the generational boundary, the family is relatively functional. And if they are not right, there are likely to be serious problems.

It is important to recognize that the structural model is essentially *hierarchical*. Parents and children are treated very differently, consistent with the idea of the generational boundary. This is very different from the basically egalitarian approach of a therapist like Virginia Satir, who is apt to work hard to establish the notion that all family members are equal. Indeed, Satir has argued (1979) that hierarchy is what is wrong in families, whereas Minuchin's point is that the problem typically is an inadequate or inappropriate hierarchy.

Boundary Conditions

What do we mean when we ask whether things are "right" with a boundary? In general, two conditions on subsystem boundaries must be met if the system is to function adequately:

1. The subsystem boundaries must be strong enough to allow the subsystem to get its work done. This has to do with the subsystem's "internal affairs."
2. The subsystem boundaries should not be so strong as to preclude effective communication with the rest of the system. This concerns the subsystem's "external affairs."

Obviously, the notion is that there is some middle ground between the two extremes where the boundary strength is "just right."

These ideas about boundary strength go right back to the roots of general systems thinking in cell biology. In the discussion of general systems theory in Chapter 3, a system was described as maintaining its integrity while interacting with its environment. The "maintaining its integrity" half of this description refers to the first boundary condition, whereas "interacting with its environment" has to do with the second.

Minuchin introduced a number of terms to describe these boundary conditions. A boundary that is too strong is called *rigid* and the corresponding subsystem *disengaged*. A too-weak boundary is *diffuse* and the subsystem is described as *enmeshed* in the rest of the system. A boundary that is just right, that is not too strong and not too weak, is termed *clear* by Minuchin; there is no term to describe the corresponding subsystem here.

Illustrations

To illustrate, these ideas will now be applied to the simplest possible two-generation family, the prototypic triad of mother, father, and one child. Minuchin's *structural map* of the functional family triad is as diagrammed in Figure 10A. Mother and father constitute the executive subsystem and are shown as separated from the child by a clear (dashed line) generational boundary. This is simply a graphical way of saying that the boundary around the parental dyad is strong enough to allow mother and father to work together as the leaders of the family without undue intrusion by the child, but not so strong as to preclude effective communication with the child across the generational boundary.

Figures 10B and 10C show two common ways things go wrong with the generational boundary, resulting in family dysfunction. Figure 10B might be called an enmeshed triangle. Here, the generational boundary is diffuse (dotted line) and, instead of being two distinct subsystems, the triad is a single, relatively undifferentiated system. The child in a family like this may, for example, suffer from a psychosomatic illness [e.g., the cases of asthma or diabetes treated by Minuchin et al. (1978)]. Parental attempts at executive functioning are typically and repeatedly compromised by the child's intrusion and the child's independent development is limited by involvement in the parents' marital conflict.

The difference between families mapped by Figures 10A and 10B may be evident from the earliest moments of their appearance in the interview room. In the case of the enmeshed triangle, the child is likely to sit between the parents, whereas in the functional triad, the parents are more likely to sit together with the child to one side. In addition, the sequence of who speaks after whom may alone reveal the family's structure. In a functional family triad, one is likely to see sequences like the following: M–F–M–F–M–F–C–F–C–M; that is, mother and father hold a sustained conversation without involving the child. In the case of the enmeshed triangle, however, sequences like this are more typical: F–M–C–M–F–C–

```
  M   F        M   F        M | F
  ---          .........     .....
   C            C            C |

   A            B            C
```

Figure 10. Structural maps of three prototypic two-generation families consisting of mother (M), father (F), and child (C). (A) Functional triad. (B) Enmeshed triangle. (C) Peripheral father, stable mother–child coalition.

M–C–F–M–C; here the child is always included in any transactional sequence. Furthermore, the latter speaker sequence is more likely to show up when the family is discussing highly charged issues about which there is parental conflict and disagreement.

A second form of dysfunctional triad is that of the peripheral father, stable mother–child coalition, diagrammed in Figure 10C. Here, the father is separated from the rest of the system by a rigid boundary (solid line), whereas the boundary between mother and child is diffuse (dotted line) and the two are overinvolved with each other. This family organization is the bread and butter of child guidance clinics: Mother brings Johnny to the clinic complaining that he is doing poorly in school; she is terribly concerned about it, but the father does not see it as much of a problem; in fact, he is typically little involved in the family at all and much more concerned about work and other things outside the family.

The Therapist's Job

The structural family therapist functions as a *boundary-maker* whose job is to make clear subsystem boundaries. Freud's famous dictum (1933) for psychoanalysis "Where id was, there ego shall be" might be paraphrased for the structural family therapist as "Where boundaries are rigid or diffuse, make them clear."

The structural family therapist makes new boundaries by reorganizing the family's behavior in the therapy session itself. Family members may be instructed to enact new behaviors not previously displayed (e.g., the parents may be instructed to talk together and arrive at a plan for handling the child's misbehavior). Or they may be blocked from their usual behaviors (e.g., the child may be prevented from involving himself in his parents' argument). Often rearranging the family in space helps establish new subsystem boundaries (e.g., moving the child from between his parents to a position on the sidelines).

Structural family therapy is oriented more to process than to content. Within certain broad limits, any content will do. There are, of course, some qualifications to this generalization. First, the content must be able to elicit the desired boundary-defining behavior. In assessing the nature of the generational boundary, for example, the content must, in some way, be related to the issues of parenting and family leadership.

And second, "hot," emotionally laden topics are often more useful than those less affectively colored. As the emotional temperature of the family increases, typical patterns are likely to become exaggerated, making them easier to spot. And new patterns, not seen at all at lower levels of affect, may emerge. For example, if the therapist, noticing the mother's tears, focuses on her and asks empathically about them, she may cry more and then the child may distract the therapist or the father may attack the therapist for upsetting his wife. Such maneuvers that function to protect mother (and, of course, the rest of the family as well) from painful affects may be activated only when the emotional level reaches a certain intensity.

Finally, certain contents (e.g., suicide, homicide, physical and sexual abuse) are so urgent that they must be considered in their own right and not simply as another vehicle for examining family process. In such cases, a strategic (i.e., problem-focused; see Chapter 7) approach is necessary as well.

The Use of Structural Maps

Minuchin's little pictures of family structure (Figure 10) guide the therapist throughout the treatment. There are three general uses for such maps. First, in assessment, the therapist translates the observed family interaction patterns into structural maps. This is a desirable simplification. As mentioned earlier, boundaries are defined redundantly: several behaviors typically go together to define a boundary. Thus there are fewer structural maps than there are potential boundary-defining behaviors and the world is therefore simplified. It should be stressed, however, that no family has only a single structure. Rather, the family organization changes (or should change; some dysfunctional families lack this flexibility in structure) to meet the demands of changing circumstances and family tasks. In addition, the structural maps focus the therapist's attention during the assessment. For example, if you are a structural family therapist and you have completed a family assessment with no idea about the nature of the generational boundary, then you have not done your job.

The second major use of structural maps is in treatment planning. Each map already implies a treatment goal in the form of a more functional family organization. If a boundary is diffuse, the treatment goal includes making it stronger. Where a subsystem is disengaged, the therapist aims to reconnect it with the rest of the system.

Finally, during the course of treatment, structural maps serve as yardsticks against which potential interventions can be measured. If you are working with the family diagrammed in Figure 10C and you are inspired in the middle of a session to give mother and child a brilliant homework assignment to do together, you had better think twice unless your intent is paradoxical. Figure 10C says that mother and child are already overinvolved, and it would make much more structural sense in this case to give an assignment to the father and the child or even to the father and mother instead.

The Development of Family Dysfunction

In structural family therapy, certain assumptions are made about the development of dysfunction. The *couple* or *spouse* subsystem is seen as crucial. Note that the couple subsystem is *not* the same as the executive or parent subsystem. Although the persons are the same, the behaviors are very different, involving intimacy and sex in the case of the couple subsystem and parenting and family leadership in the case of the executive subsystem.

Structural therapists trace the development of many family problems to the couple subsystem. Couple conflicts, if not solved, tend to become translated into parental conflicts, that is, disagreements about how to parent the children. Symptoms in the child then deflect attention from the parental (originally marital) conflict and onto the behavior of the child. So, for example, rather than coming into therapy complaining of their inability to settle their conflicts about who is in charge of their marriage, a couple often presents as the concerned, but discouraged parents of a teenage girl who is running with the wrong crowd and failing in school.

Structural family therapy typically works backward along this developmental route. Beginning with the family's focus on the identified child patient, the therapist engages husband and wife not in their roles as a marital pair, but rather as parents, working with them as a team to discipline or to help their child. As the generational boundary is strengthened and the child's problems diminish, then the therapy often moves to a couple focus. The child may eventually be dismissed from treatment altogether, and then the therapist helps husband and wife focus on neglected couple issues.

Many family therapists, no matter what their particular theoretical loyalties, share this assumption about the evolution of family problems from couple difficulties and as a result sometimes move too quickly to focus on the couple. Two outcomes are likely in such cases. First, the family simply drops out of treatment. After all, the parents came to get their child fixed up, not to work on their marriage. Or, if the family remains in therapy, as soon as the couples work heats up the unresolved marital conflict, the child obligingly acts out and attention is again focused where the family all along thinks it should be—on the child.

Two rough guidelines are offered here to help the therapist decide whether or not a child identified as the patient can safely be dismissed early in the treatment. First, if the child is younger (i.e., pre-adolescent) rather than older (adolescent or young adult), and second, if the problem is neurotic, "acting-in" behavior (e.g., inhibition, failure to achieve) instead of acting-out behavior, then an early focus on the marital difficulties may succeed. When the presenting complaint involves an acting-out adolescent, initial focus on the problems with the teenager is essential. When in doubt, start where the family is, with a focus on the child's problems.

The example presented next illustrates the problem of serious marital conflict in a family with three unruly adolescents. Here the initial therapeutic focus is on parenting. In the case presented in Chapter 7 on the strategic model, couple problems occurred in the context of a pre-adolescent with difficulties related to school achievement. There it was possible, after intensive assessment of the child, to begin treatment directly with couples work.

Case Example

IDENTIFYING DATA

Mr. Bach, a 53-year-old white male, was referred for psychiatric evaluation because of depression over family problems and an impending divorce. The family consisted of Mrs. Bach, age 46, and three teenage children: John, 17; Eric, 15; and Rita, 13. Both husband and wife had been married previously, with grown children by their former spouses. Mr. Bach was initially interviewed individually by the clinic social worker. He reported that he and his wife fought a lot about raising their children, about his not paying enough attention to the family, and about his wife's drinking. These fights included some physical abuse of each by the other. Mr. Bach also described religious differences between himself and his wife (he is Jewish, she is not), which often surfaced in unpleasant name-calling when they fought. The patient stated that he loved his children and the idea of getting a divorce and not having daily contact with them was overwhelming him. It was also learned that Mr. and Mrs. Bach had had a year of couples therapy with no improvement.

In this case, the intake team disagreed regarding appropriate treatment. The intake worker, who tended to favor individual therapy, suggested individual sessions now, to help Mr. Bach sort out his conflicts regarding his marriage and his religious background, with possible couples or family treatment in the future. As the family advocate on the triage team, I recommended family therapy.

Although we like to think that treatment decisions are made on rational grounds, this is, of course, not always the case. Here, the intake worker happened to go away on vacation, and the case was assigned to me for family evaluation.

THE FAMILY EVALUATION

I telephoned the family to arrange the initial session and reached Mrs. Bach. When I explained the clinic's treatment recommendation and told her that we wanted to see the whole family, I got an unexpected response. The identified patients in our setting (all veterans seeking treatment in a VA hospital) typically grumbled and balked at including the family (particularly their children) and I was prepared to deploy my usual strong-arm friendly persuasion. Instead, Mrs. Bach said: "Oh, boy. The children will like that." I should have guessed what her statement meant, but did not.

From the beginning of the first session with the Bachs we saw extensive evidence of violation of the generational boundary. This was clear immediately in their spontaneous seating arrangement, with Rita planted squarely between her parents and the two boys arranged next to father.

The disarray of the executive subsystem is dramatically illustrated by the following excerpt from the second of our three
evaluation sessions with the Bach family. At the end of the initial
interview, the therapist had assigned each family member the homework task of deciding upon the smallest change necessary to make
a significant improvement in the family. The second session began
with a follow-up on this assignment.

*(In this session, the seating arrangement is as follows (clockwise):
therapist (T), John (J), Eric (E), Rita (R), father (F), and mother (M).
Notice that Rita does not sit between her parents in this session—but is
nearby in case she is needed. Supervisor (S) and the rest of the family
therapy team are behind the one-way mirror.)*

T: You had a homework assignment. Do you remember what it was?

(Here therapist opens by addressing the whole family.)

E: Yeah.

R: I remember. We were supposed to think . . .

*(And the children speak up first. This is itself somewhat unusual. More
typically, one or both parents would speak for the family and reply
to therapist.)*

F: (Overlaps.) I think. . . . (Stops abruptly, looks at Rita, mumbles
something, and defers to her.)*

*(Father does begin to speak, but he immediately stops himself and
acts as if he has committed some grievous error.)*

R: (Glares at father.) Supposed to think of all the problems (unintelligible).

(Rita's look confirms father's sin.)

E: (Overlaps) At least we (emphasizes sarcastically, indicating himself
and his sibs) remember.

*(Eric's remark is a very direct put-down of the parents, suggesting that
the children are the only responsible members of the family.)*

R: (Continues.) . . . that were small, but really bugged us.

J: The smallest thing that we could change, I mean. . . .

*(Here Rita and John interrupt each other in their attempts to respond
to therapist's question.)*

R: (Overlaps.) No.

J: Something really small that could make the biggest difference if it
would change. Was real small.

T: I'd like to hear from each one of you what you had thought about.

Here the parents fail to function as the family leaders, and Mr. Bach's feeble and apologetic attempts to respond to the therapist are resoundingly discounted by his children, a rejection he accepts without protest. The executive duties are taken over by the children, but performed inefficiently and ineffectively.

In the next segment, from the beginning of the third evaluation session, we learn what happens when the parents do make a concerted effort to function as the family's executive subsystem.

(*In this session, therapist is sitting between the parents, with Eric and Rita next to father. John is absent today and therapist begins by inquiring about his absence.*)

(*Therapist's position between the parents tends to turn him into another child in the family and thus greatly reduces his ability to be effective. Supervisor should have phoned therapist and told him to move, but failed to notice until later in the session.*)

T: Where is John today?

R: (*Looks at Eric and giggles distractingly.*)

M: Long story. John and I got in a fight last night, and he got physical, and a (*tone sounds as father turns up his hearing aid*), left the house. He spent the night some place else. (*Mother speaks to therapist in a rather low voice and the end of her statement is unintelligible.*)

(*This is an improvement over the beginning of the previous session. Here one of the parents steps forward to respond to therapist. Father wears a hearing aid, which he turns up in an effort to hear mother's soft comments to therapist. Although he sometimes uses his hearing problem to control others, this does not appear to be the case here.*)

F: I can't hear.

M: I just told him what happened last night.

(*At this point the interaction is established as a dialogue among the adults and father emphasizes his wish to be included.*)

F: Well, I can't hear.

R: Dad, she didn't want to yell it out.

(*Rita intrudes into the adults' discussion by defending mother and putting father down.*)

F: (*To Rita.*) Pardon?

E: (*Says something unintelligible to Rita.*)

R: (*Speaks as if scolding a child.*) She didn't want to yell it out.

(*Rita persists, in a tone that is more appropriate for a parent speaking to a child than a child to a parent.*)

F: (*Leans toward Rita.*) I didn't. . . .

R: (*Overlaps.*) I mean, you know what happened, so Mom just. . . .

F: (*Interrupts.*) No, I still want to hear. Thank you, Rita, for making an issue.

(*Father attempts to close the issue with a sarcastic remark.*)

R: Why?

(*And still Rita hangs on.*)

E: (*To Rita.*) Why not?

(*Eric finally joins in to shut Rita up.*)

(*Session continues with further discussion of incident by father, mother, and therapist.*)

Here the violation of the generational boundary is obvious: As soon as the father and mother begin to act appropriately as the executive subsystem, Rita very persistently intrudes with an attack on her father.

In addition to the observational data like those presented above, the children told of being pulled into parental conflict by the parents and being asked to choose sides, and they cited their parents' violence with each other as justification for involvement. In addition, Rita described running away a couple of times a month "when the fighting gets too bad. Then they stop fighting and come looking for me." This is a very clear statement of the function of her acting-out behavior.

By now, I understood what Mrs. Bach had meant over the phone when she indicated that the children would be delighted to be included in the therapy.

ESTABLISHING A TREATMENT CONTRACT

In this case we had much trouble establishing a treatment contract (i.e., an agreement on goals, number of sessions, and who was to be included in the therapy), a difficulty related both to problems within the family and within the treatment team.

First, Mr. and Mrs. Bach disagreed over whether the children should be included in the therapy. Mrs. Bach wanted them involved, stating that she felt that she needed their protection. Mr. Bach, however, argued that he and his wife should settle their own problems and said that there were issues he wished to discuss with his wife that should not be aired in front of the children.

Second, Bill (therapist) and I (supervisor) disagreed regarding the children's involvement in treatment. This was Bill's first family case and he felt much more comfortable interviewing couples than working with whole families. He argued in the team conference that the children were already too involved in the parents' business and should therefore be excluded from treatment.

I, a diehard structuralist, insisted that because the children are enmeshed in the executive subsystem, the work must begin with the whole family: The first phase of therapy should be aimed at strengthening the generational boundary in the sessions and disengaging the children from their role in detouring parental conflict.

It is not uncommon to find that conflict within the family system is mirrored within the therapy team. Had we been unable to settle our fight, however, we would have been powerless to help the Bach family with theirs.

Bill and I argued back and forth, each trying to convince the other. Both of us are fairly stubborn and equally adept in the art of logical persuasion. I, for example, bolstered my position by pointing out that the Bachs already had had a year of couples therapy, with no success. But Bill did not budge and it was a stand-off.

A year of failure in working with another trainee using my usual straightforward, logical and educational supervisory approach had convinced me that it is necessary, at times, to use strategic maneuvers (see Chapter 7) in supervision. Determined not to fail again, I decided to apply what I had learned the previous year to my struggle with Bill.

I saw Bill as threatened by the idea of working with a family and doubting his own competence, and I felt that I had to find some way to avoid undermining his shaky self-confidence about family work. I scheduled a private meeting with him, outside the time set aside for team work. There I told Bill that it was obvious to me that he and I were engaged in a power struggle over whether family or couples treatment would occur in this case, and that it was not a question of whether or not he could do the family work (I was sure he was able to) but whether or not he would (i.e., ours was a contest of wills). In the language of Chapter 7, I had reframed the issue from one of competence, where I felt that Bill's defenses would be heightened, to one of will.

Having drawn a line in the dirt by framing power as the issue, I now had to win. So I told Bill that I, as his supervisor, had decided that family therapy would be the treatment in this case, and that it was only a question of whether he would jump in and do the work or he would jump out and I would do it. This is the second reframing: It is no longer a question of family versus couple treatment; the issue is whether you or I will do the family therapy. Furthermore, I said, it does not matter to me which you choose. This is a crucial point in such "therapeutic double binds" (see Chapter 7). It really did not matter to me which Bill chose. If he decided to conduct the therapy, I felt that I could teach him the structural model. And if he decided not to take on the case himself, it was the beginning of the training year and the Bachs would make a fine case for me to demonstrate the approach. Bill thought about my offer for a few days and then told me that he had decided to do family therapy.

When we met with the family for the third and final evaluation session we proposed an initial six-week family therapy contract to include all five family members, with the goal of "getting the children out from the middle of the parents' business." Once that was accomplished, we added, it was likely that the children could be dismissed from treatment and we could proceed to work with Mr. and Mrs. Bach on couple issues.

Despite the occurrence of occasional physical abuse of each spouse by the other, we did not see the physical violence in this case as so serious that we were required to focus our beginning treatment on this problem. (See the end of Chapter 12 for a discussion of this issue.) Instead, we focused on family conflict in general, which was usually expressed as intense verbal abuse rather than actual physical combat.

We asked the parents to discuss our treatment proposal and come to a decision, and this is what happened:

T: (*To father*). As far as you're concerned, are they clear to you?

F: This session, or our family situation?

T: Ah. The direction that we need to go.

F: Pardon?

T: The direction that we need to go.

F: Oh, I think that's a, I feel, I, I, I hundred percent agree with it. I have no objection. I think, I think that's a good direction. (*Turns to Eric and Rita sitting next to him.*) How do you feel, how do you guys feel about that? Do you think that's a good direction?

(*Father accepts the treatment recommendation. But he knows that, in general, whatever he thinks, his wife will not agree. So instead of facing her to work out a decision, father turns to his children for support. This little bit of interaction contains the central family problem.*)

M: I do, I do agree, in many ways. However. . . .

(Mother, appropriately, speaks instead. She gives qualified support to the therapist's proposal and then appears to begin to voice her objections.)

T: *(Interrupts.)* Excuse me. I'd like to point something out, right here. Um, I laid out a piece of information, about where therapy should go, and it seems to me that it's kind of a decision between the two of you *(indicates father and mother)*, that you should be making the decision as to where you want to go, and again you *(indicates father)* turned to the children.

(Therapist's intervention here is on the right track. However, this "pointing out" is not nearly forceful enough.)

F: Well, I, I think at this point that they're involved.

T: Uh-huh.

F: They're sitting *(motions to children)*, that's ju . . . , I think it's open for discussion.

R: *(Raises her hand and attempts to interrupt.)* Excuse me.

F: *(Continues.)* I think we are always divided, Linda *(mother)* and I are divided on this and un. . . .

T: Uh-huh.

F: I take the stronger role most of the time and say "Okay, I think we [parents] should make this decision." But then the whole family goes against me and says "No, that is everybody's decision." So I think I've been *(unintelligible)* to leave it up to the whole family to make this decision. Because if I don't I'll be called a dictator.

(Father rationalizes the parents' way of turning decisions over to their children when they themselves are divided.)

T: Let's see, I just wanted to point that out and let you see that. You're right, those are things that we need to discuss.

(And therapist backs down, implying that the issue of who decides on the treatment recommendation is open for discussion.)

(Rita again raises hand and supervisor buzzes therapist on phone.)

I intervened with instructions to the therapist at this point because the session threatened to get out of hand. It was essential that we obtain an agreement on a therapy contract to provide some structure for our work, and I also wished to use this decision as the content for the first structural intervention.

The therapist had the right idea here, but his "pointing out" was only one-half an intervention. If you wish to change a sequence of behavior, it is not sufficient to tell the family what they just did. You must follow up with a directive, telling them what to do instead.

I directed the therapist to switch places with Mrs. Bach (to get him out from between the parents) and to instruct the parents to talk with each other, reach a decision regarding the proposed treatment plan, and then present the decision to their children. The therapist restated the treatment recommendation to Mr. and Mrs. Bach and insisted that they discuss it and reach a decision.

As the discussion between the parents heated up, Rita and Eric began intruding. Because we felt it necessary to arrive at a decision on the treatment plan without getting too bogged down in the family process at this point, we elected to make a rigid generational boundary by sending the children behind the mirror temporarily while the parents continued their discussion. This is a handy stop-gap technique for dealing with unruly adolescents. In addition to allowing the work to go on in the therapy room uninterrupted, it also gives the adolescents some distance and a new perspective on their parents and provides an opportunity for the team behind the mirror to interview the children.

With this and after some discussion, the parents agreed to accept the treatment plan. Rita and Eric were brought back into the interview room and Mr. and Mrs. Bach were told to present their decision to the children, an exercise in clear communication across the generational boundary. At the end of the session, the therapist insisted that the parents bring John to the next meeting.

MAKING THE GENERATIONAL BOUNDARY

Chapter 9 presents a series of excerpts from the next interview, the first of the six contracted treatment sessions with the Bach family. There we took up the issue of John's fight with his mother the week before and insisted that the parents decide upon some consequence for his behavior, treating this as another opportunity to strengthen the generational boundary by providing an exercise for the executive subsystem.

The reader is advised to turn to Chapter 9 and read the transcript from that session. For now, pay attention to the structural work and ignore the comments about other models.

Success. Despite (or perhaps because of) the difficulty of the work reported in the transcript of Chapter 9, the Bach family returned the following week for their second treatment session looking considerably better. They reported that rain had prevented John from weeding the garden as planned, so the parents began the session by negotiating an alternative consequence. The therapist next asked the parents to work on another child-related problem.

(In this session, both the family and therapist spontaneously took seats that respected the generational boundary: Mother and father sat together, with the therapist on their left and Rita, John, and Eric arranged on the other side.)

(The seating arrangement reflects the improved functioning of the family and treatment systems.)

T: *(To parents.)* What we need to do now is, we need to find other problems that are occurring at the moment between the two of you and the children, and we need to go through the same type of process of having the two of you agree on how to handle the problems. Okay? So I think what we might do now is, a, maybe the two of you could talk together about a problem you might want to work on, concerning the children.

(Therapist prescribes the task for the parents.)

F: *(To mother.)* Have we resolved the dishwashing problem? I think one of our big problems is John's schedule and not being around to do jobs around the house. We get continuous complaints from Rita and Eric that they have to work around the house and substitute.

(Father turns immediately to mother instead of to one of the children. This is another sign of progress.)

M: Well, actually, Eric doesn't do any more than John. *(Unintelligible.)*

(And mother joins in the discussion of difficulties with the children, but immediately disagrees with father by defending John.)

F: *(Unintelligible.)* I mean, Eric has an opportunity. . . .

M: *(Overlaps.)* Rita is the one. . . .

F: *(Continues.)* Eric has the opportunity, but doesn't do it. *(Ten-second pause.)*

E: May I say something?

(At this point, when the parents' discussion has reached its characteristic impasse, Eric attempts to intervene.)

T: No, this is between the two of them. *(Pause.)* Okay, Mrs. Bach, he has presented two problems that you might want to work on, and it seems that neither one of them are acceptable to you. Why don't you propose an alternative?

(Eric is silenced by the therapist. Therapist then uses an intervention modeled by supervisor the previous week in an attempt to get the parents' negotiation moving again.)

M: I want to single out a child right now. (*To therapist.*) Can we work on one child? At a time?

T: Sure.

M: Do they have to be common problems?

T: A, any problem you want to pick concerning your children.

F: (*Unintelligible.*)

M: (*To father.*) Well, I'm concerned about Eric right now. He's had problems in the last few months organizing himself, in all areas of his life, and I'd like to help him somehow and I don't know how. Eric's not open when he talks about the problems, all the time. He tries to hide them. And I don't know how. . . .

(Mother's voice is much softer and gentler than in previous sessions and her concern for Eric is clear as she focuses on the problems she sees him experiencing.)

F: (*Interrupts.*) Could you speak up?

M: Alright. (*Leans toward him.*) And I don't know how to go about it. Helping him with them. Could we discuss what to do? I think right now it's my biggest concern.

F: Well, I think, a, I have, I haven't checked whether he's brought all his homework home from school, but one of the things I do know is that the teacher asked me to call him up, next week, to see that everything is turned in. I think one of the problems is that Eric thinks we are checking up on him, but I think it's something we have to do.

(Father accepts mother's proposal of a problem by joining in the discussion with her.)

M: Um-hum.

The couple's discussion continued for about 30 seconds more and then the therapist interrupted to ask whether the couple had any disagreement on this issue. When they indicated that they were in basic agreement, he suggested that they pick another issue, one about which they had some conflict. I saw this as a mistake and telephoned the therapist, suggested that the session was going just fine, and instructed him to have the parents continue with their discussion of how to help Eric. The therapist's error here reflects his focus more on the content of the session than on the process. His previous therapy training had been mainly behavioral, a largely content-oriented approach, and he took my instructions before the session about helping the family solve its conflicts a bit too literally. From a process point of view, what has been happening in the session is precisely what should happen in this family and it needs to continue.

(*Therapist returns to his seat following telephone conference with supervisor.*)

T: Well, I think I'd like to retract what I said concerning the disagreement. I think the two of you could work on that problem with Eric. Uh, maybe you could talk to each other a little bit about what the problem actually is, and maybe you might want to talk to Eric and get his perspective on it. Basically, I'd like to see how you work out a problem in your family when one comes up. And now you're allowed to talk to Eric. Okay?

(*Therapist restates the couple's task.*)

M: Right now, huh?

T: If you want to.

F: (*To mother.*) Okay, we have a, number one, if he continues in this fashion in school, he'll fail in English and. . . .

E: (*Interrupts, speaking with scorn.*) English! (*Shakes head in disgust.*)

(*Eric quickly interrupts, with a put-down of father.*)

F: (*Continues.*) And, a, history.

E: I don't even have a history class. And English, there's no problem there.

F: (*Overlaps.*) The two teachers (*unintelligible.*)

M: (*To father.*) Math and lab biology.

(*Phone buzzes.*)

F: Yeah, math and biology.

S: (*On phone, speaking privately to therapist.*) Okay, you're going to have to do a little traffic directing. See, Mr. Bach turned to Mrs. Bach, it goes okay, and then Eric interrupts. So either conversation flows back and forth across the generational boundary, do you see what I'm saying?

(*This is an example of a very unclear supervisory intervention. Supervisor was trying to tell therapist to direct the interaction either within the executive subsystem or across the generational boundary, but not to allow the boundary to be blurred.*)

T: (*To supervisor.*) Ahhh, yeah, sort of. Okay. (*Hangs up phone.*) (*To parents.*) You can keep going.

(*Therapist ignores supervisor's unclear instructions.*)

M: It's lab and math.

F: Lab biology and math. The teachers are going to follow through, I'm going to follow through. Supposedly he brought his homework with him, which I haven't seen. I think one of the problems that's going to come up is that we need to set a time limit, so that he arranges his time so that he gets it done by, say, next Tuesday. I mean, by the third of January.

M: In lab biology or in math?

F: A, in math. He has two assignments he has to make up in biology. He also has to make up some assignments in biology that the teacher says he could make up if he wanted to.

M: (*Unintelligible.*)

F: A, I have no idea, a, I don't know. . . . (*To Eric.*) Did you bring your assignments home?

E: I have one of them.

F: How many are you behind?

E: Three.

F: What happened to the other two?

E: I don't have, well, I guess (*emphasizes*) I have them at home. Yeah, I have all of them at home.

F: (*Unintelligible.*)

E: Yeah.

(*As in the transcript of Chapter 9, the parents' attempts to get information from the adolescent are met with vague and noncommittal replies.*)

F: I think the problem exists now, so we don't have to be in the position of continuous policemen. You need to set some goals for yourself so that . . . .

T: Mr. Bach, I hear you proposing a solution to Eric. . . .

(*Therapist is right on top of things here: Father has compromised the integrity of the executive subsystem by unilaterally proposing a solution to Eric. This is a characteristic problem in such families because the second parent typically fails to support the first.*)

F: (*Overlaps.*) Without. . . .

(*Here father recognizes his error before therapist has a chance to finish speaking.*)

T: (*Continues.*) Without consulting with Mrs. Bach.

F: (*Smiles.*) Alright. (*To mother.*) What do you think about that proposal? (*Unintelligible.*)

(*Father turns back to mother and the parental discussion continues.*)

M: (Unintelligible.)

F: (Overlaps.) That Eric sets, that Eric sets his own times when he gets it done or sets himself some time aside when he's going to do that. *(Unintelligible.)* Now I'm sure that, I don't know. *(To Eric.)* How many hours do you think it will take?

(Here father again turns to Eric for some information.)

E: Three.

F: Three hours it will take?

E: I don't know how long it's going to take.

(Eric fails to supply it directly.)

F: Approximately.

E: Minimum, two hours. Maximum, three hours.

M: (To father.) Alright, could we do that? For however many hours it takes *(unintelligible.)*

(Mother stops the unproductive interaction with Eric and takes up the discussion with father.)

E: What? What did you say?

(Eric again attempts to break up his parents' discussion.)

T: (To Eric.) Excuse me.

(Therapist stops him.)

E: She said five or seven.

T: Eric, uh, they're talking. It's very impolite to interrupt.

(Therapist uses a somewhat clumsy but nonetheless effective intervention.)

M: (To father.) How about, he works each day one and a half hours on his problems? Taking out Christmas and his birthday, not those days. Otherwise, every day, one and a half hours. If he hasn't done it by after dinner, he can't go out and he can't watch TV, whichever way, what he wants to do that night. Okay? He just has to find one and a half hours during the day to do that. Is that okay?

(Mother makes a specific, concrete proposal to father.)

F: Um-hum.

M: By that time it gets done by January third.

F: Um-hum. I think that's a good idea.

(He accepts it.)

M: Okay. *(Turns to therapist.)*

T: Are you both in, in basic agreement about that?

(Therapist punctuates the interaction by checking out and labeling the parents' agreement.)

M: Yeah. (*Pause.*) (*To Eric.*) Okay, Eric.

(*And mother spontaneously turns to present the couple's decision to Eric.*)

E: That will take two days.

(*Eric interrupts.*)

T: Uhh, wait. . . .

(*Therapist attempts to help.*)

M: (*Interrupts therapist, speaking to Eric.*) Whichever, how ever long it takes on those days. . . .

(*Mother indicates that she can handle things herself.*)

T: (*Continues.*) Excuse me, Mrs. Bach, now you need to take and present the proposal to him (*indicates Eric.*)

(*Again, therapist punctuates the interaction by engaging mother in a discussion that comments on the process and highlights the sequence of behavior that is the target for change.*)

M: Yeah, I know. I tried.

T: Oh. What happened when you tried?

M: Oh, Eric interrupted.

T: (*Looks at Eric and then back to mother.*) Okay.

M: Okay, Eric. Each day until you finish the assignments, and I guess. . . . (*To father.*) Could you check the assignments each day?

(*Mother resumes her explanation to Eric. As she begins, she realizes that she has not cleared a detail with father, so she turns to him and checks it out.*)

F: Huh?

M: Could you check the assignments each day?

F: (*Nods agreement.*)

M: Okay. (*To Eric.*) Each day you work one and a half hours on the assignments, 'til you are done. You can work more. But those days when you didn't finish the assignments by, after dinner time, you can't watch TV or you can't go out. Okay?

(*Mother then turns back to resume the discussion with Eric. This is a marvelous example of a clear generational boundary: The communication is either within the executive subsystem or across the generational boundary, but not both at the same time.*)

E: I rarely watch TV.

(*Eric makes a provocative remark.*)

M: (*Speaks sharply.*) Eric. (*Softer.*) Okay? Agreeable? And I think that would be good for after New Years too, if you kept that up. 'Cause

Dad and I were really worried about you. It's not that we want to punish you or anything. It's just that we were worried about it.

(*Mother handles this firmly, while again expressing the parents' concern for Eric.*)

E: Can I say something now?

M: Yeah.

E: How come you always bring up, whenever you're angry at me, you bring up something that I did wrong and take it to Dad so he'll get angry at me too?

(*Here Eric makes a sharp attack upon mother. And, interestingly, he attacks mother for doing the very thing that the parents are being urged in treatment to do: Stick together.*)

T: Eric, is this pertaining to something they're talking about now?

(*Again therapist rushes in to help.*)

E: Yes, because, now, after this discussion we'll go home and my Mom will say, do the same thing, what I just said.

M: Eric, you. . . .

T: (*Interrupts, speaking to Eric.*) It sounds like. . . .

M: (*Continues.*) (*Unintelligible.*) Sometimes, it's hard to handle you sometimes, okay? It's really, really hard to handle you. And I think I'd like to change that. I would like to change your behavior, make you a little more responsible, so people don't get quite so angry with you. Okay? And that's something you can do.

(*Mother demonstrates quite convincingly that she is perfectly capable of handling her son, which she does again with both firmness and warmth.*)

F: (*To mother.*) I, I, I fully agree with you. (*To Eric.*) I don't see what relationship that has, your statement has no relationship to your doing your homework. It's a completely separate issue. Ah, I think we can discuss that at a separate time. It has noth, no relationship whatsoever. We have, we have a big problem, it's a total problem, not keeping to issues. And I think we really need to do that.

(*This is the icing on the cake. Father backs mother up fully, and Eric is very clearly told that he cannot get away with attacking his mother.*)

E: (*Quietly.*) Alright.

(*Faced with a united parental front, Eric backs down.*)

M: Alright. Eric, will you say in your words what we want you to do.

(*Mother spontaneously moves to solidify the good work she and father have done.*)

E: Do my homework one and a half hours a day.

M: Okay, and if you didn't do that, what happens?

E: I get some sort of punishment.

M: Okay, and after finishing the assignments, what do you do?

E: What?

M: After finishing the assignment, what are you supposed to do?

E: Turn it in.

M: No, show it to Dad. Right? Dad's checking you out. Eric? Agreed?

E: Yes.

Failure. Now, to relieve the reader of any illusions that we miraculously transformed this family in the second treatment session, producing a solid executive subsystem able to withstand any and all assaults by the children, the following excerpt from the next session is presented.

> (*The session draws to a close in disarray. Some good work occurred intermittently, but without a consistent focus or direction. The parents turn to therapist for assistance and he wisely decides to retire behind the mirror for a consultation with the team.*)

T: I'd like to leave the room for just a minute, and I'll be back. Okay?

R: While you're back there, may I ask you something? Please? (*Therapist leaves room without replying to Rita.*)

(*This is one of Rita's typical pesky questions to therapist.*)

E: You know what I really hate?

M: Um-hum.

E: When a problem occurs with me, and Dad says (*speaks deliberately*), "What the fuck did you do?"

(*Immediately Eric opens with a harsh and provocative attack on father.*)

J: No, you know what I hate about this whole session?

E: (*Overlaps, gestures emphatically to father and says something unintelligible about swearing.*)

J: (*To parents.*) You two are just, you two, are sitting here. . . .

(*And John takes over and begins to criticize both parents.*)

M: (*Overlaps.*) Um-hum.

J: (*Continues.*) Talking back and forth, and I know. . . .

R: (*Overlaps, mumbles something.*)

J: (*Continues.*) This is going to be all bullshit when we get home. None of this is going to get carried out. And it's, whatever happens here, you guys aren't open enough right here. And whenever, right now you guys, you know, you're so tense because you're holding back so much, from everything you want t, you do, you're not saying, Dad, you're not saying a thing. You keep on saying nothing back to Mom, and Mom, Mom's saying, just arguing with you. You haven't said a thing the whole hour.

F: Well (*unintelligible.*)

J: (*Interrupts.*) And I think this whole thing, we're going to get home and it's all going to kinda go into the ground, until next week. I mean, you guys don't even remember what you guys were supposed to do over the vacation.

M: (*Quietly.*) I remember.

(*Mother manages a weak defense of herself, not mentioning father.*)

R: You guys, I have a problem with Dad. He is jealous constantly of Mom, Eric, and me, that we all like John better than the rest of us. I was out there getting a drink, and John went, and Eric went, and you (*indicates mother*) said I should get a drink, so I said "Okay." So Dad says to me and Eric, "Oh, just 'cause John comes, you all have to follow him."

(*Immediately Rita pipes up and again singles father out for attack.*)

M: (*Interrupts.*) That's sarcasm, and that's what I don't like.

(*Mother joins Rita in attacking father, signaling to the children that it is open season on him.*)

R: (*Continues, now sharply scolding Father.*) I thought that was a terrible remark.

M: (*Interrupts.*) Rita.

R: (*Continues.*) It made us all feel bad.

M: (*Interrupts, speaks to father.*) That's what I mean about sarcasm. (*By now, father has his arms folded defensively across his chest and he attempts to speak for himself; Rita, Eric, and John echo mother's critical remarks as she continues speaking.*) It's just the most horrible thing to do. It kills every emotion. It really does.

(*Mother intensifies her criticism of father, with all three children supporting her.*)

R: (*Overlaps.*) It makes us all feel terrible.

(*Rita then takes over for mother and continues the attack on father while mother sits back.*)

J: (*Interrupts, words unintelligible.*)

R: (*Continues.*) And I really thought it was terrible.

F: I think it's (*unintelligible*).

R: (*Interrupts.*) Good. I hope you never say. . . .

F: (*Interrupts.*) After I realized (*unintelligible*).

R: Okay. (*Scolding.*) You should never say those remarks about any-body.

E: (*To Father.*) And besides, I do, this discussing part. I can't discuss anything with you. I can discuss some things with Mom. I can discuss nothing with you. I can, you just, you just flat out tell me something, and you say "Punishment." And that's all I hear. I don't have any, I don't have any communication with you.

(*Eric picks up the barrage.*)

J: (*Overlaps, speaking simultaneously with Eric's last sentence.*) And then you say, "This is the end of this discussion. This is the end of it. And we're not going to discuss it any more."

(*Then John begins to take over the assault on father.*)

E: I don't have any communication.

R: (*Overlaps, speaking simultaneously with Eric.*) Even if we have some-thing else, too. You walk off.

E: And even if there is discussion, it's always scream and argue. There's no discussion with you, Dad. There's no logical. . . . Even if I do have to discuss I have to scream and holler and swear.

R: Just to get over your voice.

J: (*Overlaps.*) And ev . . . , and even right now you're not really, I mean. . . .

F: Hum?

J: Even right now, you, you're not really listening to us.

F: (*Leans forward to hear.*) I'm not what?

(*This is a good example of the power of father's hearing problem.*)

J: Listening to us.

F: John, I think that's the kind of remark (*unintelligible*).

J: (*Interrupts.*) No, no, no, I, no, you didn't understand what I said. I know you're hearing us.

F: (*Interrupts.*) (*Unintelligible.*) Not listening. Yeah, I know what you. . . .

J: (*Interrupts.*) No.

R: (*Overlaps.*) (*To father.*) Let him talk.

J: (*Continues.*) I know you hear us. You hear us fine.

F: (*Speaks louder.*) I said "listening."

R: (*Interrupts.*) Dad, let him talk.

J: (*Overlaps.*) Dad, dad, dad, dad. . . .

M: (*Overlaps, speaking to father.*) You keep interrupting.

(Mother intervenes again, making it perfectly clear that she is on the children's side. This is a good example of how a parent can use the children to fight with a spouse.)

J: Dad, listen to what I said.

F: Um-hum.

J: You hear it fine. But all it is doing is going into your head and bouncing back out.

F: That's an accusation you can't make.

J: I know.

(Therapist enters interview room and returns to seat.)

R: But it happens a lot, Dad.

F: *(Overlaps.)* You have accused me of, that's like assuming that I do not want to listen to you.

J: That's right.

T: *(Sits down.)* Okay. Excuse me. We're way out of time. I have a homework assignment for you.

(Session ends.)

The above segment is a good example of an insidious process that characterizes the Bachs and other families with similar problems: The children have learned that they can split the parents and dominate the family by attacking one parent; the other parent supports the children against the spouse under attack and the generational boundary is breached. Through such a process, the parents wage war with each other, using their children to do the dirty work. And the children maintain power in the family over a weak and divided parental dyad.

Contrast what happened here with the transcript segment from the previous session. There Eric had attempted to divide and conquer his parents (in the face of their decision regarding making up his schoolwork assignments) by attacking Mrs. Bach. Based upon his prior learning in the family, Eric had every reason to think that his father would use the opportunity to attack his mother, ending the parents' coalition against him. Instead, Mr. Bach firmly supported his wife and Eric backed down immediately.

Another success. We were, in fact, so impressed by the contrast between these last two segments of family interaction that, although we did not routinely provide videotaped feedback, we decided in this case to let the family see for themselves.

We began the fourth treatment session by showing first the segment where the parents decided how to deal with Eric's school problem and stuck together to successfully defend against his attack on Mrs. Bach. "This is an example," we said, "of how things go right in your family when you two parents stick together and work as a team."

We then showed the second excerpt, taken from the interview just presented above, where the children succeeded in breaking up the parents, which we prefaced with the comment: "And this is an example of how you parents have trained your children that they can divide and beat you."

The parents were then asked to continue using the sessions to straighten out the problems with their children. Mrs. Bach, perhaps smarting from the implied criticism that she had failed to support her husband in the face of the children's attack, promptly balked at the task, objecting that the children were being left out of the sessions and were not being given an opportunity to air their grievances. The therapist simply turned her complaint into an opportunity to continue with the structural work:

T: Okay, Mrs. Bach, this is the place to work on it.

M: (*Overlaps.*) Alright. Now, what should we do?

(*Mother now accepts therapist's directive without further ado.*)

T: Ah, the thing to do is, for the two of you to listen to some of the complaints of your children and for the two of you together to discuss it and deal with it.

(*Here the therapist very simply and directly tells the parents exactly what he wants them to do.*)

F: (*To children.*) Who wants to be first?

(*And father accepts and turns right to the children to begin. Notice how well the three adults are working together here as the leaders of the treatment system.*)

R: (*Raises hand.*)

F: Rita.

R: I have, I have, one complaint, from this week. Me and my dad, I, I think. . . .

(*Rita, ever eager to complain, singles out her father.*)

T: (*Overlaps, speaking to Rita and gesturing to father.*) You're talking to him.

(*Therapist smoothly directs Rita to speak to father.*)

R: (*Continues.*) Okay, I think this is the worst thing Dad could have done. (*Speaks in scolding tone of voice.*) And I don't think you should be smiling about my problem.

(*Rita voices her complaint in the parental tone of voice she typically adopts at moments like this.*)

F: Rita, you just (*gestures to "Come out with it"*).

R: Okay. This weekend. . . .

F: (*Overlaps.*) I'm going to have a hard time understanding you if I don't see your face (*unintelligible*).

(*Again father invokes the power of his hearing impairment.*)

M: (*Overlaps, speaking to Rita.*) Why don't you lean a bit close.

(*Mother sides with him, although she could have used this as an opportunity to attack father or put him down.*)

R: I, I, I was, I went out of the kitchen. I guess you thought I went to bed. I was brushing my teeth. And me and you had gotten into a fight earlier, an argument, or a discussion or whatever you want to call it. And we had been arguing, I don't even remember about what, and both of us are stubborn, I mean, neither one of us is, we're both, stubborn. And you were telling. . . . We had, we had a guest over. Mary, Mary was over. And you were telling Mom and Mary and mimicking me about what I had done in the argument, to them, behind my back, mimicking me. And I heard it, 'cause I was just brushing my teeth. I walked in the kitchen and you sort of smiled and laughed at me. And then you guys stopped, of course, because I walked into the kitchen. (*Voice becomes shrill and scolding.*) Now, I don't do that to you, dad. So why do you do it to me? You should be the more mature one, shouldn't you?

(*Rita recites her complaint.*)

(*Five-second pause.*)

F: Okay. Are you through?

R: Yeah.

F: Okay. I want to answer you. If I hurt your feelings, I'm sorry. (*Therapist raises hand to start to interrupt and then father turns to mother.*)

T: Wait, Mr. Bach. . . .

F: (*Overlaps.*) Huh?

T: Maybe you should, maybe you should talk it over with Mrs. Bach.

(*Father begins to respond unilaterally and is directed back to mother by therapist.*)

F: (*Interrupts.*) Well, we were both there. (*To mother.*) I think, I felt a little bad when Rita walked in and (*unintelligible*). But, I think one of the things that Rita's missing is that I was relating to Mary that we're trying to solve the family situation that we have. (*To therapist*). She's a very close friend and we explained to her that we're going to a psychiatrist, and so forth, and having group sessions. . . .

R: (*Interrupts, again speaking in a very critical tone.*) But you embarrassed me.

(*Rita attempts to interrupt the parental discussion and provoke father into taking her on by himself.*)

F: (*Interrupts.*) Wait a minute now, Rita. (*Gestures for Rita to "Stop."*) Just hold it. (*Turns attention back to mother.*)

(*Instead of falling for it as he ordinarily would, father firmly stops Rita and turns to mother.*)

T: (*Nods head vigorously.*) Good.

(*He gets a stroke from therapist and continues the discussion with his wife.*)

F: (*To mother.*) We were, di discussing. And one of the things came out, that Rita (*unintelligible*) and that Rita talked and talked and I listened and she talked and talked and talked and she never stopped and she made a mention of. . . . (*To Rita.*) I did not mimic you, by the way. (*To mother.*) And, a, she continued, and you said "Well, she's just like you. (*Here Rita claps her hand to her head and whispers something under her breath.*) You're his father and she's just as stubborn as you are." And we went on like this. And at that moment, as I was carrying on and I said, Rita just rambled on and on. She complained about interrupting her, but I didn't get a word edgewise in. So, unfortunately, (*to Rita*) it was not a matter of talking behind your back, Rita. . . .

(*Here father slips.*)

T: (*Interrupts, pointing back to mother.*) Wait, wait, wait, you're talking to Mrs. Bach now.

(*Father gets an immediate assist from therapist.*)

F: (*Overlaps, to mother.*) We were talking about everybody, and a, so, I don't know, how do you feel about that? I think it was rather unfortunate, but I, I think a, you know, I'm sure we'll be talking to our closest friends. Obviously they're aware of family problems, and a. . . . Maybe we should not talk to anybody. I don't know. What do you think?

(*Father directly asks for mother's opinion of his actions. This is very courageous on his part, because he knows from bitter experience that she rarely approves of what he does.*)

M: Mary's close enough. I don't know. Rita feels bad. Maybe you shouldn't have done it. (*To Rita.*) Well, I may have done it too, Rita.

(Mother momentarily supports father, then begins to take it back. She switches again, supporting father, but talking now to Rita rather than directly to him. This hesitation suggests conflict on mother's part.)

T: *(Interrupts.)* Wait, wait, wait. You're still communicating with Mr. Bach, here.

(Again therapist is right on top of the process, directing mother back to father.)

R: Should I give an answer when they're done?

(Rita makes one last-ditch bid.)

F: *(To Rita.)* Well, I think you'll have to wait until we're through *(unintelligible)*. *(Turns attention back to mother.)*

(Rita is firmly stopped by father.)

M: I think it was sort of okay.

(Mother makes an—almost—unequivocal statement of support for father.)

F: Huh?

M: I think it was sort of okay.

F: I don't think it was vicious or anything. I think it was in a loving way. We discussed the problems that we're having. And I don't think, a, there was anything derogatory. Did you feel it was derogatory?

(Again father asks directly for mother's opinion of his behavior.)

M: No. Well, in a way. . . . *(Pause.)* Maybe if it had been me you discussed that way I probably would have felt it was derogatory. This way it was humorous.

(And she again supports him.)

F: *(Nods head in agreement.)* *(Unintelligible.)*

M: 'Cause, Mary afterward came and said, "Well, Frank's *(referring to father)* always complaining about Rita and Rita's always complaining about Frank, but they're both so much alike, it's funny." *(Mother speaks in very warm tone of voice here. Father smiles and then mother laughs warmly. Father turns to therapist and back to mother.)*

(This is a moment of real warmth between the parents, the first seen so far in the sessions.)

R: *(Interrupts.)* *(Unintelligible.)*

M: It was, she took it humorous.

F: *(Unintelligible.)*

M: *(Unintelligible.)*

R: (*Interrupts.*) The thing is, I complained. . . . (*Therapist bolts upright in chair as if to intervene and looks to parents, to Rita, and back to parents.*)

(*Again Rita attempts to intrude.*)

M: (*Turns and speaks to father.*) Should we talk to Rita now?

(*With only nonverbal cues from therapist, mother checks with father for closure before responding to Rita.*)

T: (*Interrupts, speaking to mother.*) L, le, let me ask you. I notice that you were talking to him and then she. . . .

(*Therapist underscores the sequence by commenting on it.*)

R: (*Overlaps.*) She said "Alright."

T: (*Continues.*) She murmured some stuff and then you turned and said "Alright." And, when you did that, I was wondering if you were really finished talking with Mr. Bach.

M: (*To father.*) Are you finished? Are we finished talking?

F: Yeah. I can't, I think we are through. I think Rita has something further to say.

T: (*To parents.*) Yeah. I want the two of you to be very clear that you need to be finished with each other before you turn to the kids. 'Cause both of you have a tendency to turn to the kids very, very quickly, and interrupt what you're doing. And I think that's something you're going to have to guard against very carefully. And that's why I bring that up. So you're aware of that. Okay? (*Mother and father exchange glances in agreement and then mother nods her head toward Rita.*)

(*Here mother and father are functioning together so well as a parental team that nonverbal behavior alone is sufficient to confirm agreement and switch the interaction from within the executive subsystem to across the generational boundary.*)

F: (*To Rita.*) Alright, Rita.

(*Five-second pause.*)

R: What was I going to say?

(*In the face of parental unity, Rita completely forgets her complaint against father.*)

Rita's complaint about her father might be handled very differently by a family therapist using another approach. For example, some therapists would see in it a problem in the father–daughter relationship and might have used the complaint as an opportunity to work things out between Rita and her father. From the structural point of view, this is an error because Rita's relationship with her

father exists within the context of a parental relationship in which
the children are used as pawns in the parents' ongoing battles. The
issue is a triangular one involving father, mother, and child and not
a dyadic father–daughter problem.

FOLLOW-UP

By the end of the initial six-week treatment contract, it was evident
that some important changes had begun to occur in the family as
the generational boundary was strengthened. The children, in particular, reported feeling more relaxed, with less pressure to become
involved in their parents' fights, and more time for appropriate
involvement with peers.

After some additional weeks of treatment the children were
dismissed from therapy and the sessions focused on the couple.
Here we failed. Nothing we tried made more than a dent in the
couple's bitter battles. Had we known how to use the structural
model in couples therapy, as outlined in the next chapter, we would
at least have had a fighting chance.

The Structural Model and Family Variations

FAMILY VARIATIONS

Much of the family therapy literature assumes a "traditional" or
"standard" family with the following general characteristics:
(1) white, middle-class American; (2) mother, father, and 2.5 children; (3) the parents meet and marry as adolescents or young
adults and stay together "until death do us part"—and the latter
happens only in old age; and (4) everyone accepts socially prescribed
roles, e.g., men work, women have babies and raise kids; men are attracted to and marry women, and women are attracted to men.

In reality, however, families come in at least 57 varieties and
therapists must be prepared to work with many different "non-
traditional" or "alternative" families as well. The notion of *family
variation* recognizes the diversity of family life without implying
that there is a single standard against which "deviations" are to be
measured.

Several important classes of family variations can be identified, including premature illness, disability, or death of a family member; divorce, single-parenting, remarriage, and adoption; extended families; sociocultural variations; variations related to sex role and sexual preference.

Alternative families differ from "standard" families not in their basic processes and functioning, but because of their internal *complexity* or the particular sociocultural *context* in which they are embedded. Regarding their complexity, a child in a remarried family, for example, may have four parental figures and as many as eight grandparents and step-grandparents. Or an adolescent may be attempting to become emancipated from the family and go away to college while her father is dying of cancer.

Contextual factors are related to both ambiguities in sociocultural expectations and to differences between subcultural norms and the norms of the larger society. Walker and Messinger (1979) emphasize that roles in remarried families, for example, are less clear than in intact nuclear families and tend to be "achieved" through the family's individual efforts rather than "ascribed" by the larger society. Rapid sociocultural changes often result in ambiguous expectations regarding family structure and functioning. For example, there is no doubt that our society's expectations about the structure and permanence of the nuclear family is changing as the divorce rate rises. However, society has yet to come up with a clear prescription for just how families are to manage divorce, single-parenting, and remarriage. Similarly, as fewer and fewer mothers stay home to raise their children rather than work outside the home, the old sex-role assignments no longer fit, but there are no obvious models available for combining the roles of mother and worker, father and worker. Faced with such ambiguity, families must find their own ways of being a family.

In addition to complexity and ambiguity, differences between subcultural expectations and those of the larger society also create family variations. For example, Falicov and Karrer (1980) note that the traditional Mexican–American family tends to be more firmly embedded within an extended family structure than does the middle-class "all-American" family. And Shon and Ja (1982) describe the importance of hierarchy in the Asian–American family, not only as reflected in the generational boundary, but also within the couple subsystem (with the father as the leader of the family) as well as the sibling subsystem (with sons valued more highly than daughters and the oldest son the most important of all the children).

This concluding section offers some tips on applying the structural model to family situations that vary in important ways from the prototypic mother–father–child triad that has been the main focus above. The final section of Chapter 6 continues this discussion by considering the impact of family variations on the family life cycle.

THREE GENERATIONS

The generational boundary between mother and father and their parents is as crucial for the functioning of the nuclear family as is the generational boundary with their children. And often problems with the boundary separating the family from the parents' families of origin create generational boundary problems within the nuclear family as well.

Typically, one spouse has failed to separate adequately from his or her parents and often feels torn between the two families. The other spouse then sees the in-laws as constantly intruding into the marital relationship. A spouse's difficulties in becoming emancipated from his or her own parents may instead result in a rigid rather than a diffuse boundary. For example, the spouse may have fled across the country to get away from the family of origin. And sometimes the pattern is an oscillation between periods of enmeshment with and disengagement from family. In either case, the structural goal is a clear boundary between the nuclear family and the parents' families of origin.

Such generational difficulties were very powerfully enacted in an evaluation session conducted in an inpatient alcohol treatment program. The session was attended by the alcoholic husband, his wife and children, and his parents. The latter were invited because the wife was known to resent her mother-in-law's intrusions into their family life and felt unjustly blamed by her for causing her husband's drinking problem. In the session, the generational boundary problems were revealed as the husband sat between his wife and mother, watching them battle across his head. He presented himself as torn between them, but powerless to do anything about it. In a very dramatic moment, the therapist insisted that he solve the problem "with his feet." After much pondering and more protests of helplessness, the man got up, moved from between the two women, and sat back down next to his wife.

In assessing what patterns of behavior define a "clear" generational boundary in a given family, the subcultural context must be considered. For example, Falicov and Karrer (1980) emphasize, in the case of the Mexican–American family, that child care is typically shared not only with grandparents, but also godparents, who function as coparents to the child and peers to the parents, becoming part of the extended family system. Although these additional family members may, in certain situations, be involved in dysfunctional ways, they certainly provide valuable resources as well, to be utilized as an aid in family treatment.

SINGLE PARENTS

The job of the single parent is truly overwhelming: typically, he or she must work outside the home to support the family, serve as chief, custodial parent, and also manage a personal and social life of his or her own.

Assisting single-parent families with their economic difficulties requires attention to the family's larger social context. For example, it is often necessary to put the family in touch with community agencies providing assistance with housing, jobs, and social services. And many times, the legal system affects the family in a crucial way, with unresolved questions of property settlement, child support, and alimony contributing to an overall economic insecurity.

Shoring up a sagging executive subsystem is often the most pressing issue facing the therapist working with a single-parent family. The questions commonly asked by students learning about the structural model are "What about single-parent families?" and "How can we apply it there?" The questioner typically has correctly grasped that the structural model is interested in triads composed of two adults and a child, but does not know where to find that other adult.

There are two general answers to these questions. First, look for the second adult in the life of the single parent. Most single parents are significantly involved with someone besides their children, whether it be their lover or their own parent. Get that other person involved in the therapy if at all possible, as an ally to assist the single parent in dealing with the children. When the second adult is the single parent's lover, the issues related to the "biological boundary" discussed next under the heading "divorce and remarriage" become important. If that second adult is the mother or father of the single parent, then the generational boundary issues just discussed under the heading "three generations" are central as well.

In some cases, no matter how hard you look, there is no other adult significantly involved in the single parent's life. In this situation, you are the third member of the triad. Here the therapist must become more involved in the treatment, working with the single parent as a partner in the sessions to discipline or help the children. At the same time, it is crucial not to take over the parenting job and relegate the single parent to a position in the sibling subsystem.

A recent article by Weltner (1982) discusses this issue further. He suggests that a parental child is preferable to family disorganization and advocates organizing a "family cabinet" consisting of adolescent and young adult children to assist the single parent with younger children.

The single parent's social and personal life often suffers in the face of economic and child-rearing demands. In some cases, this becomes a problem in itself when, for example, a single mother turns to her children as her only source of emotional satisfaction. In these families, the generational boundary is blurred by the emotional overinvolvement of parent and children and the children are likely to be as underinvolved with their own peers as the mother is with hers. Here helping the mother reestablish suitable, emotionally satisfying adult relationships is crucial.

DIVORCE AND REMARRIAGE

Research indicates (Kelly and Wallerstein, 1976; Wallerstein and Kelly, 1976) that children do best following divorce if they are able to maintain an emotionally satisfying relationship with both parents. The marital conflict that led to the divorce in the first place makes this a tall order for many families. Divorce sharpens the structural issues all families face. As parents split up, children are often stuck in the middle, used as pawns in the adults' continuing battles and experiencing intense loyalty conflicts themselves. Given such a divided parental subsystem, discipline suffers and the children are inevitably placed in positions of extraordinary power in the family. These structural issues are typically enacted over such concrete problems as custody decisions and visitation rights. Some direct communication between the ex-spouses, either in person or by telephone, is generally necessary to facilitate their working together and prevent the children from being used as go-betweens.

Visher and Visher (1979) note that the intense loyalty conflicts often experienced by children in divorced families have a counterpart in intact family processes as well, in that parents have their own attachments to their families of origin. As noted above when discussing three-generation structural issues, such divided loyalties may be problematic.

The recent tendency in many states to award joint custody sometimes exacerbates the family's structural difficulties. This is particularly true when joint custody is used as a judicial solution to the parents' inability to work out a mutually acceptable custody arrangement. In such cases of intense and unresolvable conflict, the ex-spouses are least likely to be capable of the cooperation required to succeed at joint custody. Instead, the stage is set for continuing the parents' chronic struggles, with each using the children against the other.

When the divorced family's situation involves remarriage, it is helpful to conceptualize the family structure using the additional concept of the *biological boundary* defining those family members related by blood. In intact families, two important boundaries complement each other: The biological boundary separates the nuclear family from the larger society, and the generational boundary defines the major subsystems within the family. In the stepfamily, these boundaries may conflict because the child's membership in a family outside the stepfamily unit (e.g., with the noncustodial natural father or mother) means that the stepfamily is not the only source of authority, discipline, and nurturance.

The problems in so-called "blended families" formed by remarriage after divorce often include a confusion of biological and generational boundaries. The biological mother, for example, may feel protective of her children and be reluctant to allow her new husband to discipline them. Or the stepfather may have reservations about becoming involved in parenting his wife's children. Sometimes the two boundaries clearly conflict. For example, Visher and Visher (1979) note that cooperation between ex-spouses is good for their children, but also may interfere with the cohesiveness of the stepfamily and compromise the reorganization of the family to include the new stepparent.

Two generalizations about boundaries in the case of the stepfamily appear appropriate. First, in order for the new family unit to function adequately, the biological boundary must not be allowed to interfere with the establishment of a clear generational boundary. Although it is important that the children maintain a relationship with both biological parents, this must not prevent the formation of a functional executive subsystem within the stepfamily. Visher and Visher (1979) stress that a strong couple alliance is essential for the successful functioning of the stepfamily, and Stern (1978) emphasizes the important role of child discipline issues in the integration of the stepfamily unit. She notes that the stepparent must first join the child, establishing a bond, before attempting to discipline the child. Visher and Visher also emphasize that the role of the stepparent in the family's executive subsystem may depend upon the age of the child. Young children often accept a stepparent's discipline quite easily, whereas in the case of the older adolescent, it may be appropriate for the natural parent to continue to carry out the main parenting functions, with the stepparent in a supporting role.

The second generalization about stepfamily boundaries is that they must be more permeable than in intact nuclear families (Walker and Messinger, 1979) due to the child's membership in multiple families with two sets of parents often sharing decisions and providing nurturance. Visher and Visher (1979) note that the child may indeed profit from the loosening of family boundaries, making individuation from the family easier to achieve.

The following case illustrates some of these stepfamily issues. A mother consulted a family therapist about her 12-year-old daughter who had missed more than 50 percent of the school days so far that year, complaining of a sore throat. The family doctor, as well as the specialists he consulted, found no medical illness, but the girl's mother was so unsure that her daughter was well enough to be in school that she regularly gave in to her complaints and kept her home. In the family therapy session, attended also by the mother's live-in boyfriend of 11 years, the mother was very ineffective as she attempted to talk with her daughter about the problem. After a few minutes, the boyfriend broke in and proved to be much more successful in talking with the girl. With this, the therapist insisted that the couple work together as a team to get the child back in school. Previously, the mother had always refused to allow her lover to help with the parenting, except for crisis situations when she typically became helpless and dumped the whole responsibility in his lap. After two weeks in which the mother and her boyfriend worked together as parents, the daughter miraculously recovered and was back in school. The girl confided to her mother: "Maybe the family sessions will help you and Jack [the boyfriend] get closer, too."

In cases of divorce and remarriage, therapists often wonder who to invite to the family therapy session. For example, do you ask the stepfather who is living with the children and their mother? Or the natural father who takes the children every other weekend? Or both? A good rule of thumb is to begin with the children's usual living unit (the mother and stepfather, in this example) and assess the clarity of its generational boundary as well as any issues related to the original biological system. When the problems are chiefly those related to the functioning of the mother and stepfather as executive subsystem, therapy may be possible without involving the natural father. On the other hand, when the problems involve the biological system of natural parents and children, including the father in treatment may be crucial. This is particularly true in the common situation in which the divorced parents' unresolved marital conflict is still being enacted through the children. Here it is important for the therapist to keep in mind the distinction between the couple and the parental subsystems. The divorced parents are still a parental subsystem even though they are no longer a couple dyad. The therapist must help the ex-spouses solve parenting problems, but not get bogged down in the old marital issues that they finally decided to resolve through divorce.

SOCIOCULTURAL VARIATIONS

Finally, socioeconomic and cultural variations significantly influence the application of the structural model. Uncritical and mechanical application of the structural approach is rightly condemned as an attempt to turn all families into nice, white, middle-class families. When this occurs, it is generally a case of putting the cart before the horse. The structural model does not prescribe an ideal family structure. Rather, it requires that the therapist observe the family's actual workings, abstract its current organizational pattern, and then assess whether or not the present structure is adequate to meet the tasks facing the family.

In assessing the adequacy of the family's organization, the therapist must always take into account the cultural and subcultural context within which the family lives. Structural family therapy is a product of late twentieth-century America, with its cultural emphasis on the nuclear family, on producing independent children who emancipate from the family, and on considerable equality between husband and wife. When subcultural norms vary significantly from these expectations, such variations must be considered when evaluating family structure and establishing treatment goals. A few brief examples will illustrate this.

Many of the parents who consult us in clinical practice for problems with their children do so because the children are, to varying degrees, out of control and the parents need help in establishing a stronger generational boundary. In working with some Chinese–American families, however, one sometimes encounters the opposite problem. Here, the children may have learned their roles in the traditional Chinese family (where they are subject to the absolute authority of the parents) so well that they appear inhibited, dependent, and sometimes depressed and have difficulty functioning within a larger culture that expects independence and rewards competitiveness. Therapeutic work with these families often includes helping the parents relax the generational boundary by getting them to share their authority with their children to better prepare them for life outside the family.

An interesting twist on this phenomenon occurs in the Vietnamese refugee families who came to this country during the past decade as well as among other cultural minorities. In many cases, the position of the parents as heads of the family has been eroded by the fact that the children typically become acculturated more quickly than their parents. The children are in school and learn English, for example, and very soon gain power in the family beyond their years by virtue of their superior ability to communicate with the larger culture. In some cases, this reversal of power results in out-of-control behavior by the children. Here it is necessary to help the parents regain power in the family while still recognizing that members who can deal with the larger society are a valuable resource for the family.

In working with multi-problem poor families using a structural approach, Aponte (1976a,b) emphasized their "underorganization." He sees such families as lacking both the internal stable, yet flexible organization necessary to carry out their functions, as well as the necessary connections with the larger social system. Initial work with these families often requires strengthening the family's links to community resources that provide housing, jobs, child care, and other services. Much of the therapy, especially early in treatment, is crisis-oriented. Many of the structural variations already discussed in this section, particularly three-generation and single-parent issues, are also central in working with lower-class families.

Among poor urban families one sometimes sees teenagers, who

are preparing to leave the family for school or work at the culturally prescribed age, become fearful and withdrawn, developing neurotic symptoms such as phobias. Often these families have successfully protected their children from the negative impact of their immediate context by drawing a very rigid boundary around the family unit. On one hand, this is a successful adaptation to a difficult environment, and children in such families are less likely than their peers to become delinquent, drug addicted, etc. The price, however, is a view of the outside world as an excessively hostile place, with a resulting inhibition and withdrawal. Here it is necessary to help the family relax its outer boundary and permit the children to interact with and master the larger environment.

Sociocultural variations in expectations regarding sex roles are also important. Contrast an upper-class, liberal Berkeley family in which the couple's relationship is scrupulously egalitarian with the traditional Mexican–American family, for example, which stresses complementarity of marital and parenting roles. Here again, in evaluating a particular family, the therapist must take into account its subcultural context.

Although first-hand knowledge about families from different sociocultural groups is certainly desirable, no therapist's own personal experience is broad enough to cover the range of family variations encountered in many practice settings. A recent edited volume *Ethnicity and Family Therapy* (McGoldrick et al., 1982) helps fill this gap.

5

Couples and the Structural Model

For a long time after learning about Minuchin's structural work, I knew how to apply it to families consisting of two or three generations, but could not figure out how it worked for couples. I understood that structural work essentially involves triangles. (Chapter 4 focused on its application to the prototypic triangle mother–father–child.) But, I wondered, where is the triangle in couples therapy?

I suppose that to many readers the answer is obvious, but it was not until I saw Minuchin interview a couple at a workshop (Minuchin, 1980) that I finally understood the answer: You are it. The therapist is the third member of the triangle.

The Basic Idea

In its application to work with couples, the structural model is perhaps best described as a process of *sidetaking*. The therapist first joins the family and becomes a part of its interactional process and then changes that process by siding with one spouse against the other to restructure the couple system.

The notion of sidetaking was already implicit in Chapter 4 where the therapist typically strengthens the generational boundary by joining with the parents either to discipline or to help their children (e.g., "We're going to work together so that you two parents can help Johnny succeed in school.").

With a couple, however, the structural therapist's sidetaking tends to be more dramatic and prominent in the treatment. Minuchin (1980), working with a couple engaged in symmetrical, escalating conflict, said something like this to the wife: "You've got a husband who's unsatisfying to you in a number of ways. Change him to make him a more satisfying husband. I think that, of the two of you, you've got the energy and enthusiasm to do that. I'm with you."

Of course, this intervention goes against everything most of us learned early on about family therapy: One must be above all fair and even-handed, treating all family members as equals. For example, Haley (1962), writing in the first issue of *Family Process*, states the consensus of the field in those early days:

> Taking sides in family rows is dealt with by different schools of Family Therapy in different ways, but all are in agreement that the therapist should not side consistently with one family member against another. (p. 73)

The trouble is that fair-minded therapists regularly fail to help couples locked in symmetrical conflict. The interaction grinds on and on, with the therapist's shots from the sidelines bouncing harmlessly off their targets like rubber bullets. Picture such marital interaction as a couple on a see-saw. Husband and wife are of such equal weight that they go on see-sawing forever. First one is up, then the other, but the process never changes. The even-handed therapist spends the sessions running back and forth along the see-saw or perches precariously in the middle afraid to move either way, with no impact on the interaction.

By taking sides, the structural therapist dramatically changes the picture: Sitting on one side of the see-saw or the other immediately alters the entire interaction process. Escalating, unresolved conflict requires two evenly matched protagonists. By making it two against one, the therapist forces something else to happen. Minuchin (Minuchin and Fishman, 1981) calls this technique *unbalancing*.

Unbalancing

Here are some practical tips on unbalancing.

WHEN

Minuchin initially joins a family by getting them to *enact* their characteristic patterns (their "dance") in the session. In a first interview with a couple, for example, he might begin by asking them about their problems and when he hears an issue that seems hot enough to generate a few sparks he will say something like "Talk about that with each other and see if you can get it settled." He then disappears in his chair, becoming absorbed in his thoughts or involved in smoking a cigarette, and allows the couple's dance to unfold. When they turn to him for help, Minuchin typically urges them to continue with a word or two of encouragement, or he simply waves his hand in a gesture that suggests that he is not about to help out at the moment. Often he allows the pattern to escalate, or even exaggerates it, until the couple is begging for a change.

WITH WHOM

When the enactment has gone far enough and he has identified the couple's typical patterns, Minuchin begins to restructure the couple by "courting" each to see with whom it will be productive to side in order to unbalance and, thus, change the system. So he might say to the husband, "See if you can get her to change her mind." He then observes what happens, assessing whether a coalition with the husband will succeed in changing the pattern. He may then switch sides, attempting to get something going with the wife and this time examining the productiveness of forming a coalition with her.

Minuchin (1980) emphasizes that the matching of therapist and the spouse sided with is an idiosyncratic one. It is not with the "healthiest" of the pair or with the opposite-sex spouse, nor is it governed by any other absolute rule. Rather, the therapist sides with the spouse with whom he or she can get some change going. This cannot necessarily be predicted in advance. Hence the courting process: Try one spouse and see what happens; try the other and observe the results; then decide.

WHAT HAPPENS

Successful unbalancing results in immediate, observable change in the interaction. This is, of course, tautological: If the change does not occur, the attempt was not successful. In addition to expecting a change in behavior, the therapist must also be prepared for an increase in everyone's level of anxiety. No matter how aversive long-standing marital conflict can get, the pattern is at least familiar. When the system is unbalanced, that comfortable familiarity is suddenly gone.

The predictable response to such an increase in anxiety is a bid to rebalance, reestablishing the old, predictable pattern. This move may come from the couple or be initiated by the therapist. The left-out spouse, for example, may begin to flirt with the therapist in an attempt to seduce the therapist away from the partner. Or the therapist may experience the anxiety as a fear that the left-out spouse will flee the treatment and, as a result, rebalance the system by moving out of the initial coalition.

The fear of driving the left-out spouse from treatment is common among therapists learning this structural approach to couples work. Minuchin's notion that every intervention consists of both a "kick" and a "stroke" (Minuchin, 1980) is helpful here. We stroke people for what they are doing right and kick them for what is getting them into trouble. The therapist strokes the left-out husband, for example, just enough to keep him in treatment, all the while making it clear that he is on the wife's side.

HOW LONG

Minuchin stresses that if the anxiety increases as a result of your unbalancing maneuver it means that you are on the right track and should continue. Once a coalition is established with one spouse, it should be maintained until there is a definite structural change in the system. This sometimes means maintaining an alliance across several sessions. Once data from both in and outside the sessions clearly indicate that the system has changed, then you have a new system with which to work. This new system should then be assessed in terms of its potential for unbalancing. At this point it might prove productive to side with the other spouse.

Therapists first learning this unbalancing approach often make the mistake of changing sides much too quickly, hopping back and forth several times in a session and managing only to help keep things balanced.

Case Example:
Unbalancing an Alcoholic and His Wife

IDENTIFYING DATA

Mr. Morgan, a 46-year-old white male, was totally disabled by an arthritic condition for which he had had several surgical procedures on his neck. A chronic alcoholic, he was at the time of family assessment about to be discharged from his first inpatient alcohol treatment program. Mrs. Morgan, 41, was not working at the time and stated that she was thinking of "retiring." The couple had one son, age 21, who had recently moved out of the house and was living on his own.

Mr. and Mrs. Morgan had had two family interviews during his inpatient stay, before the evaluation for outpatient family therapy presented here. In these sessions the couple's problems were defined as "poor communication."

CONFLICT AVOIDANCE

In the opening minutes of the session the couple demonstrated and described their characteristic modes of conflict management.

> (*The female therapist (T) has just finished collecting face sheet data from husband (H) and wife (W). Supervisor (S) and the rest of the family therapy team are observing from behind a one-way mirror. Therapist now orients the couple by explaining the purpose of the evaluation.*)
>
> *T:* What we'd like to do is to, a, for the first couple of sessions, is to evaluate, kind of evaluate whether we see that we can, a wo, we can deal with a problem and be able to work with you on that. And that usually takes maybe one or two sessions. And then we can decide whether this would be the place that would be suited to you. And if it is, then we'd decide on a contract. So that's basically the structure that we work in.
>
> *H:* (*Turns to wife as though expecting a response. She shakes her head, looking puzzled.*) What do you think of that?
>
> *W:* That's fine.
>
> *H:* Okay.

T: (*To husband.*) What do you think of that?

H: I think it's great.

T: Okay. Fine.

H: We need help. (*Wife smiles and begins to laugh and the couple shares a bit of humor at their own expense.*)

(*The base-line affective tone during this initial getting-acquainted phase of the interview is quite relaxed and comfortable. This will change dramatically as the session proceeds.*)

T: (*Joins laughter.*) That's the, a, you're one step ahead of me. Uh, I guess I'd like to know, a, what the problem is.

(*Therapist makes a typical strategic opening here, see Chapter 7, moving to define the main problem.*)

H: Well, she probably can explain it better than I can.

(*Husband does a masterful "metacomplementary" maneuver, controlling the situation—getting his wife to start—by putting himself one-down: "She can explain it better."*)

T: Actually, I'd like both of you to explain it so I kinda get a sense of how each of you see the problem.

(*Without challenging husband directly, therapist deftly makes it clear that she wants a response from each of them.*)

H: I see. (*To wife.*) You start it.

(*Husband now openly defines the relationship with his wife as complementary by directing her to begin.*)

W: (*Laughs.*) Well, it came up, it came up in our meeting today (*the inpatient family session completed an hour earlier*), we have a problem communicating with each other. We'd like to improve our communication. Uh, I interrupt Fred (*husband*) a lot, and I know that disturbs him. But I think that I've become ingrained in that habit because, a, in the past, I don't feel that Fred listens to me.

(*Wife accepts husband's definition of the relationship by responding to therapist's question. This opening complaint by wife will later become the basis for unbalancing the couple.*)

T: Um-hum.

W: And I feel that he turns me off and I think I've gradually gotten into the pattern over the years of interrupting him in the middle of his speech to be included and also because I have a lot that I want to give and share and it just comes pouring out. I just, you know, don't g give, get to share with him I guess on a regular ongoing basis and this has got to the point where I interrupt him a lot and further explain what he's, he's saying or comment on what he's saying and this is irritating to him.

(By this point, as Mrs. Morgan speaks of it "pouring out," it is clear that she is demonstrating the problem even as she describes it: The words rush out in a torrent, with hardly a pause for breath. The impact on the listener is: How can I ever shut this off? People listening to the videotape often comment at this point: "She'd drive me to drink, too.")

T: Um-hum. Let me just ask, what, what, you said you haven't been able to share with him on an ongoing basis and I guess I'm wondering what has happened that you haven't been able to share.

W: Well, ah, he's here in the alcohol program, and drinking is a lot of it. I, I, when he drinks it's not, we're not able to have good communication. And I think that I have not been able to communicate with him or share with him on a regular basis and probably his drinking problem has contributed greatly to it.

(Wife implicates husband's drinking in their communication difficulties.)

T: Uh-huh.

W: Is that what you meant?

T: Yeah. I, I guess I was wondering what came in between.

W: *(Begins speaking immediately after therapist, but without overlapping.)* And the other thing is, at work, a, constantly they were at me to try to learn to communicate better. I'm a person that has always gravitated toward work with a lot of detail, and, uh, I explain things in detail. *(Unintelligible)* would say people ask me what time it is and I tell them how to make a watch. *(Smiles.)* Okay?

(This is a good example of wife's transactional style: She overloads the listener, piling one detail upon another.)

T: Um-hum.

W: And, I, I'm very, very much aware of this and also very aware Fred and I in many ways are very different, so when I try to explain things to him I'm not quite sure that I'm explaining things correctly and then I'll ask him if he understands and he, he acts like, you know, I'm talking down to him, or I'm overloading him with details or something like that *(slight pause to catch her breath, then continues)* so I guess what I really need to know is, you know, what amount of detail and how to express myself to him so that he will listen, you know, doesn't shut me up, and that he can maintain interest and be interested in what I'm saying.

T: Um-hum. Um-hum. Okay. Now, Fred, what do you see as the problem?

H: *(Overlaps.)* Well. Just what she said. When she, a. . . .

T: *(Overlaps.)* How do you experience it as a problem?

(Therapist persists in getting husband to describe the problem.)

H: Well, it's boring to listen to her.

(Husband confirms wife's view of the problem. Notice the extreme contrast in the couple's transactional styles: Wife has rattled on about the problem for paragraphs whereas husband succinctly states "It's boring to listen to her.")

T: Uh-huh.

H: And a lot of times, because she makes, she just keeps rattling on and on about what you could say in a few sentences, she's still talking about it and I just get. . . . But now a lot of times I've been hung over. . . .

(Husband, too, sees his drinking as playing a part in their communication patterns.)

T: (Overlaps.) Um-hum.

H: (Continues.) Or intoxicated. Then I'm not completely *(unintelligible)* I've got my mind completely closed to what she has to say to me.

T: Um-hum.

H: And I hate to have her tell me what to do and things like that. Which is selfish, I know.

(Here husband specifically identifies the control issue, which was played out in the opening moments of this segment. This is a frequent theme in the families of alcoholics, as well as many others.)

T: Does she do that often?

(This is a very interesting response by therapist: She accepts as fact husband's statement that wife tells him what to do and asks if she does it often. Without doing so deliberately, therapist has sided with husband against wife.)

H: No. I tell her. . . . No. Ah *(squirms uncomfortably in chair and then turns toward wife as if to turn floor over to her.)*

(Husband immediately becomes very uncomfortable, apparently because therapist has accepted his implied criticism of wife, and he stops in his tracks and turns the floor over to her. This nicely demonstrates the impact of sidetaking: Following unbalancing, the interaction changes and the anxiety level increases.)

W: (Accepts husband's cue.) I, I think sometimes, I, I don't know, I have a feeling sometimes I'm saying something to him and sometimes, a lot because of the drinking *(unintelligible)*, I've thought it out, what I'm going to say and how I'm going to present it to him, so there won't be any emotional problems, and I think perhaps it sounds so well thought out that it turns him off because he, you know, maybe he thinks that I'm going to tell him what to do. I don't know, 'cause sometimes I'll

tell him something and at the end he'll say "Well, you're not telling me
what to do" and I haven't, nothing in the content of what I said was
telling him what to do. But that's what he seems to have received. But
I don't think that's what I sent out, at least that was not my intention
anyway to send it out to him. . . .

(*Wife responds with a defense of her behavior, confirming that she
saw husband's statement as an attack on her. As is her style, the
defense is lengthy.*)

T: (*Overlaps.*) To tell him what to do.

(*Here therapist joins wife by speaking for her and finishing her
defense.*)

W: Right.

T: (*To husband.*) And sometimes you think she's, telling you, th, that
you experience sometimes when she's talking is her giving you a
direction of what to do.

(*Therapist immediately flops over to husband's side by talking for him
and restating his charge. This is a beautiful example of triangulation:
Therapist is acting as a go-between. Responding to the shared anxiety
following her initial siding with husband, therapist has now succeeded
in reducing everyone's anxiety level by becoming triangulated and
rebalancing. See discussion of triangulation in final section of this
chapter.*)

H: Sometimes.

T: Um-hum.

H: Lot of times she'll talk over my head, you know, where she just keeps
talking on (*unintelligible*) interrupting from talking. Sometimes I just
sit out and she carries the whole conversation for the whole night. Not
that bad, but it seems that bad 'cause it's just like a record that you
can't turn off (*smiles and looks to wife who does not smile back*).

(*The affective tone of the session has now begun to change and this
attempt at humor by husband, which would have worked earlier, is
now rejected by wife.*)

T: Uh-hum.

W: (*Overlaps.*) When Fred talks to me I try to listen, and, if it's something
that he's interested in and that he wants to share. But, at least in the
past, when I want to share something with Fred, he's not interested.
Many times in the past he's come out and said "I'm not interested in
that at all. Let's not bother talking about it." And that sort of hurts
my feelings and makes me feel frustrated.

(*Instead of good humor, wife now takes over the floor and attacks
husband.*)

T: Uh-huh. Uh-huh. So you get frustrated and, angry?

W: Well, n, I notice it more, because, last y, in 1978 my mother passed away and our son moved away and I think, a, a lot of times in the past when he (*husband*) didn't listen to me I'd go down and talk to my mother who was a widow and she'd listen to me and I'd listen to her and it didn't bother me so much then. I think the interrupting him might have become more prominent in the two years because I really don't have this outlet for somebody who will listen to me.

(*Here wife places the couple's current problems in a developmental framework—see Chapter 6: Husband's lack of attention was less of a problem as long as she could talk to her mother and son instead. This is very common. Certain long-standing family patterns become problematic only following a developmental change or when such a change is imminent.*)

T: Your mother was living downstairs?

W: No, she was living down the street but it was within walking distance, so it was very easy for me to go down there.

T: (*To husband.*) What do you think? Has this increased in the last couple of years?

H: I'd say so, yes.

T: Do you share her theory about the reasons it's increased or do you have other ideas about that?

H: Well, I'd say because of drinking.

Here Mr. Morgan focused on his drinking rather than on the family's developmental changes cited by his wife. The next segment of the session is interesting because it links the initial presenting problem (husband's alcoholism) to the couple's interaction patterns observed in this interview.

(*Following the previous segment, husband spends a few minutes describing to therapist how he "manipulates the conversation" to topics about which wife knows little, in an effort to shut her up. The discussion then continues.*)

T: What's some other way, things you've done to deal with the problem up to now?

(*"The problem" here is wife's long, boring conversations.*)

H: Just walk away.

T: Uh-huh. So that's another way.

H: (*Unintelligible.*) Go and get a drink.

T: Uh-huh. So sometimes you drink because of it, do you think?

(*Here therapist again inadvertently sides with husband by suggesting that wife is the cause of his drinking.*)

H: No. I didn't drink because of her. No, I, a. . . . (*Hesitates, rubs face, and squirms in chair.*)

(*What follows is an exact repeat of the unbalancing noted above: Husband becomes acutely anxious.*)

W: (*Interrupts.*) I think. . . .

(*Wife starts to speak.*)

H: (*Interrupts.*) Well, wait a minute (*Therapist gestures for wife to be quiet*), let me explain. Not originally. When I started drinking, it wasn't because of her. But then the latter part of it. . . . But she's trying to help me, I can see that, I couldn't see that, I can see it now because I'm taking this program there (*inpatient alcohol treatment*).

(*This time, however, therapist and husband together succeed in maintaining control of the floor for husband.*)

T: Uh-huh.

H: Lot of times I, she would nag at me because of the ass I made of myself. And of course I didn't want to hear that 'cause I felt that she was making a lot of it up, because she doesn't drink.

T: Uh-huh.

H: Other than a little. But I've never seen her intoxicated. So I thought she was making a lot of this stuff up so I just closed my ears to it. Or, go have another drink, to (*unintelligible*) her or "I'll show her." I don't know.

T: Uh-huh. So sometimes you left and had a drink and that was one of the ways you. . . .

H: (*Overlaps.*) Shut her off.

(*Here again, husband and therapist finish each other's sentences, indicating joining.*)

T: Shut her off. What are some other ways you dealt with it?

It is now apparent that the husband's drinking plays a role in the couple's current interactional behavior. With this information, it is possible to speculate on the reasons for Mr. Morgan's having sought alcohol treatment at the present time. As long as the son and the wife's mother were available to listen to Mrs. Morgan, she put less pressure on her husband and the couple were able to manage their difficulties without outside assistance. However, within the past two years, after the mother died and the son left home, the wife began pushing for more attention and responsiveness from her husband. The more she pushed, the more he turned to alcohol as a way to shut her out. And the more he drank, the more isolated and lonely she became, pushing even harder for his attention. As this deviation-amplifying process spiraled further out of control, Mr. Morgan's drinking problem eventually became acute enough that he sought treatment.

OPEN CONFLICT

As the supervisor listening from behind the mirror, I had by this point become rather bored hearing Mr. and Mrs. Morgan talk to the therapist about their problems. Although we had seen features of their characteristic interaction enacted already, I now wanted the therapist to intensify the couple's interaction patterns so I instructed her to ask Mr. and Mrs. Morgan to talk directly to each other. Very quickly, the affective tone changed dramatically and open conflict emerged for the first time in the session.

> (*Therapist returns to her seat following phone conversation with supervisor.*)

T: A, one of the suggestions they have is to, a, that you both talk, a, about your view of what the problem, so maybe we could have, (*to wife*) why don't you tell him, you've heard how he. . . .

> (*Therapist is having a very difficult time telling the couple to talk together. Part of it is simply the difficulty beginning family therapists often have with being directive. In addition, therapist at some level knows that the sparks will really fly if she allows them to talk directly to each other and she is apprehensive about it. She should have said simply "Talk with each other now about these problems," instead and turned the interaction over to them.*)

H: You mean like ad lib?

T: (*Continues to speak to wife.*) You heard how he, a, some of the ways that he's turned you off, or been able to deal with (*here therapist's gesture suggests that husband holds wife off at an arm's length*) what you did, so I'd like to have you tell him how that affects you, how that's handled. And (*to husband*), let you respond to what she says.

W: Okay. Well, the thing that occurred to me when he said that he. . . .

T: (*Interrupts.*) No. "The thing that occurred to me when you (*emphasizes*) said." (*Gestures from husband to wife.*) Talk to him.

> (*Here therapist effectively uses a simple directive to get wife to talk directly to husband. Wife next opens immediately with a sharp attack on husband.*)

W: Oh. The thing that occurred to me, Fred, when you said you would, a, go out and get a drink, I think you manipulated the conversation to a subject that would allow you to (*unintelligible*) and go out and get a drink. So maybe I wanted to start out talking about something that happened at work or something about our life and you would manipulate the conversation to my housekeeping or nagging about drinking or something that gave you (*emphasizes*) an excuse to pick a fight, to walk out of the house and drink. That's what you did constantly when we went up to Blue Lake.

H: (*Looks down, hand in front of face.*) Well, I don't believe that. Because I didn't a, those things, not keeping the house clean didn't bother me.

(*Husband defends himself.*)

W: Yes, but what I'm saying is, Fred. . . .

(*Wife persists, reiterating her charge: "Yes, but. . . ."*)

H: (*Interrupts.*) Like I come home I had nothing in my mind about drinking.

(*Husband refuses to allow her to continue and instead embellishes his own defense.*)

W: (*Shakes head "No."*) But Fred, our conversation which you ended up picking a fight with me about the housekeeping didn't start out about housekeeping. I made a comment to you that didn't have anything to do with the house and you made a comment back about my housekeeping which didn't match what I had said to you at all.

(*And the symmetrical battle continues to escalate.*)

H: Well, maybe I wasn't listening to you.

W: Well. (*Shrugs shoulders and glares at husband, as if to say "I rest my case."*)

H: (*Unintelligible.*)

(*Husband is momentarily unable to mount a counteroffensive.*)

W: Well, you know, what can I say to that? If you don't feel that you were looking for an excuse to have a fight to drink and that you. . . .

(*Wife seems to sense her advantage and zeros in for the kill.*)

H: (*Interrupts.*) Not all the time. Heck no.

(*Husband flatly contradicts wife.*)

W: But many times?

(*Wife persists.*)

H: Could be. (*Slight pause.*) The thing that gets me with you is when you, you gotta go into every little detail what you're talking about. Like, don't ever ask you to, "I didn't see that movie that was on TV. What was it about?" That's the worst thing I could ever say to you. First of all you'll talk about the actors who play in it, their careers, their, and it goes on and on and on and pretty soon, why, hell, I've lost interest. I could care about that movie any . . . (*shifts uncomfortably in his chair*).

(*This is a very important moment. When husband says "could be," wife has achieved a victory by getting him to cry "Uncle" and accept a one-down position. This is how fights end. But instead, husband mounts a vigorous counterattack by opening up a new battleground. Notice how symmetrical the couple have become: Husband's speeches are now almost as long as wife's. This is a marked change from the earlier part of the interview where the couple's relationship was complementary: Wife rambled on and on about how husband failed to listen to her; husband spoke little and largely accepted her view of his shortcomings.*)

W: Well, if you are interested in something, Fred, don't you do the same thing but yet I listen to you? I mean, if you wanted to talk to somebody that you're interested about, and you wanted to go into high detail level and people listen to you and when other people want to talk to you you're not as interested in that as what you wanted to talk about. Do you think it's right that you just say "Well, I want very brief descriptions when you talk to me about something you're interested in but I can go into as much detail as I want when I talk to you about something I'm interested in?" Because, for example, just that movie. I saw you go into more detail than I would have gone in to explain that movie with Mickey Rooney to, a, Bill Jones (*a friend*) the other evening. Yet if I did the same thing about a movie to you, you would be very angry with me. I don't think that's fair.

(*Nine-second pause.*)

(*Wife takes on husband on this new ground, turning the attack back by accusing husband of doing the same to her.*)

H: Well, you still go in. . . . Oh, boy, how can I explain it? You just. . . . Alright, something here (*Wife has been leaning forward ready to respond, but now settles back in her chair*), here's a good example. How about this weekend? I know these people that I've been in the alcoholic clinic with and I told you but you took over the whole conversation. You know those people better than I do.

(*Here again it appears for a moment that husband will capitulate and the fight will be over. He even labels his one-down position: "Oh, boy, how can I explain it?" But he is not about to be counted out yet, and instead seizes upon a new example with which to attack wife.*)

W: (*Interrupts.*) Okay, be. . . .

(*Wife attempts to interrupt.*)

H: (*Continues.*) You had to relate what I said, which I should have had the podium there because I'm the one that was. . . .

(Husband overrides. Again, the couple's symmetry is demonstrated. Wife has previously established her ability to hold the floor, but this is the first time in the session that husband has successfully beaten back her attempt to take over the floor without an assist from therapist.)

W: (*Overlaps.*) That's true. But don't you think maybe th. . . .

(Again wife attempts to take over.)

H: (*Interrupts.*) You shut me off two or three times, telling about, I was trying to tell Bob about, what alcohol can do to you, which I didn't understand before, 'til I came in here.

(And again husband shuts her off.)

W: Well, I can see that, Fred. But don't you think you were doing just what you explained to Carol (*therapist*), you manipulated the conversation. . . .

(Again wife's defense is a symmetrical counterattack, accusing husband of doing the same to her.)

H: (*Overlaps.*) No, our con, no, no, we were discussing that 'cause we was talkin' to Al, your brother-in-law and sister. . . .

(And the fight continues to heat up.)

W: (*Overlaps.*) Well, mostly. . . .

H: (*Continues.*) About how you did it there. I didn't manipulate that conversation.

W: Well, most of the time you were talking to Al. Mary and I were in the other room. You talked to Al mostly by yourself.

H: Yeah, but when we was having coffee there at the table.

W: Yeah but, whe, what did you wa, don't you think when we were all there together you could have picked a subject that we could t, all talk about? And yet you picked a subject which you could talk about and other people could listen to? I never thought of that, but I think maybe you do that a lot.

H: No, I jus, what could I talk to those people about? He's a banker. I don't know nothin' about finances. I tried to talk about that cottage we're remodelin'. He went over and looked at it. I thought that, a, some of those stories or experiences from some of these people that's here would have been interesting to those three people. But evidently it wasn't. You took it right over.

W: Well I'm sorry. I didn't mean to do that. But maybe I wa. . . .

(Here wife suggests momentarily that she's willing to take a one-down position: "I'm sorry." But in the next breath she continues the struggle.)

H: (*Interrupts.*) You do it all the time. I'm just a, I just sit there like a bump on a log.

(Husband cuts off her new offensive and attempts to press the advantage he gained from wife's brief expression of remorse.)

W: Now Fred, you know that isn't true. . . .

(But wife will not stand for that.)

H: *(Interrupts.)* Most of the time, most of the time. It's just like we had to do business transactions, the real estate guy comes over. Hell, I might as well not be there.

(Husband appears to sense that he has the upper hand here and presses his point with a new example.)

W: I re. . . .

H: *(Interrupts.)* Those properties and that, ahh, humf.

W: I don't know what to say to that, Fred, *(therapist, who has been sitting back in her chair, begins to squirm and leans forward as if to intervene)* because you handled most of that with Randy. I don't know, I know very little about that.

(Again wife suggests a one-down maneuver, "I don't know what to say," but quickly recovers and launches a defense against the charge.)

S: *(Enters interview room.)* I want to interrupt.

What happened here at the end of this segment is a nice example of what Minuchin (1980) calls *calibration*, the idea that all participants in an interaction mutually regulate or calibrate each other's behavior. The level of anger and anxiety had reached a fever pitch (total time for the previous segment was approximately six minutes, but it seemed much longer) and the therapist and I were both responding to it. By the time the therapist had started to move in her chair, I had already left the mirror and was walking to the interview room. Both of us were simultaneously preparing to intervene in the couple's war, calibrated by their behavior.

This segment provides additional confirmation of our hypothesis about the relationship between the original presenting problem (Mr. Morgan's alcohol abuse), the recent family developmental changes, and the couple's interaction as enacted in the session. As long as the therapist was available in the session so the couple could interact through her, they managed to avoid open conflict and instead we saw Mr. Morgan assume a one-down position relative to his wife. The therapist's role during this phase of the interview was presumably similar to that played in the past by the couple's son and the wife's mother. The above segment demonstrates vividly how quickly this couple's interaction could become a symmetrical, escalating battle once a third person was no longer available to help manage their conflict. In the face of such unresolved conflict, the symptom of husband's drunkenness became more and more necessary to introduce complementarity into the runaway symmetry of their interaction, turning Mr. Morgan into a one-down drunk and Mrs. Morgan into a nagging wife.

What I did next was inspired by Minuchin's (1980) demonstration interview in a workshop I had attended the previous week where I discovered for the first time how to apply the structural approach to work with couples. I used this session with the Morgans as an opportunity to try the approach myself and to demonstrate it to the students. My lines below were lifted almost verbatim from Minuchin's interview (described briefly above), revised to fit this couple's situation. What followed proved to be a powerful demonstration of the generality of Minuchin's sidetaking technique and convinced me that his workshop intervention was based upon a very keen understanding of how systems work and was not simply an artifact of Minuchin's personal charisma or his reputation: Mrs. Morgan (with whom I sided) responded to me in precisely the same way that Minuchin's patient had responded when he sided with her.

(Immediately after previous segment.)

S: I've been listening back there. I, I gather, my guess would be that the conversation the two of you just had in the last few minutes is fairly typical for you. Is that right or wrong?

(Supervisor moves to establish the previous interaction as typical for the couple. His task here is to join the couple as a prelude to unbalancing.)

H: I don't think we've ever discussed this topic before.

(Mr. Morgan is so concrete that supervisor must work hard to establish his point.)

S: But I meant the way you went about it.

H: (Overlaps.) Oh really, right.

S: (Continues.) Kinda the back and forth. *(To wife.)* That's pretty, probably pretty typical.

W: I guess.

S: (To wife.) Am I right?

W: I hadn't thought of it but I'd guess so. *(Looks to husband for confirmation.)*

H: I think, yeah.

S: (*To therapist*). I think we probably got a pretty good picture of their characteristic communication.

(*Supervisor joins therapist by including her as well.*)

T: (*Overlaps.*) The way they (*unintelligible*) on.

H: I'm glad you stopped us 'cause I was starting to get mad.

(*With this spontaneous remark, husband attempts to establish an alliance between himself and supervisor by approving supervisor's behavior.*)

S: Really?

H: At her.

S: Really. (*To wife.*) I, my perception from back there was that you (*emphasizes*) were angry at him.

(*Supervisor ignores husband's bid and instead moves to engage wife.*)

W: (*Looks at husband.*) I was angry at him, yes.

S: Yeah. Yeah, yeah I felt like it had gone on about as far enough, f, far enough to give us a picture of how you, you communicate. One thing I noticed was, the minute the two of you started talking, the atmosphere changed dramatically. (*Pause.*) And when you each were talking with Carol (*therapist*) individually, ah, it was kinda relaxed, there was some humor, some smiles, some joking. But when the two of you went at it with each other, I felt like (*snaps fingers*) things changed like that.

(*Here supervisor uses an observation about the affective tone of the interaction to frame—see Chapter 7—what has been happening, both for the couple and for therapist and the rest of the team behind the mirror. This is also a joining maneuver. Supervisor says, in effect, "I was paying very close attention to you, and this is what I saw."*)

H: I had a feeling different, than when I was talking to her (*gestures toward therapist*).

(*Again husband makes a spontaneous overture to supervisor.*)

T: Um-hum.

S: Yeah.

H: Sort of anger feeling.

S: Yeah. That's what I, I was seeing too. (*Pause.*) I want you to do something different, but first I have a question for you, Mrs. Morgan. Um, during that five minutes or so when you were conversing with your husband, do you think he was being a good listener, to you?

(*Again supervisor accepts husband's statement, but immediately turns to wife. The question supervisor now asks Mrs. Morgan is crucial for what follows. Wife's opening complaint was that husband does not*) *listen to her, so supervisor knows that he can get wife to state that she believes husband was not listening during the previous five minutes.*)

W: I don't know. I was lis . . . , I was listening to what he said. I was not reacting really to him listening to me as much as I was listening to what he said (*pauses for quick breath*) I, I, I don't know, I have a, a strong belief and it might be totally wrong and this may be part of the problem, I don't think so.

(*But it is not easy to get a simple statement from wife and in what follows supervisor must work very hard to pin her down.*)

S: You don't think so.

W: I don't think he listens to me and this goes back to. . . .

S: (*Overlaps.*) Um-hum.

W: Years before, when his answers don't answer. . . .

S: (*Overlaps.*) Uh-huh. So. . . .

W: (*Overlaps.*) The response.

S: So in the last five minutes you did not really feel that he was listening to you.

W: If I had to say if I had a feeling, yes or no, I'd probably say "No." My first answer is "I really wasn't thinking that much about whether he was listening to him, whether he was listening to me. I was thinking more about whether I was listening to him." That would be my first response.

S: (*Overlaps.*) But now that I, I press you?

W: I would have, I would have to say more that he wasn't listening to me than he was, I guess.

(*At last, an almost-definite response.*)

S: Uh-huh. That, that would have been my guess, too, that you would, you would think that. Okay. (*Pause.*) I want, I want the two of you to try something different this time. I want you to have a conversation again. But I want you, Mrs. Morgan, to change things to make him into a better listener this time (*wife's head raises with a slight start*). 'Cause I sense there's quite a bit of enthusiasm and energy on your part for changing this guy you're married to to make him a better listener.

(*Supervisor decides wife's response is good enough. Then he makes a mistake. Instead of saying that he thought wife would say that husband was not being a good listener, he should have responded: "I think you're right. I don't think he was listening to you." This would have indicated much more clearly that supervisor had moved over to wife's side in her battle with her husband. As it turns out, the unbalancing worked despite this technical flaw.*)

W: You mean, a better listener, okay.

S: Uh-huh.

W: You're not saying changing him as a person.

(*This is precisely the way Minuchin's patient responded when he told her to change her spouse to make him a more satisfying husband.*)

S: No. No, to make him into a better listener. So I want you to have another conversation.

(*Here supervisor side-steps the issue by being very concrete and wife is satisfied. Minuchin took the wife head-on, responding to her statement "You can't change another person" with "You learned that in your TA group, didn't you?" Here Minuchin was referring to the position of individual psychologies such as transactional analysis whereby you can change only yourself, not another person.*)

W: Okay.

S: And (*still speaking to wife*) this time your job is not only to have the conversation with him, but to make him into a better listener.

W: (*Smiles coyly.*) Do you have any hints?

(*Here wife attempts to seduce supervisor into being too helpful and taking over for her. Again, this is precisely what Minuchin's patient did.*)

S: No, I think that you probably already have an idea of some techniques to try. (*To couple.*) And that's what I would like you to do. (*To therapist.*) And, I don't know, maybe I'll have some more ideas from back there, or, a, I think we should give them a shot at it for five minutes or so and see what happens. Alright?

(*Supervisor paraphrases Minuchin in responding to Mrs. Morgan. Before leaving, supervisor orients therapist, who is seeing such an intervention for the first time.*)

T: Okay, that's fine.

S: And then maybe we will want to have a conference behind the mirror and make some recommendations about treatment before we wind up.

T: Okay.

S: Okay. (*Gets up to return behind mirror.*)

W: And I'm supposed to know something to make him listen, huh?

(*Wife makes one last effort to secure more help from supervisor.*)

S: (*On way out the door.*) I think you do. (*Door closes with wife, arms folded, deep in thought.*)

(*And supervisor reiterates his faith in wife's competence.*)

Two comments about therapeutic choices. First, regarding my decision to side with the wife, I think I knew I would side with her before I entered the room. I am not aware of the cues I used in arriving at this decision except that I recall being struck early in the interview by Mrs. Morgan's complaint that her husband fails to listen to her. I just felt that I could unbalance by siding with her on this issue. The above interaction does not illustrate the elaborate "courting" process Minuchin typically uses before deciding with whom to side (see discussion earlier in this chapter). In reviewing the tape, it became clear to me how hard Mr. Morgan was working to get me to side with him once I entered the interview room. I may have been reacting negatively to his approaches without realizing it at the time. I distinctly remember being impressed from behind the mirror by how angry Mrs. Morgan looked as she was fighting with her husband. So when Mr. Morgan attempted to engage me by emphasizing *his* anger, I naturally, it seemed, turned to her instead. Since the couple's interaction was symmetrical at the point of this intervention, but for my own idiosyncrasies I could have chosen either spouse.

Second, I would like to emphasize how different this side-taking approach is from more familiar, "balanced" interventions. As I pressed Mrs. Morgan to come out with the statement that she did not think her husband listens to her, she said, in passing, that the fact that she does not think he listens might itself be part of the problem. Family therapists have traditionally been very even-handed in assigning blame, insisting either that no one is to blame or that everyone is. So a fair-minded therapist might see the wife's statement as a therapeutic opportunity and get her to look at just how she fails to give her husband credit for listening to her when he does do so (for, of course, he *does* sometimes listen, and wife herself is hardly a good listener). If one chooses structural unbalancing instead, then the couple's symmetrical battle about who is to blame must instead be tilted (here, in the direction of the husband being at fault) and the wife's statement about her responsibility is seen as an attempt to rebalance and must be rejected.

(*Immediately following previous segment.*)

W: (*To therapist.*) But I can select any topic I want? Is that it?

   (*Wife makes another bid for help.*)

T: (*Nods head " Yes."*)

(*Therapist turns job back to wife with a minimal response, supporting supervisor's expression of confidence in wife's competence.*)

(*Six-second pause. Wife again appears to be deep in thought.*)

H: I'm waitin'.

(*This six-second pause, along with husband's "I'm waitin,'" already demonstrates wife's success. This is typical of successful unbalancing: The interaction changes immediately and dramatically.*)

W: Yes, I'm, I'm trying to think, think of something that could be, think of something that he, that he could listen to.

(*Supervisor buzzes therapist on phone and therapist gets up to answer. The following conversation between therapist and supervisor is recorded directly on tape; the couple could not hear supervisor's voice.*)

T: Yes.

S: Tell Mrs. Morgan that she succeeded already.

(*Supervisor wants therapist to stroke wife for her achievement. It is generally much more productive to catch family members with their successes and praise them than to point out their failures.*)

T: (*Overlaps.*) Right.

S: (*Continues.*) Because she had him waiting on the edge of his chair listening for what she was going to say.

T: Okay, w. . . .

S: (*Overlaps.*) So it's only uphill, it's only a. . . .

T: (*Overlaps.*) Downhill from here.

S: (*Continues.*) More success, yeah, more success from here.

T: Okay. (*Hangs up phone and returns to seat.*) (*To wife.*) One of the things that Steve (*supervisor*) just mentioned was that you have already succeeded in, in one way. And that was that he was waiting. So. . . .

(*Therapist should have been even more generous in her praise here.*)

H: (*Overlaps.*) So I was listening, waiting to hear some. . . .

(*Husband's comment validates wife's success, but is another attempt by him to rebalance, this time by courting therapist. It would have been more useful to discuss with wife what had happened here.*)

T: (*Overlaps.*) Waiting to hear. So, so I mean, that's a. . . .

H: Progress.

T: Exactly. (*Husband, wife, and therapist simultaneously break into comfortable, relaxed laughter.*)

(The fact that therapist and husband are finishing each other's sentences suggests an alliance between them, which tends to work against the sidetaking established by supervisor.)

H: *(Still laughing.)* But maybe I won't be so interested once I hear what she's got to say.

(Husband continues to press his alliance with therapist.)

T: Well, that's the second step. So *(gestures toward wife)*, I give it back to you.

(Therapist deftly turns husband's comment aside and signals for wife to continue.)

W: *(Turns to husband.)* Well, a, *(to therapist)* I just thought about something *(turns back to husband)*, you know, Fred, tomorrow I'm going to give Spot and Red *(the couple's two dogs)* another flea bath, and Spot doesn't have any ointment left. Do you think that I should go up to the vet's and ask if they have any more ointment like that, take the can up there? What we could. . . .

(Wife introduces a new topic.)

H: *(Overlaps.)* Well, that's a stupid question.

(Wife succeeds in getting a response from husband. Although it is a put-down, husband clearly is listening.)

W: Why?

H: 'Course take the can up. Well, I can't manufacture that salve. Take it up there and see if you can get some more salve. That's what he needs.

W: Okay. And when Red, now he only has two more pills left, and when are you gonna take. . . .

H: *(Interrupts.)* I already told you.

(The interaction continues in the same pattern: Wife asks husband a question and husband responds, but in a rather gruff way. Notice how different this transcript looks on the page than did the opening minutes of the interview: instead of wife's long monologues, husband and wife are actually taking turns in the discussion.)

W: Yeah, you told me. . . .

H: *(Interrupts.)* I'll tell you again. Give her an aspirin, one a day.

W: Uh-huh.

H: And when I get out of here, I'll take her to the veteran. Veterinarian. Veteran. *(Laughs to himself at his slip.)*

W: Okay. Well, now when I, when I'm removing the rug from the floor, okay, and if the tile breaks around the edge. . . .

H: (*Overlaps.*) Don't worry about it.

W: (*Continues.*) Should I leave it there or should I pick it up? You know, where the strip is. . . .

H: (*Overlaps.*) You mean, like, a little chip comes out of it?

W: Well, you know where that. . . .

H: (*Overlaps.*) Just leave it there. I'll take care of it.

W: Yeah, okay. Just leave it there?

H: Yeah.

W: And there's a couple of tiles that are loose. You want. . . .

H: (*Overlaps.*) Just. . . .

W: (*Overlaps.*) Just leave the whole thing like it is?

H: Yeah. (*Tone softens and husband's voice becomes warmer.*) If you get that rug off that will be a good job well done by you.

(*Here wife has succeeded not only in getting husband to listen to her, but also gets a genuine stroke from him.*)

W: Okay.

Because it falls far short of our notions of ideal, healthy couple dialogue, it is easy to quibble with this new interaction between the Morgans. Its importance should be judged not in terms of some absolute standard, however, but in contrast to both the initial complementary relationship pattern observed at the beginning of the session and the later symmetrical conflict.

Haley suggests (1976) that therapy does not proceed from a dysfunctional family organization directly to a functional one. Instead, one moves from dysfunctional structure A to dysfunctional structure B (different from A, but still dysfunctional) and finally on to a healthier family organization.

Following this segment, Mrs. Morgan engaged her husband in a discussion of one more detail of their current affairs and then asked the therapist if she should continue the discussion. The therapist chose instead to discuss with the wife what had just happened. Mrs. Morgan said she felt she succeeded in getting her husband to listen better than he had listened during their earlier discussion, and spontaneously cited two techniques she used: she chose topics she knew he would be interested in and she asked questions that required answers. ("So, perhaps, he had to listen.") Therapist stroked the wife for having monitored the conversation so well, checking her husband's attentiveness as they talked, and keeping in mind her task to engage him. Mr. Morgan also agreed that he had been listening more, explaining that his wife did pick topics (e.g., the dogs) that interest him and also citing the supervisor's intervention as having influenced his behavior.

Mrs. Morgan then attempted to dismiss her success by stating that her husband listened only because he was interested in the topics she chose and claiming that the problem is instead with topics which interest *her*, but *not him*. From here on, the interaction began to recapitulate the pattern of the session's beginning. Mrs. Morgan talked on and on, always with the same theme: "The problem is whether or not he will learn to listen to things *I'm* more interested in." Mr. Morgan mostly sat back and listened, but once interrupted the complementary pattern by attacking his wife: "Something else that bugs me about her is. . . ." The therapist was again triangulated, with each spouse complaining to *her* about the other. (If the therapist had not been so conveniently available to detour the conflict, it is likely that Mr. Morgan's new complaint would have touched off another couple fight.) The therapist, realizing the unproductiveness of what was happening, went behind the mirror for the planned consultation with the team.

Had she been familiar with the sidetaking approach with couples, it would have been quite easy for the therapist to turn Mrs. Morgan's dismissal of her success into an opportunity for the next therapeutic intervention by stating: "You're right. So now get him to listen to you about something *you're* interested in." And then she could have simply turned the discussion back to the wife to continue her good work. This approach would have been particularly appropriate during ongoing therapy. In the above situation, near the end of an evaluation session, the therapist might have instead turned the wife's complaint into a recommendation for treatment: "You're right. You've succeeded so far, but this is only the beginning. To get him to listen to things you're interested in is a big job, but from what I've seen already, I think you can do it. And I think I can help you." With this as an introduction, a treatment recommendation could then have easily been made.

In a final brief sequence from the very end of the interview, Mr. Morgan again attempted to seduce the therapist into siding with him instead of with Mrs. Morgan, thus rebalancing the couple system.

(*Therapist returns from conference with team.*)

T: Okay. The consensus of opinion was that we feel that we can, uh, be of some benefit, and, in dealing a, with you, a, with the situation of communication, and what we think will be probably the way that we, the track that we would, a, initially start out with, is, a, what we started out with today. A, would be for you (*to wife*) make him a better listener. Um, we feel that we've seen some success already. We feel your energy. And that's what we would like to, that would be how we will operate, probably.

(*Here again therapist is having difficulty making a simple, direct treatment recommendation. As discussed earlier, part of the problem is inexperience, likely compounded by concern about the reaction to her sidetaking.*)

H: How about her a better listener to me?

(*Husband's response is typical: The left-out spouse says, in effect, "What about me? Don't you like me?"*)

T: That may be down the line, but initially we will, we'd like to start out with, a, a, teaching her, uh, getting you to be a better listener.

(*Therapist's response says: "You're okay, but later."*)

H: How come the women always (*mutters under his breath as wife laughs to herself*).

T: (*To husband.*) Are you. . . .

H: (*Overlaps, laughing.*) I thought this would be opposite (*shakes finger at therapist*).

(*Here husband reveals his surprise that therapist and supervisor did not side with him.*)

T: (*Laughs, shaking finger back at husband.*) I know, an you. . . .

(*Therapist does not back down, become apologetic, or engage in long explanations. Instead, she vigorously matches husband's behavior.*)

(*Therapist, husband, and wife all break into roars of laughter.*)

(*The situation is diffused as all join in laughter.*)

T: (*To husband.*) What do you think about that?

H: I think it stinks (*laughs and is joined by wife*).

T: You think it stinks.

H: No, I think it's great.

T: Do you?

H: Yeah, sure. I'm going to listen. (*Unintelligible*) in the past. And I'll try not to do this in the future.

(*The exchange ends on a serious note that suggests that husband will accept the treatment recommendation.*)

The follow-up to this evaluation session illustrates the hazards of doing this type of therapy in a large treatment system with multiple therapists where the potential for working at cross purposes is magnified. A few days after we saw the couple, Mr. Morgan had an interview with the intake worker for the outpatient alcohol program. He made a strong bid to ally himself with her by complaining about the family therapy program. The intake worker accepted husband's offer, rebalancing the couple system we had unbalanced by siding with wife, and suggested family sessions in the alcohol clinic instead; the husband then canceled our appointment and was lost to further follow-up by us.

I wish to emphasize here that the responsibility for the ultimate failure of our intervention lies with the family therapy team. If this kind of work is to succeed, it is essential that the family systems therapist be able to anticipate and manage the response of the entire treatment system. The husband's behavior, as well as that of the larger treatment system, was an absolutely normal and predictable response to sidetaking interventions. If sidetaking is to work, the family system's efforts to rebalance must be blocked throughout the treatment system.

In this case, the situation was certainly overdetermined. There was long-standing competition between the alcohol clinic and our family program. They complained that we got all the good family treatment cases. So when Mr. Morgan came along to complain about us, they were only too happy to oblige him. But this rivalry only increased the likelihood of our failure. To see it as the cause neglects the generality of the lesson of this case.

Cautions

Like any other powerful intervention, sidetaking can be misused by the therapist. In particular, it can be used as a rationale by a therapist with some sort of axe to grind (e.g., the recently divorced male therapist who sides with the husband out of anger at his own ex-wife).

To do effective and ethical unbalancing, the therapist must potentially be able to side with either spouse. If you find yourself so unsympathetic with one or another of the couple that you cannot imagine convincingly joining that person, then you need either to work that issue out first or refer the couple to someone else.

Only by operating from this initial flexible position is the therapist free to court each spouse as a potential partner in change.

Based on the actual results of such attempts at unbalancing rather than on extraneous factors, the therapist can then decide with whom to side in order to help the couple system change.

Unbalancing, from a Systems Perspective

After Minuchin (1980) told the wife with whom he was working to change her husband, he was accused by someone in the audience of intervening paradoxically. After all, the questioner insisted, the wife will of course realize that the only way she can change her husband is by changing herself, so the intervention was just a paradoxical maneuver to get the wife herself to change. (See the discussion of paradox at end of Chapter 7.)

Minuchin insisted that his intent was not at all paradoxical, explaining that the wife is the husband's context. According to systems thinking (see Chapter 3), if the context or whole changes, the part changes. Therefore, she can change him.

The heart of this controversy is the shift from individual, non-systemic to systems thinking. It is perfectly true *from the point of view of individual psychology* that one can change only oneself, not another. From this point of view, Minuchin's intervention truly is paradoxical. *From the systemic point of view*, however, the intervention is straightforward and nonparadoxical.

Minuchin's systemic point of view inherently differs from individual psychology in another way, this time from behavior therapy. Behavior therapists frequently assume that their patients have deficiencies in their behavioral repertoires and so therapy must teach them new behaviors. Minuchin (1980), in contrast, believes that the individual's repertoire of behavior is much larger than is enacted in any given relationship context. So the therapeutic task is typically not to build in new behaviors, but instead to change the context so that more competent behaviors (already in the patient's repertoire) are displayed. This is often done with a kick and a stroke. For example, a mother came for help with an unruly 11-year-old daughter, arriving alone and helpless and stating that her husband refused to come in. I told her: "You're a very competent operating room nurse. How come you leave your competence on the doorstep when you get home? I know that you can succeed in convincing your husband to help you with your daughter." After a couple of sessions in which the mother and I struggled over whether I would treat her as indeed helpless, and agree to see her alone, the woman brought her husband to the therapy and the work proceeded nicely.

Such thinking is also behind the technique demonstrated above where, once I had firmly sided with Mrs. Morgan against her husband, I then refused to do the work for her. Instead, I pulled back and insisted that she use her own resources. To restate, the assumption underlying Minuchin's approach is that the patient does not need to be instructed in new behaviors, but instead must be placed in a new context within which more competent and successful behavior can be demonstrated. I became the context within which Mrs. Morgan could change her husband.

The Cybernetics of Conflict Management

As will become clearer in Chapter 9, where a framework for integrating family systems models is presented, the structural model has essentially to do with the management of social conflict within the family. In the concluding section here, the structural model presented in this and in the preceding chapter is linked to the cybernetics of conflict management.

Conflict, in the form of disagreement, difference, or fighting, is a given in any living organism. Conflict is both necessary for healthy growth and responsible for pathology and death.

All organisms develop more or less successful mechanisms for managing conflict. At the extremes, the least successful die from their failure. And the more successful use conflict to change and grow.

UNSUCCESSFUL MODES OF CONFLICT MANAGEMENT

The family's typical modes of conflict management are a central characteristic of its functioning. Three unsuccessful modes are discussed here: open, unresolved conflict; rigid complementarity; and involving a third person in dyadic conflict. It should be remembered that these are characteristic cybernetic *processes* rather than types of families. All occur to some extent in every family, whether clinically dysfunctional or not. And a given family may use different modes across time and circumstances.

Open, unresolved conflict. Here deviation-amplification occurs and family members engage in escalating symmetrical behaviors (see Chapter 3). Verbal abuse is common and physical abuse may occur. Families typically shift to one of the other modes of conflict management when conflict reaches a certain level. If processes within the family do not succeed in producing this shift, the result may be injury or death or, more typically, intervention by some outside control agent, such as the police.

Rigid complementarity. This is a solution to the problem of open conflict: One way to prevent escalating conflict is to set up the relationship so that the participants always behave in a complementary rather than a symmetrical fashion.

There are many ways to achieve rigid complementarity in a (two-person) relationship. One of the best and most effective is to have one person gravely disabled in some way (e.g., sick, crazy, drunk, drug-addicted). The disabled person is underfunctioning (incompetent, irresponsible, etc.). The other person overfunctions, becoming the helper and caretaker (e.g., the co-alcoholic). We talk about the disabled individual as being *one-down* in the relationship and the overfunctioning person as *one-up*, but these labels are misleading. The one-down individual has as much control over the relationship as the one-up partner does (e.g., "If you don't stop doing X, I'll drink"). The participants in the relationship exert a mutually controlling influence on each other.

For example, an alcoholic inpatient was very angry that his wife was late for a family therapy session. The wife reacted angrily to her husband's criticism of her and began to complain that he does not understand the many things she has to cope with to keep the family going since he has been in the hospital. The conflict between them, with criticism and counterattack, began to heat up, until the husband reminded his wife that he is the one in the hospital struggling to deal with the great problem of his alcoholism. Whereupon the wife dropped her criticism of her husband and the conflict subsided. Later the wife explained how she manages the family, keeps the kids quiet, and makes excuses to the husband's boss, all to keep from placing any burdens on her husband and thereby confirming his position as an irresponsible, immature drunk.

Involving a third person. Yet another solution to the problem of conflict between two people is to involve a third person. The third person is often a child, brought in to help manage parental conflict. It may also be another family member (e.g., parent) or a therapist.

Minuchin et al. (1975) distinguish a number of different ways to involve the third person (say, a child). In *triangulation*, the child is placed in the position of choosing one parent over the other or serves as a go-between, carrying messages from one parent to the other. In the case of *parent–child coalition*, the child tends to move into a stable coalition with one parent against the other. In *detouring*, the parents submerge their conflicts and unite in order to protect or blame the child, who becomes the focus of all the family problems.

To illustrate, a 40-year-old alcoholic inpatient was interviewed with his mother, with whom he had gone to live just prior to being hospitalized with acute physical problems resulting from his heavy drinking. During the interview, the thrice-married mother talked fondly of her first husband, the patient's father. She spoke about what a good man he is and it was apparent that she is still very attached to him. And she mentioned that whenever the patient has a crisis over alcohol (as had occurred recently) she telephones his father and the two of them talk about how to help their son. It is very clear here that it is only the son's alcoholic crises that maintain his (divorced) parents' relationship.

CONFLICT MANAGEMENT
AND STRUCTURAL COUPLES TREATMENT

A healthy couple relationship requires successful management of conflict and an appropriate and flexible balance between symmetry and complementarity. The couple locked in symmetrical interaction has a rigid couple boundary, with intense involvement within the dyad and great imperviousness to outside influences. When others do become involved with such a couple, they tend to be incorporated as part of the couple's conflict-reducing mechanisms. In contrast, the highly complementary couple has a rigid boundary within the dyad that separates the two individuals, who often become separately involved with others outside the couple system.

Structural treatment of couples is aimed at changing maladaptive modes of conflict management and helping husband and wife face and resolve conflicts. As discussed in the previous chapter, the approach is process- rather than content-oriented.

If the couple has involved a third person as part of their unsuccessful attempts to cope with conflict, these processes are the initial target of intervention. The third person is typically from a different generation, usually a child and sometimes a parent of either the husband or wife. Here the structural family therapist works to make a clear generational boundary. When the third person is a symptomatic child, the symptoms will typically improve as they are no longer needed to maintain tolerable levels of family tension and the child is then free to become involved with peers and become emancipated from the family at the appropriate age.

Where the spouses are rigidly complementary in order to manage conflict, these patterns become the next target of structural treatment. The couple is assisted both to work together as a parental team and to resolve their marital conflicts as equals. This requires unbalancing the couple, as discussed in this chapter.

However, unbalancing in the face of couple complementarity requires careful attention to the complementary relationship itself. As long as the couple is engaged in symmetrical interaction, they truly are equal and interchangeable and it does not matter who you side with, beyond the idiosyncratic matching factors discussed earlier. This is not at all true when the couple interaction is rigidly complementary, of course. In this case, the goal of unbalancing is to make them more symmetrical. This is done by moving the "one-up" spouse down (e.g., by attacking him or her) or more commonly by pushing the "one-down" partner up. An example of the latter occurred in a family in which the identified patient was a drug-abusing teenage son and the mother had had several hospitalizations for psychotic breaks (Meyerstein, 1974). She presented herself in the interview as incompetent and was treated by the family more as a part of the sibling subsystem than as a member of the executive subsystem. After some initial work aimed at strengthening the generational boundary by removing the identified patient from his triangulated position, the therapist was discussing with the couple the fact that they never went out together and unbalanced by siding with the wife, asking her why she let her husband get away with never taking her out to dinner. Here the therapist was treating the wife as more competent than she saw herself or was seen by her husband and children.

The matter of deciding who is "really" up versus down is not so simple, however. Consider the case of the pushy, demanding husband and the passive, withholding wife, for example. This is clearly a case of complementarity. However, it is not at all clear who is up and who is down in this relationship. One might unbalance here by saying to the wife: "How come you let him get away (so far, wife is defined as one-up) with pushing you around like this?" (but now husband is assigned the one-up position). Alternatively, the therapist might say to the husband: "How come you let her get away (here husband is seen as one-up) with never giving you what you want?" (and now wife is placed in the one-up position). Both interventions reflect the paradoxical nature of power in the complementary relationship, but each punctuates (Watzlawick et al., 1974) the relationship in a different way. The unbalancing intervention itself defines the nature of the complementarity and at the same time attempts to change it by introducing symmetry into the relationship.

Now, if you have been successful so far in removing any third person involved in managing the couple's conflict (without becoming hopelessly triangulated yourself) and have successfully challenged any rigid complementarity, you have on your hands a couple in open, symmetrical conflict. Here the goal is to help someone *win*, using the sidetaking techniques of this chapter. The desired treatment outcome is for the couple to be able to face conflicts when they arise, have a good healthy fight someone can win (but not the same person all the time), and then get on with things.

BEYOND CONFLICT MANAGEMENT

The term *conflict management* used in this section has an important limitation, suggesting as it does that conflict is something to be gotten rid of or contained. This is a powerful, "gut-issue" ultimately rooted in the realistic fear that unregulated conflict will result, if not in actual physical death, at least in drastic change in the system (another kind of death).

The work of Prigogine (1976) provides a theoretical rationale for moving beyond this negative view of conflict and allows us to examine its role in the healthy growth of the system. As discussed in Chapter 3, Prigogine looks at the way large fluctuations away from equilibrium conditions are amplified, ultimately driving the system to a totally new organization.

The therapeutic crisis introduced into family systems for the express purpose of producing change provides a good example, and none is more dramatic than the famous lunch session hosted by Minuchin for anorexics and their families. The reader is encouraged to consult *Psychosomatic Families* (Minuchin et al., 1978) in which the complete lunch interview with the Kaplan family is presented.

When Minuchin instructed Mr. and Mrs. Kaplan to make their daughter eat, he invited them to enact a process that had occurred over and over again as the family struggled with the problem of anorexia. Father and daughter engaged in an escalating struggle: The harder the father tried to force his daughter to eat, the more she resisted until both were nearly screaming at each other. Mrs. Kaplan intervened protectively on the side of her daughter, temporarily reducing the level of conflict. But her action led inevitably to another repetition of the cycle.

The intensity of the interaction at this point is suggested by the remarks of an interviewer soliciting Minuchin's comments (Minuchin et al., 1978) about the session:

> The intensity of the Kaplan's reactions at this point is shocking. Why did you elicit such a response? How will you develop it in a way that is therapeutic rather than destructive? And what happens to you when you see these people hurting each other? What do you do when they become psychologically exhausted? (p. 166)

Here the interviewer's negative frame for the conflict is clear.

So far, because Mrs. Kaplan acts as a deviation-reducing agent, the conflict between father and daughter has not reached the level necessary to propel the system to a new organization. Next, Minuchin intervened to push the family to play out its process all the way by blasting Mrs. Kaplan: "You are attacking your husband. And you are killing your daughter." (p. 165) His goal was to disable one of this family's conflict-reducing mechanisms by blocking Mrs. Kaplan's interference with her husband's attempts to get the daughter to eat.

From this point, conflict between the anorexic and her parents escalated further, with everyone screaming. Mother finally burst into tears and father, in desperation, shoved a hot dog into his daughter's mouth, which she refused, instead getting it smeared over her face. The daughter returned to the hospital ward after the lunch session, ordered a huge meal, and ate all of it. By the next family session she was eating a normal diet and gaining weight.

In Prigogine's (1976) terms, Minuchin had succeeded in amplifying conflict to the point where the system's structure was irrevocably changed. The generational boundary was reinforced by redefining the problem of anorexia as a struggle between the daughter and her parents. And the system's new organization did not include the daughter's anorexic symptoms.

6

The Developmental Model

The developmental model is a very general framework for family systems therapy based upon the developmental principle discussed in Chapter 3. Under the pressures of biology and culture, individuals enter and leave the family and the family must adapt to these changes in its membership.

The developmental approach to the family has been most systematically explored by sociologists such as Ruben Hill (1964). Within the family therapy field, Haley was among the first to emphasize developmental thinking in an influential book, published in 1973, called *Uncommon Therapy* (Haley, 1973a). This book also introduced the hypnotic approach of Milton Erickson to a wider audience of family therapists and psychotherapists in general. However, its significance for this chapter is Haley's emphasis on the *family life cycle*, the framework within which Erickson understood his patients and made his amazing interventions. The outline of the family life cycle presented in this chapter draws upon Haley's discussion.

The Basic Idea

The developmental model rests upon the very simple notion of the family life cycle, the idea that over time the family's composition and the tasks facing it change in certain predictable ways. It is convenient to describe the life cycle as a series of *stages* of family development. Roughly following Haley, the family life cycle is divided here into the following seven stages: courtship; early marriage; childbirth and child care; children start school; adolescence and the middle marriage years; children leave home; and retirement, old age, and death.

Clearly, the number of stages as well as their precise boundaries is somewhat arbitrary. Five or six stages rather than seven would work and one might wish to define as many as eight, or so. In their comprehensive new book on the family life cycle, Carter and McGoldrick (1980), for example, define six stages: between families; the joining of families through marriage; the family with young children; the family with adolescents; launching children and moving on; and the family in later life.

What is important is to get an idea of the predictable changes confronting families across their life-spans. As will be clear below, many of these stages could be further subdivided in ways consistent with other developmental typologies [e.g., Freud's (1930) stages of psychosexual development and Piaget's (Piaget, 1951, 1954; Inhelder and Piaget, 1958) conceptualization of the child's cognitive growth occupy the three family life cycle stages from childbirth through adolescence]. For some purposes, these finer-grained views are useful and even necessary. But the power of the family life cycle notion lies in standing back to view the broad changes in the family over several generations.

Each stage of the family life cycle will now be outlined, paying particular attention to the characteristic boundary issues (see discussion of the structural model in Chapters 4 and 5) and typical presenting problems (see Chapter 7 on the strategic model).

Stages of the Family Life Cycle

COURTSHIP

This discussion of the family life cycle could conceivably begin at any point in the circular unfolding of the generations, but it is convenient to start with two young adults deciding whether or not to form an enduring couple unit.

The courtship period is certainly important as the time when crucial patterns of interaction are first negotiated by the young man and woman, many of which will continue to characterize their relationship in subsequent years. See, for example, the discussion in Chapter 7 of Jackson's (1965) notion of the *marital quid pro quo*. This emphasis on the formation of the couple dyad during the courtship period looks ahead to the new family unit being formed.

An equally important perspective on this stage looks back to the young person's family of origin. Here, the courtship period is seen as a time of emancipation from the family of origin to become an adult in the larger society. Many cultures employ rites of passage signaling a young person's achievement of adult status. Although our own culture does things a bit more informally, we do have a handful of culturally sanctioned routes to adulthood.

In middle- and upper-class families, children often leave their families by going away to school. And particularly among lower-class males, entering military service has long been a traditional road to adulthood. For girls, getting pregnant has always served as one escape from home. To this list, Haley (1973a) adds individual psychotherapy for the adolescent: "It is one way the culture helps ease the young person out of his tight family organization and into a marriage and family of his own" (p. 47).

Whether or not the attainment of adult status has already been marked by one such event, serious courtship means a significant change in how the young adult relates to the family of childhood.

The boundary issues crucial in the courtship period are those defining the new couple dyad (e.g., Do they date only each other or do they see various potential marriage partners? Do they socialize alone as a couple or in a group of peers?) and regulating the involvement with each young adult's family of origin (e.g., In what way are parents and siblings included in the couple's life together?).

Presenting problems at this stage typically concern either the serious dysfunction of the young adult (e.g., psychosis, delinquent behavior, drug addiction) or the young person's difficulties with the family of origin (e.g., parental disapproval of the prospective mate).

Couples rarely present with couple-focused problems at this stage. Usually, the future together looks rosy and it is easy to overlook difficulties when one is young and in love. Occasionally a couple seeks out a therapist to help them decide whether or not to get married, indicating their awareness at some level of basic difficulties in the relationship that need to be dealt with.

EARLY MARRIAGE

This stage begins with the couple's decision to form a permanent couple unit and continues until the birth of the first child. For our purposes here, "marriage" indicates the couple's commitment to the relationship, whether or not their arrangement is formalized in a legal marriage.

As with the courtship period, this stage of the life cycle focuses both inward, on the couple dyad, and outward, toward the families of origin and the worlds of peers and work. Haley (1973a) notes that "a crucial difference between men and all other animals is that man is the only animal with in-laws" (p. 45), and he reminds us that marriage is the joining of two family systems, not just two individuals.

The boundaries between the new couple dyad and their families of origin must be negotiated, often around such concrete and practical matters as phone calls and whose house the couple visits for holidays.

The meaning of the couple's commitment to each other is worked out and tested during these early years. In some cases, couples enter treatment with commitment as an issue. For example, a couple who have lived together more or less successfully and happily for months or even years may suddenly find themselves unable to deal with new tensions that arise in the relationship when a quick and easy exit is no longer as available as it was before the wedding.

The young couple must also work out the details of their marital relationship, including issues of sex, money, household responsibilities, and conflict resolution. Rules about socializing with friends, both as individuals and as a couple, must be negotiated. And roles in the work world must be integrated into the couple's life together.

Many of the problems that present later in the family life cycle as marital difficulties or as dysfunction in one spouse or in a child can be traced to unresolved problems that began at the early marriage stage. (See Chapter 4 for a discussion of this point from the perspective of the structural model.)

CHILDBIRTH AND CHILD CARE

This stage of the family life cycle is ushered in by the birth of the first child. It is a crucial point in the family's development because, for the first time, the nuclear family consists of a triad instead of a dyad and because it now contains not just one but two generations.

Essentially different systemic phenomena can arise in triads that cannot arise in dyads. For the first time, jealousy and two-against-one coalitions are possible *within* the nuclear family. And the child is available as a convenient third person to use in managing the couple's marital conflict (see discussion at end of Chapter 5).

The in-laws are now grandparents as well as mothers- and fathers-in-law, and arrangements negotiated earlier regarding interactions with families of origin must often be revised to accommodate these new relationships.

Husband and wife become father and mother as well, requiring that the couple work out a whole new set of agreements regarding the care of the child. The new parental roles, in turn, affect the marital relationship (e.g., the woman who abandons her role as wife to devote herself to being a mother, drastically altering the couple's earlier pattern of sexual activity), as well as the way the couple deals with work responsibilities outside the home (e.g., the woman who stops working to focus on the care of her child).

Expressed in terms of boundary issues, the generational boundary between parents and child is crucial at this stage of the life cycle, with rearrangements occurring within the couple dyad and at the boundaries with their families of origin as well.

Yet another boundary is important at this stage of life: the child's individual boundary, the extent to which the parents see the child as a person separate from each of them, and the degree to which the child eventually comes to view himself as a separate person. The blurring of the child's individual boundaries, which at adolescence or young adulthood may result in the clinical symptoms of schizophrenia, begins at this early stage. Haley (1973a) cites the example of the mother of an 18-year-old psychotic girl who stated in a letter written when the daughter was only a few months old that her husband and daughter always sided against her. The letter clearly reveals the mother's inability to separate her own thoughts and feelings from those of her daughter, a condition that severely limits the child's ability to develop the sense of a separate self.

Families sometimes present for treatment with problems related to this stage of development. The classic postpartum depression is an obvious illustration, but such experiences are by no means limited to new mothers. For example, a 23-year-old man sought psychiatric help complaining of anxiety attacks and suicidal ideation at the time his wife was about to give birth to their first child (she had a 4-year-old daughter by a previous marriage). Initial sessions focused on the husband's annoyance about the behavior of the daughter and the couple's difficulties in dealing with her. As the sessions progressed, it became clear that the young man experienced even greater apprehension about his own child's imminent birth and his soon to be increased parenting responsibilities. Young adults who are still very unsure about their ability to take care of themselves often become acutely anxious when faced with the prospect of assuming responsibility for a helpless infant.

CHILDREN START SCHOOL

A new stage in the family life cycle begins at the time the first child starts school. Haley (1973a) suggests that this stage is important for at least two reasons. First, conflicts between the parents over childrearing may arise at this point because their product, the child, is put on display for the larger society. And second, parents get their first preview of the child eventually leaving home. In fact from the time the child enters school, the parents occupy a position of diminishing importance and influence as other adults and, increasingly, the child's peers become more important.

Family problems at this stage of the life cycle are the bread and butter of child guidance clinics. One often sees the overinvolvement of one parent (often, but not always, the mother) with the symptomatic child, with the other parent peripheral and underinvolved. Haley's (1973b) famous dog phobia case is a good example.

ADOLESCENCE AND THE MIDDLE MARRIAGE YEARS

In one sense, this is a boring period of the family life cycle: Typically, no one is entering or leaving the family and the parents tend to be settled in their personal and work lives.

For the parents, Haley (1973a) suggests, this is typically a time when personal issues have their impact. For example, the parents are often either disappointed at not having achieved more in their careers or else have to deal with the consequences of success (e.g., increased responsibilities at work, less time for the family). And particularly for mothers who have devoted themselves to caring for the family and have not worked outside the home, the absence of young children who need constant attention forces a reconsideration of goals and activities.

These are also typically the years during which the grandparents die and members of the nuclear family, particularly the parents, are faced with issues of loss and grief and of their own mortality.

What saves this stage of the life cycle from being too uninteresting are the beginning struggles of the adolescent children to become emancipated from the family. Haley (1973a) writes: "What is known as adolescent turmoil can be seen as a struggle within the family system to maintain the previous hierarchical arrangement" (p. 59).

Families in which the parents have over the years been able to influence and control the lives of their children appropriately are forced by the adolescent's push for independence to renegotiate power issues within the family, to endure the young person's healthy testing of limits, and, when necessary, to insist upon their adult prerogatives to still set the rules. At least some parent–child conflict at this stage of the life cycle is generally necessary for the adolescents to eventually separate from the family and to leave home.

In other families in which parental control and responsibility has at best been tenuous while the children were younger, this is often a time of increasingly out of control and irresponsible behavior on the part of the teenager. This family typically presents itself in the therapist's office as helpless parents and defiant adolescent, all angry. The therapeutic task here is first to help the parents regain control of the family so that the adolescent can eventually leave home properly instead of being shoved out prematurely and inappropriately by the family conflict. This issue is discussed further in Chapter 9, using the Bach family as an example.

CHILDREN LEAVE HOME

The crisis (if one occurs) of this stage of the family life cycle may happen, Haley (1973a) suggests, when the first child leaves home, when the last child goes, or when a child who for some reason has been "special" departs.

The couple is eventually left alone in the home again and must confront head-on marital issues that were not resolved before the arrival of the children and that had, over the years, gone underground and been expressed instead as parenting conflicts.

Society's expectation that at this stage of the life cycle young adults assume adult responsibilities outside the family may precipitate the breakdown of a young person inadequately prepared for life outside the family. To illustrate with an extreme example, this is the stage of the family life cycle at which schizophrenia, the most severe form of psychological dysfunction, becomes manifest. Haley (1973a) writes

> Adolescent schizophrenia and other severe disturbances can be seen as an extreme way of attempting to solve what happens to a family at this stage of life. When child and parents cannot tolerate becoming separated, the threatened separation can be aborted if something goes wrong with the child. By developing a problem that incapacitates him socially, the child remains within the family system. The parents can continue to share the child as a source of concern and disagreement, and they find it unnecessary to deal with each other without him. The child can continue to participate in a triangular struggle with his parents, while offering himself and them his "mental illness" as an excuse for all difficulties. (p. 61)

In the case of schizophrenia, the child, now late adolescent or young adult, often remains within the family and is unable to become successfully emancipated. Particularly in the case of serious, but nonpsychotic problems with the young person, one also encounters the opposite extreme, when the child is expelled from the family or flees from it, never to return. Both are failures of this stage of development. The goal at this point of the life cycle is for the child to become emancipated and to establish a separate life, yet remain involved with the family in age-appropriate ways. Here as with earlier stages, the generational boundary occupies center stage.

RETIREMENT, OLD AGE, AND DEATH

During the final years of life, the couple tends to encounter either a period of new interests and experiences, freed from the old obligations of family and work, or a time of isolation, ill health, and depression. Their new roles as grandparents often bring fresh satisfactions to balance the typical losses of this stage of life.

The retirement of one or both spouses can be a time of stress for the couple and requires considerable readjustment. They are suddenly together 24 hours a day, usually for the first time in their marriage. Old conflicts and even minor annoyances, which were tolerable before, may suddenly loom large. For example, a 54-year-old man who had been forced to retire early when his company went out of business sought treatment for his angry outbursts. Careful questioning revealed that these had *not* increased in either frequency or intensity during the years of the couple's marriage. What *had* changed and precipitated the request for treatment was that the wife, who was a few years older, was very dissatisfied with her job and was seriously considering retirement herself. However, her husband's outbursts had given her second thoughts, leading her to wonder whether she could stand being around him 24 hours a day.

Brief couples therapy focused first on simple transactional techniques (e.g., teaching the wife to tell her husband "I understand" instead of nodding her head appreciatively as he rambled on and on while she fumed inside). The couple also negotiated time and activities for each spouse apart from the other and settled a long-standing conflict regarding visits by the wife's son. With this, the wife set a date for her retirement and was able to look forward to a new life with her husband.

The loss of the work role, particularly for the husband, may be experienced as a severe blow to self-esteem, resulting in serious depression. Haley (1973a) tells of the wife who developed an incapacitating symptom at this stage of life in order to give her newly retired husband a new job and purpose in life.

Advancing age often confronts couples with declining health and dwindling financial resources. And the entire family is faced with the issue of how the aging parents will be cared for (i.e., within the extended family or in a nursing home). At this stage of the family life cycle, the relationship of the generations is turned on its head as the now-adult children begin to care for their elderly parents.

Finally, when one parent dies the surviving spouse is left alone and there is one less person standing between the children and their own eventual deaths.

Loss, Grief, and the Family Life Cycle

LOSS

An important *psychological* theme of the family life cycle is loss. As society's reproductive system, the family is created, carries out its function of producing and caring for the young, and eventually dies, leaving the next generation to carry on. For family members, and particularly the parents, this process is continually one of giving up and letting go.

At the moment of birth, a child is totally helpless and dependent upon the parents for physical and emotional survival and will quickly die without their constant care, or that provided by some other adult. But from that time on, this is less and less true. As the child learns to walk, for example, she will never again totally depend upon her parents for a trustworthy and efficient means of locomotion. As was mentioned above, the day the child enters school marks a shift from parental influence to that of the peer group. Finally in late adolescence or early adulthood, families in our culture are expected to give up their children and help launch them into lives of their own.

Unlike the marital relationship, which is created to endure and serve as a continuing source of emotional support and satisfaction over the years, the parent–child relationship must, in a sense, self-destruct (or at least change *drastically*) if it is to be successful. For parents particularly, the psychological consequence of such a relationship, in addition to being a source of pride and satisfaction, is a feeling of loss.

When the loss of the child is experienced by one or both parents as the loss of a part of the self, the child, or in some cases a parent, is vulnerable to psychotic breakdown at the time of expected emancipation from the family. If the personal boundaries of family members are intact, but the child has become a part of the parents' mechanism for regulating conflict within the couple dyad, then the child's emancipation may be compromised and nonpsychotic but serious symptoms, including delinquent behavior, drug or alcohol addiction, or psychosomatic illness, may develop.

If, on the other hand, the child will be sorely missed by the parents, but they also have alternative sources of satisfaction in their lives, both from within the couple relationship and from their pursuits in the world outside the family, then the parents are able to let go of the child and take pride and vicarious satisfaction in the offspring's life independent of the family.

UNRESOLVED GRIEF

Psychologically, letting go of children means working through a process of grief and mourning in the sense first identified by Lindemann in his classic 1944 paper. When normal grieving occurs, the process is typically brief and nonproblematic and does not come to the attention of mental health professionals. In cases where the normal grief process is for some reason delayed or altogether fails to occur, however, family development is often compromised and the family may wind up in the therapist's office. The importance of grief for family therapy was first emphasized by Paul (e.g., Paul and Grosser, 1965).

Unresolved grief is a "masked" disorder. That is, it is not something people come into therapy complaining about, but typically presents disguised as some other problem. A brief clinical vignette will illustrate.

The Franklin family was referred by a local neurologist. James, age 12, had been sent for neurological consultation because of increasingly disruptive and irresponsible behavior both at home and in school. He would have been kicked out of school months before had it not been for a principal who liked the family and felt that James had "so much potential." Early in grammar school the boy had been diagnosed as hyperactive and was placed on Ritalin. Neurological examination, both at the time of the current referral as well as two years earlier, was entirely normal.

The neurologist requested psychological testing of the boy and a recommendation for treatment. As I discussed the case briefly on the phone with the neurologist, he mentioned that an older son Jeff had died five years before at the age of 16, and that when Mrs. Franklin mentioned this to him, she began sobbing so intensely that he did not pursue the issue further.

When I met with Mr. and Mrs. Franklin and James for the first time (they failed to bring a younger daughter Debbie, age 10, to the session although I had requested that the whole family come in), I inquired about Jeff's death near the end of the session, which was mainly devoted to the parents' angry recounting of James' misbehavior. Immediately Mrs. Franklin began crying, and soon her husband and son were also in tears. I learned that Jeff had died in an apparent suicide, although the parents believed (persuaded, in part, by the school principal) that the death was accidental. Moreover, the death occurred immediately following Mrs. Franklin's refusal to allow Jeff to go out, insisting instead that he stay home and finish his homework. Mr. Franklin, it turned out, disagreed with his wife's decision and felt that she was being too hard on the boy.

Psychological testing revealed that James was extremely bright, but did have some moderate attention and concentration difficulties, which were consistent with either a mild organic attention deficit disorder or functional symptoms of anxiety and depression. In the one-to-one testing situation, at least, he demonstrated very adequate impulse control and the ability to tolerate frustration and to act in a responsible, goal-directed manner.

After presenting these findings to the family, I recommended family therapy and discussed my belief that their unresolved feelings of grief over Jeff's death were related to the current problems with James and needed to be worked out. They agreed to treatment.

My previous experiences with unresolved family grief had convinced me of its importance, and I fully intended to begin the therapy by focusing on the grief work. However, I quickly became caught up in the family's anxiety about this issue and involved in their characteristic defense against it: the focus on James' misbehavior. I was also afraid that I risked losing the family from treatment if I neglected to pay attention to the problem that, after all, had brought them to see me.

James cooperated beautifully by managing to do outrageous things just before each family interview so that his parents came to the sessions steaming about what he had done and I felt I had no choice but to spend 15 or 20 minutes allowing them to express their outrage. My attempts to help the parents be more consistent regarding discipline produced not even a dent in James' behavior.

Finally after the second or third of these sessions, as James' transgressions each week were worse than the last, the family revealed that the previous day had been the anniversary of Jeff's birth and that Mrs. Franklin had been very depressed and upset. Mr. Franklin attributed his wife's distress to James' behavior and said that although he had tried to get his wife to feel less responsible for James, he had been unable to get her to relax. I seized upon this opportunity to press Mrs. Franklin about what she had been experiencing, and the impact was dramatic. She tearfully spoke of her sadness about Jeff's death, her feelings of guilt for having been too harsh on him, and her great fear that James was headed toward serious problems with delinquency and drugs (as had Mrs. Franklin's brother). Mrs. Franklin cited the latter as the reason that she has been unable to back off, instead finding herself constantly berating James for his misbehavior and desperately attempting to control him. She also admitted her fear that James, too, might take his life.

By this time, the whole family was once again in tears. Debbie was particularly upset by her mother's distress, reluctantly admitting that she feared that her mother might "go crazy." I reassured

Debbie that her mother was only experiencing normal, but long-delayed grief.

As the session ended, James spontaneously hugged each of his parents and Mr. Franklin remarked confidently to me as he left the office: "I think maybe we got somewhere today."

The family returned the following week, looking much more relaxed than on any previous visit. They reported a dramatic improvement in James' behavior that week and felt that if this continued, their problems with him would be solved. The family was about to turn to focus on Debbie's misbehavior (which had formerly been greatly overshadowed by what James was doing) when I stopped them. I reiterated my belief that James had been helping the whole family avoid its grief by being so bad and insisted that instead of now going to work on Debbie, we still had some talking to do about Jeff's death.

Mrs. Franklin reported that she had spontaneously initiated a conversation about Jeff's death with a family friend following last week's session. This was the first time she had allowed herself to discuss it with anyone outside the immediate family, and she felt that, despite the pain and tears of that conversation, it had been an important step for her.

The family also revealed that the father had experienced an intense grief reaction immediately following Jeff's death, with extreme withdrawal, sadness, depression, and anger. Mrs. Franklin stated that she had believed that she had to be strong at the time, not even allowing herself to cry, but felt that "my time [for grief] will come too. Only it never came."

In subsequent sessions, the grief work was completed, including helping the family come to terms with the death by suicide. (I learned that the school principal who had helped the family avoid facing the suicide issue and had subsequently overprotected James at school had himself lost a son to leukemia the year before Jeff's death.) I suggested that the family devise a ritual to mark the end of their mourning for Jeff. Mrs. Franklin decided that they should get out all the old pictures and home movies that they had put away when Jeff died and finally allow themselves to have their happy memories of him. Mr. Franklin spontaneously resurrected Jeff's bicycle from the attic where it had been placed as a kind of somber shrine, lovingly repainted it, and allowed James and Debbie to use it.

Treatment ended with a single couples session to check out the marital dyad. There it appeared that, despite the loss of their son,

Mr. and Mrs. Franklin had been able to maintain a healthy couple relationship that had sustained them during the past five difficult years. James' behavioral problems had not reappeared and the family left satisfied with the therapy. In a follow-up note several months later, Mrs. Franklin indicated that things were still going well.

GRIEF AND FAMILY DYSFUNCTION

I had been alerted to the importance of unresolved family grief by previous work with the family of two young adult heroin abusers and a 14-year-old son who had begun to become involved in delinquent activities. The father was desperately afraid that his youngest son would follow in the footsteps of the two older brothers. This family had lost their eldest son, the parents' pride and joy, ten years before at age 18, when he died in an auto accident on his way to register for college. The mother began sobbing as soon as this was mentioned in the session, and the rest of the family cited her tears as the reason they had never been able to talk about the boy's death. The evidence for unresolved grief here was striking. For example, the family moved out of the house in which they were living at the time of the boy's death without the mother ever going back to it. And they severed all contact with the family of the boy who was driving, a family with whom they had previously been very close. Grief work with this family revealed that although she had never before been able to admit it, the mother deeply blamed her husband for having been too harsh on the son who died. As a result, she found herself unable to support her husband in setting limits for the remaining sons in the years that followed, always protecting them in the face of his firmer stand. Gradually, the boys' behavior became more and more out of control.

I subsequently learned of the important work of Stanton and his associates (Stanton et al., 1982) at the Philadelphia Child Guidance Clinic. These investigators report that in a striking percentage of the families of young adult heroin abusers with whom they worked there had been the premature loss of a family member (e.g., child, grandparent), and the death had not been adequately mourned by the family. See, in particular, the discussion by Coleman and Stanton (1978).

How can we understand the connection between unresolved grief and the subsequent development of family problems? Because loss and grief are a continuing psychological theme in the *normal* process of family development, families that have not adequately mourned earlier losses are more or less unable to successfully prepare for, face, and work through subsequent losses.

Unresolved grief typically shows up in the guise of behavior problems in the children and/or as difficulties in allowing them to become emancipated at the appropriate time. The process involved goes something like this: The premature death, particularly of a child, may divide the parents, with one parent taking a hard line in matters of discipline and the other parent becoming protective. With the parental dyad thus split, effective limit-setting is impossible and behavior problems in the child are likely to develop. The child's behavior then becomes the focus of parental concern, allowing the whole family to avoid having to deal with the unresolved grief as well as permitting the couple to ignore and contain their marital conflict.

This process is likely to intensify in adolescence as the time for the children to leave home approaches. If the young person's behavior problems become severe enough, emancipation can be aborted, protecting the family from yet another loss. Stanton et al. (1982) see heroin abuse in young adults as failed or pseudo emancipation.

I should note here that not all family systems therapists agree with my emphasis on unresolved grief. In discussing families in which there has been a death Minuchin (Minuchin and Fishman, 1981) for example, states:

> Problems in these families may be experienced by family members as issues of incomplete mourning. But if the therapist operates on this assumption, she may crystallize the family instead of helping them move toward a new organization. (p. 57)

Minuchin appears to view a focus on grief as an impediment to change, whereas I see grief as part of the process of change itself. In fact, grief, with its mixture of sadness, sorrow, depression, and anger, may be seen as *the emotional component of important life change.* By amplifying the emotional process of grieving, a skillful therapist can use grief work to help the family make necessary organizational changes and to move on in its life cycle.

Family Development and Family Dysfunction

With this excursion into the issue of unresolved grief as an introduction, it is time to discuss, in general, the relationship between family development and family dysfunction. As with the other clinical models presented in this book, the developmental model implies a particular view of family dysfunction and prescribes a direction for treatment.

In the case of the developmental model, these can be stated very simply: Family problems arise when the family, for one reason or another, is unable to shift to a new stage of its development at the appropriate time. And the therapist's job is to help get the family life cycle moving again.

The following case example illustrates the assessment of family developmental problems in the typical situation when the presenting complaint itself does not necessarily indicate family developmental difficulties.

Case Example

IDENTIFYING DATA

Mr. Stuart, a 51-year-old white male, was referred to the outpatient psychiatry service for treatment of back pain and depression. He had reportedly suffered two ruptured disks in his back during chiropractic treatment for headaches. Because of the subsequent back pain he had taken disability leave from his job as a skilled craftsman and slipped into a deep depression during the following six months. Mr. Stuart's previous psychiatric history included hospitalization for a psychotic episode 30 years before, while in the military. Although a diagnosis of schizophrenia was made at the time, his negative psychiatric history since then, as well as his adequate family and work adjustment, made such a diagnosis questionable.

Mr. Stuart was initially seen individually by a psychology intern who was so frightened by the depths of his depression that she managed to get rid of the case by arguing that Mrs. Stuart, age 53, who always accompanied her husband to the clinic, should be seen as well. So she referred the case to the family therapy program.

The family evaluation session was attended by Mr. and Mrs. Stuart together with their three sons: Bill, 25; Gene, 24; and Art, 19. A daughter Lisa, age 22, married and living an hour's drive away, was described as unavailable for one vague reason or another.

Although Mr. Stuart's presenting problems of pain and depression do not necessarily suggest family developmental problems, we quickly got some hints that there might be difficulties in this area. The three sons all lived in the family home. Bill, we learned, had been living on his own while attending college and, more recently, working. However, about three months before our initial contact with the family, he had been asked by his mother to come home because of his father's difficulties. Although college educated, Bill currently worked as a dishwasher and hoped to go to chef's school. Gene was described by the family as "neurologically handicapped" due to dyslexia, a condition that was implied to be extremely serious, although upon clinical interview it was impossible to detect any gross abnormalities. Despite his handicap, Gene held a much more responsible job than Bill. However, Mr. Stuart drove Gene to and from work every day.

Before showing how the developmental issues in the family emerged, the Stuarts will be discussed from the perspectives of the strategic and structural models.

STRATEGIC ASSESSMENT

Strategic therapy (see Chapter 7) typically begins with an assessment of the "main problem" as seen by each family member (Haley, 1976). This is how each member described the family's problems.

(*The therapy system includes father (F); mother (M); Bill (B); Gene (G); Art (A); male therapist (T1); female therapist (T2).*)

F: Not knowing if I can keep working.

M: My husband's depression, and not knowing if I can help him adjust to the pain.

B: Lack of communication and lack of knowledge about my father's back problem.

G: My father seems to have a serious back problem. I don't know whether it affects him more physically or mentally.

A: My father is having trouble with his back and it hurts him more than physically. This is weakening the bond that holds the family together.

It is interesting that as the therapists went around the circle soliciting each family member's view of the problem, the focus moved from external issues (work) to the family itself, from a concern with physical pain to emotional distress, and finally, with Art's statement, to the very bonds that hold the family together.

It was clear that Art was the family member most closely identified with father and most distressed by his pain and disability. We learned that Art and his father were both volunteer firemen in the small town in which the family lived. Art cried as he talked of what it meant to him that his father was no longer able to do this work with him.

The family therapy team saw vigorous treatment of Mr. Stuart's depression as the first order of business. In all cases of serious depression, a thorough evaluation of suicide risk is necessary. Conducted in the presence of the family, it revealed that Mr. Stuart was carrying a loaded shotgun in the trunk of his car, unbeknown to the other family members or the therapists.

The therapists employed a very useful technique, described by Drye et al. (1973), for obtaining the patient's assistance in assessing the risk of suicide. It involves asking the patient to make a no-suicide decision in the following form: "No matter what happens, I will not kill myself, accidentally or on purpose, at any time" (p. 172). After an agonizingly long silence during which this extremely depressed man pondered the therapist's sentence, Mr. Stuart repeated the statement and spontaneously added: "And I expect to die a natural death," a clear affirmation of his decision to live. He also agreed to give up the shotgun.

The rest of the family and the therapy team alike were much relieved by Mr. Stuart's statement. His reassurance regarding the issue of suicide was the minimum necessary for us to feel comfortable treating Mr. Stuart as an outpatient. He was depressed enough that we seriously considered hospitalizing him. However, Mr. Stuart was so frightened of psychiatric hospitalization, as a result of his experience 30 years before, that we wished to avoid it, if possible. Instead, we contracted to meet with the family for six weekly sessions, began Mr. Stuart on antidepressant medication, and referred him to a pain clinic for his back pain.

STRUCTURAL ASSESSMENT

In our structural assessment of this family we were drawn not so much to the generational boundary, as is typically the case, but instead focused upon the personal boundaries of each individual family member.

The most striking feature of the family was their profound dependence upon Mr. Stuart. As individuals, each person looked reasonably intact. Yet within the family, they appeared otherwise. Now that the father's ability to function was severely impaired by his pain and depression, the functioning of the entire family was seriously compromised. This assessment was based upon a number of observations.

All family members were closely identified with the father and his pain and depression. Each reported back pain. The mother insisted that her pain was every bit as great as the father's. The therapists became so intrigued with this phenomenon that at the end of the evaluation session they assigned each family member the task of rating his/her back pain during the following week on a scale ranging from one to ten. In the next session, Bill, the first family member to report on the homework, rated the severity of his pain as "7." When all the other family members subsequently rated their pain as "9" or "10," Bill revised his rating, claiming that he had underestimated his own pain.

The family reported that conversation at the dinner table had all but ceased since Mr. Stuart had become so depressed because he had always been the one to keep the talk going.

This report was clearly confirmed in the session itself. Bill and Gene were instructed to have a dyadic conversation. Mr. Stuart continually intruded with more talk whenever the interaction between his sons wound down. Afterward, Mr. Stuart described sitting out and listening as "agonizing. I wanted to put my oar in, you know, and row the boat."

To summarize, our structural impression was of an enmeshed family with very diffuse individual boundaries (as well as a diffuse generational boundary).

DEVELOPMENTAL ASSESSMENT

Four excerpts from the first of the six initially scheduled treatment sessions demonstrate the emergence of developmental issues in the Stuart family.

(*Father sits to the left of therapist 1 and therapist 2, on the edge of the family circle. The rest of the family therapy team is arranged in a "back row," behind the family, but still in the interview room itself. The therapists have been commenting on father's apparent isolation from the rest of the family.*)

T1: Is this, does the, does the family feel comfortable sitting in this arrangement?

 B: Yeah.

 G: Yeah.

 M: I do.

 F: (*To mother, seated next to him.*) You do?

  (*Father indicates indirectly that he may not be quite so happy with his position in the family circle.*)

M: Um-hum.

T1: (*To father.*) Do you feel isolated off on the end there?

  (*And therapist 1 picks up on this and questions father directly.*)

M: (*To father.*) Want me to trade you?

  (*But before father has a chance to answer for himself, mother offers to relieve his apparent discomfort.*)

 F: No. There's one thing, I realize, when we go to Mass, is that (*to mother*) you wouldn't leave (*half laughs*) me, uh, right at the end. You all troop off, uh, going to Mass, and I end up bringing up the rear.

  (*Here father picks up on the theme of his isolation introduced by the therapist and voices a complaint about the family. Notice, however, that with his laugh father softens his complaint even as he makes it, suggesting that it need not be taken seriously. This is the first spontaneous statement by Mr. Stuart in the two family sessions so far. Whenever a patient as depressed as this spontaneously says these many words, pay attention.*)

M: (*Laughs.*)

  (*Taking father up on his offer not to take his complaint seriously, mother dismisses it with a laugh.*)

 B: Yeah, I noticed that. It's happened, I tried to make it. . . .

  (*Bill, on the other hand, takes father seriously and attempts to respond.*)

M: (*Interrupts, speaking to father.*) That's 'cause you're walking slower now, right?

  (*Bill is interrupted by mother who blames father for the problem.*)

 B: Yeah.

  (*Bill then accepts his mother's version of reality.*)

 F: (*To mother, speaking quietly.*) Or you're walking faster, maybe.

  (*Father timidly contradicts mother, blaming her, or the whole family.*)

A: (*To father.*) Well, you used to lead us in and Mom would pick the row and you'd just stand next to it waiting for us to file in, and. . . .

(*Here Art intrudes into the parental discussion at the moment when conflict between them makes its first appearance in the sessions.*)

M: (*Interrupts.*) Everybody followed me into church every Sunday.

A: That's 'cause you know what benches don't squeak. (*Laughs.*)

(*Working together, mother and Art deflect the parental conflict and dismiss father's complaint by turning the discussion into a pleasant little joke.*)

M: Just like a bunch of sheep. (*Laughs.*) (*To therapist 2.*) I'd, I'd hold back some Sundays, to see if they'll go in ahead of me. Nope.

T2: (*Laughs.*)

(*Therapist 2 accepts mother's invitation and joins in the laughter.*)

M: Wait for mother to go in first. (*Long laugh.*)

This is a good example of the structural model discussed in the preceding two chapters. Therapist 1 unbalanced the system a bit by inviting Mr. Stuart to state his complaint. Despite Mrs. Stuart's initial attempt to dismiss it, her husband persisted, revealing couple conflict. At that point the system's conflict management processes were invoked as a son intervened to assist his mother in diffusing the tension. A sign of the intensity of the shared anxiety in the treatment system at that moment is therapist 2's joining in the tension-reducing laughter.

In the next segment, after several distractions by family and therapists alike, the discussion was steered once again to Mr. Stuart's complaint and the developmental issues in the family began to emerge.

T1: (*To father.*) Picking at the details of what it was about this going to church this Sunday that a (*Art anxiously kicks table upon which microphone sits*), you would have liked to have seen differently.

F: Well, a, it's nice to see a family, wa, like when all the kids were younger, we all used to (*turns and speaks to mother*) more or less walk in togeth-th-er (*father has a life-long stammer*).

(*Father connects his complaint about being left behind when the family goes into church with the past, when the children were young. The intensity of the affect associated with his memories of family "togetherness" is indicated by the emergence of his stammer.*)

M: Yeah. I carried one and you carried one and we had one in between us.

(Mother joins in father's reverie.)

F: Yeah. I always kept up back then. But I don't know, somewhere there in the past it seems like we, you'd bolt out of the car and take off at a fast clip and I wouldn't catch up with you until we got to the front of the door there. I, I don't know if, if I was just thinking of appearance's sake, or what.

T1: What about appearances? How does that appear, do you feel?

F: Well, it's, it's nice to see a family all walking together.

T2: What does it mean when they don't?

F: Well, they're all indi *(stammers)* individuals that are going to be going their own separate ways, which is healthy. In other words, maybe what I'm trying to say is I hate to see the, I hate to see the family a, finally grow up, I guess.

(Here father states the developmental issue explicitly: "I hate to see the family grow up." Again, the stammer suggests the intensity of the arousal associated with the idea of his children as "individuals that are going to be going their separate ways.")

(Eight-second pause.)

T1: *(Leg starts to move anxiously as he begins speaking.)* So you're treasuring some of your memories of the boys being smaller and. . . .

(Therapist 1's nonverbal behavior too indicates the shared anxiety as this issue is pursued.)

F: *(Overlaps.)* I guess that's right.

T1: *(Continues.)* And raising them.

T2: It's hard to see them pass you by. *(Long pause. Father looks down with chin in hand. Bill mirrors this posture, which is shortly taken up by Art as well.)*

Notice in this segment the dichotomy Mr. Stuart sets up: "a family all walking together" versus "individuals that are going to be going their own separate ways." It suggests the (psycho)logic: If the children are individuals, then they will go their separate ways and we will lose them.

As the therapists continue to pursue this issue, a very touchy subject emerges: the emancipation of Gene, the "neurologically handicapped" son.

(Shortly after previous segment.)

T2: *(To father.)* Looking around now, at your sons, realizing their ages and thinking of their futures, what is the feeling that comes up for you?

F: Well, they'll all be gone in a few years, with the exception of Gene. And I always figured Gene would want to live with us the rest of his life if he wanted to. How do you feel about it, Gene?

   (*Notice the bind in this statement: Gene would want to live with us if he wanted to. The effect of such a transaction is mitigated somewhat by father's immediate invitation for Gene to respond.*)

G: No.

T2: (*Speaks quickly, addressing father.*) Let me just hold you to that question. Looking around at your sons, thinking of their futures . . . .

So not only is Mr. Stuart distressed about the thought of his children growing up and leaving home, but he actually plans to keep Gene there forever. It is not uncommon in families where a child has some kind of handicap for there to be problems with emancipation (see discussion in last section of this chapter). Here, however, there is an extreme mismatch between the objective facts of Gene's handicap and the family's subjective evaluation of it and their conclusion that he will never be able to live independently.

Notice here how therapist 2 ignores the conflict introduced by Gene's firm rejection of his father's plans for him and instead attempts to pursue her question about Mr. Stuart's *feelings* about his sons growing up. She is proceeding here more like an experiential therapist (the model in which she was first trained) who wishes to engage the patient in a discussion of his feelings than a family systems therapist who uses affect to reveal process (see discussion of this point in Chapter 3). What Mr. Stuart will say about his feelings (e.g., sadness) is less interesting systemically than is the fact that when the father is pushed on the emancipation issue, open conflict emerges between father and son. It would have been more productive to pursue the conflict here. Instead therapist 2's move diffuses this tension.

The session subsequently focused back on Mr. Stuart, but did not succeed at any deeper exploration of his underlying feelings about his children growing up. At that point, I intervened as team supervisor, complaining that the session was too focused on Mr. Stuart and directing the therapists to return to the issue of the family "growing up." The following then occurred.

T1: How can the family grow up? Well, that is the question, "How can the family grow up?" I think that the connecting link is "When everybody is so concerned and dependent upon Dad."

(This is a very nice statement of the developmental dilemma in the family: How can the family continue to grow despite father's problems?)

B: Uh-huh.

T1: Is that a clear enough statement? What I'd like you to respond to is Dr. Schultz's thinking has been missing. You're so damn generous and giving, to the point of giving in to your own pain, *(to Bill)* coming home from *(names town where Bill was living)*, whatever it takes, a, and yet, the family has to grow despite a chronic problem.

(Therapist 1 has already made a nice clear statement. But rather than just letting the family wrestle with this important issue, he questions the clarity of his inquiry and then begins to muddle it with a tangential remark before finally returning to a clear, simple restatement. Again, this betrays the shared anxiety about the developmental issue.)

B: Uh-huh.

T1: *(To sons.)* I think the floor's open to the, the growing men of the family here. Growing up men.

A: What's the question?

(This is a classic maneuver. Faced with a hot issue, Art plays dumb.)

T2: *(Says something unintelligible and laughs nervously.)*

(Once again the tension of the moment is revealed.)

T1: *(To Art.)* Why don't you ask your brother *(indicates Bill)*? He can, he might be able to say it in terms the family can understand better than I can put it.

(This is a masterful move on the part of therapist 1. Rather than assume he has failed to make his question clear, he suggests that Art can learn the question from his brother Bill who understands it. Bill's backchannel uh-huh's—see Duncan, 1972—earlier suggested that he did understand. Furthermore, therapist 1 graciously does a one-down maneuver—"better than I can put it"—rather than implying that Art is somehow deficient for not understanding.)

B: *(To Art, speaking slowly and thoughtfully.)* Well, I guess for you, a, I would ask, a, how are you going to feel about going away to school and living here in the city *(the school Art will attend is a half-hour's drive from the family's home)*? I mean, aside from normal feelings of breaking away, how are you going to feel about not seeing us every day?

(And Bill comes through, demonstrating his very clear understanding of therapist 1's question and indeed saying it "in terms the family can understand" by rephrasing the question for Art in a very concrete and personal way.)

A: Not seeing the family, or a. . . . .

B: (*Overlaps.*) Yeah.

A: (*Speaks slowly, with sad affect.*) It's going to be a change. I don't look forward to it, but it's one of the things that has to happen. You're not going to be around all the time.

(*Contrast this family in which growing up is viewed sadly as one "of those things that has to happen" with another in which the children's emancipation is experienced with excitement and a shared sense of pleasure and opportunity.*)

T2: What did you ask. . . ?

A: (*Overlaps.*) I said, "The family's not going to be around all the time." There's certain times when I gotta go out and (*pause*) do stuff on my own.

(*Eighteen-second pause.*)

T1: How do you feel about the idea, you're, are you going to be leaving, to begin school and moving out? Is that the plan right now?

A: Uh-huh.

T1: And when's that going to occur?

A: August (*three months away*).

T1: In August.

T2: And where are you going to go?

A: (*Names school.*)

T2: So you'll be living in (*names city in which school is located*).

A: Um-hum.

T1: (*To mother.*) And the family home is?

M: (*Names city, 30 minutes from school.*)

(*The therapists do an amusing double take here. As Art talks he gives the impression that he will be traveling to the other end of the earth to attend school. The therapists shake their heads in mild disbelief when they realize that he will be only 30 minutes from home.*)

T1: In (*names city*). Art, how do you feel about, we know that you have qualms about being out on your own. Like you say, "Well, it's only natural." How do you feel about leaving everybody else home without you, the refrigerator mover, the football star?

(*Here therapist 1 attempts to focus on Art's feelings about leaving the family at a time when father has serious problems.*)

A: Well. (*Fifteen-second pause.*) I'd like to get out of the house, but, it's kind of fifty-fifty. It's something I have to do and something I want to do. I've never been away from home other than summer camp, and I'd like to see what it's like.

(The long pause suggests Art's conflict about leaving and possibly about admitting that he wishes to go.)

T2: That the fifty-plus side?

A: Yup.

T2: What's the fifty-minus side?

A: Not seeing these people for *(pause)* weeks.

T2: What about that?

A: Well, I've been with them for 19 years. It's going to be a switch.

F: It will be a feeling of loss, I guess, huh, Art?

(Here father responds very empathically to his son, accurately labeling the feeling of loss that Art has not articulated directly.)

A: Yeah.

F: But you can always come back.

(Father's solution for Art's feelings of loss is simple: He can come back home.)

A: Yeah.

(Ten-second pause.)

T2: Is it any harder leaving now that your dad's got such a, bad back?

(Therapist focuses specifically on the impact of father's problems on Art's emancipation from the family.)

A: Yes.

T1: I bet.

F: It's an awful burden I've thrown on the family.

(Here father intrudes with a depressive statement that shifts attention away from Art and onto himself.)

T1: You've thrown on the family.

F: Well, I. . . .

T1: *(Interrupts.)* You mean, when you went out and robbed that bank and. . . .

F: *(Overlaps, speaking in very depressed tones with head bowed.)* No, my bad back.

T1: Oh. I'm, I'm being a little facetious. It's, it's like you planned it to happen.

F: No, I didn't really, it's just. . . .

(Therapist 1 attempts to use humor to block father's maneuver. But it does not go over well with this very depressed man and instead the therapist becomes stuck in a long, drawn-out discussion with father.)

T1: *(Overlaps.)* I'm nitpicking but I think the words are important.

F: (*Continues.*) Circumstances. Those things happen. The chiropractor ruined the whole family.

T2: You know what I think is happening right now? Is that, we tried to turn the focus (*gestures toward sons and as she does so, therapist 1 sighs in recognition of what is happening and dramatically changes his position from inclining toward father to leaning way back in his chair with his arms raised above his head*) onto the boys, and, Mr. Stuart, you jumped in and rescued Art from dealing with his sorrow and the difficulty by refocusing back on you. Somehow, you're willing to be the problem.

(*Therapist 2 is right on top of things here, labeling father's move as protective of Art.*)

F: You mean, I want to take all the problems onto my shoulders.

(*Father clearly understands therapist 2.*)

T2: Uh-huh.

T1: (*To therapist 2.*) You mean, he's as generous as they are, but in the other direction.

(*Therapist 1's effort to clarify what was a perfectly clear statement by therapist 2 is tangential and only muddles things.*)

T2: That's right. He's willing to take on the pain and refocus the pain back on himself.

(*Therapist 2 graciously accepts the "clarification" and restores her remark to its original clarity.*)

T1: You know that, there is actually (*knee begins moving up and down very nervously*), when I asked what common things there were in the family, there've been several references, and correct me if I'm wrong, to religion. Uh, and we discussed, one of the main things was church. You remember two sessions ago you were talking about Christ and, and those burdens. And there really is a sense of, of, a, sort of the positive side of martyrdom, of taking on each other's burdens, and carrying the, the pain.

(*Here again therapist 1's nonverbal tension indicates the extent to which he has joined the family and participates in their rising anxiety as therapist 2 once more turns the interview toward family development. In the face of this anxiety, therapist 1's remarks are tangential and disrupt the focus on family development.*)

T2: So maybe what, what we should do right now is (*to therapist 1*) try and, go back (*gestures toward Art*), to where we were before.

(*This time more forcefully, therapist 2 brings the discussion back on track.*)

T1: That may seem a little bit rugged when we do it, but I think we ought to get in the habit of it. (*Leg again begins to move anxiously, then turns to therapist 2.*) It's been so effective I forgot exactly where, where we were. We were talking of, of the flip side, of what it was like to go when Dad is having trouble.

(*Here therapist 1 begins to get some distance by commenting on how "rugged" it might seem—to the family—to resume the discussion. Realizing that he has forgotten what the topic was, however, therapist 1 must reorient himself, first by turning to therapist 2 who is less enmeshed in the family's emotional field at the moment, and then by labeling his temporary amnesia. As he pulls back, he is once again able to track the issue of the Stuarts' developmental dilemma.*)

A: Well, it's going to be hard not to be seeing them every day.

(*Discussion with Art continues.*)

The Stuart family was chosen to illustrate the developmental model because these issues are expressed so clearly in the interview excerpts presented above. The intensity of the anxiety in both family and therapists is an indication of the threat that emancipation of the children poses to this family's security. The follow-up to the interview presented here helps put these developmental issues in context.

FAMILY CRISIS

In subsequent sessions, the treatment focused on how individual family members could do more to take care of themselves and depend less on Mr. Stuart and on the issue of the children's emancipation from the family.

After about a month of therapy, a flurry of phone calls from the family announced a family crisis. Mrs. Stuart phoned to report that her husband had been talking incessantly for several days, laughing, crying, singing, sleeping poorly, and quoting Shakespeare in the garden at 5:00 A.M.

Mr. Stuart's sister, about whom we had so far heard nothing, telephoned to report her distress about what had been happening to her brother. She complained that Mr. Stuart had devoted himself too much to his family, who, in turn, depended too much on him. She singled out Mrs. Stuart, who had never even learned to drive despite the fact that prior to her marriage she had worked competently as a surgical nurse.

The patient's sister went on to tell us that her brother had been very hurt and disappointed by his children: Bill went to college, but currently works as a dishwasher; Gene is "retarded" and has to be driven to and from work. Furthermore, the sister explained, Mr. Stuart had gone "into a decline," becoming depressed a year before the current treatment began when Lisa "crushed her father's heart and dashed his dreams" by becoming pregnant and then marrying someone her parents disapproved of.

Thus we learned that not only was Mr. Stuart's depression a *cause* of some of the family's current developmental difficulties (e.g., Bill had to come back home to help care for him; it was now more difficult for Art to go away to school as planned), but also that the onset of the depression was six months earlier than we had been led to believe and appeared to be the *result* of family developmental troubles (e.g., Lisa's departure from the home under unhappy circumstances).

An emergency family session was scheduled for the next day. There Mr. Stuart appeared manic, with pressured speech, flight of ideas, grandiosity, difficulty sitting still, and disruptive and interruptive behavior. Again we seriously considered hospitalization. However, Mr. Stuart was still very frightened of psychiatric inpatient treatment. Moreover, the family convinced us that the father's extreme behavior had peaked and was already declining. So we arranged to see the family again in two days at the regularly scheduled appointment time. We also used the family crisis to insist that Lisa be present.

By the next session it was clear that Mr. Stuart was in the midst of a full-blown manic episode and that there was no longer any alternative to hospitalizing him. We had begun to see him as a case of manic-depressive disorder who had had one psychotic episode while in the military, but had managed to function adequately during the intervening years. Antidepressant medication is known (Physicians' Desk Reference, 1982) to precipitate a manic episode in some manic-depressive individuals. We intended to have Mr. Stuart worked-up in the hospital for treatment with lithium carbonate.

We also made plans to continue meeting with the family during this crisis period. Lisa, who met with us a time or two, turned out to be a very immature, distracting young woman who appeared to be the most psychologically dysfunctional of all the children.

Shortly after his admission to the inpatient unit, Mr. Stuart became clearly organic: He was grossly disoriented, failed to recognize his family, and eventually suffered a seizure. He then developed chest pain, which was finally diagnosed as due to pulmonary emboli, and was transferred to a medical floor.

Reconstructing the sequence of events, it appears that the anti-depressant medication, in addition to precipitating the manic episode, may have produced the pulmonary emboli which, when they reached the patient's brain, caused his organic brain syndrome.

Remarkably, during the following two weeks on the medical unit, Mr. Stuart became totally free of both his back pain and depression. (A colleague has suggested that such an organic brain syndrome may function to relieve depression much as does electro-shock treatment: Any massive insult to the brain will do.) He was discharged from the hospital on no psychiatric medication and subsequently went back to work. Although we attempted to work on family developmental issues in a few follow-up sessions, the family did not wish to continue and family therapy was stopped.

FURTHER PROBLEMS

Five months later, Mrs. Stuart called to request an appointment, saying that her children were doing fine and the couple wished to come in alone.

At that session I obtained a follow-up on the family's development in the intervening months. Bill had moved out of the family home and into an apartment down the street. Gene was still living at home and showed no interest in leaving. Art lived at school during the week and came home on weekends. Mrs. Stuart reported that she was planning to have her nursing license reactivated and was considering a part-time job.

The couple stated that the problem was again Mr. Stuart's back pain and depression, which had once more become so serious that he had been unable to work for several weeks. And this time, the focus was on the patient's claim that his symptoms and resulting disability were the result of an injury at work. We heard no more about how the chiropractor had caused the back pain, which caused the depression. Instead, Mr. Stuart told a puzzling story about how his tools were stolen at work and his employer not only failed to replace them promptly, but also began harassing the patient by accusing him of malingering. This emotional stress, Mr. Stuart argued, caused his depression. His claim for work-related disability had already been denied and Mr. Stuart was considering legal action.

Up to now this fascinating case had involved an astonishing range of problems, ranging from definite organic pathology to difficulties involving the family system. Here, with the emergence of "compensation neurosis," yet another systemic level (society's disability compensation programs) was seen to play a part in Mr. Stuart's complex problems. [See, for example, Hirschfeld and Behan's series of articles (Hirschfeld and Behan, 1963; Behan and Hirschfeld, 1963) that examine industrial injury and subsequent disability and compensation-seeking behavior as a solution to the patient's life problems.]

My experience in the compensation-oriented VA system had convinced me that, in many cases, disability compensation provides a very powerful negative feedback mechanism, which maintains the patient's symptoms. In the face of such homeostatic involvement of the larger social system, the therapist's efforts to produce symptomatic change are often fruitless. So I advised the couple that improvement in Mr. Stuart's pain and depression was unlikely until the issue of disability compensation was settled once and for all and elected to follow them with monthly check-up visits instead of attempting vigorous treatment.

In the subsequent two months, there was little change either in the patient's pain and depression or in the status of his quest for disability. However, family developmental issues again attracted my attention.

After the first month, Mrs. Stuart reported that Lisa was getting a divorce, which greatly troubled the mother: "I would like to go up there and get those babies and bring them home with me. But I know I can't do that." She went on to talk about a friend who raised a grandchild, got no thanks for her efforts, and recently died of a stroke. One month later, the mother revealed that Lisa, her two babies, and Bill (living in a tent in the back yard) were all back home. She added: "I guess we're back to square one."

I again attempted to explore the developmental issues in the family. For example, I tried to talk with Mr. Stuart about his reaction to Lisa's original departure from the home, but got nowhere. I did learn a bit more about the context for Mr. Stuart's insistence that Gene could never leave home: The father felt guilty because, as a young child, his son fell down a flight of stairs, presumably causing his neurological difficulties; the father had neglected to fix a gate at the top of the stairs and therefore felt responsible.

However, it very quickly became clear that these parents were delighted to have their family all back home once again. I saw no way to engage them in further work on developmental issues. And

Mr. and Mrs. Stuart were mildly insulted that I even suggested that their house full of 20-year-olds might indicate a problem. We discontinued further couple sessions at that point because I was leaving the hospital, and follow-up for Mr. Stuart was arranged with another therapist in the clinic.

An amusing postscript occurred a week later. Mrs. Stuart triumphantly sent me a newspaper clipping that she had forgotten to bring along to our final session. The article, from a local newspaper, described a new sociological phenomenon peculiar to the affluent area near which the family lived: Children, who had grown up with the luxuries their middle- and upper-class families could afford, were finding themselves unable as adults to support themselves in the style to which they had become accustomed and so were returning home to live with their parents. So much for my suggestion that the Stuarts had a family developmental problem.

The Developmental Model and Family Variations

The developmental model should not be thought of as a rigid sequence of stages through which all families must march in lockstep fashion in order to be considered healthy. In fact, the family life cycle as sketched in this chapter is not a "normative" model in the sense of prescribing an inevitable sequence of stages. To understand this, it is necessary to go back to the developmental principle articulated in Chapter 3. The family life cycle is not itself a given, but is instead a consequence of biology, on one hand (in particular, birth and death), and culture, on the other (especially society's expectations regarding emancipation of children). This means that when significant variations from the typical biological or cultural conditions occur, the course of the family life cycle must also change substantially.

In fact, there are many family life cycles, depending upon just how and when the family adds and subtracts members. Several paths can be traced through the family life cycle, including: (1) the couple with no children; (2) the "standard" family with children; (3) divorce and single-parenthood; and (4) remarriage.

I will discuss briefly here how some of these variations affect the family life cycle, my purpose being to demonstrate the flexibility in thinking necessary for applying the developmental model rather than to describe exhaustively the model's application to the whole range of family variations. The reader is urged to consult Carter and McGoldrick's (1980) volume on the family life cycle, and in particular, their collection of papers in Parts 4 and 5 of the book, including articles on the impact of death and serious illness; separation, divorce, and single-parents; remarriage; women in families; multiproblem poor families; and Mexican–American families. See also McGoldrick et al. (1982), *Ethnicity and Family Therapy*.

DIVORCE AND REMARRIAGE

As outlined so far in this chapter, the family life cycle presumes a "'til death do us part" view of marriage, which is less and less characteristic of our society's current expectations of its members. Divorce is another way through which members are lost to the family, thus drastically altering the family's subsequent life cycle. As with all losses and, in particular, those that may be considered in some way "premature," grief is a healthy, adaptive response, and unresolved grief may be pathological. The issue of grief in both its normal and pathological forms should be part of the evaluation of *every* family in which divorce has occurred. To the extent that grief is a shared family process it is desirable to do grief work in family sessions. Sometimes this is not possible, however. For example, a parent's anger toward an ex-spouse may make it impossible for the children to mourn the loss of the other parent openly. Here it may be necessary to do grief work with the sibling subsystem alone, at least initially.

Remarriage is a family variation that adds family members, in many cases, several at a time. Developmentally, this complicates family adaptation by presenting it with a number of different tasks simultaneously. In particular, the couple must work out the nature of their relationship to each other, including the important issues of intimacy and conflict management, and at the same time, they are forced to negotiate their relationship as parents to the children. Similarly, adolescent children in a stepfamily are struggling to become emancipated from the family at the same time as the new stepfamily is attempting to establish its cohesion (Visher and Visher, 1979).

PREMATURE ILLNESS, DISABILITY, AND DEATH

When a family member becomes prematurely sick or disabled or dies, the family is subjected to pressures that tend either to retard or to accelerate its movement through the life cycle.

The serious illness or disability of a child inevitably tends to slow or even to prevent that child's successful emancipation from the family. In cases of severe impairment, of course, it is necessary and realistic to abort the child's emancipation. Often however, the family reacts overprotectively and the child is left with a social handicap that is out of proportion to the actual impairment.

The case of the Stuarts and their "neurologically damaged" son Gene, presented above, is an example. A more successful treatment outcome occurred in a family with a 20-year-old mentally retarded daughter referred by their family physician for evaluation and treatment. The daughter had been in special education programs beginning early in grammar school, and since finishing high school at age 18, she had spent all her time at home, going out only with the family. The parents finally sought help after their daughter had increasingly frequent outbursts of rage and frustration and the parents realized that they could no longer ignore the issue of her future. Psychological evaluation revealed that the young woman's IQ was 69, just low enough to validate the view that she was retarded and to qualify her for vocational and social rehabilitation programs for the mentally retarded, yet high enough to permit her considerable independent functioning. From the family interview it became clear that the mother, father, and 21-year-old brother all infantilized the daughter, talking for her, taking over tasks that she could perform, and tolerating her immature behavior. In the course of brief family therapy, the family members were able to become less protective. With the therapist's encouragement, the young woman herself contacted social agencies that would assist her in achieving the independence from her family she desired.

When a parent is disabled, ill, or dying, family development is typically accelerated, in the sense that life cycle tasks overlap, occurring simultaneously rather than sequentially. This too occurred in the Stuart family. It appears even more clearly in the case presented in Chapter 11. There, a 17-year-old girl about to graduate from high school and go away to college developed psychogenic vomiting when faced with the conflict of leaving her father who was dying of cancer. Leaving home is difficult enough in many families, but it is much tougher when the child leaves behind a father who may die at any time and a mother who faces an uncertain life alone.

Herz (1980) notes, as well, that the life stage of the ill or dying person affects the impact of such an event on the family. Because it is seen as an appropriate time, the impact of death or illness in old age tends to be less than when it occurs at other life cycle stages. The death or disability of young or middle-aged parents has probably the greatest instrumental impact on the family, since it requires a reorganization of the executive subsystem. The death or illness of a child, on the other hand, is often seen as a great tragedy, with emotional consequences that far outweigh its practical effects on the family. This, Herz suggests, is because a child's death is seen as very much out of place in the family life cycle, and because with the child's death, the family loses part of its hopes for the future. Finally, Herz notes that the death of an adolescent is complicated by the fact that the family is already in the process of losing the child through the normal process of emancipation, often accompanied by turmoil and conflict. In such cases, the normal weaning process is necessarily left uncompleted, and the family is often unable to resolve its grief over the death as well.

CHILDLESS COUPLES

Couples who do not have children, including many gay couples, have a life cycle without some of the middle stages of the family life cycle precipitated by the addition of children to the family and their eventual departure.

Nevertheless, universal life cycle issues should not be neglected in work with such couples. These include the courtship period, with its emphasis on emancipation from families of origin and on the formation of the couple dyad; the consolidation of the couple relationship, with the development of an enduring commitment and the necessity of working out patterns of sex and intimacy, issues of work and money, and modes of handling conflict; the impact of career successes and failures and of the deaths of parents in the middle years of life; and the effects of aging, illness, and death of the partner.

Childless couples sometimes face particular difficulty negotiating a developmental transition that is forced in other families by the arrival of children. For example, emancipation from family of origin may be harder without children to underscore the young person's undertaking of adult responsibilities. Indeed, for some individuals it takes becoming a parent to stop being a child.

Just as courtship and marriage involve processes of individual and couple identity formation, as well as emancipation from families of origin, the "coming out" process (e.g., Morin and Schultz, 1978; de Monteflores and Schultz, 1978) for gay people is both an individual developmental process and part of becoming emancipated from and redefining the relationship to family. This is often a time of considerable personal and family distress, including grief over the gay person's failure to meet parents' hopes and expectations.

SOCIOCULTURAL VARIATIONS

Chapter 4 discusses the influence of cultural factors on family boundaries and family role behavior. The impact of cultural and subcultural expectations on family development occurs chiefly through the social group's expectations regarding emancipation of the young.

Among certain Italian–American families, for example, it is still normative for young adult children to live with their parents until married. When such subcultural norms exist, one must be careful not to pathologize this arrangement unless there is evidence of dysfunction apart from the living situation itself.

This caution is even more important when attempts are made to export American family therapy models to very different cultures. For example, Japanese society is traditionally built upon the values of cooperation and interdependence, rather than competition and independence, and as a result, has very different notions of "emancipation" of children from the family than is normative in American families. And ideas regarding emancipation may vary according to the child's sex and birth order. These varying cultural expectations essentially alter the life cycle of the Japanese family and the family therapist's approach must be modified accordingly.

Colon (1980) suggests that among poor urban families the family life cycle is often truncated. People tend to marry sooner and die younger. They often experience more premature losses, which in turn, force other family members to take over vacated roles. Boundaries of life cycle stages tend to be blurred, and individuals have little time to resolve the tasks of a given stage before being thrust into a new one. Colon notes that adolescents and young adults tend to be prematurely pushed out of their families or lured away by their peer group or instead hung onto as an economic resource for the family. Parents may fail to assume parental functions, remaining immature individuals with ties chiefly to peers. Many factors interfere with the formation of the couple dyad, including the welfare system, which stops aid to mothers with dependent children if it can be shown that the father is still involved in family life.

7

The Strategic Model

Although he has recently demonstrated (Haley, 1981) that anyone who attempts to establish his paternity in the field risks his wrath, I think it accurate to say that Jay Haley is the father of strategic therapy. And, to continue the family tree a bit further, Milton Erickson is the grandfather and John Weakland, Paul Watzlawick, and Richard Fisch, at the Mental Research Institute (MRI) in Palo Alto, are the respected uncles. A quick excursion into history reveals much about the roots of strategic therapy.

John Weakland once told about the exciting early days at MRI when he and Haley (then at MRI) used to make a pilgrimage to Phoenix once or twice a year to sit at the feet of Erickson and learn about his therapeutic magic. It was Haley, in fact, who through his books *Uncommon Therapy* (1973a) and *Advanced Techniques of Hypnosis and Therapy* (1967) made Erickson's work available to family therapists and psychotherapists, in general. Haley eventually went East, to Philadelphia and now Washington, D.C., and began writing about "strategic therapy." And Weakland remained at MRI and was joined by Watzlawick and Richard Fisch and together they developed the MRI's current "brief therapy" approach.

The Basic Idea

So far in presenting the clinical models in this book, it has been possible to begin with a single basic concept that could be neatly stated in a few words and then elaborated further. I have found that the strategic model is best taught a bit indirectly, by introducing it with an analogy. According to Watzlawick et al. (1974), it is no accident that this approach lends itself to teaching by analogy. The MRI group suggests that strategic interventions essentially involve right-brain as well as purely left-brain thinking. The right hemisphere is the side of the brain thought to specialize in nonlinear, analogic thought.

In *Change*, Watzlawick et al. (1974) present the following "nine-dot problem" (Figure 11). Try it now, before reading further.

Many people fail to solve this problem. If you have tried and need help, consult Figure 12 at the end of this chapter.

The nine-dot problem contains a number of lessons. If you understand its lessons, you will have grasped the basic concept underlying the strategic model. These will now be discussed in some detail.

One, all *problems* are defined within a particular *frame* or context. The frame may be explicit or implicit. The nine-dot problem is explicitly defined by the pattern of nine dots together with the instructions (Figure 11). In addition, most people assume an implicit frame: The dots form a square within which the solution

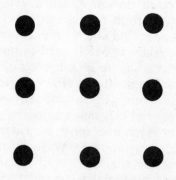

Figure 11. The nine-dot problem. The nine dots are to be connected using four distinct straight lines without lifting the pencil from the paper.

It turns out that there is more than one way to violate the usual assumptions and thus find a solution to the nine-dot problem. Most people assume that "straight line" means a Euclidean straight line. If so, then a solution of the type illustrated in Figure 12 is required. If, on the other hand, you are willing to shift to a non-Euclidean geometry, in which a curve is a "straight line," then other solutions are possible as well. Readers who enjoy such puzzles can must be found. No problem exists in a vacuum; it always has a frame as well.

Two, a problem that is unsolvable in one frame may have a *solution* in a different frame. The nine-dot problem is unsolvable as long as one assumes the usual frame, including the idea that the dots form a square within which the solution must be found. Once this assumption is abandoned and one is willing to go outside the square, the problem can be solved (see Figure 12).

convince themselves that judicious use of four of these new straight lines permits a solution to the nine-dot problem entirely *within* the square. And lest you assume that these two types of solutions exhaust the possibilities, someone once showed me yet another way to violate the usual assumptions: Instead of assuming that the dots are infinitesimally small points (despite the fact that we cannot draw them that small), let them instead have some thickness; then it is possible to get two non-parallel straight (in the Euclidean sense) lines through a single dot without having them intersect in the dot itself.

The crucial points here are (1) that the constraints of a particular frame may preclude a solution to a given problem and (2) that there are often several alternative frames within which the problem can be solved.

Three, a change in frames often requires input from outside the frame. In fact, the harder one tries to solve the problem from within the frame, the more one tends to get locked into the assumptions of the frame and the more difficult or indeed impossible it becomes to break out.

This lesson is often nicely illustrated when I present the nine-dot problem in lectures. Some brave soul comes up to try the problem at the blackboard, while the rest of the group works on it at their seats. The volunteer typically attempts a solution within the implicitly defined square. When this fails, he or she generally tries another solution of the same type, and sometimes another and another. The more this goes on, the more locked into such failed

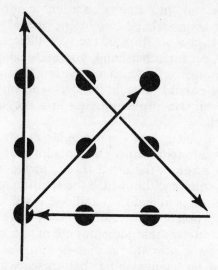

Figure 12. One example of a class of solutions to problem shown in Figure 11.

solutions the person typically becomes. It often takes someone from the audience who is not quite so locked into these futile attempts to come up to the board and present a solution.

Four, a change in frames occurs suddenly, in an all-or-none fashion. One either sees it or one does not. This is a very different model of learning than the one that is commonly employed by behavioral psychologists who see learning as a gradual accumulation of habits over many trials and speak of "shaping" behavior with progressively closer approximations to some desired response.

And five, once the problem is seen in the new frame, it is almost impossible to revert back to the old frame along with the helplessness and hopelessness about finding a solution.

I have presented this problem to hundreds of persons in lectures and find that it is not uncommon for someone to say things like "I saw that in third grade and haven't seen it since" and then immediately produce a correct solution. Other times people remember that there is a "trick" to it or even remember that "you have to go outside the square" without being able to come up with quite the right way to make the trick work.

In other words, there is something about seeing things in a new way that tends to stick.

Definition of the Strategic Model

Here the analogy of the nine-dot is translated into a linear, verbal definition of the strategic model. Rabkin (1977) attributes the term "strategic" to Jay Haley who wrote a book called *Strategies of Psychotherapy* in 1963. In it Haley was interested in the power aspects of therapy and compared the major psychotherapeutic approaches in terms of the strategies employed by the therapist to bring about change.

Writing in *Uncommon Therapy* ten years later, Haley (1973a) succinctly defined strategic therapy in the book's first sentence: "Therapy can be called strategic if the clinician initiates what happens during therapy and designs a particular approach for each problem." (p. 17) This definition has two important parts.

First, the strategic therapist is *active.* In his provocative way, Haley (1975) contrasts this active approach with what he calls "helpless" therapy. In helpless therapy, the therapist relies on passive interpretation to bring about change and the therapy depends more upon what the patient does than upon the therapist's actions. In strategic therapy, on the other hand, the therapist intervenes actively to change sequences of behavior and social relationships.

Second, strategic therapy is a problem-solving, goal-oriented approach. Haley emphasizes (Madanes and Haley, 1977) that strategic therapy is a treatment without a method. Unlike many other approaches, for example, systematic desensitization, there is no cookbook package into which the patient can be neatly fitted. The therapist is forced to be imaginative, creating a particular intervention out of the details of each case. This lack of a set method makes strategic therapy both interesting and fun to do but difficult to teach and learn.

I define strategic therapy as follows: The strategic therapist is a *problem-definer* whose job is to take the presenting complaint or symptom and frame a *solvable* problem. If the patient presents with a problem that can be solved as defined, then by all means go ahead and solve it. If not, then reframe it so that it can be solved. Or refer the person to someone who can solve it. It does no good to frame a problem in such a way that it is insolvable.

For example, within the past 10 years or so, many brief, effective treatments for common sexual problems have been developed. If a patient presents with such a problem, say, impotence, in which organic factors have been ruled out, then your job as a strategic therapist is to apply your knowledge of these intervention approaches to solve the problem. If you are not familiar with these simple, effective techniques, then refer the patient to someone who is.

The fact that you can prescribe the exercises that will likely be successful in curing the patient's impotence does not guarantee your success, however. For example, the impotent man may insist on viewing the problem as physical, despite the lack of evidence for an organic basis. If so, your first job is to help him redefine the problem as a psychosocial one, amenable to psychotherapeutic treatment. And the patient may agree to your psychological approach, but still not carry out the prescribed assignments. In this case, you must use all your knowledge of individual and couple behavior plus all your psychotherapeutic skills to obtain his compliance. That is, you must create a therapy context within which the new behavior necessary to alleviate the impotence can occur. (This point is discussed further in Chapter 10, using the concept of the treatment frame.) I have found Kaplan's two books (1974, 1979) helpful in thinking through the relationship between sex therapy and individual/couple therapy. Her approach is, I think, strategic, in the sense described here.

Reframing

Watzlawick et al. (1974) use the term "reframing" to describe the change from one frame to another. These authors aptly call reframing "the gentle art."

The man-in-the-street example of reframing is the proverbial glass of water, of which the optimist exclaims "half full" and the pessimist laments "half empty." The amount of water is the same, but because of the way it is viewed, two very different meanings can be ascribed to the same situation. And these meanings are important. It makes a difference, for example, whether one views one's life as half full or half empty.

Watzlawick et al. (1974) give an excellent and rather pithy definition of reframing:

> To reframe . . . means to change the conceptual and/or emotional setting or viewpoint in relation to which a situation is experienced and to place it in another frame which fits the "facts" of the same concrete

situation equally well or even better, and thereby changes its entire meaning. The mechanism involved here is not immediately obvious, especially if we bear in mind that there is change while indeed the situation itself may remain quite unchanged and, indeed, even unchangeable. What turns out to be changed as a result of reframing is the meaning attributed to the situation, and therefore its consequences, but not its concrete facts. (p. 95)

Two points are crucial in this definition. First, both cognitive changes and emotional changes occur with reframing. For example, early in an initial interview, the therapist may reframe a parent's "intrusiveness" (e.g., taking over and speaking for a child) as "helpfulness." The behavior referred to in both cases is the same, but the affective connotations of the two are very different. It is, generally, much easier to get the parent to stop being "too helpful" than "too intrusive."

Second, the new frame must fit the concrete facts as well or better than did the old frame. Not any new frame will do. It must be fashioned from the details of the family's life and problems. And the therapist must believe in the new frame enough to get the family members to abandon their old view of the problem and join him in a new, more productive construction of reality. Notice that truth in an absolute sense has nothing to do with reframing. The new frame is neither more nor less true than the old. The strategic model is ultimately pragmatic: The new frame is better because it works better.

A case example will now be presented to illustrate strategic reframing.

Case Example: Reframing a Depression

BACKGROUND DATA

The Green family included father (age 42), mother (age 39), daughter Molly (age 12), and son Tim (age 9). They were referred to our family therapy program from the university's child psychiatry service where Mrs. Green had taken Molly, complaining that the girl had a learning problem. Molly was making average grades in school, but Mrs. Green believed she should be doing better and was spending three hours an evening drilling Molly on her homework. Mr. Green was a policeman who spent many hours outside the home involved in such child-related activities as the Little League and PTA.

The university child service is a very traditional, psychoanalytically oriented place and the Green family had the thorough work-up typical in such settings. This included psychological and educational testing as well as psychiatric interviews for Molly, plus interviews with each parent separately and with the couple. Molly was found to be of average intelligence, without any learning disability. Mrs. Green was seen as depressed and overinvolved with her daughter's school development and the couple was felt to have a poor relationship. A math tutor was arranged for Molly, and Mr. and Mrs. Green were referred for couples therapy.

In this case, we chose to begin treatment with the couple alone instead of starting with the whole family. In general, when the identified patient is a child, one cannot so easily get away with a move like this. In fact if one shifts too quickly to a couple focus in the therapy, the family will often either promptly drop out of treatment or the child's problem will get worse and refocus the therapist's attention back where it is "supposed" to be—on the child. Chapter 4 offers some guidelines for determining when the child should initially be included in the treatment sessions.

In the case of the Greens, we not only never saw Molly or Tim, I do not think they were ever mentioned in the therapy except perhaps in passing. The credit for easing Molly out of the patient role and focusing attention onto the couple really belongs to the resident who handled the case at the university clinic. Although he was not a family therapist, he had been exposed to some of our work and was skillful enough to negotiate not only the difficulties of the family system, but also those of that analytically oriented child psychiatry clinic, delivering an excellent and appropriate treatment case to the family therapy program.

Given this good preliminary work, we were able to use the composition of the treatment system itself to reinforce the generational boundary: By excluding the children from the sessions, we reduced Mrs. Green's overinvolvement with Molly and increased the couple's interaction with each other.

EVALUATION OF THE COUPLE

We began the first session by asking Mr. and Mrs. Green what each saw as the main problem in the family at the present time, a typical strategic beginning (see section of Chapter 10 on conducting the first interview). Mr. Green, demonstrating that he had learned something at the university clinic, replied, "My wife seems to have a problem with depression." (He had not realized that she was depressed.) Doing him one better, Mrs. Green answered: "Lack of communication between my husband and myself."

We also assessed what Jackson (1965) called the *marital quid pro quo*. Jackson borrowed this legal term, which literally means "something for something else." He believed that from the moment of first meeting the couple begins to negotiate an implicit bargain of the sort: "I'll give you this (e.g., sex) if you give me that (e.g., financial security) in return. Jackson saw the marital quid pro quo as a basic relationship definition that is typically very enduring, continuing to define couple behavior five, ten, or thirty years later when they first show up in your office.

The marital quid pro quo is evaluated by asking the question: "How, out of all the people in the world, did the two of you get together? And I want to hear from each of you." The therapist then interviews each spouse in turn (usually beginning with the one who speaks up first) about the first meeting and subsequent events. Probes are used (e.g., "What was it that was so attractive about her?" "How did you decide to go out with him a second time?" "When did you decide that this was the woman you wanted to marry?") until the therapist has obtained enough detail to formulate the quid pro quo.

This is not a good time to evaluate couple interaction. It generally requires active questioning of each spouse to elicit enough information to infer the quid pro quo. If one spouse interrupts while you are interviewing the other, simply say "Your wife spoke up first, so I think I'll hear from her and then get your side of the story."

It is perfectly appropriate to ask the quid pro quo question in front of the children. Sometimes they have already heard the story, other times not. Rarely are children uninterested in learning about how their parents met. It is important to structure this part of the evaluation to define the children as listeners (e.g., "I've now got a question for you two parents, and I want you kids to listen").

Often the marital quid pro quo question rekindles the honeymoon, stimulating positive affect. As such, it is a nice question to ask midway through the initial interview, after you have found out about all the family's current problems and pains.

With the Greens, either little of the honeymoon was left or there had not been much of one in the first place. Mrs. Green reported that she met her husband at the time her mother was dying of cancer. She was working for a credit company at the time and promptly checked out his credit rating and found him to be financially responsible. (Many of the quid pro quo responses are extremely humorous.) Mrs. Green told us that the couple married after knowing each other only briefly. In fact, she said that she decided to marry her husband on the very night her mother died. And then, as if realizing the interest we might take in such a statement, she immediately tried to take it back. Mrs. Green stated several times that she felt it had been a mistake to get married so soon, before they really knew each other. And she was still very angry at her father for having remarried within a year after her mother's death, but made no connection to her own quick marriage. Mrs. Green summarized with a sigh: "The marriage was a thing to look forward to. There was nothing else in my life."

Despite the therapist's persistent questioning, Mr. Green stated only that he was tired of being single and that his wife came along at a time in his life when he wished to be married.

Besides the couple's view of the main problem and the marital quid pro quo, we found in the evaluation session that the couple had experienced sexual problems dating from the birth of their first child. Mrs. Green stated that she lost interest in sex and her husband reported that she became involved in caring for the baby and no longer had time for him.

Finally, we learned of Mrs. Green's somatic complaints and fears. She reported multiple psychosomatic problems since the birth of her children, including stomach, back, and head pains. She also described much fear of cancer, with good reason. Mrs. Green told us that her mother was depressed the last ten years of her life and then developed breast cancer, of which she died. Mrs. Green's grandmother also died of cancer at age 42 (Mrs. Green was 39 at the time we saw her). Our patient had been treated with X-rays for acne as an adolescent and was concerned about the resulting increased cancer risk. And, if that were not enough, Mrs. Green herself had already had some benign lumps removed from her breasts.

Perhaps unduly impressed by what we learned from the marital quid pro quo question, plus Mrs. Green's many current woes and worries, we contracted with the couple to work for six weeks on the issue of the wife's depression. To Mrs. Green we said: "You never really had a chance early in your marriage to work through the loss of your mother. We will help you." And to her husband we stated:

"You don't know what to do to help your **wife when she's** depressed **[he** minimizes the problems or attempts to **cheer her up].** We'll help you, too."

It soon became apparent that we had failed miserably to frame a solvable problem.

REFRAMING THE DEPRESSION

In the first of our six contracted sessions, the therapist had assigned Mrs. Green the task of drawing her depressed feelings on paper. (The best explanation for this art therapy assignment is that we had had an art therapist in the family therapy program the previous year and had tried for months to get the hospital to buy art therapy supplies. After the art therapist left, the government came through with several hundred dollars' worth of materials. These were sitting around unused, and the therapist working with the Greens decided to put them to work. Interventions are often fashioned from such idiosyncratic occurrences.)

The second treatment session began with Mrs. Green's discussion of her "cancer" drawings. The first transcript excerpt provides a good sample of the wife's behavior at this beginning stage of treatment.

> (*The therapy system includes wife* (W); *husband,* (H); *therapist* (T); *supervisor* (S). *Husband, wife, and therapist sit in an inner circle of chairs. Supervisor and a third member of the family therapy team sit behind the couple in an outer circle. Wife speaks in a soft, whiny, child-like voice.*)

W: It's, it's hard to talk about death. A death like this. I guess (*pause*), death is something everybody has to face, a, a fear, and you never, anyone can never really resolve. Their fears. Whether it be through religion or being a realist. It's always there. (*Speaks melodramatically.*) It's the last, the last big trip for all of us.

T: Has it helped at all to talk about it here?

W: A little bit, but it will always be there for me. Also, I have a, a lot of, at an early age I had a lot of religion and somehow cancer and death and my religion are all entwined in my mind.

T: And so my sense is it helps you a little to talk, but not very much.

W: Yes, it does, it helps. But six months from now I might wake up with a cancer fear again.

> (*These last four exchanges are an early indication of the difficulties one encounters in interviewing wife. If you say A, she says B.*

And if you then agree that it is B, then she says no, it is A. This pattern proves to be crucial in what happens below.)

T: Uh, huh.

W: Or if I ever do develop cancer, I'll probably have horrible anxieties. I see the whiteness (*refers to drawings in lap*) often appears in my dreams.

T: The whiteness is death.

(*Here wife offers therapist what she likely thinks every therapist wants from patients—dream symbolism. And therapist obliges with his interest, even offering a quick interpretation of the dream symbol. And the two of them are off and running, doing "dream work." In what follows, wife's statements have a very melodramatic quality.*)

W: I guess the white landscapes, with the white skies, gray, no blue clouds. Like there's a sheet over the sky, like a shroud. I can see that would come from looking at the paper. That's why I wanted to do my pictures in white instead of the paper that you had. White has a special meaning for me.

(*Wife also explains why she rejected the colored drawing paper given to her by therapist, substituting her own white paper. This is yet another sign of her "resistance" to therapist's interventions.*)

T: It means, the meaning is death.

W: Yes. Always. In fact, the other day we were in a used car basement. It was all white. And that really affected me. 'Cause I've seen that in my dreams before. A hospital or an operating room that was all white.

T: So when you see white and brightness it reminds you of death.

W: (*Overlapping.*) White. Hospitals. Death. Sheets. White sheets.

By this time I (the supervisor sitting in the back row) was already bored with the therapy and wondered how I would manage to sit through six sessions with Mrs. Green droning on and on while we attempt to help her with her depression. Fortunately, things began to get more interesting.

I had become impressed with how well Mrs. Green managed to *control* the session by talking endlessly about cancer, whiteness, death, etc. Soon the issue of control emerged in the content of the session as well as in its process.

(*Husband has just talked about the death of his father within the past year, a subject that made him teary. Therapist asks wife about her response to seeing husband's tears.*)

W: Well, I was surprised to see him so emotional, at that time.

T: How about now? How does that affect you now when you see your husband close to tears when talking about his father? What is your reaction inside? What is the feeling?

W: Well, I think that, that I feel (*abrupt cough*), well, that he, I feel relieved that he can show his feelings. He has a very hard time showing his real feelings. He masks everything.

(*It was subsequently learned from viewing more samples of wife's interaction that she uses this characteristic cough as a linguistic marker meaning "What I am about to say is not true." So here she is saying that she is relieved that husband can show his feelings but she means that she is far from relieved.*)

T: And how does that make you feel?

W: It makes me feel better inside that he can show his feelings.

T: Could you show him that? How it makes you feel better.

(*Until now therapist's attempt to get wife to talk about her reaction to husband's tears goes nowhere. Here, he asks her to show him her reaction. This leads the couple to enact their difficulty with intimacy.*)

W: (*Looks at husband.*) I'll just (*pause*), I'll just look at him, I guess.

T: Maybe you could take his hand.

W: (*Giggles.*) I would be embarrassed to.

T: You would be embarrassed to?

W: Yes.

T: You're easily embarrassed?

W: Yes.

T: Maybe you could try. If we all turned around.

H: (*Offers hand to wife.*)

W: (*Takes husband's hand.*) Okay. (*Attempts to pull hand from husband's grasp. Husband holds firm, but in what follows wife slowly begins to worm her fingers from his grasp.*)

T: That's hard for you, isn't it?

W: Huh?

T: That's hard for you.

W: Yes, it is.

T: Is it because of us here?

W: Or maybe anytime.

T: It's hard for you.

W: To reach out. I (*pause*) don't. And I get embarrassed when I do do it.

(Wife pulls hand from husband's grasp and delivers a stylized slap to his hand, succeeding in pushing it away. Husband withdraws his hand.)

(Here the action is not in the words spoken, but rather the non-verbal hand play between husband and wife. This minuet must be seen on tape to be fully appreciated. The transcript fails to do it justice.)

T: You get embarrassed when someone reaches out to you.

W: Yes. Or, I, not embarrassed. But I don't like to be touched and I don't, I'd rather be in the solitary state, sometimes, than to be twined with people.

(Notice the dichotomy wife sets up here: "solitary state" versus "twined with people." This describes an important feature of her frame for intimacy.)

T: Have you, do you have any understanding of that feeling? Of wanting to be very solitary and not be intertwined with people?

W: It's lonely.

T: Yeah.

W: Selfishness.

T: Selfishness?

W: Um-hum. A certain selfishness. *(Pause.)* Habit.

T: Habit?

W: If you don't get involved with people. . . .

T: *(Interrupting.)* If I don't. If you don't.

W: Right. I'm sorry. I meant for me. It's easier to control your life. A way of controlling things for me. 'Cause once you, once I, reach out you've given up something of yourself. You have to share with other people.

(Wife has just named in words the issue, control, which has by now become clear in the process of this session. Wife also paints a clear picture of the frame within which she lives her life: "Once you . . . reach out you've given up something of yourself. You have to share with other people.")

By this time I had concluded that Mrs. Green's depression as we had framed it was indeed not solvable and had decided instead to reframe the therapy around the issue of control. As the session neared its end, I was waiting for my entrance cue. That is, I wanted to intervene when the control issue again came up, so I could use the fresh occurrence to introduce the new frame. As is always the case with a central therapy issue, it did not take long for control to raise its head again in the session.

(Therapist has just asked the couple whether they had ever considered separation or divorce.)

H: Not really, I, I really don't seriously worry about her leaving me.

W: And I don't really, maybe, giving up, or something, but I don't see him leaving me physically. You can leave people mentally, emotionally, just give up on them. Keep busy and forget about them. You can go on. . . .

T: If he knew the real you he'd just let you drift away?

W: No, he wouldn't drift away. He'd be angry and try to control me and make me another kind of person. He is that way. He tries to, you know, say "You will not do this" or "You will go skiing." He has that kind of a personality. He thinks by telling people he can change them. Or try to.

(The control issue again.)

H: But, I've never insisted you do anything.

W: No, but *(cough).* . . .

(Here is wife's cough again. She says "No, you don't insist" but her cough indicates she believes otherwise.)

H: (Interrupts.) I've suggested.

W: (Continues.) You've suggested in a very forceful way. The powers of persuasion.

T: Do you feel overpowered now?

(Here therapist accurately reflects the theme of wife's statements.)

W: No.

(She promptly denies it.)

T: What kind of person do you want to be?

W: I don't know. I just want to be, a, I'd like to be more outgoing, less afraid of people. I'd like to be able to, fear, feel, when I attempt to do something I won't fail, or I would just do it and enjoy it anyway. I would like to be less afraid. Less fearful. I would like to enjoy people more. I would like to be. . . .

(Therapist's question elicits the entrance cue supervisor has been waiting for: "I would like to be less afraid.")

S: (Enters circle from back row. To therapist.) Can I interrupt here? *(To wife.)* This has been an important session for me, from my perspective in the back row, because for the first time in the sessions I have realized that you, Mrs. Green, are not at all the fearful person that you portray yourself as.

(The first reframing: "You are not at all the fearful person you portray yourself as." Here supervisor is turning on its head Mrs. Green's statement "I would like to be less afraid.")

W: No? (*Slight smile.*)

(*Wife's response immediately tells supervisor that she has made the leap with him into the new frame.*)

S: You've said some very important things today that have made me realize that you are not at all as fearful, as timid, as you, as you portray yourself. And I have a special homework assignment that I would like to give you today, to send you out with, to maybe begin to help you figure out the ways in which you are not nearly as fearful and timid and all as you. . . .

(*To maximize his impact here, supervisor speaks slowly and builds in redundancy. His very simple message is said several times in slightly different ways. Beginning therapists typically try to say too much using too many words and as a result lose their impact.*)

W: (*Overlaps, nodding.*) Um-hum.

S: As you portray yourself. Are, are you willing to take on an assignment like that?

(*Supervisor already knows from observation that wife is likely to resist his direction, so he does everything he can to secure her compliance ahead of time. This technique is borrowed wholesale from a therapist named Harold Greenwald.*)

W: Probably, if you tell me what the assignment is before I (*big smile, pausing*). Will I have to do something physically dangerous (*beams*)?

(*Wife is clearly involved at this point and very excited.*)

S: I can guarantee that it won't be something physically dangerous. It will involve only you thinking and doing some writing.

(*In the process of reassuring wife, therapist introduces a bit of mystification: "It will involve only you thinking and doing some writing."*)

W: Oh. Okay.

S: You're willing to do that?

W: Yes.

S: If, after I give you the assignment, you decide that you won't do it, will you tell me before you leave today?

(*A further step to ensure compliance. If, after all this, wife fails to comply, supervisor can easily frame her failure as a willful decision and not let her get away with an excuse like forgetting. Again, borrowed from Greenwald.*)

W: Yes, I will.

S: You will. Okay. I've noticed, especially in this session but I also saw a tape of the last session, I've noticed that, or I've realized that you have been in almost complete control of these sessions (*wife nods agreement*) since the beginning.

(This is the second stage of the reframe: from "you are not at all the fearful person" to "you have been in almost complete control of these sessions." This new frame is the opposite of the frame within which wife characteristically experiences her actions.)

W: *(Again nods agreement.)* Um-hum.

(Again, wife's immediate, affirmative response indicates that she has bought the new frame.)

S: And I want you to go out this week and think about the ways in which you have almost completely controlled these sessions *(wife smiles, nods)*. And to write down your techniques.

(It is not enough to simply create the new frame. Now supervisor fashions a homework assignment to get Mrs. Green to act in the new frame.)

W: *(Big smile, nods vigorously.)* Okay, I will complete your assignment.

(Again, wife signals that she is still with supervisor in the new frame. Wife and supervisor are, to use Minuchin's—1980—term, calibrating each other's behavior. If she were not sending out these signals, supervisor would have to back up and do some more work to get her with him. Or, failing that, abandon the frame altogether.)

S: You're willing to do it.

W: *(Smiles, nods.)* Yes, I will.

S: And I want you to bring that list in next week. Because I think there are some very important things for you to discover about yourself and for the two of you to discover about your marriage and for all of us to discover about the therapy so far, if you do your assignment. Alright?

(A final effort to seal the new frame and ensure the success of the intervention.)

W: Okay. *(Looks from husband to therapist, beaming.)*

(Supervisor returns to back row and therapist concludes session with couple.)

I stressed, when introducing the strategic model above, that the job of the strategic therapist is to take the presenting complaint and frame a solvable problem. In this case, we took the wife's depression (the complaint by the time the couple was referred to us) and initially framed that as the problem to be solved in treatment. And we very quickly discovered that we had made a terrible mistake, that the problem as we had defined it was unsolvable. So we turned it on its head, taking this poor, depressed, whining woman and transforming her into a powerful figure who so far had managed to control the therapy. And she accepted the new frame, with considerable enthusiasm and even delight. Clearly, the new frame fit the facts as well or better than the old did. And it already promised to make the therapy more interesting and productive.

The homework designed to implement the new frame was set up so that whether she carried it out or not, Mrs. Green could be held responsible for her behavior. As it turned out, she fulfilled the assignment beyond even our wildest expectations.

(*The beginning of Session 3.*)

T: Ah, we sent you out with an assignment.

(*Therapist appropriately begins the session by soliciting a report on wife's homework assignment. Unless there is a pressing crisis that must be handled first, always begin by getting a report on the homework. You must clearly indicate that the homework is important or the family will not take it seriously.*)

W: Um-hum (*beaming again*).

T: Last week.

W: Yes.

T: And I'd like to see what you did.

W: Okay. (*Reaches into purse, pulls out a piece of paper, and hands it to therapist.*)

T: Oh, you typed it. (*Takes paper, looks at it, and then hands it back to wife.*) I'm going to let you, I want you to read some of it to me. What was your understanding of the assignment before you. . . ?

(*Here the therapist does a good job: He takes wife's paper from her, looks at it, and then hands it back to her. It is important to touch it, but then to hand it back and not get stuck with reporting on the homework yourself. The patient should do the reporting. The therapist also clarifies wife's understanding of the assignment before proceeding. This helps avoid misunderstanding about what was done— if you were careful to make sure initially that the patient had indeed understood the assignment, then you can comfortably frame subsequent "misunderstanding" as a decision, e.g., "How did you decide to forget exactly what I told you to do?"*)

W: To write how I manipulate therapy.

(*Here, by changing from "how I control therapy" to "how I manipulate therapy" wife is demonstrating how much she has bought the new frame for her behavior.*)

T: How you (*Here therapist and supervisor lean far forward as they strain to catch wife's words*).

(*The nonverbal behavior of therapist and supervisor as they listen incredulously to wife is another example of "calibration": Both dance to her tune at the moment.*)

W: (*Overlaps.*) Manipulate therapy.

T: How you manipulate the therapy.

W: Yes.

T: Okay, and you were going to write down your techniques for us.

W: Yes. Well, how I. . . . Shall I begin?

T: Go right ahead. Just do one at a time.

> (*Here wife fires the first shot and the therapist immediately joins, in what will be a colossal control battle that runs throughout the rest of this excerpt and mars the otherwise good work being done here. Wife and therapist now lock horns in a competitive struggle to control the reporting of the homework. Therapist could, and should, have avoided this by doing a gracious one-down, saying simply "Go right ahead." Instead, he had to have the last word by adding "Just do one at a time." and so was hooked into the battle.*)

W: (*Reads from paper.*) "I play one against the other. In the first session I tried to play the therapist against Dr. Schultz. I watch the therapist and I observe his reactions. I am inclined to try to play him against my husband."

> (*Again wife presents convincing evidence that she has accepted the new frame and performed the homework assignment.*)

T: Really.

W: Yes. (*laughs.*)

T: That's, um, you're inclined. . . . How do you do that? How do, how do you play me against. . . .

W: (*Interrupts.*) No, I said I was inclined (*emphasizes*) to, I didn't say that I did it. It would be my inclination, to pick up an opportunity. I can't remember specific incidents, but it would be my inclination, to try and do something.

> (*Now wife clearly has therapist's interest, but when he goes after more details she withholds.*)

T: So, so you watch me carefully.

W: Uh-huh. Yes.

T: And what kind of things do you pick up that are helpful?

> (*Again, therapist asks directly for more information. . . .*)

W: (*Interrupts.*) Nothing.

> (*And wife withholds it.*)

T: In controlling the therapy.

W: Nothing.

T: Nothing?

W: Nothing.

T: Okay.

W: Shall I go on?

T: I, I'm still not very clear on what you do. About how you control the therapy.

W: Well, if I could, uh, if you're talking to my husband and if I could try and make him look bad, I would be in control, wouldn't I?

(The struggle to control the pace of the homework report continues as wife proposes going on and therapist blocks her. Notice, however, that here therapist gets more information than on his two previous attempts. He succeeds by doing a one-down maneuver, "I'm still not very clear. . . ." Wife rushes in to help this poor, befuddled man.)

T: By making your husband look bad. To me.

W: *(Overlapping.)* Yeah. Or saying things, adding on. I'd be kind of directing the course of the therapy, wouldn't I?

T: *(Pause.)* So, by putting him in the down position.

W: Uh-huh. If I'm doing all the talking, I'd be controlling the therapy, wouldn't I?

T: If you talk about him.

(Here therapist consistently avoids a direct answer to wife's question: "I'd be controlling the therapy, wouldn't I?" This likely has the effect of prolonging such questioning.)

W: Talk about him or get you to change your direction, then I'm controlling, or, not controlling, but I'm manipulating. *(Wife again opens paper in front of her.)* Shall I go on?

T: That's another way you control the therapy.

(Here therapist takes a different tack in response to wife's moves to control the reporting, commenting on her behavior.)

W: I wouldn't say controlling. Try to.

(She deftly turns it aside by doing a masterful one-down—"I wouldn't say controlling. Try to.")

T: *(Pause.)* Read the last one.

(Therapist is then left without much else to say besides his rather desperate "Read the last one.")

W: The last one? Of my three?

(Again she subtly jabs him with her question "Of my three?")

T: Um-hum.

W: Okay. *(Reads.)* "I misconstrue homework assignments. I used the first assignment *(to talk about her depressed feelings)* to express hostilities toward my husband. With the next assignment *(the art therapy task)*

I drew only the emotions which I wanted to discuss." (*Looks at therapist, smiling triumphantly.*)

T: Okay. So, so you're doing the assignment right now, by only putting out the things that you want us to see.

(*Although therapist says wife is doing the assignment right there, he really implies that she has not done the assignment adequately because she has selectively listed things. This is a strategic error. At this point he should be heaping praise on Mrs. Green, congratulating her on how extraordinarily well she has done.*)

W: Yes. No, this assignment (*refers to paper*) is true. I mean, I'm sincere about this assignment. Okay. I mean, maybe if you see other things, I would like to hear about them. But this is sincere. I'm not using this particular assignment.

T: You didn't misconstrue this one.

W: No, I did not misconstrue this. Unless I misunderstood it.

T: But you're talking about the first assignment and instead of talking about your down feelings you talked about your hostile feelings.

W: Yes.

T: You probably knew I'd be happy with that, too.

W: No, but I didn't have too many hostile feelings that particular week.

T: Uh-huh.

W: Okay?

T: Okay.

W: (*Looks down at paper.*) Shall I read the second one now, or. . . .
(*More of the tiresome battle.*)

T: I'm still confused about the first one.

(*Again, therapist does a one-down, prevents wife from moving on, and nicely succeeds in getting more information from her.*)

W: Okay.

T: (*Overlaps.*) I'm still confused about that one. About, especially about the part about Mr. Schultz, Dr. Schultz.

W: Huh?

T: The part about Dr. Schultz.

W: Oh, okay. A, I think the end of the first session he came up and he said that, I believe that Tom (*husband*) was playing therapist and shouldn't be. But you were bringing out a point that I thought was important. I countered that the point was important, so, I was sort of playing you against him.

(*And again, wife's response indicates that she understood the assignment perfectly.*)

T: You, you're even doing it again. You're very good at this. . . .

W: (*Slightly flustered now, overlaps.*) What, I, I'm not realizing it. . . .

> (*Here therapist does seem to succeed in winning a round against wife. But he achieves it by putting her down, too high a price to pay to win. And perhaps worse, he then drops it and does not use it to further the therapy in any way. There is nothing wrong with fighting with a family member. But you had better win and put your victory to good use in the service of the therapy.*)

T: (*Overlaps.*) I'd be real curious about this point. You've got me real curious about this point that was so important to you. You see that as just a control maneuver.

W: Well it's, unless I don't understand. Unless I'm naive about manipulation. This is how I understand how I do it. Now maybe you have, you see it differently. I don't know what you're trying to draw, what you want.

> (*Wife again reveals that she is a master of the one-down, for she has clearly demonstrated that she is hardly naive about manipulation.*)

T: Um, okay, what's the second one?

> (*Finally given the "expert" role by Mrs. Green, the therapist now fails to use it to any therapeutic advantage.*)

W: Okay. The second is (*reads*): "I also compete with the therapist by analyzing my own thoughts. Often I speak from a rehearsed script. I feel that I have played to the gallery."

T: So you. . . .

W: (*Interrupts.*) Performing.

T: You perform. This is my depression and this is how smart I am about my depression.

W: Probably, yes.

T: So you have three techniques that you were aware of.

W: That I was aware of.

T: (*Pause.*) How long did you work on the assignment? How long did you think about it?

> (*Therapist still appears to be looking for a way to bust wife for not quite having done the assignment.*)

W: Several days. I worked on it, wrote it out. I had a longer form. Then I condensed it.

> (*And again her response shows just how well she did do it.*)

T: You had a, so, did you throw some away?

W: No, I, uh, I went into detailed examples and then I uh, added to it, and as I did it I added, I think I became more honest but, it seemed to me, more concise. But I worked on it for several days and it was very difficult 'cause I wrote it out and was very embarrassed. . . .

T: (*Overlapping.*) I see.

W: And I had trouble thinking so I did a little bit each day.

T: Uh-huh.

The therapist runs into two main difficulties in the above segment. First, there is the troublesome process throughout in which wife and therapist struggle for control of the homework reporting. The very first transcript segment given above indicated the difficulties Mrs. Green presents for a therapist. Such interaction behavior quickly leads to the label "resistive" patient. The present example demonstrates both the pitfalls in taking such an individual head-on and the ease with which one can slip under such resistance by doing a "metacomplementary" (Watzlawick et al., 1967) one-down maneuver.

The second trouble the therapist encounters here results from his failure early on in the homework report to tell Mrs. Green exactly how well he thinks she did on the assignment. Much of wife's behavior can be seen as her attempt to elicit the therapist's evaluation of her performance.

In general, a therapist has two alternatives when evaluating a patient's performance on homework. A grade of "A" can be given, heaping praise on the patient for how well the homework has been done. Or an "F" can be assigned and the patient beaten over the head for not having completed it satisfactorily. Intermediate evaluations are not useful. Remember, reframing is an all-or-none change.

Usually, the therapist will choose to frame the patient as in compliance with the homework, selectively attending to whatever aspects of the performance are consistent with such a frame. More rarely, it will be productive to bust the patient for having failed to comply. If this approach is adopted, however, one must be prepared to chastise quite soundly. A slap on the wrist will not do. For example, I once worked with a couple who, in the first few weeks of treatment, came in two weeks in a row without completing my homework assignment. The third time I decided I could not stand for this any longer. I berated them, telling the couple that my assignment was no different than any other doctor's prescription and that if they would not take the medicine, I could not help them. To emphasize my point, I ended the session after ten minutes and sent them packing back home, an hour's drive. (Since it was free

VA therapy, the question of refunding part of the fee did not come up.) The couple came in the next week with their assignment completed and the therapy progressed nicely from then on.

AN ENCORE

One of the problems in strategic therapy is figuring out what to do for an encore. Strategic interventions are often flashy and can (as here) have a dramatic impact on the treatment. But single interventions are rarely the whole therapy, and the therapist is often left wondering what to do next. This might be thought of as the difficult "midgame" of strategic therapy. Too frequently, beginning therapists are unable to capitalize on the therapeutic advantage gained from a successful reframing maneuver. Instead of working persistently in the new frame, they grab at whatever comes their way, often taking the therapy in yet another new direction.

The following excerpt from the fourth treatment session illustrates some of our difficulties in following up on our successful reframing of the therapy with the Greens. Here we began to see a chronic couple pattern emerge: Wife complains about husband, husband defends himself, wife complains, husband defends, etc. The process ground on and on and the therapist became involved in helping it continue. After many repetitions of this cycle, the following occurred:

> (*Couple are discussing what happens when husband comes home from work. Wife begins to complain that she does not get enough attention from husband.*)
>
> *H:* I usually say "Hello." (*Laughs.*)
>
> (*Husband defends self against wife's complaint.*)
>
> *W:* (*Speaks in whining voice.*) Sometimes you just, a, you're really busy, Tom.
>
> (*Wife complains again.*)
>
> *H:* Well, that may be. Quite often I'll go on to something else.
>
> *T:* Let's, uh (*to wife*), maybe it would be good if we let you talk more about your sense of him being busy and how you react to that. (*To husband.*) Give her a chance. It seems that you do not quite understand what it is she's exactly been wanting from you.
>
> (*Therapist invites wife to complain more. This might be a useful strategy if therapist were encouraging enactment of the pattern in order to then unbalance the couple—Chapter 5—or if his approach*

*were paradoxical and he wished to prescribe the symptom—see last
section of this chapter. However, therapist is working according to
neither of these plans here, and his move is another round in an
unproductive pattern with this couple.*)

S: (*Enters from back row.*) I want to intervene here. (*To couple.*) I think
that right now the two of you have gotten stuck in an old pattern that
you have. And the old pattern as I see it from the back row is that
you (*wife*) complain and kind of whine. . . .

(*Supervisor is frustrated that therapist has just invited couple to continue pattern of complaint/defense.*)

W: (*Overlaps.*) Uh-huh. (*Nods agreement.*)

S: (*To wife.*) You have a whiny quality in your voice and you kind of
complain and whine and look a little sad (*wife is nodding agreement*).
At least a little sad, right? (*Wife nods head in agreement.*) And
(*to husband*) you feel "Oh, my God, what did I do again?" and get
defensive and helpless. (*To couple.*) And you two get stuck. Okay?

W: Um-hum.

S: (*To therapist.*) I think, better than Mrs. Green doing more complaining about him (*husband*), so that he will understand the complaints, it
would be much better if Mrs. Green would start making some statements about herself and what she wants from him. So, no statements
about her husband, but statements about herself and what she wants.

(*Supervisor instructs therapist to have Mrs. Green behave differently.*)

T: Um-hum.

S: See where that goes. (*To wife.*) Pay some attention to your voice as you
make statements about yourself rather than statements about him.
And (*to therapist*) see if something different can happen than the old
cycle of complaints and sadness and all that. (*Supervisor returns to
back row.*)

T: (*To wife.*) That may be a difficult task for you, to turn your complaints
into what you want.

(*Here therapist errs by framing wife as likely to fail rather than succeed.
He should have said "I think you can do that."*)

W: (*To husband, voice now stronger.*) I guess I want to be acknowledged.
Physically, my presence and I'd like to be recognized for the person I
really am, and not somebody that you think I ought to be. I think that
sums it up.

(*Wife begins to speak more assertively.*)

T: There's a little maneuver there that I think you need to pay attention to
(*wife nods in agreement*). "I think that sums it up. That's it." It's almost
like "Whatever you say to me I'm not going to say anything else after
that." This is an old pattern and it seems to be a hot one. So hot it's
quickly shut down.

(Therapist calls wife on a maneuver she uses to shut off discussion. This succeeds in getting her to continue, but wife appears to feel criticized by therapist and switches back to complaining about husband.)

W: Well. (*To husband, again whining*) I think you're trying to make me into somebody I'm not. Uh, you don't, you don't really pay any attention to who I really am. You, a, sometimes you give me things for Christmas, like perfume, which I never wear.

(Wife complains about husband, again whining.)

S: (*Comes up behind Mrs. Green, to coach her. Therapist unsuccessfully attempts to wave supervisor back.*) Tell him who you are rather than telling him what he doesn't do.

(Not seeing therapist's gestures to "back off," supervisor again intervenes to stop wife's complaints.)

W: (*Slumps to side in her chair, hand to forehead.*) I don't know. I'm really confused sometimes as to who I really am, but I'm a person who, I like to read books, and I like to learn and study, and I like to, uh, I like to do my own thinking. I like to decide, be the one to decide if I'll go skiing or if I'll do this or if I'll go someplace. I like to be the one to decide what I want to do. Although I'm willing to, certainly, give, make compromises. But I don't want to be told (*emphasizes*) what to do. Like I'm a child. You're treating me like a child, and I don't like it. I don't like to be told what to wear. I like to decide what I'm going to wear.

(Wife again begins to make assertive statements. At the end of this exchange, wife introduces the issue that will inspire the next homework assignment: "I like to decide what I'm going to wear.")

T: (*Overlaps.*) You made some real strong statements about some of the things you want and who you are. And then you shifted back t. . . .

(Therapist praises wife, but then undercuts the praise with criticism. It is the latter that wife seems to hear.)

W: (*Overlaps.*) I didn't mean to (*hangs head*).

T: I want you now, Mr. Green, to respond to some of the statements that she made.

(Again therapist's intervention amounts to an invitation to husband to defend himself against wife's complaints.)

H: (*Clears throat.*) I don't see myself as telling you to do anything. I don't see myself as telling you what to wear. You buy what you want. (*Wife shakes head "no."*) If you ask me if I like it or not, I say "yes" or "no." (*Wife shakes head "no."*) What do you shake your head for?

(Husband accepts therapist's invitation.)

W: You have the final say whether or not most of the things go back.

H: No, I don't.

W: Yes, you do. If I buy something I like and you don't like it, you tell me and, you're the one that's paying for it. And it goes back.

(*Argument continues back and forth for several more minutes.*)

To work directly and successfully with this couple's chronic interaction pattern the therapist would need to have used the structural unbalancing techniques discussed in Chapter 5. (For example, the therapist might decide to side with wife, insisting that she get the attention she wants from husband.) Instead, he became triangulated by the couple and ended up helping to maintain their unproductive pattern.

Rather than work with the couple dyad at this point, we continued to bypass their interaction and again intervened strategically with Mrs. Green. The above segment gives the content from which this next strategic intervention was formulated. This is important in view of Haley's (1973a) admonition about strategic therapy: The therapist designs a particular strategy for each case. The intervention is not picked from the air (or borrowed from a recent workshop), but rather must always be constructed from the details of the case at hand. Still working within the frame in which Mrs. Green is in control of and responsible for her life, wife's statement that she wishes to decide what to wear leads me to the next strategic intervention.

(*Supervisor now sits with therapist and couple in inner circle of chairs. All have been discussing wife's "little girl" act and how it puts husband in the role of the "heavy."*)

S: (*Looks at watch—it is near end of session—and then speaks to therapist.*) I can think of something kind of crazy and outrageous that the two of them might do this week to explore this further. Um, I'm not sure though that they want to go any further with it. It might be so scary to think about changes and so comfortable the way things are that they would rather not try anything crazy and outrageous to see what that would be like.

(*Here supervisor is definitely teasing couple, deliberately tantalizing them with a homework assignment he hopes they will request as he withholds it from them.*)

T: You're not sure whether they can take it. Whether they want. . . .

(*The correct frame here is important: One generally frames things in terms of will and decision rather than ability.*)

S: (*Overlaps.*) Whether they want to, risk trying something new on for size. (*Husband and wife look at each other. Wife turns to supervisor.*)

W: I'll try it.

(*Supervisor's strategy has paid off: Wife is ready to undertake the new assignment.*)

S: You're ready.

W: Uh-huh.

H: (*Gestures "go ahead."*)

(*And husband passively goes along.*)

S: You are, Mr. Green? (*Husband again nods.*) Okay. (*Supervisor has been slouching way back in his chair, so far. He now leans forward and zeros in on Mrs. Green.*) I want you to tell me right now how much money you want to go out and buy something for yourself this week. (*Pause.*) Quick.

(*Supervisor's change in posture coincides with a shift in his entire approach, from provocative but withholding to directive and authoritative. Notice how the content of the intervention itself is linked to wife's statement from the previous excerpt about wanting to decide what to wear.*)

W: A hundred dollars.

(*By her response, wife signals that she has wholeheartedly accepted the new assignment. Had she said $5 or $10 her agreement to participate would have been much more equivocal.*)

H: (*Nods slightly.*)

S: (*To wife.*) Did he say "yes" or "no"? Did you get an answer?

W: Well, he's smiling. . . .

T: (*Interrupts, to supervisor.*) I would, you pretty much, she said, just said the amount of money she wants. (*To wife.*) I want you to make the whole statement about, you want to go out and have a hundred dollars to buy something for yourself.

(*This unnecessary and distracting intervention by therapist is an expression of the underlying competition between therapist and supervisor.*)

W: I'd like a hundred dollars to buy some clothes.

H: Okay. That's what you want. (*To therapist and supervisor, laughing.*) Am I obligated to give it to her?

T: This is real. . . .

S: (*Overlaps.*) Yeah, we're talking about something that you will do this week.

H: Oh, realistically. (*Waves hands in air.*) (*To wife.*) Okay. You got it.

W: Thank you.

S: Okay. Now, here's how I want you to spend the hundred dollars. I want you to go out this week and spend it all on only things that you want.

(*Supervisor now reveals the paradoxical nature of the assignment. Here is a woman who complains that men—her husband—tell her what to buy. Supervisor directs wife to spend some money on clothes for herself and then tells her exactly how he wants her to spend it.*)

W: Okay.

S: If you don't like something, don't buy it. The only time I want you to take his wants into consideration at all is to buy at least one thing that you guess he won't like, but you do anyway.

W: Okay.

S: Okay. So I don't want you to buy anything because he likes it. I want you to buy things only because you like them except for one thing that you buy because he probably won't like it but you do anyway. Alright? (*Wife nods agreement.*)

(*Again, the message in the strategic intervention is very simple, and supervisor repeats it to make sure wife understands exactly what she is being asked to do.*)

S: And then I want you to come home with your new stuff and to put on a fashion show for him.

(*Here with the "fashion show," supervisor prescribes wife's provocative behavior.*)

W: Okay.

S: With your new things.

W: Okay.

S: Okay. Um (*to therapist*) what do you think we should do about his, about getting Mr. Green's reaction to this?

T: I think he, I think he should guess what the thing is that he's not supposed to like.

(*Supervisor has been so focused on wife and her assignment that he is genuinely at a loss as to how to include husband in the homework. Therapist comes through with help.*)

S: Okay. (*Pause.*)

S: (*To wife.*) You're sitting there smiling (*wife and husband break out into huge smiles and both begin laughing.*) What does that mean?

W: (*Laughing.*) I just thought of something funny.

H: (*Laughing.*) She knows when we leave here I'm going to tell her "You manipulated this whole thing to get some extra dough." (*Continues to laugh heartily.*)

S: (*To husband.*) Do you think she did?

W: No, we're real serious about this. That will be the joke between us.

(*Session ends with softness and even warmth between husband and wife for first time during treatment.*)

This intervention was intended to transcend the pervasive process of complaint and defense between husband and wife and continue working in the new frame of Mrs. Green's control of the therapy, her marriage, and her life.

MAKING THE MOST OF SUCCESS

It was evident from her initial reaction ("a hundred dollars") that wife was enthusiastically involved in her new assignment and that the intervention would likely prove productive. But we were not prepared for the unexpected bonus in Mrs. Green's reaction to the assignment, which we learned about the following week (the fifth treatment session).

(*Therapist begins session by reminding couple that next week is the last of the six contracted sessions and that together they will then review progress to date and decide whether to terminate or recontract.*)

T: Also, you had a homework assignment that I'm curious about, we're all curious about. And I'm sure you're excited to tell us. What, what happened? From the beginning. You were to ask for some money.

(*Again, therapist begins session with homework report.*)

W: Yeah, well, I bought some new clothes. I bought a skirt, blouse, new shoes, and. . . .

T: (*Interrupts.*) Wait, before you go on. . . .

(*Here therapist risks setting up the same kind of struggle for control that marked the homework report in the earlier session. It does not happen this time, however.*)

W: (*Overlaps.*) What?

T: One of the things I'm really, really itching to hear about is, uh, how did you get the money from Mr. Green? How did you do that?

W: Charge card.

T: A charge card. Uh-huh. Did you talk about what you were going to do, how you were going to do it, at all, before you went out. . . .

W: No.

T: So you utilized the agreement. . . .

W: (*Overlaps.*) Uh-huh.

T: That we had made up here, about the hundred dollars, and just went out and did it.

(*Here therapist subtly frames wife as in compliance with homework assignment.*) (*Wife's immediate agreement signals to therapist that he is on the right track. Perhaps this succeeded in heading off the control battle.*)

W: Yes.

T: Great. Okay.

W: And I showed it to him yesterday. I bought shoes and he said he didn't like the way the shoes fit me. And, um, I said I like the way the shoes fit me, so I think I'll keep the shoes. And, a, he hasn't really told me what he thought of the clothes yet.

(*Wife's voice has lost the whiny, little-girl quality of earlier sessions as she reports on her assignment.*)

T: Um.

W: (*Looks over at husband.*) And I did buy one thing that I think he doesn't like.

(*Here wife's glance to husband underscores the provocative nature of her remarks. Of course, this time the context is different: She is being provocative at supervisor's direction.*)

T: You, you did buy one thing that was just for you and that knew you liked but were pretty sure he didn't like.

W: That's right. Yeah. (*To husband.*) It was the blouse. (*To therapist.*) It's made in India. It had kinda like embroidery on it. I didn't think he'd like it.

T: (*To husband.*) And you were to guess which one it was that she wasn't going to like.

H: Um-hum. I gues, I guessed it.

T: You did guess it.

H: But, I, uh, like the blouse. It's not that I disliked it. I just, I guessed that that was the one, because of its style. It looked like it needed an ironing (*laughs*), and I said so. That's the way the thing was made, I guess.

(*Here husband displays his own covert maneuvers. Given an opportunity to express his dislike for wife's purchase, he insists he really likes it and then proceeds to get in a backhanded dig.*)

T: (*To wife.*) So, did you take the shoes back?

(*Therapist playfully teases wife.*)

W: No.

T: You didn't?

W: No, I haven't taken them back.

T: Why not?

W: It's my, my decision. I'm going to keep 'em. I'm not taking them back.

(*And she responds by firmly asserting herself.*)

T: Well, from what I can gather so far, you did the assignment quite well. Both of you.

(*Here therapist shows that he learned from supervisor's instruction following an earlier session: He promptly gives the couple his evaluation of their performance on the homework, clearly framing them in compliance here.*)

W: It was easy (*smiles broadly and laughs; husband joins in laughter*).

(*And this praise is received with pleasure by the couple.*)

T: I'm surprised about that. I'm surprised it was so easy for you. It seemed that, I was under the impression that it wouldn't be easy.

(*This is a nice, graceful one-down maneuver by therapist, which further reinforces wife's competence. Therapist says, in effect, "I was certainly wrong in underestimating you."*)

W: (*Voice again has a bit of the old childish, whining quality.*) Well it, it took me about an hour looking in stores to finally figure out what I wanted to buy. I was starting to buy things that I knew Tom would be pleased with. And then I, I caught myself (*voice now becomes stronger and more adult*) and I said "If you were going to sell your clothes, what clothes would you buy?" And then I started picking out other kinds of clothes. Things and fabrics that I liked, colors and things I had never worn before. Then the assignment brought on a bad fit of depression.

(*Freed of any need to defend herself to therapist, wife now goes further to tell just how difficult the assignment really was for her. Notice how her voice reflects the frame: She whines as she describes behaving within the old frame—"starting to buy things that I knew Tom would be pleased with"—and then her voice becomes more assertive as she tells of the switch to the new frame—"picking out . . . things that I liked." Wife then reveals the unexpected bonus in her response to the homework: "The assignment brought on a bad fit of depression." The skillful handling of this new turn of events is absolutely crucial for continuing progress in the case.*)

T: Hum.

W: Which lasted two or three days.

(*Therapist quietly elicits more information about the depression.*)

T: Really?

W: Yeah.

T: And you connected your depression to the assignment?

(*By emphasizing that the depression occurred in the context of the homework assignment, therapist opens up the possibility that this depression can be reframed. This is very important, especially since wife's main complaint was depression. Unless the therapist is somehow able to frame the "new" depression as different from the "old" one, it is back to square one.*)

W: Yes.

H: To, to what?

(*This spontaneous remark by husband is crucial. Although he has sat quietly through much of this and other sessions, husband speaks up here and makes a bid to seduce wife back into the old pattern where she blames him for her depression and he proceeds to defend himself against the charge. The stimulus for husband's question is wife's statement that her depression was brought on by the assignment and not by something he had done or failed to do. It is not really clear from this exchange alone that all this is happening, but in a minute husband will try again and the pattern becomes obvious.*)

W: To the assignment. It triggered a really bad fit of depression.

T: (*To husband.*) Did you know that?

H: Um-hum. No, I didn't know it was tied to the assignment, but I knew she was down for two days now. And I couldn't figure out why.

T: Ask her now.

(*Therapist invites husband to continue the seduction.*)

H: Why were you down?

W: (*Tone of voice is again slightly whiny.*) Because I really realized that (*voice now again becomes stronger*), how much I've been selling myself short, doing things to please other people. I've been doing it for so long, you know, and it really depressed me. I end up feeling bitter, about the whole thing.

(*Wife resists husband's invitation to blame him and instead focuses on her own self-defeating behavior, a frame that emphasizes her personal responsibility and control. The shift in her tone of voice here indicates a point of conflict between the old and new frames.*)

T: How depressed are you right now?

W: Somewhat depressed.

T: Somewhat. Compared to the two days that we're. . . .

W: (*Interrupts.*) Better today. I've been rather depressed since the weekend.

T: And you see the assignment and the experience of going out. . . .

(Here again therapist appropriately emphasizes the connection between the depression and the assignment, paving the way for a reframing of the depression.)

W: (*Overlaps.*) Um-hum.

(Wife's responses indicate that she is right with therapist.)

T: And taking care of yourself in a new way as bringing up depression about how you've sold yourself short. . . .

W: (*Overlaps.*) Um-hum.

T: Up until now.

W: Uh-hum.

T: And some of that, and there's some bitterness connected with it.

W: Uh-hum. Lots of bitterness.

H: (*To wife.*) Can I ask a question?

(This talk of "bitterness" is too much for husband.)

W: Well, yeah.

H: Is, is that bitterness directed at me? Are you bitter at something I did?

(Husband again invites wife to blame him—the old pattern between them and wife's old frame.)

W: No, I think ultimately I have to be bitter at myself. That, you know, it's been kinda like a whip. The anger is really directed at myself.

(And instead wife remains firmly in the new frame.)

T: (*To wife.*) You know, I think that's true, your decision about where the anger belongs. (*To husband.*) But I'm concerned that you don't feel that your question has been answered. Is that accurate, for yourself?

(But here therapist slips. He pays lip-service to the new frame, but then suggests that husband try once more to seduce wife back into the old frame within which her unhappiness is his fault.)

H: Yeah, I think you're probably right. I think, uh, I just feel it's as if I have caused her to be that way, and I don't feel that way. But I think she does feel that way. (*To wife.*) I think you feel that I've caused you to, to do that.

(Husband follows suit, insisting that wife should blame him for her troubles.)

W: (*Speaks now in her full-blown, old, whining voice.*) I think that your preoccupation with how much everything costs has caused me to buy things that, buying clothes in such a way that I can save money. Buying clothes of all one color, and all match . . . Coordinating outfits, never keeping up with the new styles because they cost money. It costs money to be fashionable.

(*Too much to resist, this time wife joins in the old pattern.*)

The therapist's mistake here is in prematurely involving the husband and assisting him in entangling his wife in their old behavior pattern of complaint and defense, thereby reframing her unhappiness back to that of the helpless victim.

At this point the therapy is still essentially dyadic, between the therapist/supervisor and Mrs. Green. Powerful and unexpected changes are occurring in wife's view of the world. But this new frame for her experience is still too fragile to survive in the couple relationship without skillful support from the therapist.

After allowing the couple interaction to continue for awhile in the old frame, therapist again focused on wife's recent depression. A very brief exchange illustrates the impact of carrying out the "shopping spree" assignment.

T: How does, how do you see yourself changing, having sold yourself short for so long?

W: I don't know. I, I was really depressed this weekend, so I, I sorta went, you know, started feeling sorry for myself and really feeling hopeless. I think I'm sort of at a, I'm going to have to go one way or the other. Either lay down and die, or start living. I'm going to have to make a lot of changes. I don't know.

(*Wife's melodramatic behavior from the early sessions is completely gone. She speaks thoughtfully and with real affect. She appears, perhaps for the first time, to experience herself as having a choice about how she lives her life.*)

The seeds of a new frame for wife's recent depression have been sown. At the end of the session, I intervene to forcefully reframe wife's experience and prevent it from being assimilated back into the old frame.

(*Therapist again gets stuck in supporting the old pattern: Wife complains that husband does not understand and does not help her. Husband defends himself against the charges.*)

T: (*To husband.*) Let's see what we can do right now to help you deal with your wife when she's down.

(*Therapist is clearly operating within the old frame here: Husband is to learn to help wife with her depression.*)

H: Well, I asked her, I asked her yesterday. She says, uh, well, I forget what the words were. Anyway, she wants me to understand her. So I say, "Okay, what do you want me to understand?" And I got nothing back. So. . . .

(*Husband describes the couple's characteristic impasse in the old frame.*)

S: (*Enters from back row.*) I really don't like what's been happening for the last 15 minutes. (*To therapist.*) I think the three of you are hopelessly stuck in the old pattern. The old pattern is you (*indicates wife*) complain, he's (*indicates therapist*) helping you complain, ah, you're (*indicates husband*), you're defending yourself. And it's all back where we were (*speaks to therapist again, throwing hands up in despair*) three months ago, six weeks ago (*wife nods vigorously in agreement*). Okay?

(*Supervisor's frustration and annoyance with therapist shows here as he moves in to interrupt the old pattern.*)

S: (*Speaks very deliberately now, emphasizing each word.*) Something different needs to happen. It began to happen this week when you (*to wife*) had what I was hearing was a totally different kind of depression than you had had before. (*Wife nods agreement.*) My guess is that you have never had one like it before. (*Wife continues to nod agreement.*) Do you know what I mean?

(*Here supervisor begins the "something different" by reframing wife's depression of the past week as a totally different kind of depression than she has ever had before. Because supervisor does not feel he has the data yet to pull off the reframe, he uses the probe "Do you know what I mean?" to try to elicit the necessary information from wife. Wife's nods suggest that she is with supervisor and will supply the data he wants.*)

W: What, this week? The kind of depression. . . .

S: (*Overlaps.*) Yeah, your depression.

(*Supervisor is doing a lot of "back-channeling"—Duncan, 1972—here, nodding and agreeing to urge wife to continue.*)

W: It was more severe.

S: Uh-huh.

W: Yeah. It was, was really a depression. Before I didn't know I was depressed.

S: (*Overlaps.*) Yeah.

W: (*Overlaps.*) This time I know I'm depressed.

S: Yeah. Were there. . . ?

W: (*Overlaps.*) I went into tears all the time.

S: Were there qualitative differences as well as the severity?

(*So far, so good. But wife still has not given supervisor the data he needs to convincingly maintain that this was a totally different kind of depression and not just a worse one.*)

W: Yes.

S: Tell me about those.

W: There's a, extreme sense of hopelessness, not, about my situation but not, not directed at myself. And then there'll be breakthroughs, where I, I could look at a flower and just enjoy it or something. And that, that doesn't stay for long. There was more intense feelings. A, my feelings are coming out more to the surface now. They're coming out more. But it's more depressing. Uh, somehow I'm sadder but wiser. That kind of thing.

S: Uh-huh. So, it was very intense. The depression and the moments of enjoyment.

W: Yes. Uh-huh. The moments of enjoyment were few.

S: But they were there.

W: They were there. The depression it, it's very bad.

(*Here wife and supervisor are finishing each other's sentences, indicating that they are calibrating each other and are both working within the new frame, in which the new depression is a totally different kind of depression.*)

S: As you were talking about it at the beginning I had the impression that maybe for the first time in your life you were depressed for a good reason. Do you know what I mean?

(*This is the second step in the reframing: It is not just a totally different kind of depression, but for the first time in her life, wife is depressed for a good—rather than a bad—reason. Again, supervisor attempts to get data from wife to support the reframing maneuver.*)

W: Maybe.

(*This time wife's initial response is equivocal.*)

S: What are your thoughts about that?

(*Here supervisor fails to heed wife's signal that she is not with him and he continues to try to get her help to build the new frame.*)

W: (Pause.) I'm depressed because I'm not getting any real love and affection. I've been getting a lot of other things, but if someone won't listen to me about my depression without giving me a lecture, there's something wrong. (*Some of the old melodramatic quality creeps into wife's voice.*)

(*Wife flops back into the old frame. A pause often signals a shift in frames. It appears that extra cognitive processing time is required to make major shifts in frame.*)

S: I think those are the old reasons to be depressed, and that's not what I heard before you got into this thing with your husband. (*Circular gestures indicate the nature of that couple interaction.*)

(*Supervisor moves quickly to repair the damage of his failed move. It is sufficient here to merely remind wife of the old frame, the old reasons for her depression.*)

W: (*Immediately.*) About how I (*emphasizes*) cheated myself.

(*Wife immediately and decidedly flips back into the new frame.*)

S: Exactly.

W: That's very depressing. It's as if you find out you're going to die or something. And you do come to the realization that, maybe you don't have that much time left, and 39 years of, doing what other people want you to do (*sighs wearily*). It's depressing.

(*As wife continues in the new frame, her affect becomes congruent with the mood she is describing. Gone is the intellectualized and melodramatic tone. For the first time in the sessions, her depression is convincing, i.e., elicits the listener's empathy.*)

S: What I heard you say at the beginning was that the good reason that you were depressed this week is because you've been selling yourself short, for years.

(*Here supervisor uses wife's words from earlier in the session to consolidate the shift in frames.*)

W: (*Emphasizes.*) For years.

(*And wife is very much with supervisor.*)

S: And that's a damn good reason to be depressed. (*Again speaks very slowly and deliberately.*) And I think it's very useful that you had that experience this week. And I don't think it's going to go away immediately. But it's very important that you stay with that experience. And I think at this point there's not a lot he (*indicates husband*) can do to help you out. You're facing some things that you have to face, about yourself, first of all. And the old way of handling those things would be to go to someone else like your husband. . . .

(*Supervisor now gives a different emotional connotation to this new depression: It is no longer bad, something to be rid of, but is instead a very useful experience, one from which wife can learn. And supervisor prescribes how she is to behave in this new frame: Instead of turning to husband for help, wife must learn to rely upon herself.*)

W: (*Overlaps.*) Um-hum.

S: (*Continues.*) To help you out. That's what the fight was about. . . .

W: (*Overlaps.*) Yeah.

S: (*Continues.*) Last weekend. That was an old way of handling it. But I really think that you need to stick with this intense depression, all the feelings that are coming out, and with the moments of new enjoyment that you have. 'Cause you have a whole lot to learn for you from that.

(*Long pause. Husband shifts uncomfortably in his chair.*)

(*Husband's nonverbal display of discomfort indicates that he experiences the real threat that the new frame poses to the couple's characteristic, familiar relationship.*)

W: I felt that, no matter what I feel, I won't ever suppress my, my feelings anymore, about anything. I catch myself doing it, and I stop myself. But I can't go back that way anymore.

S: It would be safer to go back that way.

(*Supervisor warns wife about the discomfort and risk associated with change.*)

W: I it mi, I might have felt that way a little while ago. Now I see that I cannot do that any more. And I won't. (*Speaks forcefully.*)

(*And she indicates that she is up to the challenge.*)

S: (*Overlaps.*) And you wi, you will get scared. And you will fall back into the old patterns and get him to help you fall back, momentarily. Which is all right.

(*Supervisor prescribes the failure at times to maintain the new frame and frames this failure as permissible and only temporary.*)

W: (*Speaks thoughtfully.*) I can see what I'm doing to myself sometimes. I may suppress something, but I let it come out later. But before I never did that. I was, my whole life has been lies and compromises.

S: That's a pretty depressing thought.

W: (*Sadly.*) Yeah. Yeah.

(*The excerpt ends with wife precisely where supervisor wants her: Experiencing the sadness of realizing that she has so far lived her life in a self-defeating way.*)

Following this session, therapist and couple contracted for additional sessions. Initially, the work continued to be mainly with Mrs. Green and was conducted within the frame of her personal competence and responsibility. For example, she had complained for years that although she wished to go back to school, husband's disapproval prevented her from doing so. In the new frame, the therapy focused instead upon the anxiety and phobic reactions that stood in her way. She was given specific help in managing her fears as she carried out assignments such as going to the college registrar's office to obtain information.

Eventually, the personal changes wife had been making began to reverberate through the couple relationship. At this point, the focus of the therapy shifted from essentially individual work conducted within a couple context to more typical marital treatment. Husband and wife began to use the sessions to negotiate some basic changes in their relationship. After several months of treatment, therapy was terminated when the therapist completed his training rotation. Although it would have been very easy to seduce this couple into longer-term therapy, we felt that the Greens had made enough progress so that they could maintain and extend the changes in their marriage without further treatment.

The only follow-up data available in this case is anecdotal. About a year later I was having lunch at my favorite taco stand near the hospital when I happened to look out the window and noticed Mr. and Mrs. Green walking by holding hands. I suppressed a strong urge to rush out and ask them how they were doing, feeling that this would be too intrusive. I therefore had to be content with what I had just seen.

CONCLUDING COMMENTS

This case illustrates several features of the strategic model I now wish to emphasize. First, strategic interventions are essentially dyadic, between the therapist and one other person. This does not mean that the strategic model applies only to individual therapy, however. All therapy has a strategic aspect so that no matter which other models are employed one is always working in some frame and, explicitly or implicitly, changing frames. For example, when intervening structurally in a family with out-of-control adolescents, the therapist generally frames the parents as responsible for disciplining their unruly children (rather than accepting the family's frame that the parents are helpless to do anything). Here the "other person" in the "dyadic" exchange with the therapist is the family as a whole. Such strategic reframing typically lacks the intensity of a truly dyadic intervention involving the therapist and only one other person. And these reframes are generally not the main thrust of the intervention, but accompany and support other types of work (e.g., structural).

It must be emphasized that, with many couples, when there is significant marital conflict, one cannot get away with intervening strategically with one spouse—the other simply will not sit still for it as Mr. Green did here. Instead, one is forced to deal directly with the couple's interaction patterns from the beginning. I argue in Chapter 9 that the structural model is necessary in work with this latter type of couple. On the other hand, when it is appropriate (for now, read "when you can get away with it"), strategic intervention is a quick and effective means for initiating change in a marital relationship.

However, it is quite important that such strategic work be done in the context of couple rather than individual therapy. One danger of individual treatment in the face of marital conflict is that the treatment may fail. The case of the Greens clearly demonstrates how this can happen. A new frame within which the therapist works with one spouse is extremely fragile at first and can easily be destroyed as the couple resume their characteristic interactional behavior. When both spouses are present, the therapist can observe this occurring in the session and intervene to stop it.

Another danger of individual therapy when there is marital conflict is that the therapist, who unavoidably sides with the spouse in treatment against the absent mate, will tip the balance in favor of divorce when this is not a necessary or desirable outcome. In their exhaustive review of the literature on outcome in marital and family therapy, Gurman and Kniskern (1978a) conclude that when there is marital difficulty and one spouse enters individual treatment, therapy is less likely to produce improvement and much more likely to result in deterioration than is couples treatment in such situations. Although one could certainly argue that there is a self-selection factor operating here and that when one spouse refuses to participate in therapy or neglects to bring the other to treatment it means that the marriage *is* doomed, the role of the therapy in this process should not be ignored. Gurman and Kniskern do, in fact, conclude that such systematic sampling bias does not account for the inferiority of individual treatment for marital distress.

Individual therapy for marital conflict is essentially an uncontrolled structural intervention. The therapist (again, unavoidably) sides with the patient against the spouse and supports the patient's competence and self-esteem. As the patient becomes more competent and feels stronger, he or she often decides that it is silly and unnecessary to put up with the unsatisfactory marriage any longer and typically begins to demand more of the spouse, which often results in increased conflict and, in some cases, divorce.

A second general point, illustrated by the Green family, is that the shift in frames during a successful strategic treatment often occurs in a sequence of steps. Each new frame must be built from the particulars of the patient's concrete situation at the moment. And as new frames allow the emergence of new behaviors and affects, subsequent reframes build upon preceding ones.

The therapist does everything possible to control and predict the direction of treatment in constructing the sequence of new frames. However, this prediction and control is never complete, nor should it be. With Mrs. Green it was the (at the time) unanticipated depression in response to the "shopping spree" assignment that provided the crucial turning point in therapy. The strategic therapist must be prepared to take advantage of opportunities for continued therapeutic progress presented by such unexpected turns of events.

This leads to a third general point. At the time we worked with Mrs. Green, her "new" depression was totally unexpected. From this case I learned that such a reaction is, in fact, normal and predictable. If you are successful in helping a patient change a major frame that has interfered with their living a productive and fulfilling life, the natural and appropriate response is grief, including depression (about having lived so long in the old, self-defeating way) and anger (that they did not change sooner and so wasted years of their lives). A student who viewed the videotape of our work with Mrs. Green commented perceptively that I should have framed her new depression as "sorrow" instead of "depression." This is exactly right, only I was not quick enough to see it at the time. In the case of the Vietnam combat veteran presented in Chapter 12, I was able to take advantage of what I learned from Mrs. Green.

A therapist who is prepared for the normal grief reaction following a successful major reframe can help the patient work through the grief process over the course of a few weeks and then get on with life. When the therapist is unable to make this shift, the danger is that the patient's sadness and anger at having lived unsuccessfully for so long will be assimilated to the old self-disparaging and self-defeating frame, and any therapeutic progress will be lost.

Fourth, the work with Mrs. Green helps us put the concept of "resistance" in a systemic perspective. From the interactional data presented above, one might easily conclude that Mrs. Green is indeed a very resistive patient. On the other hand, it is clear that she appears compliant in other social contexts (e.g., when the therapist solicited information from a one-down position instead of using a head-on, direct approach). In other words, the "patient's resistance" is a part of the *interaction* between patient and therapist rather than a characteristic of the patient.

Finally, I wish to comment upon the supervisory aspects of this case. Haley has suggested (1979) that if supervised therapy fails it is the supervisor's fault. This case was recently concluded and fresh in my mind when I heard Haley say this, and his remark forced me to examine my supervisory role here. This is a case of successful therapy despite failed supervision. I was successful at intervening strategically with Mrs. Green, but failed in the supervision because I did not employ strategic approaches there. Each time the therapist failed to successfully carry out my directives and instead became enmeshed in the couple's chronic, unsatisfactory interaction pattern, I patiently took him aside to explain his errors, using detailed videotape playback to instruct him in alternative behaviors. When that failed, I tried harder to educate him, with more explanation and instruction. Thus I became, in the words of Watzlawick et al. (1974), part of the problem: My ineffective behavior maintained the therapist's ineffective behavior. Fortunately, I learned enough from this failure to strategically and successfully resolve the similar therapist–supervisor impasse presented in Chapter 4.

Reframing versus Insight

Therapists learning the strategic model for the first time often wonder: "Isn't reframing just a new name for old-fashioned insight? After all, you are just trying to get the patient to understand." There is a crucial difference between insight and reframing, however, which I wish to highlight here. And the difference is not always evident from the content of the intervention (e.g., strategic reframing versus interpretation), but rather depends as well upon the frame within which it occurs.

The goal of insight is to get the patient to understand (intellectually and emotionally) *what is.* The goal of reframing is to get the patient to see (again, in both the cognitive and affective realms) *what can be.* From the point of view of strategic therapy, the trouble with insight approaches is that they tend to freeze reality; turning it into a thing makes it harder to change.

This difference is rooted in very different epistemologies. In the epistemology underlying insight therapies, it is assumed that reality is given in the concrete facts themselves and exists apart from the attributes of the observer and the frame within which the observations are made. The strategic approach locates meaning and, hence, reality not in the concrete facts alone, but insists that the context, including the observer, also be included.

Insight approaches to therapy are interested in truth. Strategic therapy is ultimately pragmatic: Some realities *work better* than do others.

The case of Mrs. Green presented above helps make the contrast clearer. This patient presented herself as timid and helpless. An insight-oriented therapist might accept this as reality and help Mrs. Green understand how this reality came to be, typically searching her past for the formative influences. Or, such a therapist might see the reality quite differently, interpreting the patient's controlling behavior as a defense against her *real* underlying feelings of powerlessness. In either case, the *frame* for the work is the same: There is a reality there that must be understood.

With Mrs. Green, I was not interested in whether she "really" was in control (of her life, of the therapy, etc.) or not. The point was, she *could* be. The patient was enough in control (that is, the concrete facts were such) that I could get away with (that is, she joined me in) constructing a frame within which she was "in almost complete control." My goal was utterly pragmatic: The new frame permitted Mrs. Green to display more productive, competent, self-satisfying behavior than did the old. Of course, another therapist might have obtained similar results using a different frame. There is no single "correct" new frame.

The Mechanism of Reframing

How reframing actually "works" is rather obscure. A recent comment by a student in my family systems workshop got me thinking about *cognitive dissonance* (Festinger, 1957) as a possible underlying psychological mechanism for reframing.

Reframing appears to introduce dissonance by interjecting an alternative and often in some way contradictory view of reality. The patient is thus presented with two choices for relieving the resulting discomfort: He can reject the new frame, keeping the old frame as well as his old behavior or he can instead discard the old frame and accept the new, changing his behavior to make it consistent with the new frame. In the first case we would say that the reframing has failed to produce a shift in the patient's behavior, whereas in the second case we would say that the strategic intervention succeeded.

Some evidence from the learning literature (e.g., Kintsch, 1970) suggests that conflicting or inconsistent sets increase response latencies in experimental tasks, data that support the idea that a change in frames requires extra processing time. See the excerpt from the Bach family in Chapter 9 for a clinical example of this phenomenon.

Postscript: About Paradox

Paradox is a sometimes misunderstood and often maligned form of strategic intervention. Many people mistakenly think that all strategic therapy relies on paradox. And paradox is seen by some as the ultimate in manipulation of the patient by the therapist and are so put off and even outraged by it that they unfortunately dismiss strategic therapy from further consideration. Strategic therapists like Haley (1976) often point out that all therapy is manipulative. Perhaps because with the use of paradox it is more difficult to pretend that one is not attempting to influence the patient, strategic therapists tend to be more open about their manipulations than are other therapists.

In the past five years or so, paradox has enjoyed a surge in popularity among family therapists, in part due to tremendous interest in and enthusiasm for the work of the Milan group (Selvini Palazzoli et al., 1978). At least one full-length book on paradox (Weeks and L'Abate, 1982) has appeared and the March, 1981, issue of *Family Process* devoted a section to a lively debate among leading practitioners about just how paradox should be viewed (e.g., Dell, 1981; Selvini Palazzoli, 1981; Watzlawick, 1981). A very complex theoretical explanation of paradox can be found in a recent paper by Cronen et al. (1982).

What I hope to demonstrate in this final section on the strategic model is that paradoxical intervention is simply a special type of strategic reframing rather than a totally different and mysterious class of interventions. Compared to all the learned discussion on paradox just mentioned, the modest approach I take here will likely be dismissed by some as too simple-minded. Yet I think it has much clinical utility. Omer (1981) independently came to a conclusion similar to that expressed below when he described paradox as "symptom decontextualization."

PARADOXICAL REFRAMING

Paradoxical intervention involves a sudden and generally unexpected shift in frames that takes the problem or symptom out of one context or frame and places it in another frame. In the case of successful paradoxical intervention, the old context is one within which the problem is unsolvable, whereas in the new frame the problem indeed has a solution.

The solution is paradoxical, that is, contradictory or contrary to common sense, only from the perspective of the initial frame. In the new frame, the solution is straightforward and makes perfect sense. That is, it is not paradoxical at all.

Such shifts in frames have occurred in the history of physics. For example, take the phenomenon of refraction, the bending of light when moving from one medium to another. We have all seen this when observing a pencil "bend" at the point it enters a glass of water. Geometrical optics was able to account for this phenomenon perfectly well using Snell's law, named after the Dutch mathematician who discovered it in the 1600s. Then, some sailors brought back from Iceland crystals of spar, which had the property that anything seen through them appeared double, producing two images instead of the single "bent" image predicted by Snell's law (Feynman et al., 1963). This was promptly termed "anomalous refraction." The term "anomalous" just means that the phenomenon did not behave properly. That is, it could not be explained within the prevailing frame used by physicists of the day. Within that frame, light was seen as "rays" moving in certain geometrically definable paths.

Years later, however, with the development of the classical theory of electromagnetic radiation, the old frame of light as rays was replaced by a new and more powerful point of view in which light was conceived of as "waves." And from this new point of view, it turned out that anomalous refraction was not "anomalous" at all, but a straightforward application of the new and more powerful thinking. (In particular, light waves may be "polarized." Some substances—such as Icelandic spar crystals—can make light waves that are polarized in different directions obey different laws of refraction and, hence, produce two images for the two possible polarizations.) As long as light was seen within the frame of geometrical optics, polarization phenomena had to remain "anomalous," or not understandable.

THE PARADOX OF CONTROL

To illustrate how an intervention that seems paradoxical in one frame can appear straightforward in another, consider the issue of the control of a symptom. By definition, a symptom is something that the patient cannot control: "Gee, Doctor, I just can't help it." Thus every symptom has the implicit frame: "This (symptomatic) behavior is out of my control."

Treatment of a symptom often involves teaching the patient that he/she can, in fact, control it. This can be accomplished using paradoxical or nonparadoxical strategies. For example, in Chapter 12 I demonstrate a nonparadoxical approach to teaching a combat veteran that he can control the symptoms of a post-traumatic stress disorder.

Here a paradoxical strategy is considered. Suppose a woman comes to you complaining of headaches. Thorough medical examination has revealed no organic basis for the head pain. In order to cure her of the headaches, you prescribe three headaches in the next week and tell her when and how to have them. This is an example of a paradoxical technique referred to as "prescribing the symptom."

Such an intervention is paradoxical within the usual common-sense frame where, if you want someone to stop something, you certainly do not tell that person to do more of it.

The nonparadoxical explanation of this intervention is as follows. The therapist's directive (to have the three headaches) creates a new context for the symptom. It is no longer something done outside the patient's control, but rather it occurs (or fails to occur) at the bidding of the therapist. So the first reframe is from patient-out-of-control to therapist-in-control.

The therapist next reframes from therapist-in-control to patient-in-control. If the patient follows the therapist's instructions and has the headaches as prescribed, she is demonstrating her control of the symptom (by producing it on demand). The more the patient follows the therapist's detailed instructions on when and how to have the headaches, the more she proves her control of the symptom. For example, the therapist may congratulate the patient on how well she has performed the assignment (the therapist-in-control frame) and even more on the remarkable degree of control over her symptoms that she has shown (the patient-in-control frame).

If the patient fails to follow the therapist's instructions and does not have the headaches or has them, but not as prescribed, she is again demonstrating her control of the symptom. For example, the therapist may say: "How did you decide not to have the headaches as I told you to?"

Once the frame of the patient-in-control has been established, then the therapist works on helping the patient learn "even better control" over the symptom.

This is an example of the use of a *therapeutic double bind*. The term "double bind," introduced into the family therapy field in Bateson and Jackson's (Bateson et al., 1956) classic paper (see Chapter 2), refers to a no-win situation in which the individual is "damned if he does and damned if he doesn't." In the therapeutic double bind, the patient is "changed if he does and changed if he doesn't" (Watzlawick et al., 1967), a no-lose proposition. In our example of the lady with the headaches, if she has the headaches as prescribed she is changed (i.e., she has demonstrated her control) and if she fails to have them as prescribed she still is changed (i.e., she has nonetheless shown her control over the symptom).

OTHER PARADOXICAL REFRAMINGS

There are other implicit frames for symptoms or problems (besides the patient-not-in-control frame) that lend themselves to paradoxical reframing maneuvers.

Sometimes symptoms occur within an I-can-lick-this frame: The patient tries harder and harder to solve the problem, persisting with the same ineffectual attempts at a solution. Watzlawick et al. (1974) give the example of the insomniac who tries harder and harder to fall asleep, but fails because he is trying to accomplish deliberately what is, in fact, a spontaneous occurrence. Watzlawick characterizes this as a "solution is the problem" situation. Here the patient's attempted solution forms part of the context for this problem and the problem together with the solution form a cybernetic circuit: The solution is the feedback loop that maintains the problem (or even makes it worse).

The general intervention strategy in such cases is to get the patient to *stop* the old solution. Watzlawick's paradoxical intervention with the insomniac is to instruct him to stay awake. The harder the patient tries to stay awake, the more likely he is to fall asleep. (I used to wonder if this really worked until I recalled something I had observed as a child, but never understood. If I lay awake at night trying to fall asleep without success and someone returned home late, I would listen carefully for them to come upstairs but invariably fell asleep before they reached the top step.)

Another common implicit frame for problems or symptoms is the symptom-is-bad frame, in which the problem behavior is seen as bad and must be gotten rid of. This frame often has a second part as well: But-you-can't-make-me-stop-it. This sets up a struggle with the therapist for control of the symptom. Here it is the behavior of the other person vis-à-vis the symptom that forms the crucial context for the symptom.

In this case the therapist may adopt the paradoxical strategy of *positive reframing*. The offending behavior is defined as positive rather than negative. And since it is so positive, the therapist cannot see any reason why the patient should stop it and instead tells her "Maybe you should do more of it, and I'll even help you." For example, the therapist may remind the woman with headaches that despite the pain, the headaches *do* have the benefit of keeping her husband from bothering her for sex and it seems like a good idea to keep having them. The therapist could add that it would be even better to have "painless headaches" rather than the painful variety. These will work just as well for avoiding the husband, without the unpleasant side effect of the pain. This reframing technique plays an important role in the work of the Milan group (Selvini Palazzoli et al., 1978), where it is termed "positive connotation."

THE USE AND MISUSE OF PARADOX

Paradoxical intervention is perhaps more susceptible to misuse by inexperienced or grandiose therapists than are some other treatment approaches. Paradox is flashy and some therapists assume that it is a magical answer to all human problems and every therapeutic impasse. It is not.

Inappropriate use of paradoxical interventions can make some people worse rather than better. (I will argue in Chapter 9 that this is more of a problem the *lower* the patient's overall level of functioning.) But paradox is by no means unique in this respect. *Any* intervention can do harm if used inappropriately. Psychotherapists are only recently beginning to own up to their responsibility for the possible "negative effects" of their interventions. See, for example Gurman and Kniskern's (1978b) article on deterioration in marital and family therapy.

Beginning therapists often fail to understand that the appropriate and successful use of paradox requires a correct understanding of the *particular context* of the patient's problem. You cannot simply borrow that nifty paradox you heard about over coffee with a colleague last week or saw at a weekend workshop. This crucial point should not be overlooked despite the fact that Selvini Palazzoli's most recent therapeutic approach involves giving the *same* prescription to *all* families (Simon, 1982a).

Therapists who wish to add paradoxical intervention to their therapeutic repertoires must obtain competent supervision or consultation.

8

The Transactional Model

Chapter 2 described how the family therapy field began with the study and treatment of schizophrenics and their families. Over the years, as the early enthusiasm about curing schizophrenia gave way to a more realistic view, most of the original pioneers, as well as those who followed in the field, moved on to more tractable problems. Only Lyman Wynne (at NIMH in Washington, D.C. and now in Rochester, N.Y.) and Margaret Singer (in Berkeley) have pursued the original focus on schizophrenia. This chapter translates their research approach into a clinical model applicable to family therapy.

The Basic Idea

The concept of *shared focus of attention* underlies the transactional model. This idea is Singer and Wynne's interpersonal adaptation of Schachtel's (1954) intrapsychic notion of "focal attention." Singer and Wynne see the ability to *share* an object of focal attention as central and crucial to the communication process. Singer (1967) defines the concept as follows:

> We apply the concept of sharing foci of attention to four main sequentially related processes which begin with (1) one person's effort to *select* some event, feeling, perception, or idea; proceeds with (2) his

effort to *orient* the other person to the same "set," or frame of reference and to a particular focus within this "set"; continues with (3) a sustained transaction in which the same "set" and focus of attention is *shared* if all goes well; and optimally concludes with (4) *closure* around meaning or "point" which is understood by both. Not only do foci of attention need to be shared, but also need to be linked through time in order for sensible communication to occur. Some foci are quite brief, others more sustained, some interrupted but held in abeyance, others disrupted permanently. (p. 148)

Here Singer and Wynne view the family simply as a collection of members *transacting* with each other. The transactional model has no interest in, for example, the generational boundary, the presenting problem, etc. The term, suggesting the transactions of a business deal, is an apt metaphor for this very pragmatic, task-oriented approach to family communication. What is exchanged is not money or goods and services, but attention and meaning. Singer and Wynne argue that successful transactions require the establishment and maintenance of shared foci of attention.

As discussed in Chapter 2, Wynne et al. (1958) introduced the notion of *pseudomutuality* to describe the relationships within families of schizophrenics and suggested that the disturbed perception and communication of the young adult schizophrenic could be understood as an internalization of disturbances in the family's social organization.

The trouble with ideas like pseudomutuality (and many of the other pioneering notions discussed in Chapter 2), if one is interested in doing empirical research, is that they are very abstract and difficult to operationalize. In fact, of the four early research groups, only Singer and Wynne developed an ongoing research program that has produced solid and replicable findings. Their success is due, in part, to their use of "middle-level concepts," like shared focus of attention, which bridge the gap between abstract ideas and concrete research (or clinical) data.

Singer and Wynne selected the process of sharing foci of attention for study because they believed that it is at this very basic level that communication breaks down in the families of schizophrenics. In a very real sense, communication fails here before it ever gets off the ground. To document such failures in the communication process, Singer and Wynne catalogued the *communication deviances* that occur in the families of young adult schizophrenics to disrupt transactions and thus prevent the sharing of attention and meaning.

Communication Deviance

Singer and Wynne's purpose in defining communication deviance was research. To produce reliable, replicable empirical data, they had to be able to teach their research assistants to listen to the transactions of family members and spot the kinds of things that went enough wrong to prevent the sharing of foci of attention. A communication deviance "manual" was developed (Singer and Wynne, 1966), listing the various communication deviances together with the criteria for identifying them.

Singer and Wynne used the Rorschach task to generate samples of family members' transactional behavior (instead of using the ink blots as a test for inferring intrapsychic processes). This task is an excellent choice for studying those features of transactional behavior that distinguish the families of young adult schizophrenics from control families because its lack of structure maximizes opportunities for communication deviance to occur.

What follows in this section is an adaptation of the latest version (Singer, 1977) of the Singer-Wynne manual for scoring communication deviance in the Rorschach task, modified here for the kind of free-running interaction characteristic of family therapy interviews. See Figure 13 for a convenient summary of these communication deviance categories.

Singer (1977) identifies five types of communication deviance: commitment problems; reference problems; language anomalies; disruptions; and contradictory, arbitrary sequences. A sixth category, turn-taking problems, is added here. Each category will now be discussed in turn.

COMMITMENT PROBLEMS

Singer (1977) states:

> When a listener is confronted with . . . commitment problems . . . he is apt to wonder: *Does he (the speaker) really mean what he is saying?* The way in which the idea is phrased by the speaker leaves doubt in a listener's mind about the status of the idea—has he abandoned it, disqualified it, down-graded it, or intended it to be taken seriously. The speaker in various ways seems less than fully committed to the idea. The following items class ways in which a speaker causes a listener to wonder if he should really pay attention and heed what the speaker is saying: (pp. 464–465)

A. Commitment problems
   1. Abandoned, abruptly ceased remarks
   2. Unstable remarks
   3. Remarks in negative form
   4. Questions
   5. Avoidance
   6. Derogatory, disparaging remarks
   7. Nihilistic remarks
B. Referent problems
   1. Unintelligible remarks
   2. Gross indefiniteness and lack of specificity
   3. Inconsistent and ambiguous references
   4. Cryptic remarks
C. Language anomalies
   1. Ordinary words or phrases used oddly or out of context
   2. Odd sentence construction
   3. Peculiar, quaint, or private terms or phrases
   4. Euphemisms
   5. Slips of the tongue
   6. Mispronounced words
   7. Clang associations, rhymed phrases, and word play
D. Disruptions
   1. Extraneous questions and remarks
   2. Nonverbal disruptive behavior
   3. Humor
   4. Swearing
E. Contradictory, arbitrary sequences
   1. Contradictory information
   2. Odd, tangential, or inappropriate responses to a preceding
      speaker
   3. Non sequitur reasoning
F. Turn-taking problems
   1. Holding the floor
   2. Interrupting

Figure 13. Communication deviance. Types of communication deviance observable in free-running family interaction such as family therapy interviews. (Adapted from Singer, 1977)

1. Abandoned, abruptly ceased remarks: A speaker communicates a bit of an idea but then abandons it.

2. Unstable remarks: A speaker indicates that what he is saying is changing so rapidly that the listener is not sure just what to pay attention to.

3. Remarks in negative form: The speaker withholds commitment by stating what he does not think, feel, wish, etc.

4. Questions: The speaker expresses himself in question form rather than making a statement.

5. Avoidance: The speaker avoids commitment in a transactional context that requires it (e.g., in response to a "What do you think?" type question, the speaker avoids committing self). This category is added to those described by Singer to accommodate a form of commitment problem often encountered in family therapy interviews.

6. Derogatory, disparaging remarks: Statements are made, but then down-graded so the listener does not know if they are to be taken seriously.

7. Nihilistic remarks: Statements that deny the possibility that meaningful communication could occur at all in a particular context.

REFERENT PROBLEMS

Here Singer (1977) says:

> When referent problems occur the listener hears things worded in ways that cause him to ponder: *What is he talking about?* From what the speaker says, a listener cannot be sure he is sharing the proper referent point. What is being alluded to is ambiguous or inconsistent, in any of a variety of ways. (p. 466)

Referent problems include:

1. Unintelligible remarks: Remarks are simply not followable at all.

2. Gross indefiniteness and lack of specificity: Statements are so indefinite and vague that a speaker could be talking about almost anything—or nothing at all.

3. Inconsistent and ambiguous references: Within one or more related statements, the speaker shifts referents or changes tense,

gender, or number, and thus leaves the listener unsure about what is intended.

4. Cryptic remarks: The speaker makes a cryptic statement and the listener must guess the intended meaning.

LANGUAGE ANOMALIES

This category describes (Singer, 1977)

> oddities in word choice, word order, and word usage. When a speaker uses words peculiarly and places them in odd order, plays with their sounds, and even invents words, he reduces the likelihood that a listener will be able to follow his remarks. Again if we ask what is the experience of the listener when he hears a language anomaly, we can see the impact. He asks himself mentally, "Do I know what he is talking about?" The listener knows roughly what the speaker is talking about, but has to stop to process or puzzle over the words and feels he has not kept up with the flow of the transaction. (p. 467)

Singer (1977) cautions that grammatical errors, local dialects, and common slang expressions do *not* impair the sharing of attention and meaning, but rather it is the peculiar and *idiosyncratic* words and phrases that puzzle and distract, causing the listener to wonder: "*Did I really hear that? Did I get that right?*" (pp. 467–468).

The following are classified as language anomalies:

1. Ordinary words or phrases used oddly or out of context: Here ordinary and correctly pronounced words are used in odd, incorrect, or unexpected ways.

2. Odd sentence construction: Word order is peculiar and seems loose and at times almost random.

3. Peculiar, quaint, or private terms or phrases: The speaker makes up words or modifies common sayings in private, idiosyncratic ways.

4. Euphemisms: Rather than stating his meaning directly, the speaker expresses himself euphemistically.

5. Slips of the tongue: Here the listener must guess about the speaker's intended meaning.

6. Mispronounced words: These distract the listener.

7. Clang associations, rhymed phrases, and word play: Here the speaker shifts the listener's attention away from the message itself to the sounds of the words involved.

DISRUPTIONS

According to Singer (1977), certain remarks

> have a distracting, disrupting effect upon the listener. The listener as he hears these types of remarks says in effect to himself: *I can't keep up, I am losing track.* The speaker in one way or another diverts himself and the listener away from the shared task they set about to do. (p. 469)

The following are classified as disruptions:

1. Extraneous questions and remarks: Here the speaker disrupts the task or topic at hand, shifting to other issues instead.
2. Nonverbal disruptive behavior: The task is disrupted by nonverbal behavior that distracts or interferes.
3. Humor: Although in some contexts humor is an important social facilitator, it may also interfere with the accomplishment of a task and in these cases is seen as a disruption.
4. Swearing: When the use of profanity changes the general tone of transactions, it may be disruptive to the shared task.

Of all the categories of communication deviance, disruptions are the most intimately linked to the particular interactional context. The transactional model assumes that there is some task or job to be accomplished and examines the extent to which particular communication behaviors facilitate or impede getting the job done. This assumption is totally inappropriate for a cocktail party, for example, where there is no particular task at all, and rather than interfering with a job to be done, humor and wit are the order of the day. It does apply, however, to much of the day-to-day business of family life and survival: taking out the garbage, balancing the checkbook, and getting the kids fed and clothed.

CONTRADICTORY, ARBITRARY SEQUENCES

Singer (1977) describes this category of communication deviance as follows:

> The speaker contradicts himself, or violates the laws of logic in a variety of ways. The impact of these types of occurrences is to make a listener think: *I got it, but how can I deal with it?* He hears what the

speaker says, but it contradicts what he heard before, or the speaker is violating the rules of logic and the listener is caught not knowing quite what to do about what he hears. (p. 471)

Three types of contradictory, arbitrary sequences are identified:

1. Contradictory information: Remarks contradict what the speaker said earlier or statements, in themselves, are internally inconsistent.

2. Odd, tangential, or inappropriate responses to a preceding speaker: Non sequitur *replies* to a previous speaker.

3. Non sequitur reasoning: Reasoning fails to conform to the usual laws of logic.

TURN-TAKING PROBLEMS

A very basic feature of communication is that participants take turns at speaking (Duncan, 1972). Singer and Wynne do not distinguish this category of communication deviances because the prototypic interaction context used in their research is the individual Rorschach in which the subject interacts with an examiner and turn-taking behavior is quite rigidly prescribed (although they have studied couple and family Rorschach interactions as well). Two types of turn-taking problems can be distinguished:

1. Holding the floor: Here, a speaker keeps on talking rather than relinquishing the floor to give the listener an opportunity to respond.

2. Interrupting: In this case, one speaker attempts to take the floor before another has relinquished it, distracting from the message of the original speaker (Singer classifies interruptions as a type of disruption).

The Empirical Findings

Before applying the transactional model to an actual family case, let us examine Singer and Wynne's main empirical findings about communication deviance in the families of young adult schizophrenics.

These investigators have compared families in which there is a young adult schizophrenic with those in which the index offspring is diagnosed as borderline, character-disorder, neurotic, or normal. In a series of studies spanning more than 20 years, Singer and Wynne [see Wynne (1977) for a summary] have found that the sheer density of communication deviance (i.e., number of communication deviances per word spoken) in the speech of the parents successfully differentiates families of schizophrenics from those with index offspring with less severe diagnoses. The occurrence of *any* communication deviance in parental communication is not pathognomonic for schizophrenia in a child. In fact, communication deviance occurs at a low level in everyone's communication, without a pathological impairment in the ability to share a focus of attention. But, in the families of young adult schizophrenics, communication becomes so *saturated* with transactional difficulties that meaning is not transmitted.

In addition to this main finding, a few more specific results will be mentioned here. First, one parent may have a corrective influence on the communication of the other so that the impact on the child is less pathological. Singer and Wynne find (Singer, 1979) that if one parent's communication is full of communication deviance, while the other parent communicates in an essentially normal fashion, then the offspring's diagnosis will at worst be borderline, not schizophrenia.

Second, the parents of young adult schizophrenics who transact in such deviant ways themselves tend to be diagnosed as borderlines rather than schizophrenics (Singer, 1979). This finding helps explain the fact that the concordance rates for schizophrenia between parents and child are modest: When one parent is schizophrenic, 10 to 15 percent of their children will eventually be diagnosed as schizophrenic; when both parents are schizophrenic, the probability of a schizophrenic child increases to 30 to 40 percent (Mosher and Wynne, 1970). Although schizophrenics frequently have disturbed parents, the parental disturbance tends to stop short of clinical schizophrenia. It also lends some support to Bowen's (1966) oft-quoted statement that it takes three generations to make a schizophrenic (see discussion in Chapter 2).

Third, there is actually *more* communication deviance in the transactions of the parents of schizophrenics than in the speech of their offspring who have the more severe diagnosis (Wynne, 1977). This finding seems contradictory until one realizes that Wynne and Singer's original research goal was to predict the diagnosis of the child from parental communication samples. Communication deviances are those critical features of the family language environment that impair a young child's ability to learn to communicate effectively and, in adolescence or young adulthood, result in clinical schizophrenia. Singer argues (1974) that the Rorschach task used as an interaction prototype in much of their research is, in fact, an analogue of the kind of learning that goes on every day in families with young children. Children are always asking "Mommy, what's that?" and "Why do they call it that?" Parents are thus required to help their children name, explain, and reason about objects in their social environment in consensually validatable ways. These same types of naming and reasoning skills are tapped in the Rorschach task. Singer goes on to suggest that the subtle forms of thought and language disturbance seen in the (often borderline) parents of schizophrenics actually have a more insidious and pathological impact upon a young child than if the parent were frankly psychotic. In the latter case, it is much easier for the child to realize that "Mommy is talking crazy again" and turn elsewhere for help in testing reality.

Case Example

The Holmes family illustrates the application of the transactional model. Mr. Holmes was a white male in his forties with a diagnosis of chronic undifferentiated schizophrenia. His manner of speaking suggested a rural, Southern, lower-class background. He was referred for family consultation by the inpatient psychiatry unit where he was hospitalized following an incident in which he exposed himself to some young girls.

Mr. Holmes's therapist on the inpatient unit saw Mrs. Holmes and the couple's daughter Diane (age 13) as aligned against the patient. His solution to this problem was to request a family session to explore the issue of divorce. This is not an atypical *individual* approach to a family problem and such consultation questions are routinely presented to family therapists. You will see at the beginning of the interview how the family therapist (my colleague, Neil Scott) reframed the consultation question into one more appropriate and workable from the family therapy point of view.

Approach this transcript as an exercise in transactional assessment. In fact, pretend you are a coder hired to work on Singer and Wynne's research project. You have been given a coding manual (see the communication deviance section of this chapter, summarized in Figure 13) and your job is to mark the occurrence of all communication deviances in the transcript. Check your own observations with the commentary.

> (*The beginning of the consultation interview with the Holmes family: mother (M); father (F); daughter (D). Besides the family therapist (T), two other members of the family therapy team as well as the inpatient therapist Dr. Holt are sitting in on the session.*)

T: Maybe we could start with Mr. Holmes. The question that Dr. Holt has raised, he's saying that there's some question in his mind about whether the marriage will continue. And he's, I guess, done his part to get everybody rounded up so that question can be discussed. Is that. . . .

> (*Therapist begins by attempting to clarify for the family the context of the consultation interview.*)

F: (*Overlaps.*) Yes.

T: (*Continues.*) The way you understand it?

> (*So far, so good. Therapist and father appear to be sharing a focus of attention.*)

F: Yes. Ah, well I, see I usually sleep during the daytime to avoid fussing with her. Everything like that. And she, she constantly is on my back about something, about not doing chores right and stuff like that. And she's constantly fussing at me (*throws hands up in the air in a helpless gesture*). And I couldn't get my thoughts together or anything like that.

> (*Father's second "Yes" again leads a listener to believe that Mr. Holmes is sharing a focus of attention with therapist. Then father abruptly veers from the apparent shared focus without giving the listener any warning. This tangential response is scored E2, using the communication deviance codes in Figure 13.*)

T: Was it your expectation, uh, that that issue would get talked about here today? About. . . .

> (*Therapist tries again to focus with Mr. Holmes on the context of the interview.*)

F: (*Overlaps.*) Yes.

T: (*Continues.*) Ending the marriage.

F: Yes.

> (*Again, it appears that a focus of attention is being shared.*)

T: Did you want this session yourself?

F: Yes, I did. And she takes all the money and I never see but about twenty dollars a month. And all the money goes to her.

(And just as in the previous exchange, father indicates that he is tracking therapist in one breath only to respond tangentially in the next, E2.)

T: *(To Dr. Holt.)* It a, it's awkward to start out a family session with such a, a gangbuster of a question. Particularly when there are three people here *(indicates the family)* who don't know three other people *(gestures toward the family therapy team)*. Um, it also goes frankly, Dr. Holt, against one of my deepest convictions as a family therapist. And that is, at least to begin with, until I know a family really quite well, a matter of months, I never get involved in that question. In fact, I take the position that my job is to keep people together. If they want to separate it's something they have to do on their own. I'm not going to help them with that. I do that for a variety of reasons, some of which we can talk about later. But it's a very awkward position, at least as a family therapist, not as an individual therapist, but as a family therapist, to wade into a system where that's the question on the table. And before I turn to other members of the family and go ahead a bit, I, I feel I have to do a little more work to get to know the family. Of course, the question is on the table and we can't ignore it, I guess.

(Two strikes and he is out: Therapist gives up on getting anything clear with father on this point and turns instead to the referring therapist. Here therapist does a bit of teaching of the intern therapist and reframes the interview in a manner consistent with his own family therapy perspective. The particular position that therapist takes here is in part inspired by an article by Carl Whitaker—Whitaker and Miller, 1969.)

T: *(Turns back to family.)* Let, let's get acquainted just a little bit. *(To daughter.)* Can, can you tell me your name, please? *(Daughter turns her head away.)* Are you shy? *(Daughter continues to look away.)*

(Therapist now begins to join the family by getting acquainted first with the daughter. Daughter's shy, reluctant behavior is not altogether atypical for an adolescent in an initial family interview, although her reluctance to respond is more extreme than that of most teenagers.)

M: Yeah. *(Laughs.)*

(Here mother speaks for daughter in a protective way, breaking the tension with her laugh.)

T: Let's just sit for a minute. We don't have to say anything.

(Seventeen-second pause during which daughter steals a glance at therapist.)

T: *(To daughter.)* Can you draw?

(When his backing off produces no more verbal response from daughter than did his questioning, therapist decides on another tack.)

D: (*Looks again at therapist, giggles and gives an equivocal reply, and looks away.*)

T: (*Therapist asks another family team member to get drawing supplies from the next room. He then turns again to daughter.*) What is your name?

D: (*Barely audible.*) Diane.

(*This time therapist succeeds in getting the barest response from daughter.*)

T: Diane?

D: (*Nods agreement.*)

T: Diane. And you're how old?

D: Thirteen and a half.

T: Really. Let's see, I have to think. Thirteen and a half. That must mean you're in the eleventh grade?

D: No.

T: (*Emphatically indicates surprise.*) No? What?

D: Seventh.

T: Seventh. Eleventh, ugh. (*Knocks on head in a how-could-I-be-so-dumb gesture.*) You're right. That's, that's about where you should be. You just started school this fall?

(*Here therapist does a deliberate one-down maneuver in an attempt to reduce the gap between daughter and himself and make her more comfortable.*)

D: (*Nods agreement.*)

T: Seventh grade. You like seventh grade?

D: Yes.

T: You go to a junior high?

D: Yes.

T: Uh-huh. You have girlfriends?

D: Lots of 'em.

(*Daughter appears to be warming up a bit by now.*)

T: Lots of them, yeah. (*Team member returns with art supplies. Therapist continues to speak with daughter.*) Would you mind drawing me a picture?

D: Of what?

T: I'd like for you to draw a picture of the family, including yourself, with everybody doing something.

(*This is a classic art therapy task called the kinetic family drawing—Burns and Kaufman, 1970. Even if you ignore the expressive aspects of the task and make no interpretations of the drawings, it is very useful to have this task—along with some drawing materials—in your bag of tricks. Then when confronted with a shy adolescent or with a rowdy four-year-old, you have the option of giving them something else to do in the session. If you do ask a family member to draw during a session, make sure that you look at the drawings and make the appropriate murmurs before the sessions ends.)*

D: I can't do that.

T: It's no art contest. It doesn't have to be anything uh, for anybody but you and me. But a picture of the family, including yourself, with everybody doing something. (*Hands paper, crayons, and colored pens to daughter.*) Are you surprised at this meeting today? (*Daughter giggles and hides her face.*) I'm trying to think if I were thirteen or fourteen and I came to a meeting I'd probably be scared to death.

(*Daughter's response here is typical and therapist reassures her that an artistic production is not expected. Finally, therapist makes one last attempt to engage daughter verbally.*)

D: I don't know what to draw.

(*And daughter chooses to ignore therapist's last statement and responds instead to the less threatening drawing task.*)

T: Well, think about it a bit. I don't mean to put pressure on you. I just want to get acquainted a little better.

M: (*Speaks to daughter in very staccato style which is difficult to understand.*) Well, draw what he asked you to draw.

D: What are you supposed to be doing?

M: I don't know. Whatever you draw comes to your mind.

(*Here mother's odd sentence construction is a language anomaly, C2, of an especially insidious kind. We normally would say "draw whatever comes to your mind," which implies that the direction is from inside (the mind) to outside (the paper). Mother's statement "whatever you draw comes to your mind" reverses this sequence, suggesting that instead inside follows outside. The impact of such a statement is to distort the usual notion of personal boundaries, inside versus outside.*)

T: Anything at all is perfectly okay. (*To mother.*) Mrs. Holmes, tell me, uh, I want to talk just a little bit with you. Uh, tell me your name please.

M: Mary.

T: Mary?

M: Right.

T: You have other kids?

M: No. Just the one.

T: Diane. And how old are you?

M: Forty.

T: Forty. Let's see, you guys live in (*names town about an hour's drive away*)?

(*By now therapist and mother have fallen into a stereotyped interaction pattern. Mother is withholding and unresponsive; therapist asks closed-ended questions that maximize the likelihood of a response, but also make it easy for mother to continue to give only minimal replies.*)

M: Right.

T: So you had to drive down here today.

M: Right. (*Abruptly laughs very loudly in a manner completely out of context. Laughter ceases as abruptly as it began.*)

(*A disruption, D3.*)

T: Was that a hassle, problem?

M: No, not really.

(*Here mother avoids committing herself in a transactional context that requests commitment, A5. This particular occurrence appears so benign and ordinary that it might not be scored as communication deviance at all. However, you will quickly see that it is part of a developing pattern.*)

T: Have you been coming down here often?

M: Well, we were down here Saturday.

(*Again mother avoids committing herself, A5, and the listener is left to guess at her intended meaning.*)

T: How long have you and your husband been married?

(*By soliciting personal information, therapist is attempting to join mother.*)

M: Twenty years.

T: Uh-huh. Twenty years?

M: Twenty-one next month.

T: You, you've lasted a lot longer than most people.

(*Here therapist intensifies his effort to join by complimenting mother.*)

M: I guess.

(*Another noncommittal response, A5.*)

T: (*Laughs.*) Were you, uh, surprised, a, or did you know that this session was some way set up to talk about continuing the marriage or not?

M: No.

T: (*Begins to speak.*)

M: (*Overlaps.*) I didn't have a foggy what was going on.

    (*Here mother uses another language anomaly, C1. The ordinary phrase, "I didn't have the foggiest notion. . . ." is transposed into the odd form "I didn't have a foggy. . . ."*)

T: Really?

M: Right.

T: What was you, what did you expect might happen here today?

M: I don't know.

    (*Mother avoids commitment, A5. Here again, this might not be scored as communication deviance except for the context of commitment problems within which it occurs.*)

T: Do you have anything particular you'd like to have happen?

M: Well, I don't know if separation's going to solve the problem what he's been doing. And I think it's more that, you know, the excuse of getting out to solve the problem what he's been doing.

    (*This very difficult-to-follow response contains several communication deviances. First of all, it's a tangential response to therapist, E2: If we work at it we can see the connection between mother's response and therapist's question, but she does not give the listener much help. Second, the first sentence is oddly constructed, C2. And finally, her final sentence contains abandoned, abruptly ceased remarks, A1.*)

T: Uh-huh. Do you think that question of separation is something we should be talking about here today?

M: Whatever.

    (*Mother again avoids committing self, A5.*)

T: If you didn't know about it, I, I'm concerned that you not feel like you're walking into some kind of an ambush.

M: Well (*laughs*), that's what it feels like.

    (*Therapist's empathic response results in an emotional breakthrough in the interview. Mother clearly relaxes and softens as therapist succeeds in joining her. You will see shortly, however, that this change in the affective tone does not cure mother's communication deviance.*)

T: Does it? Le, let's, let's hear a little bit more about what it feels like.

M: Well, it just feels like you're walking in and don't know what the heck's going on.

T: And your husband comes in the hospital and the next thing you're invited to a family session. . . .

M: (*Overlaps.*) Right.

T: (*Continues.*) And the next thing you're talking about, a, separation. This for a woman who's been married 21 years.

M: Right. But, you know, it's just the thought of bringing him down here to, uh, turn around and get his problems solved out.

(*As with father in therapist's first exchanges with him, the therapist's successful sharing of a focus of attention with mother is abruptly ended by her tangential response, E2. In addition, her speech contains a language anomaly, C3: The peculiar expression "problems solved out." Here mother has combined two common phrases, "problems solved" and "problems worked out," into a single odd usage.*)

T: Uh, huh. (*Daughter glances at mother several times.*) You are doing fine, Diane. (*Daughter hides her face behind the drawing paper and whispers to her mother. Therapist again speaks to mother.*) Do you think that part of your daughter's shyness is that maybe she feels a little ambushed, too?

M: (*Nods agreement.*)

T: Yeah. That's what I think. Is she normally shy?

M: Oh.

T: A little?

M: A little bit with people until after she gets to know you from let's say the first time then the second time she's pretty well, uh, from walking into something like this here it's. . . .

(*This response is so difficult to follow that even after dozens of close listenings it is not possible to be sure that this is an accurate transcription of what mother said. It is an extreme example of abandoned, abruptly ceased remarks, A1, which leave the listener with no idea of what the speaker is committed to and is therefore worthy of attention. There appear to be at least four fragments of ideas in this short speech. But mother hops so quickly from one to the next that the listener cannot keep up. And she gives the listener no help at all in following her intended meaning.*)

T: Uh-huh.

What is remarkable in the above interview segment is that Mrs. Holmes, who is not the identified patient and, so far as is known, has never been psychiatrically labeled or treated, shows as much (or more) communication deviance as does her diagnosed schizophrenic husband. This illustrates Singer and Wynne's success at identifying subtle forms of thinking and language difficulties. It also suggests that, with two parents who transact in deviant ways, the daughter is at risk for the development of clinical schizophrenia in adolescence or young adulthood.

In a further attempt to join the family, the therapist turned at this point to Don Jackson's (1965) marital quid pro quo question (see discussion in Chapter 7). Notice in the following segment how therapist sets the stage for the quid pro quo question in order to enhance its impact.

> *T: (Speaks to Mrs. Holmes.)* Well, I'll tell you what I'd like to do to begin with here. Rather than talk about separation right now. As an opener that's not a particularly good way to open up a session. I'd like to take you back to earlier times. I have a question that I frankly like to ask everybody. I've asked, maybe, five hundred people. And I'd like to ask both you and your husband. And I want you to listen, Diane, because kids love to hear this question answered. Sometimes they know it already. The question is, "Of all the millions of people in the world, how did the two of you get together?"
>
> *(Therapist labels a clear shift from one topic to another as he moves to obtain the quid pro quo. This generally works better than attempting to slide into it on the heels of something the family has been discussing. Therapist then frames his question by informing the family that he routinely asks it and that he has asked it of many people before. And he sets the stage structurally by indicating that the question is for mother and father, but daughter will likely wish to listen in. Finally, therapist pops the question, in a somewhat formal, dramatic manner.)*
>
> *(Twelve-second pause. Daughter giggles quietly.)*
>
> *M:* Through a girlfriend of mine.
>
> *(Eventually, mother begins.)*
>
> *T:* Let's hear your side of it. I'm interested in. . . .
>
> *(And therapist indicates that he wishes to speak with mother about the question.)*
>
> *M: (Overlaps.)* Well, she just up and called one night.
>
> *T:* Uh-huh.
>
> *F:* She called and I picked took the phone away from her. We was at the same house. And I talked to Mary.
>
> *(Here father's inconsistent and ambiguous references—she, her, we—leave the listener totally adrift as to who he is talking about, B3. In an attempt to clarify the matter here, therapist now abandons his usual strategy of interviewing the first spouse who responds.)*
>
> *T: (Confused.)* Who called?
>
> *(Therapist is genuinely confused, with good reason.)*

F: Her girlfriend.

T: (*To mother.*) Your girlfriend.

M: Right.

T: Phoned?

(*And therapist must plod along to try to make sense of what is being said.*)

M: Oh, well, a girl that I knew goin' through school.

T: Uh-huh. She phoned who?

F: She phoned Mary. And then I took the phone away from her 'cause we was at the same house and I knew the girl and I talked to Mary and told her I'd be out there in 15 minutes and she told me I wouldn't. Fifteen minutes later I was knockin' on the door.

(*Here again father's inconsistent and ambiguous references, B3, make his speech extremely difficult to follow. His use of the logical construction "'cause" is also an example of non sequitur reasoning, E3. Put yourself in therapist's shoes and imagine trying to track father here, without the aid of a transcript.*)

T: (*Slowly.*) Knocking on?

(*Therapist grabs at the last thing father says and tries to get that clarified.*)

F: Mary's door.

T: Mary's door (*turns to rest of family team*), I'm, I'm confused. Did I, what did I miss? (*To mother.*) The, the, your girlfriend phoned (*inflection implies a question*) you (*therapist answers own question*).

(*Therapist's response here is appropriate and in fact diagnostic of the communication deviance. Then, in the face of the unfollowable transactions, therapist turns to the rest of the team for a bit of reality testing before turning back to mother.*)

M: The girlfriend (*stops, then whispers to herself.*) Let's see. Okay. (*Resumes normal speaking voice.*) The fellow that he used to run around with was the girl's, was the uncle of the girl.

(*Here mother is clearly making a supreme effort to assit therapist in following. She uses subvocal speech as an aid, slowing herself down and patiently supplying the missing referents. However, she supplies detail that is only tangential to a clarification of the basic story.*)

T: (*Overlaps.*) Ahhh.

(*Therapist is very eager, even desperate, to understand.*)

M: (*Continues.*) And a bunch of the guys used to go up to the house.

T: I see.

(Therapist indicates that he follows before he likely does understand. The danger here is that therapist joins the family's pseudo-mutual system, pretending along with them that he follows the unfollowable.)

M: *(To her husband.)* Wasn't Fred the uncle?

F: Yeah.

T: *(To father.)* So you and Fred were friends.

F: *(Nods agreement.)*

M: They were in the service together.

T: Ahh. Okay. *(To mother.)* And your girlfriend phoned you, but while she was talking to you he took the phone away?

(By this time therapist really does appear to have put it together. Notice how much effort it took, both on his part and on mother's.)

M: Right.

T: Um. *(To mother.)* H, how was that?

M: Don't remember all those details that I *(laughs, and rest of sentence is unintelligible).*

T: *(Laughs.)* P, people generally do remember the details of their first meeting, actually.

(Therapist gently pushes mother to continue with the quid pro quo by informing her that most people do recall such details.)

M: That's too long ago.

T: *(To father.)* Do you remember taking the phone away?

(After pushing mother again and getting nowhere, therapist gives up and turns to father.)

F: Yeah, I was drunk.

T: Oh yeah?

F: And I took the phone away and I talked to Mary. And then I went up to her house.

T: Huh.

F: And then she said "Hi" and I was sober as if I hadn't had a drink.

(Here father uses a very interesting construction, suggesting a logical connection between mother's saying "Hi" and his sobering up. This is a form of non sequitur reasoning, C3. It will be clear in what follows that from this point therapist proceeds on the belief that father is making a logical connection.)

T: Huh. You had sobered up or you *(rest of sentence unintelligible as father overlaps.)*

F: *(Overlaps.)* Yeah, I had *(emphasizes)* sobered up.

T: Uh-huh.

F: And we went to a coffee shop and had coffee. That, that ended my drinking.

(*Here father states explicitly that there was a connection between meeting his wife and ending his drinking.*)

T: Really?

F: Yeah (*smiles broadly*).

T: Really?

F: Um-hum. I have one beer about every six months now.

T: I'm always interested in ways people find to quit drinking. How, how did that work out for you.

(*By now it is clear that therapist is in pursuit of the implied logical connection.*)

F: It worked out all right.

(*And father is not providing it.*)

T: You, you quit drinking then when you met, ah. . . .

F: (*Overlaps.*) Yeah.

T: Mary?

F: Yeah.

T: What was there, uh, about the meeting that had to do with the drinking?

(*Finally therapist asks explicitly for a statement of the logical connection.*)

F: I I don't know. I don't have any idea.

(*And there is none.*)

T: If we knew that we might be able to help a lot of people stop drinking.

F: (*Laughs.*) I know.

T: Have you ever talked to her about the effect she has on you?

F: No, I couldn't. I just, hold it in me.

T: (*To mother.*) Did you know you stopped his drinking?

(*Therapist turns to mother in one last attempt to uncover the implied connection.*)

M: Well, it doesn't show it now. (*Laughs.*)

(*Without success.*)

T: You've run out of magic?

M: Whatever. He's got a mind of his own.

(*Another commitment problem, A5.*)

T: You remember his coming that night?

M: Yeah.

T: Did you think he'd been drinking?

M: I know he was drinking.

T: Oh, you knew it? You knew it over the phone?

M: Right.

T: Uh-huh. What was your reaction to his drinking?

M: Just another dumb, drunk sailor, that's all.

T: Did you say anything to him about the drinking?

M: No.

T: At what point did you know that this was the man that you wanted to marry?

> (*Finally therapist abandons the unproductive line of questioning and returns to a typical quid pro quo follow-up question.*)

M: I didn't, did I? (*Laughs.*)

T: Well you must've at some point. You did get married to him. When did you make up your mind?

M: I don't know. Just a couple of weeks later. I don't know why.

T: A couple weeks?

M: Whatever.

> (*Here and in the following transactions with therapist, mother returns to the pattern of avoiding commitment, A5, in her replies.*)

T: What was there about him that attracted you, caught your eye?

M: I don't know.

T: There must have been something about him. His person, his personality.

M: I don't remember.

T: You're getting shy now too. (*Therapist and parents laugh together. Daughter now pushes her drawing into mother's hands. After watching mother and daughter interact about the drawing, therapist asks daughter about it.*)

> (*After several more attempts to obtain the quid pro quo, therapist gives up. Instead, he accepts daughter's intrusion into the discussion with her parents and inquires about her drawing.*)

Although we referred the Holmes family to a therapist near their home, they reportedly did not make an appointment and were lost to further follow-up.

Learning Transactional Assessment

Of the four family systems models presented here, the transactional model is perhaps the most difficult to learn. When I present the above case on videotape in a lecture, someone invariably questions the first or second instance of communication deviance on the grounds that *he/she* could understand what Mr. Holmes really meant to say. This is a common and understandable reaction, but one that so seriously interferes with learning transactional assessment that it bears discussion here.

A humorous, but absolutely on-target example of this phenomenon occurs in Peter Sellers' movie *Being There*. In it, Chauncey Gardener, a very unworldly, sheltered, intellectually limited man is suddenly thrust into circumstances of increasing prominence. He babbles nonsense no one understands, but because everyone appears to think that Gardener is Einstein and Gandhi rolled into one, none are willing to admit that they do not understand what he is saying.

An interesting preliminary observation (Singer, 1979) from Singer and Wynne's current prospective study at the University of Rochester (Doane et al., 1982) illustrates this point. In this investigation, the school-age sons of mothers of schizophrenics are being followed for five years. By the age of eight or nine, these young boys have already been identified by their peers on sociometric ratings as different and shunned, whereas teachers' ratings do not distinguish them from other children their age. Singer explains this finding by noting that the young schoolmates of these subject boys are not as well socialized as are their teachers. They have not yet learned to compensate for and fill in the gaps in the transactions of these children who are already communicating in deviant, difficult-to-follow ways. Instead of making allowances and working hard to understand as the teachers do, the peers shun these boys and seek the company of children who are easier to follow and deal with.

So the message is clear: In order to successfully assess transactional difficulties, we must become more like little children. That is, we must give up the socially learned assumption that the other person is making sense and that we must work hard to understand what he or she is saying.

This is a tall order, especially for us therapists who have been trained to be empathic and understanding, above all. Perhaps a bit of reframing will help. Suppose you have a patient whose speech is filled with communication deviance and you pretend to understand and work very hard to fill in the gaps and look for the underlying meaning (a pseudo-mutual relationship). Then this patient leaves your office and tries to go about his daily business with a bus driver, or a bank teller, who is not as empathic and understanding and good at making sense of the patient's deviant communication. How have you helped your patient survive in the outside social world? Or the patient leaves your office with his children and attempts to teach them to survive? How have you improved the social learning environment of these children?

Intervention in the Transactional Model

As with any good clinical model, the diagnosis of what is wrong with a family's transactions (communication deviance, in this case) leads logically to a prescription for intervention: Fix them. The therapist in the transactional model functions as a kind of transaction broker (to continue the business metaphor a bit further).

This job has two parts. First, make sure that *you* are sharing a focus of attention with the family member who is speaking. If the therapist is unable to grasp what the speaker is talking about, it is unlikely that other family members really understand and follow. This needs a bit of discussion, since it is a popular belief that each family communicates successfully in private, idiosyncratic ways that are perfectly transparent to its members even though they may be opaque to therapists and other outsiders. Although there is, in general, a certain amount of truth to this assumption, it simply is not true in the families of schizophrenics that people understand each other perfectly well. Rather, as Wynne and his colleagues pointed out (Wynne et al., 1958), these family members relate in a pseudo-mutual way built on a pervasive but false sense that they all understand each other.

And even if it were true that communication *within* the families of schizophrenics is thoroughly adequate, we as therapists still do these family members no favors by buying into and going along with their idiosyncratic transactional style. Such communication fails within the larger social world and thus compromises the ability of the family members to survive outside the family. The therapist in the transactional model must be the agent of consensually validatable meaning.

Second, your job as a transactional therapist is to help family members share foci of attention with each other. That is, once you are able to share a focus of attention with person A, then you help B get involved in the transaction, sharing the same focus of attention.

The specific content of the transactions is immaterial in this model, although much of the work often centers around tasks (household chores, child care, managing money) crucial to the family's day-to-day functioning. Margaret Singer often does therapy in her home around her kitchen table, a very natural place to assemble a family to help them conduct such mundane but necessary business. The interventions themselves typically have an educative flavor. For example, "Now wait a minute, you just lost me there so we need to back up. You were talking about finding a baby sitter. See if you can spell that out so that your wife can follow along with you."

Transactional work is slow, difficult, and often tedious. It is not flashy like paradox nor dramatic like some of the structural interventions. But, as I will argue in the next chapter, it is the place to begin treatment with these severely disturbed families. Such work begins to pay off as the family becomes better able to meet its survival needs. And it helps pave the way for other work to follow.

The Function of Communication Deviance

The focus of this chapter has been on communication deviance. The reason here is pragmatic: To use the transactional model clinically, one must learn to listen to an entirely new level of communication. Singer and Wynne emphasized communication deviance for analogous pragmatic reasons: Such a focus allowed them to do empirical research.

On a theoretical, rather than a pragmatic level, communication deviance is problematic because it focuses our attention on mechanistic explanation while obscuring the teleologic. To understand the *function* of communication deviance it is necessary to go back to Wynne's original paper (Wynne et al., 1958; also see Chapter 2). There he suggested that *the function of* what came to be called *communication deviance is to prevent the emergence of difference.* Communication in the families of schizophrenics is either so vague and amorphous or so fragmented (Wynne and Singer, 1963) that differences between people and, consequently, individual boundaries themselves, fail to develop. Furthermore, disordered communication and blurred individual boundaries are complementary phenomena. One way of seeing this is to invoke a formula from one of Jay Haley's early papers on schizophrenia. Haley (1959) says that every communication involves four aspects: (1) *I* (2) am saying *something* (3) to *you* (4) in *this situation*. If the "something" is unintelligible or somehow inappropriate to "this situation" because it is saturated with communication deviance, then the boundaries of the "I" and the "you" will be vague, or distorted, as well.

Ultimately, in adolescence and young adulthood when society expects offspring to become emancipated from such families, the individual boundaries necessary for the young person to leave the family and establish a separate life are lacking, and clinical schizophrenia develops.

Another aspect of the function of transactional disorder can be seen by examining the family's modes of handling interpersonal conflict. It was suggested in Chapter 5 that the hallmark of families with structural problems is their lack of effective methods for resolving conflict. The families of schizophrenics deal with conflict in a more primitive and even more pathological way: Their organization makes real interpersonal conflict *impossible*. When communication is so amorphous or fragmented that differences between people cannot even be identified, and individual boundaries are so poorly defined that people are not differentiated enough from one another to really fight each other, true conflict is simply not possible. There is, instead, the sticky kind of togetherness that Wynne et al. (1958) termed pseudo-mutuality. And it is impossible to ever really get out of such families because, no matter what the young person does, the vague and/or constantly shifting family norms are redefined so as to encompass the offspring's new behavior (the "rubber fence" phenomenon).

9

A Second-Order Model:
Systemic Psychopathology

The ideas described in this chapter began with the question: How can the various approaches to family systems therapy be differentiated from each other and integrated into a coherent framework? I suggested in Chapter 1 that it is time the family therapy field took up the question of integration. Once I began teaching family therapy as well as practicing it, I found it impossible to avoid grappling with the issue. This struggle led me eventually not only to an integrative framework for the clinical models discussed so far in Part 1, but also to a new *systemic psychopathology*, that is, a psychopathology of the individual seen from the perspective of systems thinking and cybernetics.

Toward an Integrative Framework

As I settled in my clinical work and teaching upon the four clinical models described in the preceding chapters, at first I implicitly operated from the position that the therapist is perfectly free to choose among these models, more or less to suit his/her fancy. However, my clinical work gradually convinced me that certain approaches are better suited to some families than to others. But then, how does one choose?

Two sources provided useful stimulation at this point. First, I came across a thoughtful article by Burke et al. (1979), in which the authors suggest a rationale for choosing among the various psychodynamic brief therapy models. They argue that each model is especially suited for a particular stage of the adult life cycle [as described by Erik Erickson (1963)] and advocate using these stages to tailor the therapy to the patient. Perhaps, I thought, a similar sort of "developmental" dimension could be useful in selecting an appropriate family therapy model.

And second, Mady Chalk (1979), describing her work at the Yale Psychiatric Institute with schizophrenic and borderline adolescents and young adults and their families, suggested that with psychotic patients one should begin with communication work, move on to structural work, and eventually (after a year and one-half to two years) switch to object relations work. So maybe, I wondered, the model of choice changes during the course of treatment.

I found the beginnings of the unifying scheme I was looking for in Vaillant's *Adaptation to Life* (1977). Working from a psychodynamic framework, Vaillant asks: What are the defensive/adaptive strategies used by individuals across their life-spans? And do these coping mechanisms change over the years? Vaillant places defensive/adaptive strategies on a continuum ranging from the most primitive and pathological to the most normal, healthy, and adaptive. He divides this entire range of psychological functioning into four broad levels, which he labels psychotic, immature, neurotic, and mature. This way of ordering and comparing an *individual's level of functioning* led me not only to a framework for integrating family therapy models, but eventually to a systemic reconceptualization of psychopathology as well.

In this chapter, I reverse the evolutionary process just described. First, systemic psychopathology is outlined. Second, this new point of view is used to differentiate the four family systems models presented so far in Part 1 and, third, integrate them using a *second-order model* based upon systemic psychopathology. Fourth, various therapy schools are discussed in terms of systemic psychopathology and the second-order model. And fifth, the second-order model is illustrated with some additional interview excerpts from the Bach family first presented in Chapter 4.

Systemic Psychopathology

THE FOCUS OF FAMILY SYSTEMS THERAPY

I argued in Chapter 3 that, contrary to popular belief, family systems therapy is not "about" families at all, but rather about individual persons viewed in their social contexts, in particular, the family.

The difference between family systems therapy and traditional ways of understanding human problems is therefore not a difference in focus, but rather a difference in approach to understanding and explaining a common object of interest.

Traditionally, psychopathology has been viewed nonsystemically, with disturbed behavior explained mechanistically in terms of some parts inside the person (e.g., psychic structures, biological systems). My purpose here is to recast psychopathology in systemic terms: that is, to take the same disturbed behavior displayed by the individual, but to describe it in its social context.

In particular, I assume with Vaillant (1977) that, at any given time, an individual's psychosocial functioning corresponds to some position on a continuum ranging from least healthy and adaptive to most mature and competent. Furthermore, I use Vaillant's traditional division of the level of functioning scale into four broad ranges: psychotic, immature, neurotic, and mature. The task is then to describe in systemic terms the functioning of individuals at each of these general levels. Before doing so, I first outline the view of development underlying this systemic psychopathology.

PSYCHOSOCIAL DEVELOPMENT

Heinz Werner (1948) based his view of cognitive development on the biological principle of orthogenesis. This link with biology makes Werner's work particularly compatible with systems thinking, which also grew out of biology (Bertalanffy, 1968). Except for Wynne and Singer (1963), however, family therapists have incorporated little of Werner's developmental theory.

Werner saw development as characterized by complementary processes of *differentiation* and *integration*. The developmental process begins with the differentiation of parts from the whole, followed by their integration with each other into a hierarchically organized organism of greater complexity. Further differentiation is again followed by still more integration as development proceeds. For example, the original single cell of the human embryo successively differentiates into all of the body's organ systems, which are in turn integrated at higher and higher levels of complexity. By the end of the first eight weeks of pregnancy, the embryo's biological organization is essentially identical to the adult's ("How Human Life Begins," 1982, p. 39). Werner argues that the much longer process of psychosocial development also occurs through a process of successive differentiation and integration.

LEVELS OF FUNCTIONING

I now describe the levels of psychosocial functioning in systemic terms, linking them by using Werner's developmental notion. That is, as the level of functioning rises from psychotic through immature and neurotic to mature, developmental level rises, with successive differentiation and integration and increasing complexity and organization. After defining each level, I then go back and, in the next section, discuss their interrelationships, focusing on the transitions from one level to the next.

Psychotic. The first necessary step in psychosocial development is the differentiation of the individual self from others in the social environment.

"Persons" functioning at the psychotic level suffer from a basic failure to achieve this differentiation. It is necessary to qualify their description as "individuals" or "persons" because, in the ordinary ways we use language, these terms already connote the differentiation that is lacking at this level. Because of this fundamental lack of differentiation, it is a logical error to see schizophrenia, for example, as "in" the person labeled schizophrenic. The individual diagnosed schizophrenic is a poorly differentiated part of a larger social system in which psychosocial development stopped almost before it began. (Note that this description of psychotic functioning ignores the question of etiology and does not rule out the contribution of biological factors.)

Beginning with the early days of the field, when the initial focus was on schizophrenia, family therapists have reminded us of the error of attributing pathology to the individual rather than to the larger system. More recently the Milan group, also working with psychotic-level problems, has emphasized (Selvini Palazzoli et al., 1978) the ways in which language constrains our thinking and forces us to make individual attributions.

From these observations of schizophrenics and their families, some family systems thinkers have gone on to insist that one make *no* attributions about individuals. Such thinking led to the idea that family systems therapy is about families, that the family is the patient, etc. This stance is also expressed in the anti-diagnosis position common in the field.

I will argue here that, although at the psychotic level of functioning it truly does not make sense to speak of the "individual" in its usual sense, the notion of a "person" or an "individual self" takes on meaning as one moves up the scale of functioning and the level of differentiation and integration rises. At the risk of appearing unfashionable or being imprecise, I will use the words person and individual without quotation marks, with the understanding that the meaning of these terms changes depending upon the level of functioning under consideration.

Implicit in this whole chapter is the conviction that diagnosis, in the sense of assessing an individual's level of psychosocial functioning, is essential for family systems therapy.

Persons functioning at the psychotic level have unclear individual boundaries. They do not really know where they leave off and the next person begins and do not distinguish clearly between personal (internal) and social (external) reality. In a profound sense, they are one with their social environment. In the early days of the field, Bowen (1961) introduced the phrase "undifferentiated family ego mass" to describe this phenomenon as he observed it in families of schizophrenics. And Wynne et al. (1958) coined the term "pseudomutuality" to mean a sense of relatedness based upon the lack of personal boundaries.

How is it that self/other differentiation fails in psychotic-level families? This lack of individual boundaries is related to the nature of communication in such families. For self/other differentiation to occur, the family system (i.e., the family members plus their behavior with each other) must contain information in the precise Batesonian (Bateson, 1971) sense of "a difference that makes a difference." In families of schizophrenics, the information necessary for such differentiation is lacking.

Singer and Wynne (1966) describe the "communication deviances" occurring in families of schizophrenics that preclude the establishment of difference. Using Werner's developmental notions, they see (Wynne and Singer, 1963) the most primitive kinds of communication deviance as failures of differentiation in language itself, the "amorphous" transactions that are so vague and unclear they could refer to almost anything or to nothing at all. Developmentally higher, but still within the psychotic range, Singer and Wynne distinguish "fragmented" communications, in which the speaker hops from one meaning to another so quickly and without warning, or communicates multiple meanings, so that the listener either becomes hopelessly lost or is left with contradictory messages that cannot be integrated. The latter case includes the famous double bind first discussed by Bateson and Jackson and their colleagues (1956).

Besides making self/other differentiation impossible, such communication also precludes the establishment of a coherent and consensually validatable view of reality. These twin problems of (1) blurred individual boundaries and (2) disturbances in the use of language and in the perception of reality are central and unique to the psychotic level of functioning and (by definition) do not occur at higher levels of functioning.

Immature. This discussion of immature-level functioning encompasses two classes of patients not often considered together: those traditionally labeled character disordered, in particular sociopaths, and psychosomatic patients. [Vaillant (1977), for reasons which are unclear, specifically *excludes* psychosomatics from his discussion of immature functioning.]

The cybernetics of the immature level is diagrammed in Figure 14B. At this level of functioning, it now does make sense to speak of an individual in the ordinary sense of a separate person. However, the behavior of this individual is seen as cybernetically linked directly and tightly to its underlying biological mechanisms, on one hand, and to the behavior of others in the social environment, on the other.

For contrast, the cybernetics of the psychotic level of functioning is presented in Figure 14A. There, "fuzzy" boundaries distinguish the behavior of the individual from the social context and the informational links between them are also "fuzzy."

Two brief examples, one from the research literature and one from the clinical realm, illustrate the descriptive paradigm appropriate to the immature level of functioning. Rose and his colleagues (1975) experimentally manipulated the social organization of a

SYSTEMIC LEVEL

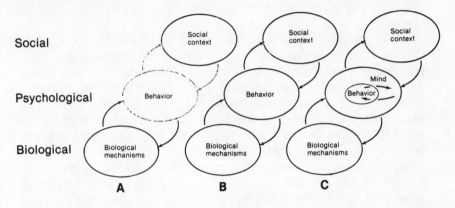

Figure 14. Systemic psychopathology at three levels of psychosocial functioning. (A) The cybernetics of the psychotic level. (B) The cybernetics of the immature level. (C) The cybernetics of the neurotic level.

group of rhesus monkeys and found that following defeat and loss of status in the group's dominance hierarchy, the males' plasma testosterone levels fell by approximately 80 percent. The authors (Rose et al., 1975) invoked a cybernetic paradigm to describe their results:

> It is possible that following defeat in a social group, the associated fall in testosterone is adaptive. We would invoke the feedback loop explanation to say that defeat produces the fall in testosterone and that this lower level decreases the probability of aggressive action on the part of the [vanquished] subject, thus precluding instigation of additional combat and repeated defeats. (p. 60)

These findings are consistent with the paradigm of Figure 14B, in which mutual regulatory processes involving both biological and social levels are seen to influence the individual animal's behavior. In particular, modifications in the social environment result in changes in behavior and biology.

Minuchin's psychosomatic work (Minuchin et al., 1978) provides an example closer to home for family therapists. Marital conflict in the child's social environment leads to emotional arousal in all family members. As this tension reaches some critical level, the child in some way or other becomes involved in the conflict.

This involvement results in *less* arousal in the parents as their marital conflict subsides, but *more* arousal in the child. A marital crisis is avoided, but often at the price of the child's psychosomatic crisis.

This was dramatically demonstrated by Minuchin and his colleagues in an experiment using psychosomatic diabetics and their families in which free fatty acid levels in the blood were monitored during conflictual family interaction. Free fatty acid level has been related to emotional arousal (Bogdonoff and Nichols, 1964) and, for the diabetic, is part of the metabolic sequence leading to the onset of the psychosomatic symptom. As the child watched from behind a one-way mirror while her parents fought, all family members' emotional arousal increased, as measured by free fatty acid concentration. When the child was brought into the room and subsequently became enmeshed in the parents' discussion (as described in Chapter 4), her free fatty acid level continued to climb while the parents' levels dropped.

At high enough levels of arousal outside the experimental situation, a psychosomatic crisis is triggered and the subsequent behavior necessary to care for the child (e.g., a trip to the emergency room) greatly alters, at least for a time, the nature of the marital interaction. In this case, the child can be seen as sacrificing his/her own internal biological regulation for the good of the family's social regulation and in order to regulate the parents' internal states.

Focusing for a moment on the role of the social context in the paradigm diagrammed in Figure 14B, immature-level individuals traditionally labeled character disordered are those whose behavior is inordinately controlled by others in their social environment and who, in turn, control the behavior of others to an extreme degree. Put another way, their behavior is tightly linked, in a cybernetic sense, to their social context. In fact, from the point of view of systemic psychopathology, character disorder is simply the ways an individual typically manages his social context (and is, in turn, managed by it). What distinguishes character pathology from normal behavior-in-context is the "tightness" of the cybernetic link between behavior and the social context. This view of character disorder is consistent with that of Ackerman (1960), who saw it as a social phenomenon requiring the complicity of others in the social environment (see Chapter 2).

Character-disordered individuals, particularly sociopaths, do not themselves experience *psychological* distress, whereas those around them are typically upset by the sociopath's behavior. That is, this type of immature functioning is characterized by *social* rather than psychological distress.

Like character disorders, psychosomatics also do not typically experience *psychological* distress. For them, the distress is instead *physiological*. Stress (e.g., interpersonal conflict) in the social environment is converted into biological distress in the psychosomatic patient. Such overstimulation of physiological systems eventually results in somatic damage (Levitan, 1978).

The picture, then, at the immature level of functioning, is of an individual whose behavior is directly "plugged into" both biology and social context.

Neurotic. The differentiation of the psychological sphere into mind (thought plus feeling) *and* behavior (action) makes it possible for the individual to move beyond the immature level of psychosocial functioning. The cybernetics of the neurotic level is depicted in Figure 14C. Comparatively speaking, things were rather simple at the immature level (Figure 14B). Thought and action were not truly differentiated, feelings were inadequately distinguished from body state, and the psychological level of systemic organization consisted of simply the individual's behavior, itself cybernetically linked to both biological and social levels.

Several features of Figure 14C are important. First, mind serves the dual function of mediating the relationship between the behavior of the individual and the social context, on one hand, and the person's biological mechanisms, on the other. Instead of, for example, physiological arousal being expressed directly and immediately as action on the social environment, the mind can mediate this link to modify or delay action. Similarly with the impact of stress in the social environment on the individual's behavior and his biological state, again the mind can modify these effects.

A second feature of the new complexity of Figure 14C is important as well. Mind and behavior themselves form a new, mutually self-regulating system linked by feedback loops: Behavior affects mind and mind affects behavior. The psychological system can be thought of as shown, with the individual's behavior seen as part of a larger whole (mind + behavior). Viewed this way, at the neurotic level *mind* can be seen *as* another *context* for behavior, along with the social context. At the immature level, on the other hand, the social environment alone was the context for understanding the individual's behavior.

And unlike persons functioning at the immature level, where distress is social or physiological, neurotic individuals are typically seen as *psychologically* distressed by their symptoms.

Description of the *mature* level of psychosocial functioning will be postponed until the end of the next section, which discusses the tasks involved in moving from one level to the next.

DEVELOPMENTAL TRANSITIONS AND DEVELOPMENTAL TASKS

It is characteristic of the view of psychosocial development outlined here that the success that allows movement up the scale from one level of functioning to another becomes the problem that must be solved at the new, higher level. This follows directly from Werner's developmental principle: Successful differentiation results in a more complex organism, requiring a high-order integration. As a result, development proceeds through a tenuous series of imbalances between differentiation and integration, in which each imbalance is an "error" to be corrected by the next step of the process.

The transition from psychotic to immature levels. If the central issue at the psychotic level is the differentiation of self and other, the core issue at the immature level is the social integration of these now differentiated persons and the key problem is that of interpersonal conflict.

At the psychotic level, the lack of self/other differentiation precludes true interpersonal conflict. This is so both because there are no distinct individuals to be in conflict with each other and because communication at this level will not support the emergence of differences. Interpersonal conflict is both necessary for self/other differentiation to occur and, unless checked by processes of integration, threatens the integrity of the system.

Given such differentiation at the immature level, the whole organism (e.g., the family) must manage conflict in order to survive. Typically in the case of immature psychopathology, it is the symptomatic behavior in one or more persons that makes this survival possible (e.g., the child's psychosomatic symptoms regulate marital conflict). In Chapter 5, three more or less successful modes for managing (dyadic) conflict were outlined: open, unresolved conflict; rigid complementarity; and involving a third person in the conflict.

Although it is convenient, for descriptive purposes, to divide the scale of functioning into categorical levels and emphasize their qualitative differences, the underlying assumption here is that this is really a continuous dimension ranging from pathology to health. The diagnostic category of "borderline" illustrates the point. On the scale of psychosocial functioning, borderline individuals fit somewhere between the psychotic and immature levels. And in terms of the systemic psychopathology outlined here, they combine features of both levels.

One of the DSM-III (American Psychiatric Association, 1980) criteria for borderline personality disorder is intense, poorly controlled anger. These outbursts produce great social distress, a characteristic of immature-level functioning. At the same time, the angry lashing out at others protects the very fragile individual boundaries of the borderline person, a psychotic-level issue. Shifting down the scale, below the level of the borderline personality disorder, one is likely to encounter pseudomutuality or pseudohostility based on fluid and unclear boundaries instead of this intense, primitive anger. And moving up the scale of functioning, interpersonal conflict does not have this same flavor of protecting personal boundaries. Instead, one finds stable differentiated individuals in conflict with one another.

The transition from immature to neurotic levels. As discussed above, immature-level functioning is characterized by the lack of psychological distress. This amounts to a lack of *self-feedback*. If, on the other hand, my behavior does distress *me* (e.g., results in feelings of anxiety or worrisome thoughts), then I can use this self-feedback to control my behavior. Such self-regulation of behavior is what we mean by *self-control*. Freud's (1926) concept of "signal anxiety" refers to this information-carrying function of anxiety and its role in behavioral self-control. With the differentiation of mind and behavior at the neurotic level, true self-control in the sense described here becomes possible.

The cybernetics of immature-level functioning and its relationship to self-control will now be examined, first for character disorders and then for psychosomatics. The behavior of individuals labeled character disordered, particularly sociopaths, is generally described as socially controlled rather than self-controlled. In cybernetic terms, the crucial feedback regulating the individual's behavior is the behavior of others in the social context rather than the individual's own behavior or psychological state.

Schachter's (1971) experimental work with sociopaths sheds some light on the cybernetic processes involved here. He notes that sociopathic individuals experience chronic states of high but indiscriminate autonomic arousal, reacting similarly to both frightening and relatively neutral situations:

> Such generalized, relatively indiscriminate reactivity is, I would suggest, almost the equivalent of no reactivity at all. If almost every event provokes strong autonomic discharge, then, in terms of *internal* [italics added] autonomic cues, the subject feels no differently during times of danger than during relatively tranquil times. (p. 179)

Without such self-feedback, self-control is impossible.

Immature individuals are also traditionally seen as impulsive persons who fail to use thought as a means for delaying action and often rely on acting-out defenses. Developmentally, this is a consequence of the lack of differentiation of thought and action at the immature level of functioning. Expressed in cybernetic terms, persons functioning at this level lack the ability to use thought in the form of internalized action as a form of self-feedback to self-control their behavior.

In addition to characterizing immature-level adults, such processes are generally seen as normal in adolescents. For example, Piaget (Inhelder and Piaget, 1958) has described how, only in later adolescence with the full development of formal operational thought, is the child able to carry out operations mentally rather than having to play them out concretely in action. And neuropsychologists (e.g., Golden, 1981) suggest that only with the full development of the brain's frontal lobes at about age 12 are the individual's biological mechanisms adequate to the task of true behavioral self-control.

Turning from a focus on character disorder to the psychosomatic individual provides additional clues about immature-level functioning. For psychosomatics, the distress tends to be *physiological* rather than psychological. Again, the lack of psychological distress deprives the psychosomatic individual of a crucial form of self-feedback and compromises the development of true self-control.

Within the past 15 years or so, much interest has been generated among psychosomatic researchers and clinicians by Sifneos's (1967) introduction of the term "alexithymia," a coined word literally meaning "lack of the words for emotion." Krystal (1979), who finds alexithymic characteristics in substance abusers as well as in psychosomatic patients, sees such individuals as unable to recognize and use emotions as signals to themselves.

Nemiah (1977) emphasizes that earlier psychodynamic models long prominent in the psychosomatic field (e.g., Deutsch, 1959; Alexander, 1950) saw physical symptoms as expressions of a repressed psychological conflict. He contrasts this view with the more recent "deficit model" (e.g., Marty and de M'Uzan, 1963; McDougall, 1974), in which the *absence* of psychological activity (experiencing feelings, forming fantasies, etc.) is responsible for the somatic symptom. Krystal (1979) sees the psychological deficits of the psychosomatic patient as a failure to differentiate feeling, as a psychological experience, from the body-bound aspects of emotion.

Where does such a deficit model leave the psychosomatic patient? The paradigm of Figure 14B suggests that stress in the individual's *current* social environment activates behaviors (e.g., pressured activity in the type A individual; see Friedman and Rosenman, 1974) in the immature individual that, in turn, must be supported by high levels of physiological activity (e.g., autonomic arousal). Unless the feedback loop between the individual's behavior and the social context changes, the ongoing cost of this behavior, is this high level of biological activity. The long-term effects of such physiological arousal include physical damage (e.g., heart disease, hypertension). Of course, the process works in the other direction as well: Physiological arousal leads to aroused behavior, which can result in increased stress in the social environment.

This view of the cybernetics of immature functioning and the issue of self-control applies as well to the addictions, yet another phenomenon characteristic of the immature level. The addictive medium may be either biologically or socially active—anything that generates an appropriate feedback loop may be addictive. For example, many people (myself included) are discovering the addictive potential of computers. Consider the process of debugging a program. The computer provides error messages to help the programmer find bugs in the program. Each new run provides additional feedback and makes it likely that the programmer will make "just one more" run, until the program finally runs correctly (or despair sets in). In this case, the computer always provides feedback that makes it likely that the operator will continue to be "hooked." Such an addict's behavior is not self-controlled. Instead, the regulating feedback is generated by the addictive medium.

Alcoholics Anonymous, the most successful treatment for alcohol abuse, works in a manner consistent with the view of immature functioning discussed here: The sometimes daily AA meetings constitute a new social context within which the alcoholic can maintain sobriety.

The transition from neurotic to mature levels. The differentiation of the psychological sphere into mind plus behavior along with the development of self-control makes movement beyond the immature level possible. These same advances become the problems of the neurotic level of functioning. Neurotic symptoms can be seen as errors in the self-control process, as differentiation of the psychological realm gone awry, and as incomplete integration of this now more complex organism.

The essential task in moving from neurotic to mature functioning is the complete integration of the new psychological complexity of mind and behavior and of the links between the psychological level and the biological and social levels.

At the neurotic level and above, it truly does make sense to talk about an "individual" in the traditional sense of the term, someone not only separate from others in the social environment, but also capable of self-controlled behavior using the mind's self-feedback. But the attempts at self-control of the neurotic-level individual inevitably miss their mark in some area of life or another, resulting in over-control and cutting off certain areas of experience in the service of this control. For example, the individual who relies on intellectualizing strategies tends to overdevelop thought (internalized action) at the expense of feeling (experience of bodily states and their mental representation) and of action itself.

When it comes to the mature level of psychosocial functioning, I suffer from the same embarrassment as do most writers on psychopathology: There seems to be much more to say about pathology than about health and optimal adjustment.

What distinguishes mature functioning is the harmony and free flow of information between "inner" and "outer" system levels, without the blocks of the neurotic level.

Most of us catch only glimpses of this congruence between our inner and outer lives. And to speak of such integration at all, it is necessary to reach for examples beyond the clinic, to the worlds of athletics and the arts and to subjects such as love and intimacy. Were I a poet rather than a psychologist, I might better do justice to the description I undertake here.

Think of the most accomplished performances of a world-class gymnast, star ballet dancers in a pas de deux, or the musicians of a fine symphony orchestra. The performer's inner experience, behavior, and social context form a seamless whole. Movement expresses the joy and vitality within and fits perfectly with the motion of others. Intense concentration permits the goal-directed behavior necessary for flawless performance. Yet the full range of continuous feedback from both within and without produce results that rise above the mere mechanical. When the gymnast executes a perfect move, kinesthetic feedback from his muscles tells him so and the pleasure of fluid motion feeds back upon and enhances the original feelings of joy and competence. Or the musician's aural feedback increases the pleasure already expressed in the first notes. And the movement of a partner in the dance both follows the dancer and leads to the next move as though there were one body and not two.

Yoga and the Eastern martial arts in various ways reflect the mature functioning I am struggling here to describe. Yoga, for example, concentrates on breathing and movement. The mind monitors and regulates the rate and depth of breathing and enhances the stretching of the muscles and the body's movements by directing in imagination the flow of breath to various parts of the body. Here breathing becomes a vehicle linking inside and out. The physiological changes in the body that occur as breathing is regulated are reflected in movement and action upon the world. And this action feeds back upon and enhances the original sense of well-being and the resulting movement.

It is even more difficult to take this discussion into the area of love and intimacy. Remember what it is like being in love and holding your lover. You are being held, but not held onto, closeness merging two bodies into one while still maintaining their separateness. Kinesthetic feedback from the muscles is an essential part of this experience, simultaneously allowing one to feel the lover's solidity and permitting a sense of warmth and merger. But this experience can never be produced mechanically by directing the muscles in a certain way. Rather, the kinesthetic experience that characterizes and enhances love and intimacy is part of a loop of experience linking one's internal and external lives with the mirrored experiences of the lover.

In cybernetic terms, this sense of intimacy is embodied in the notion of the "open" system, the organism that is able to maintain its integrity while freely exchanging information with the environment. Mature functioning is characterized by such openness at all systemic levels, biological, psychological, and social.

Differentiating Family Systems Models

Before using this systemic psychopathology in the next section to integrate various approaches to family systems therapy, I concentrate here on differentiating among the transactional, structural, strategic, and developmental models, quickly reviewing the central notions presented in the preceding chapters of Part 1 and relating them to the systemic psychopathology just outlined.

I distinguish here between these models and the schools of family therapy discussed in Chapter 1. A school is a more or less integrated collection of ways of operating as a therapist, typically one that has grown up around the person of a charismatic and innovative figure in the field. A school may include the practice of several different models. For example, Minuchin's structural school of family therapy employs the structural, strategic, and developmental models.

When the family therapy field is seen in terms of its overlapping yet competing schools, things look chaotic and confusing. What I hope to demonstrate in the remainder of this chapter is that if one first differentiates certain pure models embedded within the several schools of family systems therapy, these models can then be integrated into a coherent whole using the framework of systemic psychopathology.

TRANSACTIONAL MODEL

The basic notion underlying the transactional model is that of the *shared focus of attention.* From their studies of the families of schizophrenics beginning in the 1950s, Singer (1977) and Wynne (1977) have demonstrated that communication in these families with a severely disturbed member fails before it gets off the ground because members typically do not help others focus on an object of attention, maintain this focus across a series of transactions, and arrive at some point or meaning regarding this focus. These investigators have used the term "communication deviances" (Singer and Wynne, 1966) to describe how a shared focus of attention is either never established at all or is prematurely disrupted.

Assessment in the transactional model consists of identifying the deviances occurring in communication both within the family and between family members and outside persons. Singer's and Wynne's impressive research over the years [summarized in Singer

(1977) and Wynne (1977)] clearly demonstrates that the sheer rate of communication deviances (number of deviances per word spoken) is sufficient to distinguish the families of young adult schizophrenics from those whose offspring have less severe or no psychopathology.

The therapist in the transactional model functions as a kind of communication broker whose job is to first of all share a focus of attention with all family members and second to help them share foci with each other. Work in this model has an educational flavor. The therapist stops the process when communication deviances occur and gets a shared focus of attention established before proceeding.

It will likely already have occurred to the reader that the transactional model is tailor-made for intervening in the central problems of the psychotic level of functioning: poor self/other differentiation and interpersonal communication that lacks the information necessary for such differentiation. This correspondence between the transactional model and psychotic-level problems is hardly surprising, in view of the fact that the transactional model was developed from Singer's and Wynne's studies of the families of schizophrenics.

STRUCTURAL MODEL

The basic idea underlying Minuchin's structural approach (Minuchin, 1974; Minuchin and Fishman, 1981) is that of *boundary*. The system of interest in the structural model consists of a group of persons (e.g., family members) together with their behaviors with each other. Behaviors that define boundaries in systems are behaviors that separate the system into two groups: those persons who engage in the behavior and those who do not. Put another way, a boundary separates a "subsystem" from the rest of the system in such a way that all subsystem members are like each other (i.e., they engage in the boundary-defining behavior) and different from the rest of the system's members (who do not).

To illustrate, Minuchin is particularly interested in the generational boundary defined by executive, parenting, leadership behaviors. The generational boundary divides the two-generational nuclear family into executive and sibling subsystems.

For optimal functioning, the family system must be able to organize itself into subsystems capable of carrying out the various tasks necessary for survival and growth. And to perform its functions a subsystem (e.g., the executive subsystem) requires boundaries strong enough to permit it to get its job done but not so strong as to preclude effective communication with the rest of the system.

Optimal family organization (that is, for example, a structure that allows the family to raise competent, healthy children capable of becoming emancipated and leading productive lives of their own) is often compromised by the family's need to contain interpersonal conflict, particularly between the parents. Minuchin's important work, first with families of delinquents (Minuchin et al., 1967) and more recently with families with a psychosomatically ill child (Minuchin et al., 1978), demonstrates the role of the child's symptoms (acting-out or psychosomatic) in detouring marital conflict and thus maintaining the family while sacrificing the child's competence and development and/or his physiological integrity. Here the generational boundary is violated by the child's involvement in the business of the executive system.

A second, alternative method for managing conflict, again, for example, between husband and wife, is for one spouse to be hopelessly one-down in the relationship due to serious criminal behavior, alcohol or drug abuse, or somatic illness. Symmetrical conflict that escalates and threatens the marriage can always be interrupted by the symptomatic behavior of the compromised partner. Here the couple boundary is violated by the separation of the pair into over- and under-functioning subsystems.

Assessment in the structural model is directed at the integrity of the boundaries within the family, particularly the generational boundary, and the family's organization for managing conflict, especially between husband and wife.

The job of the structural family therapist is to make "clear" boundaries, that is, boundaries that are neither too strong nor too weak. This is accomplished from the "inside," by joining the family and then restructuring it by siding with one subsystem against the rest of the system. For example, the structural family therapist typically intervenes in the family with a delinquent adolescent by siding with the parents, either to discipline or to help the adolescent. Or in the case of the symmetrical couple in conflict, the therapist may unbalance things by siding with one spouse, directing the wife, for example, to change her unsatisfactory husband.

The correspondence between the structural model and immature-level pathology should by now be clear. The focus is on how the family's social organization functions to manage interpersonal conflict. And again, the link between the structural model and immature pathology is not coincidental in view of the fact that Minuchin's structural work grew out of work with immature level problems: first lower-class delinquents in New York and then child-hood psychosomatics in Philadelphia.

STRATEGIC MODEL

Central to the strategic model is the idea that no problem occurs in isolation, but rather always exists in some context or *frame*, which may either facilitate or preclude finding a solution. Watzlawick et al. (1974) define the important notion of *reframing* by which the mental context of a problem is changed and as a result changes the problem itself. These authors emphasize that the mental change involved in reframing includes both cognitive and affective components.

Assessment in the strategic model begins with a careful investigation of the problem as presented by the family. How does each family member see the problem? What are the historical and interpersonal contexts of the problem? And what previous attempts at a solution have been made?

The strategic family therapist is a problem-definer whose job is to start with the presenting complaint and define a solvable problem. Haley (1973a) emphasizes the active role of the strategic therapist and insists that there is no method here. Instead, the therapist must invent a unique solution for the particular problem presented by the family.

The strategic model's emphasis on changing behavior by changing its mental context corresponds to the view of neurotic-level functioning presented above. And again there is a relationship between the therapy model and the kinds of problems from which it was developed: The MRI branch of strategic therapy grew out of work with an essentially middle- and upper-class, neurotic population.

DEVELOPMENTAL MODEL

The basic idea of the developmental model is that of the *family life cycle*. Very simply, the notion is that across its life-span the family goes through a series of stages, including courtship, early marriage, childbirth and childrearing, children start school, adolescence and the middle marriage years, children leave home, and retirement, old age, and death.

As discussed in Chapter 3, the developmental model is based upon a developmental principle that is outside the scope of classical general systems theory and cybernetics (that have to do with the regulation of systems consisting of a fixed set of members). Two facts dictate the operation of the developmental principle in families. The first is biological: People are born and people die. And the second cultural: In our society, at least, children are expected to grow up, leave the family, and function as competent adults on their own.

Assessment in the developmental model focuses on the family's past and current stages of the life cycle and particularly on its *next* stage. Pathology is seen as arising from the family's inability to make developmental transitions at the appropriate times. Prior developmental problems, particularly the failure to grieve for losses, may be seen as complicating current difficulties, but the developmental model is more future- than past-oriented. The job of the therapist in the developmental model is, quite simply, to help the family move on in its life cycle.

The developmental model has essentially to do with the unfolding of chronological time rather than with the notion of psychosocial development emphasized so far in this discussion of systemic psychopathology. As such, it corresponds to no particular level of functioning, but rather cuts across and applies regardless of psychosocial level.

Integration: A Second-Order Model

DEFINING THE SECOND-ORDER MODEL

The four models differentiated above can be thought of as *first-order* family systems *models*. Each is a particular but different lens through which the family and family therapy can be viewed. At this first order, all models apply to all families all of the time.

The *second-order model* is a model that organizes and integrates first-order models. Systemic psychopathology offers a framework for constructing a second-order model aimed at answering two questions: First, are some (first-order) models more appropriate for certain families than others? And second, does this fit between family and model change over the course of treatment?

Figure 15 outlines a second-order model based on systemic psychopathology. Two central dimensions define the second-order model. The vertical axis represents psychosocial functioning, divided, following Vaillant (1977), into the four levels: psychotic, immature, neurotic, and mature. The horizontal dimension corresponds to chronological time. The transactional, structural, and strategic models apply to the psychotic, immature, and neurotic levels of psychosocial functioning, respectively. And the developmental model is related to the chronological axis.

Families at the mature level presumably do not need treatment, at least in the sense of problem-solving therapy (Madanes and Haley, 1977). Nonetheless, it is tempting to associate "growth" approaches to therapy with mature functioning (and thus fill the empty slot in Figure 15). It is certainly true that the emphasis on promoting intimacy in the work of such growth-oriented therapists as Satir (1964) is consistent with the view of mature functioning developed here. However, most of these growth-oriented schools are not based purely on systems thinking, but rather bring in other viewpoints (e.g., psychodynamic, gestalt) not necessarily consistent

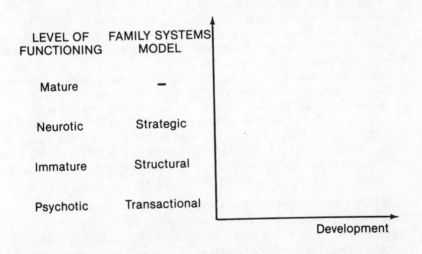

Figure 15. The second-order model. Transactional, structural, and strategic models are related to particular levels of psychosocial functioning. The developmental model represents a second dimension.

with cybernetics. Chapter 13 outlines a *systemic psychology* appropriate for conceptualizing mature functioning and may suggest new approaches to therapeutic work at this level.

SOME EMPIRICAL SUPPORT

Before discussing in detail the application of the second-order model to family treatment, I wish to present the results of the research program of Lewis and his colleagues that provide some empirical support for features of the second-order model. This section does not present a formal test of hypotheses derivable from the second-order model. However, the fact that I developed the second-order model before discovering the Lewis work suggests a convergence in thinking that encourages future empirical study.

A chapter by Lewis summarizes the research he and his colleagues (Lewis et al., 1976) have conducted at the Timberlawn Foundation in Dallas. Lewis (1980) describes the central ideas of their work:

> I wish to propose a model of family competence constructed from research data that lends itself readily to a consideration of the role of biologic and developmental variables. This model proposes that families can be distinguished by their general or overall *level of functioning* [italics added], and that this global measure may play a role in determining the susceptibility of family members to both physical and mental illness. The model suggests that, at any given level of functioning, there may be specific patterns of family organization, communication, and conflict which predispose to specific illnesses in family members. An initial or sole focus on the search for specific patterns may be obscured by the impact of the family's general level of functioning on susceptibility to a wide range of disturbances. Indeed, the model proposes that often nonfamily biologic, developmental, and cultural variables play a decisive role in the nature of the specific disorder developed. (p. 12)

Here Lewis suggests that there is an underlying dimension of family competence such that it is possible to say that one family does better than another in carrying out its central tasks. He assumes that the family's first task is to ensure its actual physical survival. Although some of the families he studied were dysfunctional enough to compromise somewhat their ability to survive, his sample of middle- and upper-middle-class families allowed him to concentrate on two other crucial (at least in mid-twentieth century

America) family tasks: "the maturation and stabilization of the parental personalities and the production of autonomous children" (p. 13).

Families were first rated on an overall global health–pathology scale and then videotaped samples of family interaction were independently scored on 13 specific variables, including overt power, responsibility, invasiveness, and expressiveness. These data suggest that the continuum of family competence can be divided into four characteristic ranges or categories that Lewis labeled optimal; competent, but pained; dysfunctional; and severely dysfunctional. The somewhat pedestrian names for these levels of competence should not obscure the important qualitative differences among them. As you will see, Lewis' four levels of family competence correspond rather nicely to the levels of psychosocial functioning of the second-order model (Figure 15).

Lewis reports that dysfunctional and severely dysfunctional families were distinguished from their more competent counterparts by their failure to produce autonomous children. This is consistent with the implication of the second-order model that structural-level breakdown is associated with generational boundary violations and the family's inability to emancipate its children successfully. Symptomatic adolescents in the dysfunctional families of the Lewis studies typically exhibited either severely incapacitating neurotic symptoms, serious behavior disturbances, with acting-out and rebelliousness, or acute reactive psychosis. The severely dysfunctional families were likely to have an adolescent with a schizoprenic disorder. These latter families were characterized by amorphous and indistinct boundaries between individuals and by communication patterns low in clarity and in the ability to achieve closure and high in invasions by one person into the thoughts and feelings of another.

The competent but pained families were characterized by marital dissatisfaction, particularly on the part of the wives. These women complained about their husbands' unavailability and inability to meet their emotional needs. Such families fail at the task of assisting with the parents' personal maturation. However, this marital unhappiness was not associated with a failure to produce autonomous children. None of the children in such families was symptomatic, and these offspring could not be distinguished from their counterparts in the optimal group by raters working from interview transcripts and Minnesota Multiphasic Personality Inventory (MMPI) results. However, the wives in the competent, but pained group often suffered from neurotic symptoms. (The one-sided emphasis here on the *wives'* dissatisfaction and symptoms likely reflects the pre-women's movement viewpoints of both subject families and researchers.) In contrast, the marital relationships in the optimal families were characterized by shared power and leadership, psychological intimacy plus well-developed individuality, and high levels of affection and sexual satisfaction.

APPLYING THE SECOND-ORDER MODEL TO TREATMENT

To be precise, the terms "psychotic," "immature," etc., apply neither to individuals nor to families, but rather specify a particular level of functioning at a given time and under particular circumstances. All families, as well as all individual family members, exhibit a range of functioning. Most families exhibit higher and lower levels of functioning as well, depending upon circumstances. And within families, individual family members vary in both characteristic level and range of functioning.

The predominant symptoms of family members are a rough guide to the family's *characteristic level* of functioning. Psychotic symptoms, particularly schizophrenia, indicate the psychotic level. Acting-out and delinquent behavior, character disorders, addictions, and psychosomatic difficulties are associated with the immature level. And neurotic symptoms, "acting-in," and inhibition define the neurotic level.

Although at the first order, all models are theoretically equal, the second-order model implies that some models are pragmatically more equal than others. The idea that family therapy approaches have limited applicability to particular populations of families is not an especially popular notion in the field today. Most of the central figures speak and act as though their school of therapy applied equally to *all* families. Minuchin (1982) commented on this phenomenon in a recent address: "The old-timers knew that their private truths were only partial" (p. 662). He went on to describe, allegorically, what happened next: Students came to study with these early explorers who had staked out their territory; large buildings were needed to accommodate all the students, and eventually castles were constructed; and because the castles were expensive to run, their landlords "needed to justify their existence. Therefore, they demanded ownership of the total truth" (p. 662).

Four principles guide the selection and use of first-order models:

First, intervention with a particular family begins with the model appropriate to the family's characteristic level of psychosocial functioning: transactional at the psychotic level, structural at the immature level, and strategic at the neurotic level. When the range of family members' symptoms spans several levels, begin with the lowest applicable model.

Second, all higher-level models also apply, but the bulk of the work is initially in the model corresponding to the family's current level of functioning. To succeed in working at the current level of functioning, interventions must be compatible with good practice within higher-level models, but the higher-level work alone is not sufficient to improve the family's level of functioning. For example, in working with a family at the immature level, the initial work is structural. However, the strategic model applies as well (*all* therapy occurs within *some* frame) and attention must always be paid to strategic as well as structural issues (see the Bach family transcript in the final section of this chapter). The second-order model does imply that strategic work alone will not succeed in moving the immature family to higher levels of functioning.

Third, as treatment progresses and level of functioning improves, therapy shifts to the corresponding higher-level model.

Fourth, the developmental model always applies, regardless of the family's level of functioning.

In Figure 15, the orthogonal relationship between horizontal and vertical axes suggests that they represent independent dimensions. This is not really true. Movement in time along the horizontal axis puts pressure on the family for reorganization, that is, for movement up the vertical (level of functioning) axis. Or put another way, the lower the family's level of functioning, the more difficulty they will have in making developmental transitions at the appropriate time.

It is possible to complicate the model of Figure 15 a bit further by adding a third dimension, which might be termed "ecological" and refers to the level of stress on the family due to extra-family factors. In this more complete model, both developmental influences arising from within the family and extra-familial ecological factors affect the family's level of psychosocial functioning.

Several corollaries follow from these principles. First, intervention at too high a level will at best be resisted by the family, either with massive defensiveness (see Chapter 11 for an example) or by bolting from treatment entirely. At worst, intervening at too high a level will provoke disorganization. This latter situation is illustrated by a case in which a middle-aged father presented with depression and gut pain of six years duration. He had not worked during this time, was taking large amounts of narcotic pain medication, and was intermittently suicidal. We had done what I thought was an especially brilliant strategic session, complete with nifty homework assignment. The family came back the following week clearly worse, apparently disorganized by our intervention. (I am grateful to my colleague Neil Scott whose comment that we had intervened at "too high a level" in this case was one of those crucial bits of information that ultimately pushed my thinking in the direction spelled out in this chapter.)

Second, strategic interventions are best suited for *higher* functioning patients. This is contrary to certain clinical lore that suggests that intensive, insight-oriented psychotherapy is the treatment of choice for neurotics and that manipulative strategic interventions are best saved for those low-functioning persons who are too sick to benefit from real therapy (or too poor to afford it). The position I take here is in substantial agreement with the contraindications for the use of paradox cited by Fisher et al. (1981).

So far I have been implicitly assuming that the goal of treatment is to move families and their individual members up the level of functioning scale. Crisis intervention is a limited form of treatment with a more modest goal: to return the patient to a pre-crisis level of functioning. The above comments about strategic interventions must be modified in this case. Strategic approaches can be successfully employed *regardless* of level of functioning, to interrupt escalating, deviation-amplifying cybernetic cycles and return the family to its pre-crisis level.

Finally, a comment about the second-order model's implications for the size of the crowd in the therapy room. In general, at higher levels of functioning, fewer people need be involved in the treatment. This notion is consistent with a remark by Whitaker (1979) that "individual therapy is the Ph.D. of psychotherapy." Whitaker was suggesting that, if you have a mess in your family, first go to family therapy to get it straightened out. Next, work with your spouse in couples treatment to fix things up there. And then, if you are still interested in therapy for your own personal growth and development, that is the time for individual therapy. Again, this is the opposite of the clinical advice typical in traditional treatment approaches. There, you first get yourself straightened out in individual therapy and after that you might wish to work with your spouse or join a group to tackle interpersonal issues. Systemic psychopathology focuses the clinician's attention first upon the social context of the individual's problems. Instead of the years-long character reconstruction attempted in individual psycho-analysis, it is possible to work more effectively and efficiently by utilizing the current social context in the treatment itself.

Models and Schools Revisited

What is the relationship between these first- and second-order models and the more familiar schools into which the therapy field is usually divided? To illustrate the power of the second-order model in clarifying this issue, I discuss the structural and strategic schools, Bowen's school, and the systemic school of the Milan group, and comment on cognitive, behavioral and psychodynamic individual therapy approaches.

THE STRUCTURAL AND STRATEGIC SCHOOLS

I indicated above that Minuchin's structural school utilizes struc-tural, developmental, and strategic models. His use of the structural model is, of course, obvious. The developmental model is em-bedded in Minuchin's discussion of the structural approach, al-though he does not recognize it as conceptually distinct. And finally, Minuchin employs reframing and what he terms "construct-ing a therapeutic reality" (Minuchin, 1979) or "world view" (Minu-chin and Fishman, 1981), illustrating his use of the strategic model.

Haley's strategic school relies, I think, upon these same three models. Haley talks about the phenomena of the structural model [e.g., "peripheral person" (1973b), and "hierarchy" (1976)] without specifically using Minuchin's structural language.

Comparing the two schools, the difference appears to be more one of degree than of kind, with each school emphasizing a different model from among those both schools employ. Minuchin uses more of the structural model than the strategic. And Haley works strategically more than structurally. This cross-fertilization of ap-proaches is not surprising, given the development of the work of these two men. For example, in his acknowledgments to *Families and Family Therapy*, Minuchin (1974) admits his debt to a twice-a-day traveling seminar he held with Haley and Montalvo as the three of them commuted to and from the Philadelphia Child Guidance Clinic. In my more despairing moments, as I struggled with differentiating the strategic and structural approaches, I wondered if perhaps Minuchin and Haley had developed a single therapy, but each needed a school he could call his own. Still as I have argued above, there are conceptually distinct models lurking in the work of these two men, and it is useful to tease them apart.

Also citing their 10-year collaboration in Philadelphia, Haley agrees (Simon, 1982b) that he and Minuchin describe families in very similar terms. He adds: "The biggest difference I see between what Minuchin does and what I do is that strategic therapy has an absolute focus on the symptom" (p. 58).

The MRI brief therapy approach (Weakland et al., 1974) represents a relatively pure application of the strategic model. And perhaps the most original and highly developed implementation of the strategic model is found in the hypnotic work of Milton Erickson (see Zeig, 1982, for an overview) in which the resources of mind become the chief vehicle for behavioral change.

BOWEN'S SCHOOL

I have largely neglected Murray Bowen's school of family therapy in this book and in my own work, I think, for two reasons. First, I have always seen his one-sided emphasis on *differentiation* of a self (Bowen, 1966) as too limiting, neglecting as it does the equally important process of integration. And second, most of my clinical cases have not seemed to require conceptualization and intervention using Bowen's approach. The second-order model places this neglect of Bowen in a perspective that transcends my idiosyncrasies and locates the Bowenian school within family systems therapy.

Bowen focuses on that portion of the scale of psychosocial functioning ranging from psychotic to the borderline between psychotic and immature functioning. At this level, the paramount issue *is* the differentiation of self from social context. From the point of view of systemic psychopathology, Bowen's emphasis on differentiation over integration is entirely appropriate for work at this level of functioning, even if it fails as a general principle applicable across all levels.

As I have struggled recently in working with a number of borderline patients and their families, I have become more interested in Bowen's (1966) techniques for assisting family members to establish and maintain their individual boundaries.

THE SYSTEMIC SCHOOL

Influenced by Watzlawick and his colleagues at MRI, the "systemic" approach of the Milan team (Selvini Palazzoli et al., 1978), with its use of paradox and positive connotation (reframing), clearly utilizes the strategic model. In its early work, the Milan team, in fact, saw such strategic elements as crucial. The interview with the family was used simply to gather the information needed to generate a systemic hypothesis. Based upon this hypothesis, the team then formulated an "intervention" (always strategic in the sense of Chapter 7, and often paradoxical) and sent the family home for a month or so.

If it is the case, as the Milan team initially believed, that such strategic interventions are the curative factor in their work with families of schizophrenics, then the second-order model as I have presented it here does not hold up: The second-order model suggests that therapy based upon the strategic model alone is not sufficient to improve the level of functioning of psychotic-level families.

However, the Milan group's more recent work suggests a change in their own view of how the systemic approach achieves its results. At the conclusion of an article on conducting the interview, Selvini Palazzoli and her colleagues (1980) wonder aloud whether the final intervention is necessary at all. Instead, they suggest that the method of interviewing may itself *be* the treatment.

It appears that differences over the role of the strategic aspects of their work were, in fact, involved in the recent split of the Milan team into two separate groups: Selvini Palazzoli and Prata, on the one hand, and Boscolo and Cecchin, on the other. In a recent workshop I attended, the latter (Boscolo and Cecchin, 1981) extended and amplified the direction suggested in the Milan group's 1980 paper. Boscolo and Cecchin currently emphasize the role of their interviewing technique in introducing *differences* into the family system (e.g., by asking questions like "Of all your brothers and sisters, who does mother prefer?"). Boscolo and Cecchin see psychotic-level families as having great difficulty perceiving and talking about differences within the family. They suggest that it is the covert, unacknowledged differences in these families that are pathological enough to drive one member crazy, whereas the overt differences of less disturbed families are not crazy-making.

In the language of systemic psychopathology, Boscolo and Cecchin have, I think, begun to emphasize how language is used in the interview to differentiate individuals within the family from one another. According to the second-order model presented here, this is precisely the type of intervention necessary for successful work with families functioning at the psychotic level.

Selvini Palazzoli and Prata, in contrast, have moved in an even more strategic direction, currently advocating the use of the same intervention with all families (see discussion at end of Chapter 7).

BEHAVIORAL AND COGNITIVE THERAPIES

Behavioral therapies are essentially concerned with the cybernetics of the immature level of psychosocial functioning (Figure 14B). Respondent conditioning focuses upon the connection between an individual's behavior and the social context. Classical conditioning generally includes a link with the biological level, as well. However, in contrast to the circular causality of cybernetics, the behavioral paradigm punctuates the feedback loop and views causality as linear.

Cognitive-behavioral approaches, on the other hand, focus upon the link between mind and behavior that emerges in the cybernetics of the neurotic level (Figure 14C). As in the case of classical behavior therapy, causality is generally seen as linear rather than circular. For example, irrational thoughts, seen as producing dysfunctional behaviors, are typically the target of psychotherapeutic intervention.

PSYCHOANALYSIS

The tension between systemic and traditional individual understanding of behavior comes down to whether one looks "outside" or "inside" the person for explanatory factors. Systemic approaches have emphasized the outside, focusing on the importance of social context and minimizing the role of mind. Psychoanalysis, on the other hand, has largely ignored the social world and instead emphasizes intrapsychic mental phenomena. This gap might be bridged if both sides budge a bit: Systemic thinking must legitimize the role of mind in the explanatory scheme of things, whereas psychoanalysis must acknowledge the importance of context, particularly the individual's social context.

The conceptualization of mind is the key to linking these two explanatory schemes. Instead of viewing mind as irrelevant *or* as intrapsychic, mind can instead be seen as an important context for the individual's behavior. In this view, mind is *not inside* the individual person in the same way that, following the mechanical explanation dominant in Western science, mind has traditionally been viewed as "intrapsychic."

Bateson's (1971) cybernetic thinking leads him to a similar conclusion regarding the location of mind. He rejects the traditional notion that the mind lies within the brain or even within the body. Using the example of a man chopping down a tree, he concludes:

"this *self-corrective* (*i.e., mental*) [italics added] process is brought about by a total system, tree–eyes–brain–muscles–axe–stroke–tree; and it is this total system that has the characteristics of immanent mind" (p. 6).

Here Bateson describes the cybernetic circuit as a single loop including biological (eyes, brain, muscles), behavioral (stroke), and contextual (axe, tree) components.

I have instead reorganized this loop in Figures 14B and 14C on three different systemic levels (biological, psychological, and social). Here mind is seen as a kind of "membrane" surrounding behavior and mediating the relationship between the individual's behavior and his biological mechanisms, on the one hand, and his social context, on the other. The metaphor I have in mind is the cell membrane that defines the cell's limits and ensures its integrity while allowing exchange of material and information with the environment.

Once the mind is seen as context for behavior, the conflict between traditional "intrapsychic" approaches to therapy and family systems thinking appears less formidable. From the systems point of view, behavior changes when the context changes. Changes in mental context as well as social context may result in behavioral change. The price of this new conceptualization of mind is giving up the idea that mind is *intra*psychic, that is, inside the person.

The concept of transference is related to the notion of mind as context developed here. Freud found that instead of responding to the current social context the behavior of his neurotic patients was often related to the *mental* contexts they carried with them from one social context to the next. The genius of Freud's original contribution lay in his ability to understand and change neurotic behavior through an exploration of its mental context. The limitations of psychoanalysis for patients functioning below the neurotic level lie here as well, in the tendency to emphasize the mental context of behavior to the exclusion of its social context (e.g., the assumption that the child's incestuous fantasies always represent a wish rather than a family reality). Although this may be fine when working with neurotic individuals, the neglect of the social context leads to failure at the immature and psychotic levels of functioning. Psychoanalysts uncovered the importance of the mental context by working with neurotics. Family therapists discovered the central role of the social context by working first with families of schizophrenics and later with families functioning at the immature level.

Case Example

This concluding section presents two additional excerpts from the Bach family discussed in Chapter 4 (the middle-aged, middle-class parents with unresolved marital conflict, three teenage children exhibiting some behavior problems, and a chaotic and verbally abusive family environment). Taken from the first of the six initially-contracted family sessions, these two segments depict an exercise in parenting for the executive subsystem and illustrate the application of transactional, structural, strategic, and developmental models, guided by the second-order model described above.

(*The oldest child John was absent from the previous session because of a fight he had had with Mrs. Bach in which he reportedly either threw a knife at his mother or attempted to choke her. The couple was given the task of bringing him to this session, which they did. In discussing the fight and its aftermath—John took the car in violation of a directive from his father and then left home—it became clear that Mrs. Bach thinks that her husband is too harsh with John, whereas Mr. Bach believes her to be too lenient. The therapist discovered that, in the case of the present incident, father assigned a tough punishment which mother undercut. As a result, there have been no consequences at all for John's behavior. The supervisor phones in, telling therapist to have father and mother come up with a suitable consequence for John's actions.*)

(*We see the old, familiar pattern here: The executive subsystem is paralyzed and cannot effectively set limits for the children because the parents are unable to agree and the couple has no way to resolve their conflict. Though the knife throwing/choking incident sounds extremely serious, our assessment of this family did not indicate a need to focus strategically on the physical violence and do a form of crisis intervention. Rather, the family therapy team addressed the underlying structural problem by prescribing new behavior for the parents.*)

T: What needs to happen now is, the two of you need to come up with one consequence that both of you can agree to impose on John for what happened. I mean, what appears to us is that John directly disobeyed you a number of times and he went off with the car and ran away and so on and so forth. And basically what John is saying is "Well, not much happened. Business as usual." And, I think in a sense what Mr. Bach says is right, in that, a, John has his own needs and so on and so forth, and that the two of you do need to impose some kind of consequence. (*Here Rita jerks her head up, dramatically tossing her long hair back from her face, and raises her hand as if to interrupt therapist, slowing shaking her head to signal "No."*) And it needs to be something you can both agree to. So the task for the two of you now is to come up with, with one consequence for that.

(*Rita lets her hand drop and continues to shake her head as in disbelief. This is followed by a long pause.*)

(*The therapist really has two jobs here: to instruct the family on the new kind of behavior he wishes to occur and to frame his instruction in such a way that he succeeds in getting them to carry it out. He makes a good start, telling the parents what he wants them to do and building a frame for the intervention out of the details of the previous interaction. But he inadvertently sides with father: "What Mr. Bach says is right."*)

M: All right. Let me say something to that. John, since grade, from sixth to ninth grade, has watched very little TV. Because every time he was deprived of TV. Four weeks, six weeks. He was grounded. It doesn't work. It does not work (*speaks slowly, with emphasis*). The problem is lack of communication. What you say may help temporarily, perhaps. Maybe. It does not help the problem. I know.

(*And therapist is immediately attacked by mother. This is quite predictable: Mother and father agree on nothing, so anyone who sides with father will incur mother's wrath. Notice that mother fights therapist's frame with arguments based on John—a way of using him against the therapist—and she counters therapist's frame with one of her own: "The problem is lack of communication."*)

T: What I'm saying. . . .

M: (*Interrupts.*) It's not a good way to go.

T: (*Continues.*) What I'm saying is that, in essence John has learned that he doesn't need to obey you. I. . . .

(*Therapist comes back and reasserts his frame: The problem is that you have taught John that he doesn't need to obey you.*)

M: (*Overlaps and drowns out therapist's words.*) He also has learned
that, he has learned so many other things, which are much (*said with
great emphasis*) more important. Obeying is of little importance right
now. (*Unintelligible phrase*) he will move out. He's almost eighteen.
And we at eighteen can't impose our will all that much anymore. My
parents could on me, sure, and even on my three brothers. At eighteen
I think we can try to communicate a different way and not say "If you
don't do this, you can't do this." I think that's past. We can do that
with Eric and Rita yet. When you're almost eighteen, that doesn't
work. You know that. You were eighteen at one time.

(*And mother displays her power by turning therapist into a child and
speaking to him in a very patronizing way. She again insists that
therapist's frame is wrong—because John is now too old—and again
reframes the problem in terms of communication.*)

T: Do you, a, see a basic issue of responsibility being involved here?
Both for John living in your house and for you as parents?

(*Here therapist shifts his frame a bit, from obeying and the consequences of John's misbehavior to responsibility.*)

M: Uh-hum.

T: That's really what I'm talking about.

(*Forty-seven second pause. The extraordinary, 47-second pause indicates that therapist temporarily succeeds in flipping mother into his
frame. His error is probably in not using his momentary advantage to
coax Mrs. Bach into staying with him. Therapist's silence appears to
allow mother to regroup.*)

M: So, Frank (*father*) and I are talking about one punishment to impose
on John and that's it? That will solve the whole thing?

(*And she comes back in fine form, attempting to demolish therapist
with her sarcasm.*)

T: (*Quietly.*) No, no one solution is going to solve the whole thing.

F: (*Unintelligible.*) I think this is a step, a, I think what's happened, I
don't think you. . . . (*To mother*) I think the article which you read
a long time ago about authority and violence, remember? That's what
(*unintelligible*). We have, because of our problems, lost authority in
the family. And the result of that is violence. (*Unintelligible.*) And I
think in order to maintain that there's a family unit going and there's
equal responsibility on all family members. That's not going to solve,
not going to make us love each other, you know (*unintelligible*) all of
a sudden. I think we need, need to play our roles for a while so we can
get along. But I think we need to play our roles in a way that there is
some kind of order. And one of the things that needs to be done is
that when we tell John "You bring home that car. You have no
business taking that car. You have no business choking your mother."

A, that should be obeyed, at that point. As long as he lives in this house as part of the family unit. If he doesn't live in the house anymore, he's not part of the family unit, then it will be up to him to come to us if he wants to. But at this time he is still part of the family unit and he still has to abide by certain rules and responsibilities for this family.

(Father, the usual target of his wife's cutting remarks, now rushes to the defense of his new ally. Most structural family therapists would likely agree with the content of Mr. Bach's speech here. Certainly his statements support the therapist's frame. However, father's remarks are not at all helpful to therapist because the more he has father's support the more flak he will get from mother. Transactionally, father's speech shows some communication deviance that interferes with the listener's ability to share a focus of attention with him, chiefly commitment problems—abandoned and unstable remarks—and turn-taking difficulties—monopolizing the floor.)

F: *(Continues above speech.)* I really feel, I don't want to be the one to hand out the punishment. I think the punishment should come from both of us. At this point you feel you should not give any punishment because John's going to be gone in a few months anyway. Now, that's, I don't see that at all. I don't see that's the logical approach.

(Here father rather succinctly and directly points out the couple's failure as an executive subsystem.)

F: *(Continues above speech.)* And I don't think John feels comfortable with the fact that he can get away with anything he wants to. I, a, in the long run he won't feel comfortable. Nobody feels comfortable in that sort of situation. You wouldn't either. If you could get away with anything you wanted to at any time, you wouldn't feel comfortable either. You would feel "Somebody's playing games with me. Why would they do that to me, that I can do whatever I want?"

(Now father ups the ante by using the technique mother used above on therapist, attempting to make her a kid alongside John.)

M: *(Interrupts.)* Frank, it's, it's a lot of talk, but you get away with everything. You don't put any brakes onto yourself. And maybe we should all have an example. Maybe John took the violence thing from you. You know?

(And he succeeds in provoking a frontal assault by mother.)

F: *(Overlaps.)* I think we both need to make examples.

M: *(Continues.)* And maybe there is, there was that, all of it, you know? You can't punish someone for something you do. *(Supervisor enters room.)* That's not possible either.

S: I want to interrupt.

This segment nicely illustrates the interplay among the four first-order models. The Bach family has all the earmarks of immature-level dysfunction: acting-out adolescents, alcohol abuse, some physical violence, and chronic unresolved marital conflict. Following the second-order model, the main therapeutic work is structural. But higher-level models (strategic, in this case) apply as well. The therapist always works within *some* frame and always has the task of getting the family to join him in the frame. And as in all cases, the developmental model is crucial as this family faces the task of emancipating the children.

What becomes clear in this segment is how work at one level can undo what is happening at another level. Structurally, the therapist wishes to draw the generational boundary, unbalancing the family by siding with the parents against the children. However in attempting to construct a plausible frame for his structural intervention (one which will succeed in gaining the parents' co-operation), the therapist inadvertently provokes couple conflict, undermining the cooperation he seeks to promote through the structural work and getting Mrs. Bach fighting with him instead of talking to her husband.

The reader may wonder why the therapist's intervention of siding with Mr. Bach against his wife is not an example of good couple unbalancing (see Chapter 5). There are at least two reasons. First, this therapist did not side with father as a carefully planned maneuver, but rather stumbled into an uneasy coalition with Mr. Bach, becoming another child in the family system to be used by the parents as an ally in their internecine warfare. (Note how mother responds immediately to therapist's siding with father by treating therapist like a child.)

Second, unbalancing the couple is for a later stage of therapy, appropriate once the generational boundary is clear. In fact, one needs initially to *balance* the couple, promoting their cooperative behavior, in order to *unbalance* the family. This will become clearer in the next transcript segment.

I commented above on the transactional-level problems that show up in Mr. Bach's speeches. This does not mean that this is a family in which some member has been or will be psychotic. Remember that the vertical level-of-functioning scale of the second-order model is a continuum. The Bach family falls somewhere between the immature and psychotic positions on the scale, but closer to the former than the latter. The communication deviance here is rather mild and is, as we will see below, at times completely absent from father's transactions.

Finally, a word about the developmental model here. Mother uses developmental arguments quite effectively against the therapist and her line of attack is both typical and reasonable enough so that one needs to be prepared for it. Essentially, the application of the developmental model to the Bachs goes like this. Although chronologically the children (particularly John) are approaching the age of emancipation from the family when they will be out from under parental control, *developmentally* this family is much younger. The Bach family is struggling with issues of limit setting and family structure it should have settled years ago. Had this been done, the parents could now be granting to John the kind of autonomy appropriate for a soon-to-be 18-year-old. If John is to become emancipated properly from the family and go off to be a truly autonomous individual, his family must first reorganize itself along generational lines. There has to *be* a generational hierarchy in the family before this hierarchy can be relaxed. Elsewhere in our work with this family, we learned what is likely to happen if things do not change soon: John is already planning to leave the family as soon as he is 18, to get away from the chaos and conflict at home. This would be a less-than-desirable emancipation, one which would likely compromise this young man's psychological functioning in the future.

As the supervisor in this case, I felt, at this point, that the therapist was not likely to succeed in getting the necessary structural work going and intervened myself to demonstrate how to do it.

(*Immediately following last segment.*)

S: Let me re, shift the focus a little. (*Supervisor sits next to mother and father, leans toward them, and speaks directly to the couple, avoiding eye contact with others in the circle of chairs.*) The reason that you two need to agree on a consequence for John's behavior doesn't have anything to do with John. Or his plans to leave out, to move out in a few months. The reason that it's absolutely necessary for you two to agree on some consequence, no matter what it is, the reason is, that it's absolutely necessary is, that you two are split on this issue. And you (*to father*) name a big consequence and you (*to mother*) said "No consequence" and (*supervisor throws up his hands*). You haven't gotten together. So the reason that you two need to assign a consequence now doesn't have anything to do with John and his plans, but it has to do with you two as parents. You two need to get together on some action as parents. That's what I would like you to do right now. Is talk together, for a few minutes, and find one consequence, however big or small, that you can agree on, for the incident last week. (*Supervisor now leans back in his chair, signaling that he is finished talking to parents.*)

(*Here supervisor works congruently on both structural and strategic levels. Structurally, using physical space, posture, and eye contact, he joins the parents, separating himself and them from the rest of the therapy system. And strategically, he shifts the focus from John and his plans squarely to the parents and their lack of agreement as parents. Remember, the goal is to make a frame within which the structural work can get done. To maximize his impact, supervisor is emphatic, has a very simple message, and builds in redundancy. At the end of his speech, supervisor again uses nonverbal cues to indicate another change in structure: From mother–father–supervisor triad to mother–father dyad.*)

M: (*Turns to father, speaking quietly.*) Uh, do you have anything in mind?

(*This is a very crucial moment. Mother does not fight supervisor, but instead follows his directive and begins the couple interaction.*)

F: Well, I think, a, that there's only one thing that, a, as far as I'm. . . . (*Father stops speaking and begins looking around the room. He has apparently been distracted by a telephone light blinking behind the one-way mirror.*)

(*Father joins her and what happens next is incredible. It is as though father says to himself "Oops, my wife and I are actually talking to each other" and quickly distracts. The evidence for the notion that he distracts in response to the couple interaction rather than to the light itself is simple: The light has been blinking frequently throughout this and previous sessions.*)

M: What?

F: Oh, I just see something blinking.

M: What?

F: I just see something blinking. It's alright. I can (*unintelligible*).

M: Oh.

F: Uh, I think the only thing that we can do, because he is seventeen, the only thing is the car issue, that will have any consequence at all. The others are, I think they're meaningless. I think this would be a meaningful thing, at this point. I think other responses might be, punishment like not watching television or anything like that, I think that was a spur of the moment decision on my part. But I think not using the car is, a, definite consequence. And I think he can appreciate that. The others, other consequences he can circumvent and it isn't meaningful to him. It almost nothing. Okay, I can make him work out in the yard. He never has time for that because that will take him away from all his activities.

(*Father makes a proposal, but then goes on, monopolizing the floor and preventing the interaction from going any further. Notice how this transactional difficulty serves a conflict-diffusing function: Father knows that whatever he says will meet with rejection by mother—a rejection he can delay as long as he holds the floor.*)

S: Let me give you a hint, Mr. Bach. You, you made a definite proposal. Now you need to stop and get some feedback from your wife about where she is with that and see if you can go further.

(*Supervisor's intervention here is transactional, a maneuver designed to promote turn-taking.*)

M: The problem with that now is that John works. (*This remark is directed to supervisor. Supervisor points to father and mother now speaks to her husband.*) John works, right? Now I'll have to pick him up every time. If he goes out he will hitch-hike at night. And I'm really afraid when the kids hitch-hike at night. I don't like them to, and you know that. So the punishment is really punishing me because I will be worrying all the time. And you're not worried about that. But it's punishing me, because he will go out. He won't stay home just because you don't give him the car. And he will hitch-hike.

(*With a simple nonverbal intervention supervisor succeeds in extricating himself, allowing the couple to continue their dyadic exchange. Now mother focuses on John, forms a coalition with him against her husband, and uses John as a club to attack father's proposal.*)

F: He hitch-hikes now, with the car, too.

M: Daytime, I don't care. Nighttime, I care.

F: Well, at nighttime.

M: Well, that's why I most of the time pick him up. So he doesn't hitch-hike.

F: He hitch-hikes sometimes from Kentucky Fried Chicken or whatever at nights, too.

M: I don't think so. No.

(*Here the couple's symmetrical conflict pattern emerges. Notice the relationship between well-oiled turn-taking and open conflict. You cannot have a battle unless both sides are throwing punches. And as long as turn-taking is inhibited, e.g., by long speeches, full-blown conflict is avoided. Of course, one-sided conversations also preclude the give-and-take necessary for cooperation as well.*)

T: (*Interrupts.*) Mrs. Bach, if you can't accept your husband's proposal, then how about proposing an alternative? Remember, the goal is that you two can agree on one thing, however big or small, that's a consequence for what happened.

(*Another transactional intervention: Supervisor reminds mother that they have a shared task to accomplish, namely agreeing on a consequence. Structurally, the maneuver balances the couple, reducing their conflict.*)

M: (*Nods agreement.*) Um-hum.

(*Sixteen-second pause.*)

M: We need to clean out the garage, because you are going to have this great (*debris*) box, right? I think John should give up one day of his work next week. (*Unintelligible*) that he can't work, and clean out the garage that day so we have it all together for that box. Could you be agreeable to that? (*Unintelligible*) that day. I think if we deprive him of one day's wages, then. . . .

(*Mother comes through beautifully with an alternative proposal. And even more, she courageously asks father to agree. But then she spoils it by rambling on and thus prevents father from responding to and, predictably, rejecting her idea.*)

S: (*Interrupts and speaks to mother.*) You did marvelous. You put it out there and then you say "Can you agree with that?" And then you need to stop and let Mr. Bach respond.

(*Another transactional intervention, an example of Minuchin's stroke, "You did marvelous," and kick, "And then you need to stop," technique.*)

F: I think that's a good proposal. The only problem about it is, a, he has already agreed to work three days next week. One day this week yet, and Saturday and Sunday. So (*unintelligible*) I'm already having difficulty even getting those days (*unintelligible*) with the box. Okay, if you, that's a fine proposal, but the problem is, all it is taking, it's just adding the three days that we've already done, we've already agreed on that he's going to do. So you're going to get four days? You'll never get four days out of him. It's impossible. He doesn't have that kind of time. Realistically speaking, I'm having enough problems right now getting him to work this weekend and work two days next week (*unintelligible*) the box.

(*Father immediately uses John to shoot down mother's counterproposal: You idea is lousy because of this or that about John.*)

M: Well, he, um, he usually goes to work at. . . . (*To supervisor.*) Is it permissible to ask John when his working days are?

S: If you need that information.

(*Now, with conflict again open between the parents, mother moves to directly involve John and presumably recruit his help in her battle with her husband. She does so in such a perfectly reasonable way that*

she succeeds at seducing supervisor into giving his blessing. After all,
how could anyone refuse such a reasonable request? Here supervisor is
accepting mother's frame—that she is making a simple request for
information.)

M: (To John.) All right, John, when do you work next week? You were
supposed to find out today.

J: He hasn't made out the schedule yet.

(*This is a very typical pattern: In the middle of a parental conflict, one*
parent turns to a child, ostensibly for information; the child inevitably
fails to produce the information sought and thereby prolongs the
interaction with the parent and so continues to interrupt the parents'
conflict.)

S: Okay, now you're in a good position. If the schedule hasn't been made
out yet then you can make your plans and the consequences for John
and then he can make his schedule around it. So you two need to
agree on some consequence, however big or small, for what happened.

(*It is beginning to dawn on supervisor that he has been had by*
mother. Frustrated, he tries a slick reframing maneuver in an attempt
to short-circuit the child's involvement in the interaction.)

M: (To John.) When is Sam (*John's boss*) going to make out the schedule?

(*Supervisor's strategic ploy fails miserably, not even making a dent in*
the process. Notice how skillfully John prolongs the interaction, in
what follows, never quite giving mother an answer, but leading her on
nicely to another question.)

J: Before Sunday.

M: Did you tell him that one day next week you can't work?

J: That's obvious. I've got finals next week.

S: (Quickly sits up in his chair and leans forward to focus his attention
again on couple.) Now, now what's happening is you're turning to
John more and more to take you off the hook.

(*Some more drastic action is needed, finally bringing supervisor half*
out of his chair. Supervisor now reframes mother's behavior as a bid
for John's help with the parental conflict, rather than as a simple
request for information.)

M: I forgot about finals.

S: You two need to agree on a consequence. (*Supervisor again signals*
that he is done speaking by sitting back in his chair.)

(*Supervisor again refocuses on the couple dyad and on the task at*
hand, a structural move.)

F: I, I, I'd like to say again. All these kinds of things, extra work, these
are problems already. We have problems getting John to work for one

day. I think we'll have to work that out. That's something we have to agree on, how we're going to work that out.

(*And father and mother resume their conversation.*)

M: (*During father's last two sentences mother has been nodding agreement.*) Um-hum.

F: But I do think to impose another day, that's fine, if that's what you want to do, but I don't feel that you're going to be able to do this at this particular moment, because of the fact if you consider, okay, a (*with only a few minutes remaining in the session, supervisor now checks his watch*) "All you can do next week, John, is to do your work, to work at Kentucky Fried Chicken, and. . . ."

(*Supervisor is aware of the time pressure and will shortly use it to push harder for the couple to reach an agreement.*)

M: (*Overlaps.*) I forgot that he had finals.

(*Mother concedes. But notice that she agrees with father—that John should not be asked to work an extra day—not because she accepts his position but rather, for reasons that have to do with John.*)

F: (*Continues.*) "And finals. Ah, and otherwise you are responsible to work in the house." We could do that. But I, I think this is the wrong week probably to do that. I still say, ah, there are certain limitations to car usage. Car usage, he can use the car to go to school in the morning and after school the car goes back in the garage. He can, if necessary, you will have to pick him up (*unintelligible*). I don't think he should be able to use the car to go out on a date. I just think, the only way, that's the only one I can think of.

(*With this victory, of sorts, in his pocket, father returns to his original proposal: Restrict John's use of the car.*)

F: (*Continues above speech.*) You can also say, okay, do some extra work around the house, but I can't think of a way to schedule that, at the moment, except to say "Okay, all the free time that you have you'll have to work around the house." And I don't know if I can cope with that. I'd be fighting both of you for the two weeks on that one. I just feel that way.

(*By emphasizing a coalition between mother and John, father again precisely labels the violation of the generational boundary in the family.*)

S: (*To father.*) So your proposal is what?

(*Another transactional intervention designed to help father make a specific, concrete focus of attention for the discussion.*)

F: Huh?

S: Make a specific proposal again to your wife.

F: Uh. (*Fifteen-second pause.*) I'd just say, I'd restrict him from using the car for two weeks for pleasure. (*Unintelligible.*) I think that would be a consequence that would mean something. I don't see any other consequence that means anything to him.

(Notice how clear father is able to be with this transitional assist from supervisor.)

M: I don't know how he can work that. I already promised him the car. He's taking Mary *(his girlfriend)* shopping. He does his Christmas shopping. Rita does her Christmas shopping. They're all going to shop. There's that. Saturday night is his office party from Kentucky Fried Chicken. He has to go there, you know, he has to. Just like your office party. *(Unintelligible.)*

(A repeat of the previous pattern: Mother uses John to attack father's position rather than saying "I don't like your idea.")

S: So that means you *(to father)* are being the hard liner and you're *(to mother)* being the soft, taking the softie position. You two have to agree on one consequence, however small. You talked before about moving toward the middle. Alright, you've got two minutes left in the session. You two need to agree on some consequence, however small. *(Rita yawns loudly.)*

(Supervisor labels couple's disagreement vis-à-vis John and insists that they reach some agreement. Notice that supervisor's sights are now lower: "However big or small" has become "however small." What mother and father settle on is much less important than that they agree on something. Supervisor ups the ante by reminding couple that the time in the session is almost up.)

M: My garden has to be weeded. How about we agree if by next Wednesday it is weeded? Would that be agreeable?

(This is successful in prompting mother to come up with an entirely new proposal.)

F: Yeah, but I don't want it to interfere with the two days I need him to take down that scaffold.

(Which immediately meets with equivocal acceptance by father.)

M: Yah.

F: You know?

M: *(Turns quickly to John.)* John, is that agreeable?

(This is another classic move: Rather than pursue their discussion to a genuine conclusion, mother prematurely turns to John, again to take the parents off the hook.)

S: *(Extends hand to block mother's interaction with John.)* Wa, wa, wait, now, don't turn to him too quick. You two have to agree first. And then together present it to John.

(Supervisor moves quickly to—literally—block this interaction, once again drawing the generational boundary.)

F: (*Overlaps.*) Okay, I think that's a great idea and I think really productive for this household, too. Okay, by Wednesday the garden has
to be weeded, okay, and. . . .

(*Father falls nicely in line, giving his wholehearted support to mother's
proposal.*)

M: (*Overlaps.*) Or by next Friday. I don't know when his final is, his
math final.

(*And, as though she does not know what to do when she and father
get together—remember father's distraction with the blinking light
earlier—mother immediately begins back-pedaling.*)

S: (*Overlaps.*) No, no, Wednesday, because you'll come here next week.

(*Supervisor first attempts to block mother's retreat by invoking the
time frame of the family sessions.*)

M: Next Thursday?

S: Right. We, we need to get it, we need something that we can check
next week and see how you've implemented. . . .

M: (*Interrupts.*) He has a really important calculus final. . . .

(*Supervisor's move fails.*)

S: (*Overlaps.*) Yeah.

M: (*Continues.*) And I don't know if, when he's. . . .

S: (*Interrupts.*) Right. What's happening is you're, you put out a proposal and then you get worried about John and then you soften it.
You said "By next Wednesday." That was your proposal to him
(*father*). Can you two agree on that?

(*Supervisor tries again, insisting that mother stick to her initial proposal, and then turns the discussion back over to the couple.*)

F: Well, I think that's a good thing. I think the only thing he is going to
lose by it is not having enough free time for leisure time. I think, uh,
you know, studying he can find time.

(*And father resumes the battle with mother.*)

M: Um-hum.

F: Or if it's necessary he can always not work. The only time that it will
take away is for leisure time. So I (*unintelligible*).

M: (*Interrupts.*) Yeah. I don't know if he can, I don't know.

(*Mother continues to use John's needs to express her objections.*)

F: (*Interrupts.*) He will have the ti, he will have the time to do it.

M: I don't know if he has because it's final week, right?

S: Okay. The issue is the, the consequence that you two can agree on and
will impose this next week.

(*Supervisor continues to press the couple to reach an agreement.*)

M: I don't want to impose anything that's not realistic.

S: (*Overlaps.*) It's his, it's his job to find the time to do it. Okay? Your job is to make the consequence and it's his job to find the time to do it. Is that a consequence that you can agree on? You two made, you made a very clear proposal to your husband, and you're (*to father*) saying, I think, "Yes." Is that right?

F: I think it, it's, you know, I think it has to be something meaningful. If you're not, you know, and I think this will create a hardship on him. There's no doubt about that. But not in terms of not being able to do his calculus test or anything like that. It may mean a hardship as far as taking away his leisure time. Now that's, you don't want to do that? Take away his leisure time?

M: He has very little leisure time as it is.

S: (*To mother.*) Okay, this was your idea in the first place.

(*Supervisor again attempts to block mother from backing out.*)

M: It was. And maybe I made a mistake about the day and I'd like to check with him what's happening.

(*Finally mother makes another move to actually draw John into the discussion.*)

S: (*Overlaps.*) No, no. You, you can't ta, go to him to take you off the hook. That's been the problem. Is that when things get tough between you, you turn to one of the kids. It's really important that you two work this out agreeably and then present it as parents to John. You made a very clear proposal, your husband accepted it, and now you're about to take it back. That's very dangerous because that's what happens over and over and over again in the family. And if I allow you to turn to John now, it will repeat.

(*Supervisor moves vigorously. Structurally, the intervention prevents mother from violating the generational boundary. At the strategic level, supervisor frames the intervention as necessary to prevent a repetition of the main family problem—turning to the children for help with the parental conflict.*)

M: (*Immediately.*) Um-hum. Okay.

(*Mother accepts supervisor's move.*)

S: Okay.

M: Alright. Let's do it that way.

S: Check with each other and make sure you're clear on what the agreement is, what the consequence is.

F: What? You tell me.

M: Well, I was proposing to say Wednesday or Friday, but if you're stuck with Wednesday and that's the only way you will go, I guess we'll go Wednesday. I think he has the final on Thursday so I would rather move it to Friday to finish, you know, to get, give him time until then. . . .

(*But she expresses her reluctance.*)

S: (*Interrupts.*) The Wednesday part is mine. I said "We meet here again on Thursday, so let's make it Wednesday." Is that something that you can agree on?

(*This intervention illustrates how much supervisor has joined the family on the side of the parents. At this point the executive subsystem clearly consists of mother, father, and supervisor.*)

F: Can you?

M: Okay.

S: Okay. Now I want you two to decide who's going to tell John. I know he's sitting here but it's real important that you two present it to John somehow. And I want you to decide how you're going to do that.

(*Supervisor now attempts to turn some of the responsibility back over to the parents.*)

M: (*To father.*) Do you want to present it to John?

F: Surely.

M: Alright.

F: (*To John.*) Uh. As you probably heard we decided that we're going to have you, a, weed the garden. Now, I, I, I recognize the problem that you're going to have. A calculus test and all of this. And everything. But I think, you know, this Dr. Schultz says, what we agree, too, is that there needs to be a consequence to, to what's been happening. And I think it's a, I think it's a fair, it's not really a harsh, I think it's a fair punishment, a fair consequence. And I think you can accomplish it, it, you, I think it will cut down on your leisure time somewhat, but I think you can accomplish it.

(*Notice how father borrows the authority of supervisor in presenting the decision to John. This is entirely appropriate at this beginning stage of treatment and indicates supervisor's success at forging a new executive subsystem of which he himself is a part.*)

F: (*Continues above speech*) Now, it depends, (*to mother*) what weeds are we talking about? (*Unintelligible.*) What weeds are we talking about?

(*Here father appropriately turns to mother to clarify an unresolved detail.*)

M: Up in the garden, you know.

(*And again the old conflict resurfaces.*)

F: Which area? There are weeds. . . .

M: (*Overlaps.*) Where I usually have the vegetables.

F: (*Overlaps.*) We have a quarter acre of weeds.

M: (*Emphatically.*) Frank, where I usually have the vegetables. Okay? That area.

F: Those two plots?

M: That's right.

F: That's it? Nothing else?

M: Well, it takes awhile.

(*This is a crucial moment. The conflict has again wound down and could either be ended here or instead rekindled.*)

S: John, are you clear on what they're asking you to do?

(*Here, under the time pressure of the session's end, supervisor moves too quickly to John, dragging him in to solve the problem and doing precisely what he has worked so hard to prevent mother from doing.*)

J: They want the two retaining walls, that were built, right?

M: Um-hum, right.

J: Those (*unintelligible*). So it's no problem.

S: (*To John.*) You're willing to do that?

J: It's fine.

S: Okay.

(*And it works. John is very cooperative and agreeable and the session ends with a sense of closure and accomplishment.*)

(*Therapist promptly ends session.*)

This segment demonstrates an interesting interplay between the transactional and structural models. When I intervene transactionally, for example to promote couple turn-taking, I necessarily became triangulated structurally. This has an immediate conflict-reducing impact on the parental dyad. At this beginning stage of treatment where my initial goal was to promote cooperative action by the parents as the executive subsystem and so define the generational boundary, I offered myself as an object of triangulation, to be used by Mr. and Mrs. Bach instead of turning to their children for help. And so I became a third member of the executive subsystem. Although this is a defensible approach at this point, it does have the potential disadvantage of making it more difficult for the therapist to later extricate himself from the couple dyad and force the two of them to face and resolve their conflict.

Ultimately, the structural work was compromised when *I* drew John in to finish the conflict and permit us to end the session. This was a case in which a frame (here, the time frame of the session itself) got in the way of the necessary structural work. Instead of using the time pressure against the couple to push them to a solution, the pressure got to *me* and I inappropriately turned to John for help, just as the parents do over and over again. At this point I had completely joined the family and was dancing their characteristic dance with them.

To summarize, following the second-order model, the main work with this family is structural, with some relatively high-level (compared, that is, to families of schizophrenics) transactional work. But to accomplish any of this central treatment work, the strategic aspects of the interventions cannot be ignored. In the first segment, the therapist failed to get the parents to join him in a frame within which the necessary structural work could be done. When I entered the room (beginning of the second segment) I *knew* I could pull off the intervention I had in mind. This confidence was not at all incidental to my subsequent success (nor was my increased power as the expert coming into the room from behind the mirror).

In other words, for success at a given level (in this case, structural), it is *necessary* that interventions succeed at higher (here, strategic) levels as well. But, to go a step further, the higher-level work is *not sufficient* to guarantee success at the lower level. This latter point is illustrated above in several instances where I intervened strategically (with reframing) when Mrs. Bach attempted to involve John in the couple's conflict. These efforts failed because by themselves they were at too high a level. When I instead dropped down a level and intervened structurally (by directly blocking those transactions that violated the generational boundary and insisting that Mrs. Bach turn back to her husband), I succeeded.

Part II

Applications of
Family Systems Therapy

10

Creating Frames for Treatment and Training

The hallmark of family systems thinking is attention to context. As discussed in the preceding chapter, the crucial context for understanding the behavior of a given person may be that individual's current social context or mental context (frame) or both.

So far in this book, we have generally focused on the family as the relevant social context, considering as well how family members frame their experiences. This chapter looks beyond the family system, examining the contexts within which we practice and teach family systems therapy. The emphasis here is practical—how to create frames within which successful treatment and training can occur.

The first section introduces the notion of the treatment frame and examines how the therapist entices the family to join in the treatment enterprise. The initial interview and the use of a treatment contract are outlined next, along with the place of cotherapy in family systems work. Finally, frames for training and for the practicing family therapist are discussed.

The Treatment Frame

The treatment frame is the overall reality or context within which the therapy is conducted. This frame is larger and more general than the specific frame chosen for the family's particular problem as described in Chapter 7 on the strategic model. All therapy occurs within *some* frame or context and necessarily has strategic elements. The therapist's overall goal is to create a viable frame within which successful therapy can occur and to get the family to participate in this new frame.

JOINING

The therapist initially joins family members in their views of the world and shares in their experiences. This is accomplished, for example, by listening carefully to family members, using their language, emphasizing similarities between therapist and family, etc. The process goes by various names depending upon one's therapeutic school. Rogerians (e.g., Hart and Tomlinson, 1970) speak of *empathic listening*. Minuchin (1974) writes about *joining* and *accommodation*. Bandler and Grinder (1975), writing about Milton Erickson's hypnotic work, talk about *pacing* the patient. In this chapter, the term "joining" is often used generically to refer to all these phenomena.

Without successful joining of the family's reality, no change can occur. This point is perhaps underemphasized in the preceding chapters. There, clinical material was chosen to demonstrate the change process in four specific intervention models and the process of joining the family was less prominent in the case vignettes and transcripts presented.

There are many different ways to join the family, depending upon the therapy model and the therapist's own personal style. A traditional way for a therapist to join the patient is by taking a long and detailed history, in this way becoming acquainted with the patient's experience. Strategic therapists typically join the family through the presenting complaint, learning about the family by exploring the problem and its social and historical contexts. Structural therapists, such as Minuchin, and experiential therapists, such as Whitaker, often join family members through a quasi-social process of soliciting personal information about work, school, daily activities, etc.

Joining is sometimes seen as something the therapist does at the beginning of treatment, as a prelude to the main job of changing the family. Minuchin (Minuchin and Fishman, 1981) provides a more accurate metaphor for the process. He suggests that all good interventions include both "a kick and a stroke" (p. 6). The stroke is a supportive statement designed to join the patient and keep him with the therapist even as the kick is delivered to push him to change. Seen in this way, the entire therapy is a process of *both* kicking and stroking, with stroking perhaps more prominent than kicking in the initial stages of treatment. Such a view is consistent with Piaget's (1950) idea that change occurs through a process of successive accommodation and assimilation: The therapist both allows himself to be assimilated by the family, changing himself to fit them, and also forces the family to accommodate to him by requiring that they change.

The treatment frame must be close enough to the family's original view of reality so that it is possible for them to join in, yet different enough to allow for the possibility of change. Minuchin (1980) emphasizes that there is some flaw in the family's reality—otherwise they would not have consulted a therapist in the first place. The therapist's job is to create an alternative, therapeutic reality. Minuchin suggests that if the therapist buys into the family's reality completely, the family will likely drop out of treatment because they realize at some level that the therapist cannot help.

ON SEDUCTION

The therapist must use his power to seduce the family into joining in the treatment frame. "Seduce" is a strong word, with sexual connotations that often make therapists nervous. I did not have the courage to use the word in this context until I once heard Carlos Sluzki talk about seducing families into treatment. I decided that if this internationally known and respected family therapist could speak of seducing families, it must be alright.

"Seduce" really is the right word. The second meaning listed in the dictionary (Webster's, 1963) is "to lead astray." And this is precisely the therapist's job: To lead the family astray from an unproductive view of reality into a new, more successful frame.

To do so, the therapist must use all the charisma and personal power he can muster. The therapist's vitality and love of his own life must be compelling enough to entice the family into the treatment frame. This crucial part of therapy training defies our usual efforts at teaching. Each therapist must develop and use those parts of the self that attract and hold others in a relationship. Only when the therapist can be powerful in the therapy can family members use treatment to learn to be powerful in their own lives.

Not all family therapists agree with this view of the place of the therapist's personal power and charisma in therapy. Selvini Palazzoli, for example, insists (Selvini Palazzoli et al., 1978) that the therapist's charisma plays no part in successful treatment. Instead, she argues, all that matters is that the therapeutic method be systemically correct. In taking this position, the Milan group is, I think, choosing to work within a frame in which their own considerable reputation and power are simply ignored.

OTHER ESSENTIAL INGREDIENTS

Other essential ingredients of the treatment frame include hope and caring. The therapist must be able to instill the hope that the family's problems can be solved in order to counter the hopelessness most families bring with them into treatment. According to Ackerman (1962): "The first responsibility of the therapist is to arouse the dormant hope of these troubled people. He endeavors to make of the interview a touching experience" (p. 34).

At times, however, the therapist may choose to counter the patient's pathological optimism with some therapeutic pessimism. Watzlawick and Coyne (1980), for example, describe the family of a stroke victim whose optimism and helpfulness toward the patient maintained his depressed and helpless behavior. In the course of brief treatment, the family was instructed to be less hopeful and helpful, even to the point of replacing unsuccessful encouragement of the patient with strategic discouragement. As the family members abandoned their pathological hopefulness, the patient gave up his depressed hopelessness.

Finally, the therapist's genuine caring for the patient makes the whole therapeutic enterprise possible. Whitaker metaphorically describes the therapist's caring as the anesthesia that permits the surgery of the therapy to take place, referring, for example, to the "'anesthesia' supplied by the therapeutic relationship" (Whitaker et al., 1982, p. 77), which allows the patient access to previously blocked fantasies. Lovaas, the behavioral therapist who has utilized spanking and electric shock to extinguish self-mutilation in autistic children, has remarked (Chance, 1974):

No one punishes who isn't prepared to devote a major part of his life to that child. Nobody punishes a child who doesn't also love that child. . . . Once you lay your hands on a child it morally obligates you to work with that child. . . . After you hit a kid, you can't just get up and leave him; you are hooked to that kid. (p. 80)

Whitaker also cautions, however, that the therapist can care too much. A therapist who *needs* his patients to change to maintain his own sense of esteem and worth risks confusing his own needs with his concern and caring for the patient. To guard against this pathological caring, Whitaker (e.g., Whitaker, 1977) emphasizes the importance of the *therapist's* growth through the family treatment, at times announcing to families that although he does care about them and their growth, he cares about himself and his own growth even more; he is there for himself and if they wish to grow along with him, fine.

EMPATHY IN FAMILY SYSTEMS THERAPY

Family systems therapists do not usually talk about such topics as the therapist's empathy. In fact, we make very different assumptions about what a person has to learn in order to be a good therapist than do adherents of some other therapeutic schools. Client-centered approaches, on the one hand, tend to believe that people who want to be therapists are often deficient in empathic listening skills and that these need to be developed in the course of training. Family systems therapists, on the other hand, are more likely to assume that trainees are empathic listeners who instead need training in particular intervention skills.

Of course, neither position is accurate. In this section, I attempt to balance family systems therapy's emphasis on change techniques with a consideration of the place of therapist empathy in accomplishing such change.

Although experts differ in their particular definitions of empathy, the various notions tend to converge on the idea that empathy includes the ability to emotionally put oneself in the shoes of another and to understand the other's experience as though it were one's own.

The therapeutic use of empathy depends upon the patient's level of psychosocial functioning as discussed in Chapter 9. In working with psychotic-level individuals and their families, the self/other boundary is crucial. Empathy involves the capacity to experience someone else's experience *as if* it were one's own without either having to flee to some safer distance, on the one hand, or being taken over and engulfed by that experience, on the other. In families functioning at the psychotic level, pseudomutual relationships (see Chapters 2 and 8) typically replace genuine empathy. The transactional model's emphasis upon sharing a focus of attention is a prerequisite for building a real empathic relationship.

Moving up the scale of psychosocial functioning slightly, into the borderline range, the self/other boundary is more intact than at the psychotic level, though still very fragile. Here, a crucial issue is the maintenance of *self*-esteem. Kernberg (1975), Kohut (1966), and others emphasize the exquisite vulnerability of borderline spectrum individuals to insults to their self-esteem in the form of "narcissistic injury." When working with such persons, the therapist uses his empathic response to the patient to help maintain that individual's integrity as a separate and valued person.

At the immature level, the central problem is social integration and the therapist's empathy emerges chiefly through his ability to join with the family and with particular family members as a prerequisite to restructuring the family. For example, in order to get Mrs. Morgan to change her husband to make him a better listener (Chapter 5), I had to be able to set aside the negative impact on me of her verbosity and empathize with her plight as a wife whose husband fails to listen. Here the therapist's empathy is a kind of "social glue" holding the therapy system together during treatment.

Empathy is used in work with the neurotic-level individual to help orchestrate the frame for the patient's experience. To keep the patient in a particular frame, the therapist becomes empathic and the patient's experience within this frame intensifies. For an example, review the last excerpt from the work with Mrs. Green presented in Chapter 7. There, when I wanted her to experience her grief at having lived a life that has been "lies and compromises," I simply reflected back her experience with an empathic "That's a pretty depressing thought." And Mrs. Green responded with more sadness, as I had intended. Thus I succeeded in keeping her in a frame that allowed her to grieve. If my goal had been, instead, to reframe her current experience in some other way, then such an empathic response would have been counterproductive.

Moving beyond the clinical realm to the mature level of functioning, empathy is a part of the true intimacy that can develop when separate persons are able to share in each other's experiences.

The Initial Interview

Confronted with a first interview with a family, therapists often find themselves overwhelmed by the tasks at hand: joining the family, as individuals and as a group; accurately assessing the problem; formulating a treatment plan; getting the family to agree to treatment; and making sure they come back for the next session. Some of these tasks are discussed briefly in this section and in the next on the use of treatment contracts. My goal here is to assist the therapist in getting treatment rolling by creating a workable frame for the initial contact with the family.

THE EVALUATION FRAME

The therapist needs time to get to know the family and to plan with them a reasonable course of treatment. The family, on the other hand, often comes to the first interview desperate for some immediate help. Unless the therapist is careful, the family's anxiety may either stampede him into well-intentioned, but premature and useless attempts to be helpful or, at the other extreme, leave him paralyzed and helpless.

The notion of the "evaluation frame" is useful for helping the therapist avoid both rash action and paralysis in the initial interview. Unless the family is clearly in a crisis and something must be *done* immediately, the best initial frame is one of evaluating the problem to see what might be done. I often say something like this:

> The way I work is to take the first one or sometimes two sessions for evaluation, to see what the problem is and how I might be helpful. At the end of this evaluation, I'll be prepared to make some specific recommendations to you, including goals and an estimate of how long the treatment will take.

It is important to introduce this frame early in the first interview. Otherwise, some families are disappointed when the initial session ends without a solution.

If it is clear right from the start that there is a crisis requiring some immediate action, the therapist can still frame the job of the initial session as "figuring out what to do about X." The first interview is then used to evaluate the problem and formulate a plan of action.

Although the evaluation frame should be made explicit to the family to orient them, its value for the therapist should not be underestimated, since it provides a breathing space within which the treatment can begin.

INITIAL INTERVIEW STYLES

There are many ways to conduct the initial interview, depending upon the particular therapy model and the therapist's personal style. Two different approaches are outlined briefly here, to guide the beginning therapist and encourage the more experienced clinician to explore additional options. The first is a strategic-model first interview style, the second is structural.

Strategic. As has been emphasized in the preceding chapters, the strategic model is essentially content-focused, whereas the structural approach is more interested in process. A strategic first interview is concerned with defining the treatment problem and devising an appropriate strategy for solving it. Haley (1976) offers a cookbook guide which is easy for beginners to learn, and provides a step-by-step plan for conducting the initial interview. Roughly following Haley, the following phases of the first session are defined:

Social phase. This typically brief phase provides a transition between the ordinary social interactions outside the treatment room and the business of therapy itself. Here the therapist's job is simply to get everyone greeted and seated, beginning the process of joining the family.

Business phase. All treatment settings, whether agencies or private offices, require that some initial business be conducted. For example in our VA setting, the business phase included collecting face sheet data, explaining the one-way mirror, introducing the treatment team, and obtaining permission to videotape the session.

Orientation phase. This is the time to clarify the purpose of the session by introducing the family to the evaluation frame, as described above. Therapists conducting consultation interviews rather than evaluating families for treatment need to pay particular attention to this phase of the interview. When a family makes an appointment with a therapist, the implicit frame is: *We* want help with our problems. A family appearing for a consultation interview is typically sent to the consultant by someone else and it is this *third party* who wants help with the family. In such a situation, it is very important for the consultant to take the time to first find out the family's expectations for the interview and then to orient them to the purpose of the consultation. For example in family consultations conducted on an inpatient psychiatry unit, families routinely appear either with no clear idea about why they have been asked to come in together, or expecting the consultant to solve their problems. In such cases, the consultant must frame the consultation interview for the family, making clear that he has been asked (e.g., by the patient's inpatient therapist) to find out how the whole family sees the problems the patient is having and to make some recommendations about the appropriateness of family therapy.

Problem definition phase. Here the therapist's job is to find out how each family member defines the problem in the family as well as to determine the problem's relevant historical and social contexts. The therapist typically begins this phase by saying something like "Now I'd like to hear how each of you sees the main problem in the family. And I'd like to hear from everyone." Starting with the person who speaks up first, each family member is interviewed in turn. If another family member interrupts, a therapist conducting the interview according to this model politely, but firmly, indicates that he wishes at the moment to hear X's point of view and will shortly turn to Y.

Interaction phase. In this phase of the strategic first interview, the therapist sits back to observe the family's interaction patterns while family members discuss their problems with each other. During the problem-definition phase, the therapist will have noted what appear to be particularly crucial, emotionally charged topics. Picking one of these, the therapist can introduce the interaction phase by stating, for example, "It's apparent that all of you are stirred up about this problem with Johnny and his behavior at school. Talk about this with each other for a while, and I'll listen and join in from time to time." In addition to observing what happens, the therapist involves himself at strategic points, making trial interventions to probe for possible ways to change the family.

Closing phase. At the end of the first interview, it is crucial to provide something concrete that the family can take back home. This should include some feedback to the family about the therapist's observations, as well as a specific plan of action. If the therapist has already completed the evaluation and is prepared to make a treatment recommendation, this is the time to do it. If not, another appointment should be scheduled "to complete the evaluation."

Structural. A process-oriented structural first interview is more difficult to characterize and harder for the novice to learn, since it does not readily lend itself to the cookbook outline just presented for the strategic initial interview style. Following Minuchin, the therapist initially joins the family and gets them to *enact* their characteristic dance in the session. When process is the main concern, almost any content will do. So an apparently innocuous question by the therapist like "Well, what's the problem?" generally elicits the opening steps of the dance. Some family member responds to the therapist's invitation and begins talking, typically, to the therapist, about the problem. After a few minutes the therapist then directs that person to "discuss the problem" with another family member and the family's dance begins in earnest.

At this point, the therapist has become an observer of the family system, abstracting the steps of the dance from the actual interactional behavior. When the dance winds down and the dancers withdraw from each other, the therapist notes this part of the process and then again becomes active for a moment, urging the family members to continue their discussion. Or when another family member is drawn into the dance, again the move is noted and again the therapist intervenes to restructure the dance and observe the effects of restructuring.

Two generic types of restructuring maneuvers are possible. First, an existing process can be *amplified* to push the system beyond its usual limits. For example, a husband attempting to convince his wife of the correctness of his position can be encouraged to continue the argument beyond the point at which the discussion typically ends in mutual withdrawal. Or, when a daughter joins in the parents' fight on the side of her father, she can be encouraged to work even harder to help her father beat her mother.

Second, an existing process can be *blocked*, forcing the system to find an alternative. To illustrate, the child who joins her parents' fight can instead be blocked from participating, forcing her parents to find a solution to their problem without involving the child.

In general, any content will shed some light on the family's characteristic processes. A topic that generates heat as well will often make the therapist's job easier because emotionally charged interactions usually display typical patterns more clearly or reveal crucial processes that are triggered only at high levels of affect.

As with the strategic first-interview style, at the end of the session, the therapist must achieve closure in the form of specific feedback to the family and a plan for action.

The Treatment Contract

The treatment contract is a useful device for formalizing the results of the evaluation in a concrete plan for therapy. The contract defines the treatment goal and frame, identifies the participants in the therapy, and sets the number of sessions.

In defining the goal of treatment, the therapist should summarize a few key observations made about the family during the course of the evaluation and link these to a direction for therapy. This should be done as concretely and specifically as is possible at this early stage of the work. For example, with the Bach family presented in Chapters 4 and 9, a treatment recommendation something like this was made to the parents: "What we see is that your children always end up involved in your problems. What we need to do as a first step in helping you two solve your problems is get the kids out from the middle." Notice that, in this case, the treatment goal is implicitly framed as a first step in a presumably longer process of marital therapy.

A second part of defining the treatment contract is making clear who needs to be involved in the therapy in order that it succeed. A good rule of thumb is to include as many family members as possible in the evaluation sessions and then decide who must be involved in the treatment itself. In the case of the Bachs, we insisted that the children be included in the initial phase of treatment because we believed that only by having them in the sessions could we successfully reduce their involvement in the parents' marital conflict.

Sometimes certain family members are crucial to the success of therapy. For example, a competent surgical nurse consulted me complaining that her 11-year-old daughter was surly and out of control and that her husband refused to help discipline the daughter and was unwilling to get involved in therapy. The mother presented herself to me as totally helpless to do anything to change either her daughter or her husband. Had I accepted the notion that the husband was indeed unavailable and agreed to see the mother alone, it is likely that the treatment itself would have further entrenched the problem. Predictably, the mother would have become even more helpless as I worked harder and harder to solve her (by then) unsolvable problem.

Instead, I stroked her for her competencies at the hospital, where she ran the operating room, and insisted that she use her considerable abilities at home, to bring her husband to the next session. She returned alone the next week to renew her pleas, and again I remained firm in my conviction that she could bring her husband to the session. The following week the patient returned instead with her problem daughter. This "surly" daughter, large for her age and dressed in an incongruously frilly dress, was reserved and even polite in the office. I told the mother that since she had brought her daughter instead of her husband, she should talk with the daughter and get the problem solved. The two carried on a restrained but unproductive discussion for several minutes, and then the mother turned to me in frustration and announced "I'm coming back next week with my husband." She did, and the two were rather quickly able to work out a plan for handling their daughter.

Finally, here are some guidelines for setting the number of sessions in the treatment contract. Some brief therapies are strictly time-limited, allowing, for example, 10 sessions and no more. Among the psychoanalytically oriented, brief therapy models, Mann (1973) makes perhaps the most persuasive argument for rigidly limiting the length of therapy. He observes that most patients have issues of separation and loss to work through and believes that, from the beginning, brief therapy should focus on termination as a vehicle for resolving these issues.

I prefer a more flexible approach in which therapy ends when the family's problems are solved (or when it is clear that no progress is being made). A typical initial treatment contract of six to eight weeks then becomes a vehicle for beginning the therapeutic work. Sometimes shortening this period to 4 sessions is useful. In other cases, 10 sessions might be appropriate. More than 10 sessions is probably too long, however, because the contracting begins to lose its time-framing power.

I usually introduce the time frame for the therapy with a little speech I learned from my colleague Neil Scott which goes something like this:

> What I recommend is that we work together to (briefly restate treatment goal) for six sessions, once a week, and then re-evaluate. You know, in this business we cannot guarantee success. What I can guarantee you is that at the end of this six weeks it will be clear to all of us whether or not we are getting anywhere. We may not be done by then, but you will know and I will know whether your time and money are being well-spent.

In some cases, I know from the presenting problems that the work will likely take six months instead of six weeks. For example, such immature-level problems as acting-out behavior, drug and alcohol abuse, or psychosomatic disorders typically take several months of treatment, whereas focused neurotic problems may be solvable in six weeks or so. When I expect that the problems will not be solved at the end of the initial contract, I often add the following, to head off the possibility that the family will use the end of the first contract to leave treatment prematurely:

> Based on my experience with families having problems like yours, I expect that we will not be finished at the end of six weeks and that more sessions will be needed. But at least we will know by then whether or not we are getting anywhere.

Recontracting

When an initial treatment contract is made, it is important to stick to it unless there is good reason to abandon it. Good reasons for abandoning a treatment contract include lack of prospects for success (as with the hopeless contract to cure Mrs. Green's depression in Chapter 7) and the emergence of a true crisis that demands immediate attention (but be careful that this crisis is not simply an attempt to avoid good but painful work already underway).

It is also important that the therapy be re-evaluated as scheduled at the end of the contract period. I often use the "highlight" exercise, also borrowed from Neil Scott, to introduce this re-evaluation. In the interview before the final session of the contract I say something like:

> Next week is the last of the sessions we agreed on so we need to re-evaluate then and see how we are doing. And I have got a homework assignment for all of us to get that review going. I would like you to think back over the sessions we have had so far, to what were the highlights for you of the work we have done together. What one or two things that happened in the sessions stand out in your minds, either positively or negatively, as the highlights of what we have done so far?

The final session of the contract usually begins with a report on the highlights homework. With some direction by the therapist, it is generally possible to elicit specific, concrete highlights. Events that happened in the session are generally preferable because their process was shared and can be examined in detail by all participants, so I usually press for these.

My own highlights are typically of two types. First, I sometimes have "spontaneous" highlights from the sessions that I choose to share with the family, events that have simply grabbed my attention. And second, I may also choose a "strategic" highlight to emphasize a particular change or to send a message to a particular family member. For example, to punctuate the change process for a daughter who is overinvolved in her parents' marital conflict, I might tell her that my highlight was when she bit her lip in the next-to-last session and stayed out of her parents' fight.

By the end of the reporting of highlights, the therapist will have a pretty good idea whether the family sees the treatment so far as successful or unsuccessful. The issue of whether to terminate or to continue treatment should then be explicitly discussed with the family, including the therapist's own professional recommendation about recontracting. Beginning therapists, often unsure of themselves and of their ability to help families, sometimes abdicate their professional responsibilities at this point and make the family solely responsible ("whether you want to continue").

Good reasons to terminate treatment at the end of the initial contract are first, the problem is solved and there is no other significant problem, or second, the treatment is getting nowhere, in which case a referral should be considered.

Good reasons to recontract for more sessions include first, partial success, when progress is being made, but more work is needed to solve the problem, and second, the initial problem is solved, but a new problem needs work. The danger associated with recontracting in the face of partial success is that of "the solution is the problem" (Watzlawick et al., 1974): The therapy itself has become part of the context maintaining the problem. The pitfall involved in recontracting to solve a new problem is that the family is having trouble giving up the therapist or the therapist is having trouble giving up the family.

With the above as a prelude, by the time it is necessary for me to make my recommendation regarding recontracting versus termination, I generally have a good idea which way the wind is blowing in the family on this issue. If the family uniformly views the treatment as unsuccessful, I generally agree, accept the blame, make the family responsible for anything positive that did happen, and send them on their way, sometimes to another therapist. Similarly, when family members strongly agree that their problem has been solved, I typically accept their judgment, congratulate them on their success, and gracefully bow out of their lives.

Sometimes, however, it is necessary to exercise one's professional responsibility and make a recommendation about recontracting that disputes the family's position. This is always the case where there are pressing but unresolved issues like suicide or physical abuse. In less extreme cases, it is sometimes necessary nonetheless to challenge the family's attempts to flee from the distress of therapy by reviewing the relevant patterns observed in the course of the work and insisting that they continue. Obviously, the family still makes the final decision, but the therapist has then done what was necessary to discharge his responsibility.

Other options besides either termination or recontracting for more regular sessions include (1) a "vacation" from therapy with an agreement to re-evaluate at the end of a specified time period and (2) periodic "check-up" visits. The latter are particularly useful for seriously impaired families (particularly those functioning at the psychotic level) when the goal is to be available to intervene vigorously during periods of crisis and to stabilize functioning in between such periods.

The power of the therapy contract is generally diminished by making too many successive contracts. When treatment will continue beyond the initial contract, the therapist faces a choice between settling into long-term work versus using one or two more short-term contracts and then ending the treatment. If there are likely to be several more months of treatment ahead (or if the therapy moves in the direction of being frankly exploratory rather than problem-solving), it is usually preferable to make an open-ended contract with the agreement that progress will be periodically reviewed. In other cases, when the scope of the work remains circumscribed and the likelihood of success with several more weeks of treatment is high, recontracting with specific goals and a specific number of sessions makes sense.

A Frame for Training

Family therapy training requires both didactic learning through books and lectures and close supervision of the trainee's actual clinical work with families. In the Preface of this book I presented a frame for the former type of learning, stressing that family systems therapy is first of all a new way of *thinking* about the world, one that is best learned by putting aside other ways of thinking and instead beginning to speak in systems terms. The practice of family systems therapy requires, in addition, that the therapist develop new forms of *action*. This section presents a frame for conducting the clinical supervision necessary for this second type of learning.

The training approach I describe here leans heavily on that developed by Salvador Minuchin and Jay Haley at the Philadelphia Child Guidance Clinic, and which is currently used by Haley at his Washington, D.C. Family Therapy Institute. The particular model presented in this section is based on my work with Neil Scott at the Veterans Administration Medical Center in San Francisco. There, clinical training was conducted in "tutorials" consisting of four or five team members, one or two trainers plus trainees. The tutorial met weekly for three hours, interviewing two families back-to-back, with 15 minutes allotted for discussion before and after each session. Team members took turns interviewing families in the tutorial, with the same therapist conducting all sessions with a given family.

THE SUPERVISION SYSTEM

Consistency demands that systemic thinking be applied to training family therapists as well as to understanding families and conducting family therapy. Traditional, nonsystemic thinking directs our attention to what's "inside" the trainee therapist, whereas systemic understanding as always asks that we examine the trainee's context. Here the term "supervision system" is used to include the supervisor and other treatment team members as well as the "treatment system" consisting of therapist plus family. The treatment system, and in particular, the therapist, is thus seen as part of a larger whole (the supervision system).

The boundary separating the treatment system from the rest of the supervision system typically includes a one-way mirror, although other arrangements are possible as well. For example in the work with the Stuarts described in Chapter 6, the supervision system was configured as an inner circle of therapist and family plus an outer circle or "back row" consisting of supervisor and observers. What is important is not the mirror itself, but rather the boundary between the business of doing therapy and the business of observing and supervising the treatment. Hoffman (1981) compares the advantages of this "bicameral" format for doing therapy to the new perspectives and possibilities that emerge when a second eye or second brain hemisphere is added to the first.

LIVE SUPERVISION

A cybernetic loop links the treatment system with the rest of the supervision system in a mutual regulatory process and provides an ideal context for clinical training often referred to as "live" supervision. The "feedforward" part of the cybernetic circuit (see Chapter 3) consists of the treatment team's observation of the therapy. Much essential family systems training occurs through such observational learning. From the vantage point of the second chamber behind the one-way mirror, trainees have a chance to observe both their supervisor's demonstration interviews with families as well as sessions conducted by their peers.

The "feedback" portion of the cybernetic loop is comprised of the supervisor's corrective interventions to redirect the course of a session. Such feedback occurs using a variety of channels. The ubiquitous telephone in the corner allows private conversations between supervisor and therapist to be initiated by either. Some settings utilize a "bug-in-the-ear" through which a supervisor can direct the therapist's activity. In addition, the therapist may leave the therapy room to confer with the supervisor in another room, or the supervisor may confer with the therapist in the therapy room in front of the family. Or, finally, the supervisor may take over the session itself in order to demonstrate a particular intervention.

Furthermore, in most cases, the relationship between trainee therapist and supervisor is clearly hierarchical. The therapist's job is to direct the family with the goal of solving their problems and the supervisor's job is to direct the therapist with the goal of teaching the trainee to do family systems therapy, and ensuring that the family receives adequate care. This hierarchical arrangement generally reflects such realities as the supervisor's greater experience and competence as a therapist and often the fact that the supervisor has ultimate clinical responsibility for the case, as well. In other situations when the treatment team consists entirely of peers of essentially equal status and experience, a consultation model may be more appropriate than the supervisory model. In this case, the treatment team's job is to observe the session and give the therapist an opinion about what is happening in the session, but the therapist is left free to accept or reject the team's views.

Videotaped replay of family interviews is a useful adjunct to both didactic training and clinical supervision. Students should routinely tape their sessions and take the time to review them afterwards. Live supervision in the tutorial format described above can be effectively supplemented with sessions in which the trainee's tapes are reviewed and discussed with a supervisor. In addition, videotapes of the master family therapists are now available from major training institutes, providing additional opportunities for observational learning.

INDIRECT SUPERVISION

More traditional, "indirect" forms of supervision in which the trainee tells the supervisor about what happened in the session are better saved for advanced family therapy trainees than used with novices. There are a number of reasons for this. First, many beginning family therapists need the structure and support of live supervision, and often the goal of providing quality care to families demands it as well. Second, it is well known that trainees are generally quite selective in reporting on sessions to their supervisors, whether out of defensiveness or lack of knowledge about what to pay attention to. Videotapes are helpful in this regard, but they are still no substitute for live supervision.

The most important reason for de-emphasizing indirect supervision in the early stages of family systems training is more subtle, however, and has to do with the frame implicit in the entire approach. Family systems work requires careful observation of behavior and well-timed action by the therapist. It is not a very inner-directed or reflective approach. The primary material in live supervision is the ongoing behavior of therapist and family, with the therapist's own feelings and reactions about the work taking a secondary position. In indirect supervision, on the other hand, the only live data the supervisor has to work with is the therapist's behavior and feelings while reporting about the session. This information tends to become the primary material in indirect supervision, with the behavior in the therapy session itself taking a back seat. For this reason, reliance on indirect supervision in the early stages of training subtly undermines the entire family systems approach.

On the other hand, with more seasoned family therapists who have already developed a basic repertoire of observation and action skills, the reflective stance of indirect supervision can be valuable in helping trainees integrate these new skills with their own personal styles and with previous therapy training and experience.

OTHER FEATURES OF THE TRAINING FRAME

Additional features of the training frame will now be noted briefly. First, a time frame. It takes at least a year of hard work before a trainee really begins to think and act like a family systems therapist. It is helpful, I think, to make this expectation explicit at the beginning of the training period: At first it gives trainees permission to bumble around and make mistakes and later in the year focuses attention on how far they have come.

Second, considerable attention must be paid at the beginning of the training period to creating a safe atmosphere within the tutorial. Even experienced clinicians become apprehensive at times when their work is under scrutiny, and the prospect of live supervision strikes terror into many trainees' hearts. It is essential at the outset to establish the ground rule that "everyone interviews families," supervisor and all trainees alike. Later in the year with a well-established tutorial, it is possible to invite others in to observe the team at work. But at first it is important to make it clear that everyone's work will receive the same scrutiny. Supervisors should also attempt to organize the rotation of interviewers during the first weeks so that everyone has a chance to conduct at least one session. Typically, each tutorial has a member who hangs back and is reluctant to jump in and conduct a session. Much anticipatory anxiety can be avoided by structuring things so that each member routinely interviews early.

Third, a trainee's discomfort with the tutorial format generally gets displaced onto families unless it is dealt with effectively by the supervisor. As long as the trainee is comfortable with the team approach, one-way mirror, videotaping, etc., and the treatment setting is matter-of-factly introduced to families as "the way we work," most families accept it as such. When the trainee is uncomfortable, however, this anxiety is invariably transmitted to family members. They, in turn, generously oblige the therapist by, for example, refusing to sign the videotaping permission form.

Fourth, the supervisor must succeed in communicating to the trainees that he is there to "help" the therapist, not to criticize him/her. This does not mean unconditional positive regard of all therapist behavior. The supervisor knows that he has succeeded in this respect when trainees experience relief that help is on the way when he phones into a session with instructions rather than steeling themselves for a critique.

Finally, supervisors must operate within the systemic frame that trainees are competent individuals whose prior life contexts and therapy training have typically not selected for those behaviors (including careful observation and directive action) required to do successful family systems therapy. The supervisor's job, then, is to create a training context that will allow trainees to demonstrate these behaviors. To paraphrase Haley (1979), if the training fails, the supervisor has failed to create such a context.

Cotherapy in Family Systems Work

The use of cotherapy is somewhat controversial. Experiential therapists such as Whitaker make cotherapy central to both practice and training. At the opposite extreme, Haley suggests (1976) that people do cotherapy because they are afraid to see a family alone. My own position, although not as extreme as Haley's, is that the solo therapist model works best for family systems therapy. In such active, directive work, two therapists tend to trip over each other's feet unless they are *very* experienced at working *with each other*.

The clear advantage of cotherapy is the corrective influence of one therapist on the other (the final excerpt from our work with the Stuarts in Chapter 6 provides an example). However, this benefit can be retained in the single-therapist approach by making the second person into a supervisor or peer consultant behind the mirror, rather than a cotherapist, thus maintaining the boundary between the therapist and family, on the one hand, and the rest of the treatment team, on the other.

In my experience, cotherapy is unsatisfactory as a training model as well. With two novice therapists, each tends to look to the other to act rather than jumping in and working with the family. And when a trainee is paired with a supervisor, their real difference in experience and competence generally precludes the symmetry necessary in a good cotherapy relationship.

The experience of the Milan group provides an interesting example of how the structure of the treatment team is often worked out in practice. Faced with the problem of how the four of them, two men and two women, could work together, Selvini Palazzoli and her colleagues originally developed a model in which a male and female therapist conduct the interview together while the other two act as consultants behind the mirror. This model was widely adopted by other groups as an essential part of the Milan school's approach. Recently, however, the Milan team split up, with the two men going off in one direction and the two women in another. As a result, both groups have now abandoned cotherapy, but have retained the use of a colleague as consultant to the interviewer.

The place of cotherapy within the various family therapies illustrates the fact that each school tends to adopt training methods consistent with its therapy approach. Experiential family therapists, on the one hand, emphasize experience, whether it be that of the family members, the therapist in the family interview, or the therapist in a supervision session. Role-playing and sculpting techniques are frequently used both in therapy and in training. Structural and strategic approaches, on the other hand, emphasize behavior over the experience of behavior (e.g., what mother is now doing rather than what she experiences as she does it). The therapist's job is to direct family members' behavior and the supervisor's job is to direct the behavior of the therapist. Videotape review and live observation and supervision of actual treatment cases are the preferred training methods.

I was reminded of this point recently in consulting with a local family agency that, for the past several years, had been conducting a successful training program in structural and strategic therapy using live supervision, a one-way mirror, the bug-in-the-ear, etc. I was surprised at the end of the first interview when family members joined the treatment team behind the one-way mirror and the latter talked with the family about their personal experiences while observing the session. This post-interview technique was, it turned out, a carry-over from earlier years when the agency's predominant treatment approach had been experiential. What tends to happen during such a process is that the direction developed during the interview is diffused as each team member comments from a personal, idiosyncratic perspective. Although such an approach is perfectly consistent with experiential therapies in which everyone's view is valued equally, it does not fit with the hierarchical systems models discussed in this book. Instead, I suggested that the consultant join the therapist and family in front of the mirror at the end of the session to provide some feedback about the session and indicate directions for subsequent work.

The Care and Feeding of the Practicing Family Therapist

Beginning family therapists in organized training programs, as well as experienced clinicians attending workshops, often become wildly enthusiastic about family systems approaches, only to be disappointed when they go to other settings and attempt to apply what they have learned. The fault here typically lies neither with the trainer nor with the students, but rather in the failure to appreciate the fact that the context in which the treatment occurs makes a crucial difference. Although the notion that context is important is central to family systems thinking, we sometimes forget that successful family systems therapy cannot be done in certain settings without first modifying the context itself. Haley's (1975) paper "Why a Mental Health Clinic Should Avoid Family Therapy" can be profitably reread as a reminder of this important point.

Therapists in institutional settings, many of which as a whole are not particularly systems-oriented, often solve the problem of context partly by creating a family therapy program within the larger institution. Often organized to provide training as well as clinical services, such a program offers the supportive context necessary to think systemically.

After leaving such a family therapy program for the insular world of private practice, it took me quite a while to feel that the work I did in my own office was as good as the work I had done in my former institutional setting. The overriding reason for this was the shift in context within which I practiced.

Private practitioners generally must work very hard to maintain a context supportive of systems thinking. I am reminded of this several times a year when I catch myself working with an individual patient for a while only to realize that there have been family issues all along, had I only remembered to look for them.

Some ongoing group context is, I think, necessary to enable therapists to continue to think systemically and to provide the feedback necessary to keep one's actions in line with systems thinking. This may take a variety of forms. Local family therapy associations permit professional and social contact among peers and support family thinking. Case consultation, whether in organized, ongoing groups or individually, provides another such forum.

11

A Case of Developmental Impasse:
Psychogenic Vomiting
in an Adolescent Girl

In this chapter and the next, the models of the preceding chapters are applied to two new cases, each offering a view of treatment from start to finish.

The Miller family, presented here, illustrates the use of all four first-order models, employed according to the second-order model described in Chapter 9.

In fact, this case came along when I was just beginning to struggle with the question of how to integrate family systems models, and stimulated my thinking along the lines that eventually became the second-order model and systemic psychopathology. Several transcript segments from the first session presented below demonstrate the problem of overlooking transactional-level pathology and intervening instead at too high a level (i.e., strategically). In subsequent interviews, transactional and then structural models were employed, with more success.

In retrospect, some of the work, particularly the structural, now seems to me inefficient and at times clumsy. More elegant alternatives will be noted below at certain points as the case material is presented. Despite these limitations, however, the Miller family drama as it unfolded in the course of therapy provides a textbook case for viewing a fascinating symptom in the context of the family's organization.

Identifying Data

The Miller family included the father, age 66 at the time of referral, the mother, age 59, and two daughters: Laurie, 21, and Nancy, 16. Laurie had been adopted as an infant after the couple gave up hope that they could have a child of their own. A few years later, Nancy was born.

Mr. Miller, a businessman, had retired from his job a year and one-half before our initial contact with the family at the time he underwent surgery for cancer of the esophagus. Mrs. Miller, a housewife, had not worked outside the home since her marriage. Laurie attended college and Nancy was a junior in high school. Both daughters lived in the family home.

Approximately six weeks before we saw them, Mr. Miller was found to have metastatic disease in both lungs. The recurrence of his cancer was inoperable and Mr. Miller was begun on chemotherapy. A week later, the family was referred to us by the oncology fellow who felt that the Millers needed assistance in coping with this new crisis in the father's illness.

The Initial Phase of Treatment

Fourteen sessions were held with the Miller family over the following 11 months. Initially, the entire family was seen. During the last three of these months, the sessions included only Mr. and Mrs. Miller.

ASSESSMENT

The early sessions with this family produced the following picture, seen through the lenses of the strategic, structural, and developmental models.

Strategic model. In the opening moments of the first session (attended by Mr. and Mrs. Miller only) Mr. Miller described the presenting problem: "I'm not sure how my daughters are handling my illness. They may be having some problems that they aren't talking about."

Accordingly, my cotherapist Barbara and I invited Laurie and Nancy to the next session. The daughters admitted that coping with their father's illness was difficult for them, but were unable or unwilling to identify any specific problems. Mr. Miller reiterated what had by then become a theme: "I don't want my illness to affect the family." The parents insisted that their daughters may have things on their minds that they are unable to discuss in front of their parents.

Our solution at this point was to schedule separate sessions for the couple and for the daughters. Seen alone, Laurie and Nancy did identify some troubling issues: Laurie's struggles to become emancipated from the family and Nancy's role as family "go-between" (see structural and developmental assessments below). However, when we attempted to bring these issues back into the family session, the daughters again minimized the problems.

We felt in a difficult bind. On the one hand, the family was clearly distressed, tugging at us for some help. But every time we attempted to get a handle on the problems the Millers were experiencing, the family seemed to conspire to deny that there was anything wrong.

The pervasiveness of the family's denial of problems while engaging in treatment is illustrated by a brief excerpt from a session more than a year later and after Nancy had developed a serious psychosomatic symptom.

F: How about you girls? Any problems. (*Two-second pause.*) None?

(*Father opens the floor to a discussion of problems with his daughters and then denies that there are any without giving them a chance to respond.*)

L: (*Unintelligible.*)

F: What?

L: (*Overlaps.*) A job, so I'm sure I get one.

(*Laurie cooperates by ignoring the family's most pressing problems—Nancy's symptom and father's illness—and offering her own dilemma about work as a safer alternative.*)

Structural assessment. The early sessions suggested two structural issues: (1) great distance in the father–Laurie dyad because of their conflict over Laurie's struggles to become emancipated from the family and (2) Nancy's job as go-between in the family.

To illustrate the first, Laurie had come home from a date at seven one morning, something that was just not done in this nice Catholic family. Mr. Miller was very angry at Laurie about this, but was unable to discuss it with her and had avoided talking with Laurie for several days. As the two discussed their difficulties in the session, the pattern became clear. Laurie, pushing harder and harder for independence, continued to live at home. And father was fighting just as hard to maintain control, while asking Laurie to assume more financial responsibility for herself.

Nancy discussed the dilemma of her role in the family as follows: "I don't like my role as go-between. Everybody tells *me* their problems rather than the person really involved." She described herself as the "cheerful" one in the family. Early work on this issue was limited to helping Nancy stay out of the conflict just described between father and Laurie.

Six months after we began working with the Millers, the father was feeling weak, tired, and discouraged and the family was willing to discuss their concerns about his dying for the first time in the sessions. In a follow-up session with Laurie and Nancy, we focused on Nancy's added burden of cheering up the family now that they were all so discouraged and depressed. We questioned Nancy about how she handled her own depression, and were worried enough about her that we asked directly about suicidal thoughts, which she denied. We also predicted that if her father's condition got even worse, her burden as family "cheerer-upper" would increase still more. We reminded Nancy that everyone has limits to the amount of stress they can manage and discussed what she could do if she began to feel very low.

Curiously, in these early sessions, our attention was not focused much on the generational boundary directly nor on the marital dyad. It seems in retrospect that the enormity of Mr. Miller's cancer prevented us from employing our usual ways of looking at families.

Developmental assessment. From the beginning of our work with this family, we framed the family's experience in developmental terms. For example, Laurie's emancipation struggles, particularly with her father, have already been described. In this case, however, Mr. Miller's illness added an additional complication to Laurie's normal and appropriate moves toward independence from the family, tending to bind her to the family home.

Nancy was already thinking ahead to the following year when

she would complete high school and was wondering what would happen when it was time for her to go away to school. (Unlike Laurie who went to school near home, Nancy was planning to attend college in another city, 500 miles away.)

Mrs. Miller spoke movingly about looking ahead to her daughters' growing up and leaving home while facing a very uncertain future with her husband in view of his serious illness.

This case illustrates how family development is complicated when a typically later stage of the life cycle (here, the issues of illness and possible death of a parent) is superimposed on the demands of an earlier life task (in this case, the emancipation of the children).

Impasse

During the final three months of the initial phase of our work with the Millers, an impasse developed in the therapy. At that point we began meeting with the couple only, approximately once a month. Mr. Miller's physical condition was unimproved or slowly worsening. And the couple's mood fluctuated between bland optimism ("I'm cured" or "I'm going to lick this") and depressed pessimism.

In one of these sessions, the couple cried together for the first time *ever* in their marriage when discussing Mr. Miller's failing condition. Father immediately apologized profusely for his "breakdown" and mother became worried that now she might find herself crying all the time. We thought it was a breakthrough. However, Mr. and Mrs. Miller avoided all attempts to discuss it further in the next session.

A follow-up session six weeks later was missed due to a mix-up in appointment times and was never rescheduled. We were as discouraged as the family was, and *mutual avoidance* set in.

About four months later we learned that the family was at an impasse as well. Barbara was about to contact the family when she happened to meet Mrs. Miller in the hospital. The mother was very distressed, told Barbara that she had been wanting to talk, and began pouring out a whole long list of problems that had severely taxed her coping abilities.

A couples session was scheduled for the following week, at which we learned:

Laurie had flunked out of college six months earlier, with only one exam and a paper needed to complete her degree. Four months before this (about the time the daughters had stopped attending the sessions), she had moved out of the family home and into an apartment of her own. Mr. Miller was still extremely angry about this and very hurt that Laurie had told him of her plans only after signing the lease. Both parents strongly disapproved of Laurie's boyfriend. And Laurie was now working at a poorly paid job much below the level her college degree would have permitted. She continued to depend upon her parents for financial assistance while rejecting their advice.

Nancy had been vomiting for five weeks and had already lost more than 20 pounds. Her medical work-up was completely negative. She had had a similar episode several years before, lasting about 14 months. Nancy was planning a trip to Europe with high school classmates in two months and intended to go away to college in the fall.

Mrs. Miller admitted that she was extremely depressed and discouraged. Her brother had died suddenly of cancer (and her mother had died about a year before). Mother stated: "I just want to hibernate for six months." She revealed with sadness that she had had no physical affection from her husband during the three years since his illness began.

Remarkably, Mr. Miller's physical condition had actually improved. There was no sign of a recurrence of his cancer without chemotherapy for the preceding five months. And he had obtained some symptomatic relief with acupuncture. However, Mr. Miller continued to complain (of tiredness plus many, many physical problems) and was totally unresponsive in the session to his wife's moving statement of her own needs.

We felt hopeless, and scheduled a family session for the next week.

The Drama and Power of Nancy's Symptom

Father, mother, and Nancy attended the next session. Mother explained Laurie's absence with the double message: "Laurie had to work but is willing to come."

That week Nancy had begun individual treatment. She reported that her therapist told her that she is vomiting because she is worried about going off to Europe and to school in the fall with her father so ill.

Nancy admitted that she worries a lot about her father, although she pretends to herself and her family that she does not. I began explaining to Nancy that her stomach was telling her that she can no longer ignore the worries and strain. At that moment she began to get nauseous and ran from the room to vomit. Immediately Mr. Miller excused himself to go to the bathroom, explaining "It's my new medication." In the previous months when he was much sicker physically, Mr. Miller had never left a session. Rather than physical distress, this sequence suggests Nancy and her father's poorly defined individual boundaries. When Nancy and her father returned, I framed the vomiting as her stomach's confirmation of my statement that she could no longer ignore the worries and strain of her father's illness.

By the end of the session it appeared that Mr. Miller had begun to soften, becoming more understanding of his family's distress about his illness. And Mrs. Miller acknowledged that the family had been avoiding facing the strain of his cancer. We continued to frame Nancy's symptom by attributing father's softer attitude to the power of Nancy's stomach.

The family agreed to an eight-week family therapy contract, to include Laurie, with Nancy continuing with her individual treatment as well. This is a good example of the usefulness of combining family and individual therapy in the case of an adolescent having trouble becoming emancipated. Both strengthen the generational boundary. We subsequently met with Nancy's individual therapist and were pleased to learn that she saw the case much as we did. Everyone had expected Mr. Miller to die the previous Christmas. Instead, he had managed to improve, which now presented Nancy with the prospect of leaving him, still very ill, to pursue her own life. Her vomiting appeared to be a response to this dilemma.

The literature on psychogenic vomiting, outside of the syndromes of anorexia nervosa and bulimia (where the vomiting is usually voluntarily induced), is sparse and of limited relevance to the present case. Most of the psychologically oriented articles describe vomiting either in young children or in a mentally retarded population. One study of a group of 14 women and 6 men, all adults with this symptom, sheds some light on Nancy's difficulties. Hill (1968) found that, among other factors, the life histories of his subjects with psychogenic vomiting were distinguished from controls suffering from psychogenic abdominal pain without vomiting by the patient being "locked in an inescapable hostile relationship with their family group." This is vividly illustrated by his description of one case in particular: "A spinster, the sole companion and support of an aged, depressed, cantankerous mother with whom she lives. The patient tolerates the position because she considers it to be her duty" (p. 351).

Binding Communication and Scapegoating

The following segment is taken from the second of the eight contracted family sessions. Read this transcript through the first time without consulting the annotations. Try to put yourself in the place of Barbara (designated *T2*) and me (*T1*) and imagine the impact of the family's communications. Later you will be directed to return to this segment and consider the interaction in detail.

(*Near the beginning of the session, Laurie sits next to her parents, with Nancy on the outside of the family circle. Father has just introduced the issue of his going back to work part-time. This leads to a discussion of family finances and Nancy wonders whether the family is prepared for and can afford her college expenses. Therapist 2 attempts several times to connect this issue with father's illness, without success.*)

T2: (*To father.*) Are you reassuring Nancy that the money for college is already there?

 F: Yeah. (*Father looks down into his lap.*)

 (*Seven-second pause.*)

T1: Is that true?

 M: Yes, it is.

T1: It is true.

 (*At this point it appears that the therapists have succeeded in pinning down a fact: The money to meet Nancy's college expenses is available.*)

 M: Um-hum.

T2: Were you aware of that, Nancy?

 N: Yeah. They've always told me, like I used to say, uh, "Well, if you want I can go to work and just start saving the money to go to school" and they say "You don't have to worry about it because we, we planned for," more or less after I was born. I always knew that they were prepared. But I don't think they were prepared for paying room and board (*laughs nervously*).

 (*Here Nancy accepts her parents' reassurance in one breath and questions it in the next. Her laugh betrays anxiety along with her doubts.*)

T1: So you have some questions.

(*Therapist 1 supports Nancy's questions.*)

N: I guess.

T1: One of them is whether they were prepared for. . . .

N: (*Overlaps.*) The room. Well, because of. . . .

(*Nancy finishes therapist 1's sentence, acknowledging that he has joined her.*)

M: (*Overlaps.*) That's all part of it.

(*Mother attempts to reassure Nancy.*)

N: (*Continues.*) Inflation, too, the money, the tuition has gone up, uh, room and board. (*Nancy turns toward her parents, having to talk across Laurie, who sits between them.*) You probably expected me to go to school. . . .

(*But Nancy continues to question her parents' version of reality.*)

T1: (*Interrupts.*) Wait a second. (*To Laurie.*) You're kinda in the middle of this. How about if you two (*indicates Nancy*) change places. (*Nancy and Laurie change seats, placing Nancy next to mother.*)

(*Therapist 1 intervenes structurally to remove Laurie from the middle of this discussion between Nancy and the parents.*)

T1: (*To Nancy.*) Now you can find out the answers to some of the questions that you have directly from your parents. Like, "What about this room and board stuff?"

N: Well, you guys were probably more prepared for me going to a school around the house.

(*Nancy persists, indicating the seriousness of her concerns.*)

M: Not especially, Nancy, we, we have a, enough, for the room and board.

(*And mother persists in her attempts to reassure Nancy.*)

N: I know, you have enough but did you think about it then. . . .

F: (*Overlaps.*) I did.

N: (*Continues.*) When you started saving for it?

F: (*Overlaps.*) I did, 'cause I didn't think you'd find a school around the area that you'd want to go to.

M: (*To father.*) When she was a baby? (*Laughs and touches father affectionately on arm.*)

(*Here mother supports Nancy by gently questioning father's outlandish effort to offer still more reassurance to Nancy.*)

F: (*Unintelligible.*)

T2: (*To Nancy.*) Nancy, I'm wondering if part of your question, in addition to your saying you don't think they were prepared for you to be going away to school, to pay the room and board, I'm wondering if part of the question is that you didn't think that they were also prepared for your father getting ill, and that maybe that changes things?

(*Therapist 2 makes another effort to relate the discussion of the family's ability to afford Nancy's education to the issue of father's illness. This time she succeeds. This is a hot issue because it challenges the family myth that father's illness does not affect the family.*)

N: I don't know.

(*Nancy pleads ignorance.*)

F: I don't think we were prepared for that.

(*Father answers for Nancy and also diverts attention from the main point of therapist 2's question: Whether father's getting ill changes the family's ability to afford Nancy's education.*)

T1: Give Nancy a chance.

N: (*Sighs and laughs.*)

T2: Everybody's very helpful to Nancy today.

(*Therapist 2 nicely frames father as "too helpful" here.*)

M: (*Laughs.*) Answer her questions.

T1: Uh-huh.

N: Um, can you run that by me again? (*Laughs.*)

(*Here Nancy pleads confusion.*)

F: (*Laughs.*)

N: I'm a little slow today.

T2: Okay. I heard the question, I heard that you accepted that they had some money for you to go to school, but that you still wondered whether they had been prepared for you to go away to school. You had some questions about that. And it flashed through my mind (*Nancy anxiously kicks table on which microphone sits*) that I also wondered if you were thinking about the fact that your father had, become ill and that that had changed their financial situation, and whether that was part of your worry. That in addition to their maybe not expecting you to go away to school, there is also this added situation of your father being sick.

(*Nancy's confusion is contagious. Rather than seeing Nancy's behavior as a defensive maneuver, therapist 2 assumes that she herself was being confusing and attempts to explain. In doing so, therapist 2 turns a concise, pointed question into a long, wordy, convoluted statement, dulling its impact. Compare this with the very effective way the therapist in Chapter 6 dealt with a similarly "confused" family member.*)

N: Um-hum.

T2: And that you were worried about that.

N: Yeah, but I don't think dad's sickness really has affected our finan, I don't really think it did affect our finances because he had already retired, and uh, he'd still be getting the same money if he wasn't sick. Wouldn't he?

(Once therapist 2 zeroes in on father's illness, Nancy drops her doubts and says what she is supposed to say, reiterating the family myth that father's illness does not affect the family. But her logic suffers a bit in the process.)

M: Uh-hum.

N: So I really don't think. . . .

(Nancy insists on maintaining the myth.)

T2: *(Overlaps.)* Okay.

(And therapist 2 drops the matter.)

N: *(Continues.)* It would make any difference. Now he can go on with what he was going to say. *(Laughs and then turns to father.)* You said, you were starting to say something.

(Nancy now moves strongly to avoid the discomfort of further discussion of this issue.)

F: I've had added expense, that's about all I can say. Going to the acupuncture.

(Once Nancy has confirmed her loyalty to the family's view of reality, father challenges Nancy's denial that his illness has affected the family and in so doing himself contradicts the family myth.)

M: And then inflation too has made quite a difference.

(And mother joins in father's repudiation of the family myth.)

F: It's created, see, we're on a fixed income, our pension, and it never varies. There's no cost of living in it at all.

(Imagine Nancy's confusion: If she voices her own concerns about the family's ability to finance her education in the face of her father's illness, she is disloyal to the family; on the other hand, if she loyally supports the family's version of reality she must give up her own perceptions and is repaid for her loyalty with her parents' immediate contradictions.)

T1: So the, the illness has affected your finances.

(Again attempting to pin down the facts, therapist 1 restates the challenge to the family's usual construction of reality.)

F: It, that's right.

(Father assents.)

M: (*Overlaps.*) In a sense.

(*Mother qualifies.*)

F: (*Continues.*) There's been additional expense. It's affecting it more and more. That's why I think I'm going to work, to, to augment what I'm not making. But it doesn't affect the provision of hers (*Nancy's*) because hers was already set aside.

(*Father now takes back his statement of a few speeches before and again recites the family myth.*)

Tl: I'm not sure whether Nancy believes that. I guess I'm not sure whether I believe it. (*To Nancy.*) I'll speak for myself rather than you. (*To father.*) You're saying on one hand the money is set aside, but you feel like it would be nice to go back to work to augment the income you're getting.

(*Therapist 1 finally begins to perceive just how slippery reality is in this family and gropes to label the contradictory messages.*)

F: Well, let me answer a double-barreled question with a double-barreled answer. But I feel that the therapy's going to be the primary purpose I'm going back to work, the therapy.

(*Father gives himself away here, acknowledging the double message while attempting to deny it.*)

Tl: For you.

F: Yeah, right. And I think that's going to be very helpful. The money is secondary. It's, it's, it's, uh, well, I wouldn't put it secondary. It's primary too, in the respect that the cost of living has gone up and I have this expense of the acupuncture per month, that I have to meet, because no insurance covers that yet. They're working on it now, the company is, but so far they haven't gotten to first base on it. See, it's been approved by the state of California, but it hasn't been accepted by the insurance companies yet. And it has done me a lot of good, but Bridges (*the oncologist*), see, I cleared this with Bridges here. He knows about it, so that she (*the acupuncturist*) contacts him and he contacts her. And they talk back and forth on my condition, so that there's nothing undercover about it at all. They both know about it.

(*With marked hesitation and stammering suggesting anxiety, father contradicts himself in the span of a few sentences. Then father becomes more and more tangential, distracting from the hot family issue.*)

Tl: But it is a financial drain.

F: Right.

Tl: And you're concerned about it.

F: Right. Right. Runs about a hundred twenty-five a month.

T2: Uh-hum.

T1: So where does all of this leave you, Nancy? About the finances?

(*Again therapist 1 attempts to establish a solid reality and then confronts Nancy with the problem it poses.*)

N: I didn't think it made any difference, I mean, him being sick, but I guess it does. Uh, it's not going to change my mind because I want to go to that school, but like if they needed any, uh, financial help or something like that, I can always, you know, apply for a scholarship or something like that. Or get a part-time job and pay for it. 'Cause I'm not afraid to do that.

(*Nancy accepts this new version of reality—the opposite of the family's usual construction—asserts her own needs in spite of it, and then immediately becomes guilty and responsible.*)

T1: That's something you've talked about with the family?

N: Not really. I mean, I've talked about I can get a scholarship or a, um, government grant, or something like that, but we haven't talked about me getting a part-time job.

F: See, she. . . .

L: (*Interrupts, speaking to Nancy.*) You, you've been thinking about it.

N: Well, if it got down to the point where they couldn't help me I would.

L: I want to clear something. The money that's set aside for college, that was done since Nancy was born. Right?

(*Nancy's responsible position activates first father and then Laurie, who again recites the family myth.*)

M: Um-hum. Right.

L: In a special (*speaks emphatically*) account.

(*Laurie becomes very excited and insistent.*)

F: Right.

M: (*Speaking simultaneously with father.*) Right.

(*Speaking in chorus, the parents join in Laurie's reiteration of the family myth. In the great flurry of activity that follows, even Nancy joins in.*)

L: (*To Nancy.*) So that has been saved for all this time for you (*emphasizes*).

M: (*Overlaps.*) Right.

F: (*Immediately.*) Yeah.

N: (*Immediately.*) Yeah.

M: So there's no, uh. . . .

F: (*Overlaps.*) So there's no need. . . .

L: (*Overlaps.*) So, I, me, it wasn't like, well, you know, suddenly. . . .

M: (*Overlaps.*) All of a sudden. Right.

L: (*Continues.*) They just put it aside. Or it's, you know. . . .

(*Notice the contrast between the earlier long, separate speeches and these short, overlapping utterances. Under attack, the family becomes much more a single organism than a collection of separate persons, reasserting its version of reality and insisting that it be accepted by all members.*)

N: Yeah, I know that, but I'm just saying that they may have accumulated so much but my tuition is still more than they've accumulated, and they can't afford to. . . .

(*But once again Nancy begins to emerge as an individual, standing her ground by challenging the family's reality.*)

M: You mean it might go over. What we saved. Well.

T1: (*To Nancy.*) You might turn out to be more expensive than they anticipated?

The discussion continued, focusing on whether or not the parents were aware all along of how much Nancy's college expenses would be. As the conversation proceeded, there were signs of Laurie's increasing irritation with her sister. Therapist 2 then shifted the emphasis somewhat, suggesting that Nancy's concern is really that she should give the money back to her parents to help them out and she could go to some other school or get a part-time job to support herself. This incited Laurie further, and with great excitement she began accusing Nancy of being too self-sacrificing, giving, as an example, a situation when Nancy refused to go out with her because it would have meant leaving their father at home alone. Mr. Miller then empathically turned to Nancy and, addressing her by an affectionate nickname, said, "It looks like you're carrying the burdens of everybody." Mrs. Miller quickly snapped "But she doesn't have to," and immediately took up Laurie's criticism of Nancy, insisting that it is totally unnecessary for her to bear the family's burdens.

Several more segments from this session are now presented, showing us groping for a handle on Nancy's problems. At this point I was so uncomfortable with mother and Laurie's scapegoating of Nancy that I attempted to protect her by reframing the situation in family terms.

M: No, I feel if Nancy's doing this, it's not necessary. She always says that she's not aware of it, and all this, but uh, I (*to Nancy*), I think that you have to think about it and realize that you don't have to do this kind of worrying.

(*Mother lectures Nancy about feeling too responsible.*)

T1: Wai, wait. I'm, you know, it's just not true that Nancy learned to carry everybody's burdens without some help from the rest of the family.

(*Therapist 1 attempts to reframe by shifting the blame from Nancy and onto the family as a whole.*)

M: What do you mean, doctor?

(*The edge in mother's response suggests that this reframe will not be an easy one.*)

T1: Well, somehow families are cooperative affairs. When someone learns a particular way of being in a family, it's always true that everyone else helped them out to learn this. There's some advantage to everyone that Nancy was, is the one that carries the burden. And you all have a piece of that somehow. What I'm saying is, I think you've all helped Nancy. . . .

M: (*Overlaps.*) Get the way she is (*laughs*).

(*At first it appears that mother has accepted the family frame for Nancy's overly responsible behavior.*)

T1: (*Continues.*) Be the burden carrier in the family because it's useful to have a burden carrier, so I don't think you can just say to Nancy "Now, Nancy (*shakes finger in accusing gesture*), you shouldn't take on the burdens. It's not necessary."

(*It is likely that therapist 1's implicit criticism of mother undercuts any possibility of success here.*)

M: I don't feel that way.

(*Needing to defend herself against therapist 1's implied criticism, mother makes it quite clear that she wants no part of the new frame.*)

F: I don't think we've thrown the burden on her at all.

(*Father joins his wife against therapist 1's new frame.*)

M: (*Overlaps.*) If she assumed it, that, that's the way she did it.

F: (*Overlaps.*) That's essentially her fault.

M: (*Overlaps.*) But I don't think there was any reason that she took on this role.

T1: You don't think you all helped her in any way.

(*Facing a solid wall of parental opposition, therapist 1 accepts defeat.*)

M: (*Shakes head.*) Not to my knowledge.

(*The theme of Nancy's responsibility reappeared a minute or two later.*)

(Therapist 1 has been pressing Laurie about whether it had been easier for her to leave home a few months before, with Nancy still at home. Laurie argues that this was not at all the case, rather that it was harder on her to go off and leave Nancy behind at home.)

T1: What about that, Nancy? What's it like to be the last kid?

 N: *(Sighs loudly, squirms in chair, and draws arms together across her stomach. Thirteen-second pause.)* I don't know. I can't put it into words.

(Nancy's anxious behavior makes it clear that this is a hot issue and the nonverbal cues suggest a link to the vomiting symptom.)

 F: She has no responsibility. . . .

(As in an earlier session when he followed Nancy to the bathroom, father is activated by Nancy's discomfort, again suggesting some blurring of individual boundaries.)

T1: *(Gestures to father to stop. As he does so, mother motions for father to be quiet.)* Just a second, Mr. Miller. You always take Nancy off the hook when I ask her a tough question.

(Here therapist 1 frames father as protective of Nancy.)

 M: *(Laughs.)*

 F: *(Joins in laughter.)* Oh, no. I'm not taking her off the hook. I think, a, your question is misconstrued. There's more into it, more meat in it than there should be, because. . . .

(Father indicates that he feels the session has entered dangerous territory.)

T1: *(Interrupts.)* I think Nancy can answer the question for herself. I really do. *(Father turns to Nancy, followed by mother who also turns to look at her daughter.)*

(Therapist 1 stops father and insists that Nancy can answer for herself.)

 N: *(Gazing at ceiling.)* Um, I guess it would be, it's harder to be the last one in the family, or the last child in the family, because, I guess I feel more responsible towards them *(gestures toward parents)* because they've had to take care o, at least care of me, well, not longer, but *(sighs)* ohhh man. cause *(Looks at Laurie who laughs sympathetically. Nineteen-second pause.)* 'Cause they don't want to let go of the little kid, the little, littlest, the youngest. And *(looks at mother and whispers)* don't give me that look.

(Nancy acknowledges her sense of responsibility toward her parents as the last child at home. Once she blurts this out, Nancy becomes more and more uncomfortable and closely monitors her parents' reactions.)

 F: In other words *(unintelligible)*.

N: You don't want, you guys get attached to the oldest and the youngest. And since we only had an oldest and a youngest. . . . (*Laurie begins to laugh, followed by mother and then father who also joins in.*)

(*Now Nancy diffuses her statement. She shifts the focus to include Laurie and reduces her concern to a joke.*)

M: (*Laughs, speaking unintelligibly.*) Something in the middle. (*Laurie laughs loudly and Nancy playfully slaps her on the shoulder.*) I can see your point. (*Unintelligible.*)

N: I don't know what I'm trying to say.

(*Nancy again attempts to get off the hook by pleading ignorance.*)

T2: I think you're doing fine. Why don't you go on with it.

T1: I think you do need to struggle with the answer to this question.

(*The therapists support Nancy and gently insist that she continue.*)

N: Um. (*Eighteen-second pause.*) I'm stuck, I can't, um (*six-second pause*), I guess they expect the oldest, you know, to be able to take care of herself, and everything like that. And the youngest still needs the protection, the guidance and all this other stuff. And then, because they give us all this guidance and all that I feel more responsible for them and so therefore it's going to be more harder to, um, go out.

(*With this support, Nancy again clearly states the bind she feels.*)

F: Break away?

N: Yeah.

T1: You feel pretty responsible for them.

T2: (*To Nancy.*) What's going to happen to them when Nancy leaves?

(*Here the therapists push Nancy to further explore her sense of responsibility for her parents.*)

N: They'll do fine. I know they'll do fine. (*Laughs.*) Um (*eight-second pause*), they'll miss me, um, screaming and yelling at them and everything like that, but, they'll learn to adjust just like I'll have to learn to adjust without them. So it will be just total separation between the two (*looks at parents*) of us for a while, three of us for a while (*glances at Laurie to include her*), four of us.

(*And she backs off, insisting that she really has no worries about her parents after all and using humor to diffuse the issue. Note how Nancy includes Laurie here as a kind of afterthought. The significance of this will be clear shortly.*)

T1: When you said that, you feel responsible for them. . . .

N: (*Overlaps.*) Uh-huh.

T1: (*Continues.*) You looked kinda worried, or something like. . . .

T2: (*Overlaps.*) Yeah. That's why I asked that question, "What will happen to. . . ."

(*The therapists try again.*)

N: Well, if anything happens to either one of them I'll feel that right away I have to go back and help them out. If Dad really, really got sick I'd leave school and come back, immediately, and help if I had to.

(*Nancy concretely states her sense of responsibility.*)

T1: How else do you feel responsible for them?

N: Financially, I guess, too. Like if they needed the money or something, I'd get a part-time job or find some way of help supporting them.

T1: How else do you feel responsible?

(*Fourteen-second pause.*)

N: I don't know. Can't think of anything else.

(*Again Nancy backs down.*)

T1: What's going on inside your body (*gestures toward stomach*) as you talk about your responsibility toward your parents?

(*Therapist 1 now moves to connect this discussion of Nancy's feeling of responsibility with her stomach symptom. Here the power of the symptom is invoked in an attempt to break a therapeutic impasse.*)

N: Scared and nervous and wonder what's going to happen.

T1: How does that feel inside?

N: Like a big ball.

T1: Right here (*points to stomach*).

N: Right (*points to stomach and laughs nervously*), right here.

T1: Scared and nervous. And it feels more that way when you talk about your responsibility to them? It gets worse then?

N: Sort of, yeah.

T1: I think that's really important. How much responsibility you feel, for your parents right now.

F: (*Has been sitting with head in hand for past several minutes but now looks up.*) Well, I can't see why it should be her to feel the responsibility, and her alone. Because I wouldn't want her to think that she was the, the sole one who had the responsibility.

(*This clear focus on Nancy's symptom and sense of responsibility now activates father who insists again that Nancy should not feel so responsible and implies that perhaps someone else, i.e., Laurie, should feel responsible as well.*)

N: (*Softly.*) I'm not.

F: Well. . . .

N: (*Overlaps, speaking much louder.*) Well, I'm not, I'm not saying it'd just be me. I know Laurie would (*looks at Laurie*) help.

(*With considerable uncertainty Nancy includes Laurie in the conversation.*)

F: (*Overlaps.*) I'd, I'd hope you'd both share it, if it came to that.

(*Father alludes to his hurt and anger about Laurie's moving out of the famly home at a time when he was so sick.*)

N: But you see, I don't know how Laurie would feel (*turns and looks again at Laurie*), if she feels as. . . .

L: What?

N: Guil, not, um (*speaks very fast*), just as responsible as I feel toward them. I don't know, 'cause we never talk about that.

(*Nancy now admits that she is not at all sure that Laurie can be counted upon. So now the context of Nancy's responsibility for her parents has been widened to include Laurie's behavior as well: Nancy became more responsible—and developed her symptom—at the point that Laurie gave up some responsibility by moving out.*)

Tl: You'd better talk about it now, then.

L: I, well, I know I don't feel all the responsibility or guilt (*to Nancy*), you were going to say "guilt," weren't you?

N: (*Laughs nervously.*) Uh-huh.

L: I know you were. I don't feel that way, you know. Feel guilty (*emphasizes*) because I've moved out and all that.

(*Laurie makes it clear that she does not feel as responsible as Nancy.*)

N: I didn't say you would feel guilty.

L: No. But I don't, I don't feel as much responsibility and guilt that you do, I don't think.

F: In other words, you don't feel any responsibility towards us at all.

(*This deadly comment by father reveals the dilemma faced by both daughters: Be irresponsible and leave, or feel guilty and stay.*)

L: I didn't say that.

N: (*Sitting between father and Laurie, Nancy looks from one to the other. She begins speaking simultaneously with Laurie's next speech.*) She said she didn't feel as much.

L: I said I didn't feel as much. The way Nancy's been going on and from what I know of Nancy, it's like, uh (*sighs*).

(*This nicely illustrates Nancy's triangulated position in the conflict between father and Laurie, putting Laurie's excitement and agitation with Nancy as well as the scapegoating of Nancy in a new light. On the one hand, Nancy's increased sense of responsibility and ultimately her symptom occurred as a result of Laurie leaving home. On the other hand, the scapegoating of Nancy for her responsibility serves to detour attention from the unresolved conflict between father and Laurie over Laurie's moving out. The family finds it safer to discuss Nancy's "overresponsibility" than Laurie's "underresponsibility.")*

N: (*Overlaps.*) I make a mountain out of a molehill.

L: It. Yeah. It's almost like you, you have (*gestures emphatically*) to do this, or else. Well, like uh, they can't survive without me.

N: I didn't say that.

L: I know. But that's how it comes across at times. To me.

(As the session ends, the conflict between father and Laurie has again been detoured as Laurie attacks Nancy for being too responsible.)

T1: Your stomach seems to be saying that.

(Therapist 1 becomes involved and shifts the focus onto Nancy's symptom.)

N: I guess so.

T1: It's a pretty hot issue.

The discussion continued and the scapegoating of Nancy by the family re-emerged. Laurie stated that it makes her angry at times that Nancy feels so responsible for their parents. Nancy jokingly suggested to Laurie that she move back in and "be in my shoes." Laurie replied: "And get an ulcer? No thanks." Mr. Miller, who again had been sitting quietly with his head down, looked up and began to speak.

F: (*To therapist 1.*) Well, isn't this mostly a figment of her imagination, this responsibility?

(Father initiates a new round of criticism of Nancy for her responsibility. Paradoxically, he confirms her position of responsibility in the family by insisting that it is imagined rather than real.)

T1: Well, the thing I was saying before, which didn't get a very good reception, was that it's not so much a figment of Nancy's imagination or her body but it's something that the family somehow has a hand in.

(Therapist 1 again attempts to reframe Nancy's responsibility as a family affair.)

M: Of helping her get into that situation.

(Mother responds sympathetically to the reframing.)

T1: (*Overlaps.*) Helping her get, get to that point. It's not that any of you wanted it that way.

(This time therapist 1 is careful to avoid any suggestion that the family intentionally did anything to Nancy.)

M: No.

T1: No, no intention implied, but that, that Nancy was available and you all said "Okay." (*Laughs.*)

M: (*Joins laughter.*) "Here she is," huh? Right?

T1: "Here she is."

M: I, I see what you mean.

(*Mother maintains her support of the new frame.*)

T1: (*Unintelligible.*)

N: (*Overlaps, speaking to mother.*) Like if you, if you ever got mad at someone and you wanted to talk to someone, sometimes you come here and you keep it up, or if dad was mad at someone. . . .

(*Nancy spontaneously connects the issue of her responsibility for the family with their patterns for dealing with conflict, focusing in particular on the parents. This is our most intimate glimpse so far into this area of the family's life.*)

M: (*Overlaps.*) But I mean the, the last several, not (*looks at Nancy who emphatically shakes head "No."*) Really? (*Laughs.*) Is that right? Well, that's possible.

(*Mother appears to be arguing here that the difficulties to which Nancy alludes are recent, presumably subsequent to father's illness.*)

N: I remember way. . . .

(*Nancy insists instead that the problems go back much further.*)

M: (*Overlaps.*) Way back?

N: Way back.

T1: She (*To Nancy.*) You're well trained, for your job.

N: (*Laughs, pointing to Laurie and mother on either side of her.*) I've got good teachers.

T2: Yeah. And that's, that's why I've been wondering if, if that isn't more of the responsibility you're feeling that you're worried about when you leave. What's going to happen? I mean, this has been a big role. Who's going to step in?

M: Um-hum.

N: Yeah.

T2: Is the rest of the family going to be in big trouble, when Nancy leaves?

(*Here the therapists are activated by the family's anxiety upon mentioning the parents' marital conflict. Good structural work requires at this point that the drama within the family be allowed to unfold. Instead, the therapists' interventions allow a retreat from the escalating tension: Therapist 1 diffuses the affect with humor and therapist 2 leads the session to the relatively safe ground of the future by framing the question "Is the family going to be in trouble when Nancy leaves?")*

M: Not likely (*laughs*).

(Here mother defines the family's reality, signaling to the others how the therapist's question is to be handled.)

T2: Well?

N: (*Looks at mother as she speaks.*) I don't think now. But before maybe.

(As Nancy monitors mother, it is evident that she has heard loud and clear what mother just said. Mother has put Nancy in a bind here with her statement that the family will not be in any trouble when Nancy leaves. Nancy abandons her own sense of what is real, loyally accepting the family's reality and relegating her own worries to the past.)

T2: You don't. . . .

N: (*Overlaps.*) I don't think s, really think so now, because we're able to communicate better, with each other. But before. . . .

T1: Before what?

N: Before we started coming to see you and, even when dad was just getting sick, we never really communicated with each other.

(Here Nancy uses the therapy to support the family's version of reality, flattering the therapists by suggesting that the family's communication problems have been cured.)

T1: So. . . .

M: (*Overlaps, speaking to therapist 1.*) It's true.

N: It was slam door, go in room, sit there and pout or go yell at someone or kick holes in walls, or whatever (*gestures toward parents*).

(The frame of the problem-as-cured does allow Nancy to give more information about conflict in the family. Here, however, Nancy has exceeded the family's limit of tolerance.)

L: (*To Nancy.*) That was all you.

(And she again becomes the family scapegoat.)

M: (*To Nancy.*) That was you, Nancy.

N: (*To Laurie.*) You slammed doors. (*To mother.*) You sulked. And dad would blow his top. Laurie would blow her top. I would blow my top.

(The pattern of conflict becomes clearer: Mother withdraws and pouts and father blows up. It appears to be unacceptable to talk

about father's anger, so Nancy immediately includes Laurie and herself along with father.)

F: We were all blowing our tops.

M: Not me. I pouted *(laughs).*

T1: I don't really believe that the family has learned to communicate to the point of where it's not a problem.

(Therapist 1 refuses to be bought off by Nancy's compliments and instead challenges the pseudo-mutuality of the family's frame by insisting that communication still is a problem in the family.)

M: I think you're right.

(Mother confirms this.)

T1: *(Overlaps, speaking to Nancy.)* 'Cause if that were the case I think that you wouldn't be vomiting.

(Again therapist 1 invokes Nancy's symptom. Without it the therapists would be—and, in fact, were—powerless to change this rigid family.)

M: I think communication's a big factor. I think I mentioned that when we first started, that we weren't a family who communicated, which is true.

(Again mother concurs.)

T2: Um-hum. *(Nancy signals her anxiety by kicking the table on which microphone sits.)*

(This appears to be dangerous ground for the family.)

L: Well, with Nancy, you know, if there's, you know, some, lots of little problems, and stuff. *(Nancy's nervous behavior continues.)* I don't really notice that, you know *(to Nancy)*, you coming out and saying what's wrong.

(So dangerous that Laurie immediately shifts the blame back to Nancy: She is the one who fails to communicate.)

M: *(Overlaps.)* That's right. Um-hum.

L: *(Continues.)* You'll keep it all to yourself and tell everyone to leave you alone. Like you have to solve it yourself.

F: Yeah. You, you, you won't share it.

(And first mother and then father join in making Nancy responsible for the lack of communication.)

N: But I can't share it because I don't know what it is. . . .

F: *(Interrupts.)* Well. . . .

N: *(Overlaps, speaking loudly to father.)* Like if I'm in school. . . .

L: (*Overlaps.*) Like if you get in a fight with Mary (*Nancy's school friend*), you won't tell us.

N: You, you guys know.

L: I, I'll find out from Mary. You know. Or mom, or. . . . We'll find out in a roundabout way because you won't tell us.

M: Come direct and talk about it.

T2: So Laurie, are you telling Nancy that it's kind of a one-way street, where she's taking it for the family so that everybody can come to her, but she doesn't really in return share anything for the rest of you?

(*Therapist 2 now begins to accept the family's frame: The problem is that Nancy keeps everything to herself.*)

L: Yeah.

F: There's no two-way street.

L: That's how it always, it always has been, kind of.

M: Um-hum.

T1: Problems go to Nancy and stay there.

L: (*Overlaps.*) Maybe, maybe because it's Nancy's nature not to tell people, that we told her our problems.

(*This sequence represents the construction of a new family myth. In the effort to defend against the notion that the family plays a role in Nancy's problems, a new explanation of reality is created.*)

N: 'Cause I wouldn't tell anyone else your problems.

L: No, that's not, it's like, when you have a problem you wouldn't complain, to anyone else. And so she became, I mean, we just naturally went to her because she never complained and she could take all of ours.

(*Because it is Nancy's nature not to complain, the rest of the family "naturally" came to see her as the one to whom they could take their complaints.*)

As this discussion continued, Laurie got her parents to join her in dumping more and more anger on Nancy, complaining that she makes them all feel guilty by refusing to discuss her problems when they can see that she is upset about something. As her comment above already suggested, therapist 2 also joined the family against Nancy and began helping them hammer the message home: "Be more open with the family and everyone else in the family will feel better." Hearing all this, I literally began to squirm in my seat and finally said: "I'm getting uncomfortable because what's happening is that Nancy's getting more messages about how she's responsible for making you feel good or you feel good. (*To Nancy.*) I'm worried about how you're hearing all this. And I'm afraid that you're going to go away feeling even more responsible." Nancy acknowledged her dilemma and mother and Laurie indicated their sympathetic understanding as well.

Although this session was a rich source of information about the relationship of Nancy's symptom to the family structure, it failed to go anywhere because our work was too strategic. The attempts at reframing were motivated by our discomfort with the family's scapegoating of Nancy and our wish to protect her. In fact, our efforts to place Nancy's problems in a family frame had precisely the opposite effect, eliciting the family's characteristic defensive maneuvers, chiefly the scapegoating of Nancy. So she ended up in a worse position than before.

Fortunately, we sat down and reviewed the videotape after this session, which allowed us to move beyond our vague sense of discomfort and bewilderment about the interview to an understanding of what went wrong. Careful analysis of that interaction revealed that the Millers exhibited serious transactional-level difficulties that we had previously failed to detect, but that had nonetheless produced in us a sense of uneasiness and perplexity.

Particularly where Mr. Miller's illness and its impact on the family were concerned, contradictory and constantly shifting messages resulted in a fragmentation of experience, making it impossible to develop a coherent, integrated sense of reality.

To put our new transactional-level observations in perspective, it is useful to recall a repetitive theme heard from the beginning of the therapy a year and one-half earlier: Mr. Miller would assert "I don't want my illness to affect my family." and the family would rush to reassure him "It doesn't." This sequence contains a *family myth* (Ferreira, 1963), that is, a belief system or frame which the family uses (often defensively, Ferreira suggests, when threatened in some way) to explain its experience to itself.

Now go back to the first transcript excerpt presented in this section and follow the comments while rereading that portion of the interview. Notice how slippery reality is in the Miller family when Nancy attempts to determine the impact of her father's illness on the family's ability to afford her college expenses.

This transactional-level look at the Miller family convinced us that our strategic work had been at too high a level for the family and we needed to shift to the transactional model. We went into the next session with the goal of changing not the family's overall reality or frame but, much more microscopically, challenging the fragmentation of that reality.

The Transactional Work: Unbinding Binds

As discussed in Chapter 8, the transactional model requires a completely different type of listening, perhaps best characterized by Singer's (1974) emphasis on the *impact* of communication on the listener. An example of transactional listening and intervention occurred near the beginning of the next session. Notice how the therapeutic focus immediately became more microscopic than in the previous session.

> (*Laurie is absent from the session and Nancy sits between her parents. It is near the beginning of the interview and the family has been discussing a hot issue: Whether father is a complainer. Mr. Miller is well known on the oncology service for his many complaints, bringing long lists to each visit and insisting that doctors and nurses listen to all of them. Nancy's triangulated position in the family is demonstrated by their choice of seating. During the session it never occurred to the therapists to move Nancy from her spot in the middle.*)

F: And I haven't been a complainer, as long as, in the three years I've had this problem, I haven't been a complainer. I'm sure the family hasn't heard me complaining every day about my aches and pains. (*Turns to Nancy and mother.*) Have you?

> (*Father instructs his family to confirm his statement.*)

M: (*Immediately.*) No.

N: (*Speaks simultaneously with mother.*) No.

> (*They do, as if with one voice.*)

F: What, what can be resolved. . . .

M: (*Overlaps.*) I, I agree with John (*father*).

T1: Wait, wait, wait a minute. Something important has just happened. (*To mother.*) You said earlier, u. (*To father.*) You're smiling. What are you smiling about?

> (*Therapist 1 moves immediately to focus on these transactions, activated by several features of what has just occurred: First, the contradiction between father's overt solicitation of mother's and Nancy's opinions and the covert message to agree with him; second,*)

the speed and synchrony with which mother and Nancy join to reassure father, suggesting a need to quickly mobilize defenses; and finally, the gross discrepancy between the family's statement of reality and the therapists' perception of it. Taken together, these suggest binding communication in which the overt message is qualified at some other level and reality is fragmented.)

F: (*Laughs.*) Maybe I can (*unintelligible*).

T1: Huh?

F: (*Continues to laugh.*) Maybe I can listen more, I don't know. (*Mother and Nancy smile broadly.*)

T1: No. (*Turns again to mother.*) You, you said to him earlier "You don't complain about every little thing." Or "Don't complain about every little thing."

(Therapist 1 begins to explore the bind by summarizing the interactional sequence that constitutes it.)

M: (*Overlaps.*) Like aches and pains.

T1: (*Continues.*) Or something like that.

M: That they can't do anything about.

T1: When I heard that at the time, I was thinking: "She's telling him 'Don't complain.'" Okay? That's how I was. . . .

M: (*Overlaps.*) No, that's isn't how I meant it.

T1: (*To father.*) And then you said "I don't complain about every little thing, do I?" and you two (*indicates mother and Nancy*) as one chorus said, like in a Greek play, "No." You guys, okay?

F: (*To mother and Nancy.*) So we're Greeks now. (*Entire family joins in hearty laughter.*)

T1: I think that, I think that's an important issue, somehow. (*To father.*) Like you were asking them for some kind of reassurance or. . . .

F: (*Overlaps.*) No. . . .

T1: (*Overlaps.*) Something's going on about complaining. (*Nancy turns and exchanges glances with mother.*) What do you think, Nancy?

(Here Nancy tips therapist 1 off that he is on the right track, suggesting a covert coalition between Nancy and mother against father who complains but cannot be accused of doing so.)

F: (*To Nancy.*) Say what's on your mind. I know what's on my mind.

(This time father explicitly instructs Nancy on how to respond. Again, a bind is implied.)

T1: Wait, wait a minute. One thing I've learned (*turns to therapist 2 and exchanges glances*) in this family is, when someone says "Say what's on your mind," it may be a message. . . .

(Therapist 1 moves quickly to challenge father's new binding of Nancy. Here therapist 1 uses therapist 2 as a source of reassurance and reality testing, nonverbally checking out his intervention.)

N: *(Interrupts.)* Not to. . . .

(By finishing his sentence, Nancy confirms therapist 1's position and makes the work easier.)

T1: *(Continues.)* Not to. . . . Yeah. *(To Nancy.)* Do you think he was just say, telling you that?

N: No, I don't think so.

(Asked directly to be disloyal to her father, Nancy declines.)

T1: But you knew what I was going to say before I said it, so you must understand something about this.

(Therapist 1 sticks to his position, but softens it a bit to make it easier for Nancy to join him.)

F: What was that? I didn't get it. Run that by me again.

(Father pleads ignorance and confusion, preventing Nancy from responding to therapist 1.)

T1: Okay. One thing I've learned about this family is that when someone says "Say what's on your mind," it might be a message to not say it.

M: Is that right?

T1: And before the words were out of my mouth Nancy knew what I was going to say. So she knows something about this. . . .

N: *(To mother, overlapping.)* It's like when you guys say "Don't worry," and I say "Okay."

M: *(Overlaps.)* Ohh.

N: *(Continues.)* Then I think there's something worrying me. It's the same thing. *(Laughs.)*

(Nancy indicates how well she understands what therapist 1 is talking about by linking this discussion to what will shortly be seen as a central bind in this family regarding their worries about the very ill father.)

M: This is very confusing to me, because a person gets so they don't want to say anything. . . .

(Mother joins father in pleading confusion.)

F: *(Overlaps.)* Well, I. . . .

N: *(Overlaps.)* No, I, you can take it that way. That doesn't, it's just that sometimes when you hear, you know, when you say "Don't touch this" you go ahead and touch it out of curiosity or whatever.

(Nancy works hard to make mother understand.)

M: (*Laughs and is joined by Nancy.*) Really?

N: Yeah.

T1: I stopped the action because I felt like the issue of complaining was a hot family issue and this confirms my guess because when I said "Nancy, what do you think about it?" you (*indicates father*) said "Say what's on your mind." And now Nancy's stuck with the dilemma of should she or should she not say what's on her mind about complaining in this family.

(*Therapist 1 labels the dilemma in which Nancy has been placed by father's statement. The intervention here follows from the original Bateson et al., 1956, formulation that one way out of a double bind is to comment upon it.*)

F: So how. . . .

T1: (*Raises hand to silence father.*)

N: (*Overlaps.*) We don't complain. I mean, if we, when we get hurt or something like that, we say, "I hurt myself," or "I have this pain here," or something like that. It's not a constant "Oh, I don't feel. . . ." For me, I'm always saying "I don't feel okay." But, um, these two don't complain.

(*Faced with this dilemma, Nancy recites the family myth about complaining.*)

T1: Who's allowed to complain in the family?

N: All of us are. Except, I just do it a little more.

T1: You do more?

T2: (*Simultaneously.*) You do?

N: Yeah. (*Therapists turn to look at each other in disbelief and Nancy laughs.*)

T2: That comes as quite a surprise.

(*Nancy's response is so contrary to reality as perceived by the therapists that both react immediately and simultaneously with surprise bordering on shock.*)

N: I do, you know, I'm always saying "I don't feel good today," a, something like that.

M: Um-hum.

F: (*To Nancy.*) Do you think that might be a crutch?

(*This is another surprising turn of events. Nancy has so effectively taken the heat from father that he is able to turn the tables and become mildly critical of her.*)

N: No, I mean, even way before, you know, you wake up on the wrong side of the bed or something like that and you go, I go "I don't feel good," or "I didn't get enough sleep," or something. But, these two hold back more of their pains or whatever and they let me go ahead with all the little aches and pains I have.

To summarize, the therapeutic strategy in the above segment was to move quickly to challenge transactions that violated either consensual reality or individual boundaries, the focus of the transactional model. When Mr. Miller asked his family if he complained, the overt message was that they were perfectly free to say "yes" or "no," yet the impact of this transaction on us as listeners in the session was to suggest a powerful covert instruction to say "no." In the course of discussing this transaction, Mr. Miller delivered an even clearer binding message to Nancy: "Say what's on your mind." In the context in which this command was issued, the overt meaning "You are perfectly free to say whatever you wish," was qualified by the covert message of the command itself: "Do as I say."

In such transactions, family members are asked to sacrifice their own personal perceptions of reality out of loyalty to the family. The process involved here is one of psychotic denial. In the families of schizophrenics, this process is pervasive. With the Millers, such gross denial of reality was circumscribed, related to the father's illness and its impact upon the family. Similar "limited psychoses" occur in such other psychosomatic conditions as anorexia nervosa when the patient insists that she is fat even as she is about to die of starvation.

The next segment reveals an even clearer example of the classic double bind:

> (*The family has reported that father has had disturbing visual symptoms during the previous week and they acknowledge their fear that these could indicate brain metastasis.*)

T1: (*To Nancy.*) What's been happening with your stomach this week, since your father's been having more problems?

N: (*Softly.*) It's gotten better.

> (*This is surprising. Therapist 1 had expected Nancy to say that her stomach was worse.*)

T1: Really?

N: Yeah. (*Turns to glance at father.*)

F: Oh, you're not worried now. That's good.

> (*Father expresses approval that Nancy is less worried about him.*)

N: It's, it's getting better. Just once in a while, now.

T1: Really?

N: Uh-huh. (*Nods head.*)

T1: (*To Nancy.*) How do you make sense of that?

T2: Yeah?

F: (*Immediately.*) Well, maybe she figures "He's not worth saving."
(*Father then undercuts his message with a deadly reinterpretation of Nancy's symptomatic improvement.*)

N: (*Pitches forward in her chair and begins to laugh.*)

M: (*Joins in laughter.*) My stomach's (*unintelligible*).

T1: Wait, wait, we can't laugh about his comment.

T2: No. This is serious.
(*The therapists are stunned and react with horror and somewhat critically.*)

M: I know. It is serious.

T1: (*To Nancy.*) How did you hear what he said?

N: (*Turns to look at father.*) Wait, I didn't act. . . .
(*Nancy acts confused.*)

F: (*Overlaps.*) Well, I shouldn't have said it.

T1: (*To Nancy.*) Yeah, you get confused when, when you don't want to pay attention to something.
(*Therapist 1 calls Nancy on her confusion.*)

N: Yeah. Um.
(*Stops monitoring father and looks down to her lap. Eight-second pause, during which Nancy again turns to monitor father's reaction.*)

T1: And how did you react to what he said?

N: Kinda, well, don't, you know. "That's funny. That's not the way I feel." (*Continues to monitor father as she speaks.*) It's, 'cause he was more or less saying that um, I should, I probably don't care about him anymore.
(*After considerable nervous hesitation, Nancy reveals that she understands father very well.*)

T1: Because your stomach's not acting up.

N: Yeah. But. . . .

T1: (*Overlaps.*) And how did you react to that?

N: I laughed at it because I knew it wasn't true. (*Turns again to look at father, who avoids her gaze.*) I. . . .

T1: (*Overlaps.*) It's a hell of a bind. (*Nancy sharply draws a breath and holds it.*) Right?
(*Five-second pause. Nancy again turns to monitor father's reaction, but does not reply.*)

T1: One way you can show that you care (*therapist 1 exchanges glances with therapist 2*) is by worrying or even more so by having a stomach that's doing crazy things. And if you stop having a crazy stomach, it might mean that you don't care. . . .

(*Therapist 1 labels Nancy's bind and makes it explicit. Therapist 1 looks to therapist 2 for support and as a means to test reality.*)

N: (*Overlaps.*) No, he wouldn't even take it that way, but, uh, I think because my stomach's been settling down, maybe I'm not worried as much, or I'm showing it more outward, that I'm worried, than keeping it inside.

(*Nancy rushes to deny the bind.*)

T2: Let's, let's go back a minute. When you, when your dad said that, you gave the interpretation that maybe he thinks "I'm not, I don't care about him much anymore."

(*Therapist 2 persists.*)

N: Um-hum.

T2: And then you said, "But, he wouldn't really think that?" And, I, how do you know?

N: I don't know. I guess maybe I get a, a gut feeling or something. 'Cause a lot of times when we say something, something serious, and we're trying to break the tension or something and make a little joke or something and we all laugh at it. But we get through to each other exactly how we feel. At least. . . .

(*Nancy's metaphor—"gut feeling"—belies her insistence that father's statement was not really as toxic as it sounded.*)

T1: The truth often does come out in those joking asides.

T2: Yeah, let me ex, what it does to me when I hear those kind of interactions is I end up getting confused. Um, and, having a hard time knowing which way to go with that. And that's why I wondered if that might happen to you a bit too?

N: I don't think so, because we always seem to know what we're feeling, with each other, I think (*turns to mother*), what each other are feeling, more or less.

(*Nancy now labels the extent to which individual boundaries are tenuous in this family: We know each other's feelings.*)

M: I have always felt that way.

N: Yeah.

M: We've been together for many years and understand each other's personality.

T1: (*Overlaps.*) You can read each other's minds?

(*Therapist 1 labels the family's reality.*)

N: Yeah, I guess it's something like that. I mean, uh. . . .

T2: (*Interrupts.*) Then what's been going on in here? For the last months?

(Therapist 2 uses Nancy's problem to challenge the family's reality.)

F: What do you mean?

T2: I mean, can you really read each other's minds? Do you. . . .

N: (*Overlaps.*) Not all the time.

F: (*Overlaps.*) think that's misquoted, reading a person's mind. I'm not psychic as yet, I don't think. But I think, what she's trying to say is perhaps the fact that she doesn't want to say things that might be misconstrued by us, or by her. She shouldn't say those things that may be misconstrued by her.

(As he rushes to challenge the therapists and speak for Nancy, father ceases to make sense.)

T1: (*To Nancy.*) You're looking puzzled.

(Therapist 1 gives Nancy an opportunity to comment on the fact that father's speech was unfollowable. This undercuts the family's pseudo-mutual belief that they always understand each other and gives Nancy a chance to test her own reality.)

N: I don't know what he means.

(Nancy makes use of the chance.)

M: I don't either, John (*father*).

(She gets immediate support from mother.)

F: Well, for example, if I were to expound on the problem I had in the last four days and say to you (*speaks now to mother*), and knowing that you would take it more to heart than I would, for example, a, I maybe hold back, or I'd give you the whole brunt of it at one time.

(In an attempt to explain himself, father becomes increasingly tangential.)

M: Try me.

F: Well, I've done that. This week I haven't pulled any punches. I was so worried about it myself at the time because this is, something's radically wrong here somewhere, with this stuff going on.

T1: I think there's a real problem in the family, and that is that worry gets mixed up with care and concern. And on one hand the message is "Don't worry. Don't let the problems affect you," and on the other hand the message is "But the worry is a sign to me that you care and that you're concerned." (*To Nancy.*) And that's the double message that you just got caught up in when you said, you said your stomach was getting better. Your father pops up with something about not caring anymore. An that's a real bind that you're in. (*Four-second pause.*) Right?

(Therapist 1 explicitly states the bind concerning the family's response to father's illness.)

N: Uh-huh.

T1: You can feel that bind?

N: I, I can't feel it, but I guess, from what you said, I can, you know. . . .

(Confronted directly with the bind, Nancy is again loyal to the family.)

F: *(Interrupts.)* Yeah, you can put that interpretation on it, but I didn't mean it that way at all. That's misconstrued. I didn't mean that at all.

(And father defends himself.)

T2: What we are talking about is the effect.

F: Yeah, I know. It depends upon if they can accept that kind of a, you might say joking response, or they can't take it. If they're going to misinterpret it.

T2: Let's go back to Nancy and how she's saying it's affecting her at this point.

F: *(To Nancy.)* Is it affecting you?

(Another binding question.)

N: It's not affecting me, because I know what he means. . . .

(And again Nancy supports father.)

T1: *(Overlaps.)* In your head. . . .

N: *(Overlaps.)* Yeah, but then. . . .

T1: *(Overlaps.)* But what about *(points to stomach)*?

(This time, rather than confront Nancy's denial directly, therapist 1 again begins to involve the power of her stomach.)

N: But my stomach fe, it. *(Four-second pause while Nancy hangs her head.)* My stomach feels fine, even when he makes those jokes, but, I, I feel that there's some sort of communication between us that we don't have to come out and say it. Oh, I don't know what I'm trying to say.

T2: You're doing alright. Stay with it.

N: We have our own communication and you guys to me seem to be interpreting totally different than we do and there's no way we can explain to you the way we feel.

(Nancy makes a very pointed criticism of the therapists, which must be taken seriously.)

F: That's it. That's it. Because we joke, well, I've always been that way. All my life. And a, I don't put any serious connotation on the joke at all. I just accept it as a joke. So that's why other people might hear us talking and they mis, misconstrue the whole issue. You remember that old expression about "You never hear the same person talking about the same person. . . ." I mean, "Two guys talking about the same person saying the same thing." They're all different interpretations. It's the same thing with us when we talk about these things. We may say them jokingly or in a joke or make some comment, but it's not ever serious. (*Unintelligible.*)

(*Father's muddled and tangential speech obscures Nancy's precise statement.*)

T1: (*To Nancy.*) I'm afraid that your stomach is more like us than one of the family. See I, I would believe what you say, that we're outsiders and we don't really understand the private communication in the family, if it were, were it not for the fact that you've been having these problems.

(*Therapist 1 responds by pulling out the big gun—Nancy's vomiting. Without this symptom there would have been no way to effectively challenge the slipperiness of this family's reality.*)

M: You mean the stomach's getting a different interpretation.

T1: I think it is. And that, I, I believe that you do not intend harmful consequences by the jokes.

F: Of course it may trigger, a, something in her mind or subconscious to, that she wasn't aware of before. That's true. It could do that.

(*Mother immediately understands and accepts, and therapist 1's assurance that no malignant intent is assumed allows father to thoughtfully follow suit.*)

T1: Um-hum.

The Restructuring Begins

Although we continued to focus on the family's transactional difficulties as they arose, in subsequent sessions our interventions became more structural, a therapeutic progression consistent with the second-order model articulated in Chapter 9.

By the next interview, attended by the entire family, it was clear that an important structural change was already in progress. The fourth session began with a discussion of the fact that Nancy had stopped vomiting. We wondered if it would recur, and Laurie responded with the family's frame: It will not happen again—Nancy used to worry about all sorts of things that she should not have worried about, but that is all over now. I attempted to reframe things: If Nancy is able to go off to Europe in a few weeks, it will mean not just that *she* has changed, but that the whole *family* has changed. This new frame was again resisted by both parents, but Nancy jumped in and provided a whole list of issues the family as a whole now needed to face: Her own leaving, the improvement in Mr. Miller's health, and the fact that the parents will be alone at home without children for the first time in 20 years. The discussion was then broadened to include Laurie.

T1: We're right, but we're leaving out Laurie. (*To Laurie.*) Because it (*Nancy being able to go off to Europe as planned*) will also mean that something has changed between you and the family. Do you know what I mean?

　　　(*Therapist 1 shifts the focus from the father–mother–Nancy triad to the entire family.*)

L: I guess.

T2: What?

L: I don't know. Maybe trying to take Nancy's place now, becoming closer to them. Like she was. I don't know.

　　　(*And here he strikes structural gold.*)

T1: What about that?

N: (*Softly, to Laurie.*) Watch out for your stomach. (*Laughs.*)

　　　(*Even the symptomatic vomiting is spontaneously linked to this shift in family structure.*)

T1: "Watch out for your stomach."?

M: (*Laughs vigorously.*)

L: I don't know. I mean, I can't, like my (*new*) job is in south city and dad keeps saying "Oh, that means you're going to move back home, huh?"

　　　(*Laurie reveals the strong pull on her to move closer to the parents as Nancy draws away.*)

T1: (*Overlaps.*) Uh-huh.

L: (*Continues.*) And I say "No."

T1: Uh-huh.

L: Yeah. So I feel bad when I say "No."

T1: (*Overlaps.*) So Nancy takes off on the plane and you move back home.

L: Right. And that's not the way it's going to happen.

As Laurie talked about the pressure to move back home and her guilt at not wishing to do so, she seemed near tears and admitted feeling knots in her stomach. Laurie stated that the issue of her living on her own, which had once seemed settled, was again called into question by Nancy's imminent departure.

What is emerging here is the clinical phenomenon that helped launch family therapy in the first place: When the patient gets better, another family member appears poised to assume the symptomatic role.

(During the discussion with Laurie, mother, and father about the pull Laurie feels to take Nancy's place in the family, Nancy sits quietly and listens from her chair on the edge of the family circle.)

T1: I want to check out a couple of things before we stop. One is *(to Nancy)* how is it for you to have the focus be on Laurie and. . . .

N: *(Overlaps.)* The pressure's off.

(Nancy expresses her relief over the restructuring of the family.)

T1: Yeah.

T2: Uh-huh.

M: *(Laughs loudly and expansively pats her stomach with her hands.)*

T1: The tables have really turned, haven't they?

N: Uh-huh. Now Laurie more or less is getting into the position that I might have, she might be trying to take problems that I've had, she's trying to take them on now. Starting with the knot in the stomach.

(Again the stomach symptoms are linked to family structure.)

T1: So there's a. . . .

F: *(Overlaps, speaks softly but unintelligibly to mother.)*

(The parents are now activated and a ripple of defensiveness runs through the family.)

L: *(Laughs loudly, apparently in response to father's statement.)*

M: But I'm beginning to feel that way. . . .

L: *(Overlaps.)* No.

M: *(Continues.)* That this worry is misconstrued. I mean there's. . . .

T1: She's *(refers to Laurie)* helping the matter along.

(But this time the defensiveness is successfully sidestepped by therapist 1's emphasis on Laurie's open-armed acceptance of her new position in the family.)

M: Yeah.

T1: Nancy's gracefully bowing out *(makes exaggerated bowing gesture while Laurie laughs loudly and with much excitement)* and turning things over to Laurie and Laurie's embracing the job.

(*Note Laurie's excitement here, which appears much more pleasurable than painful.*)

M: (*Overlaps.*) Right. Right.

Tl: (*Continues.*) And everybody's. . . .

F: (*Overlaps.*) The dog will be next.

Tl: So, I was wrong when I said earlier that if (*to Nancy*) you are able to go off to Europe on July 7 and your stomach doesn't prevent you from doing it, that the family will have changed. That's over optimistic.

N: It's just been moved over.

L: Shifted.

(*Therapist 1 again reframes the structural changes underway in the family, and this time is joined by Nancy and Laurie.*)

Tl: It may mean that the family has changed or it may be that you two (*indicates Laurie and Nancy*) have now changed jobs.

T2: The job has shifted.

M: (*Laughs.*)

Tl: That's a serious possibility. We laugh, but it's really a serious possibility and we need to pay more attention to it.

M: I don't understand this shifting though. Laurie's life is pretty much her own as far as I'm concerned. I have gone through that worry and concern.

(*Mother begins to defend against the presumed charge that the parents are responsible for pulling Laurie closer to home.*)

L: I know, but maybe the fact that things have been said all along, little chit-chat, light things, I am seeing in a different light because Nancy is going.

(*Laurie makes it clear instead that Nancy's imminent departure has changed her own perceptions of old family interactions.*)

M: And you're looking at it differently.

L: Yeah.

M: I see.

L: Just my perception has changed on that. That's why I feel more pressure right now.

Following this there was a long discussion about a suitable time for the next meeting, with the parents voicing concern about whether the session would interfere with the new job Laurie hoped to get. When they rose to leave, it was still left a bit unclear whether Laurie would attend. But as she left the room Laurie turned back and said with a wink and a huge smile: "I'll be there." Although we did not notice this bit of behavior at the time, it is quite dramatic on videotape and, in light of subsequent developments, reveals how much Laurie had already moved into Nancy's old job as the child most responsible for her parents.

Taking Care of Parents

At this point in the treatment, we felt that it was time to stop focusing on Nancy's symptom, which had now abated, and instead shift to the issue of whether or not the parents would survive without their daughters in the home to take care of them. This move was suggested by our knowledge that emancipation difficulties generally occur in families where children are involved in managing parental conflict and, particularly, by Nancy's previous hints about Mr. and Mrs. Miller's unresolved conflict. We introduced this move in a homework assignment given to Laurie and Nancy at the end of the session just discussed. They were instructed "to do some worrying this week about whether your parents will be able to make it when you kids are out of the home."

The fifth treatment session began with some discussion of the changes taking place in the family. Laurie had indeed gotten her new job and was succeeding at losing weight. Nancy was no longer vomiting. With her husband's health improved, Mrs. Miller admitted to a "letdown" feeling after having been so worried for so long. Still, she insisted that she could afford to take no time for herself because "there are always floors to scrub." The session then turned to a report on the homework.

> (*Seating is as in last session, with Laurie next to her parents and Nancy on the edge of the family circle.*)

T1: (*To Nancy and Laurie.*) In the last session I sent you two out with a special homework, to do some worrying about how your parents will make it, how your parents will survive when there aren't any more kids in the home.

F: (*Overlaps.*) Little ones.

T1: And I'm wondering what worries you came up with in the three weeks (*since the last interview*).

> (*Twelve-second pause. Then Laurie turns to Nancy as if expecting her to respond. Instead, Nancy gestures back to Laurie, turning the floor over to her. Seven-second pause.*)

(Notice how the role of "concerned child" is for a moment again up for grabs. Nancy declines Laurie's invitation to respond and instead turns the job over to Laurie.)

L: Well, I guess the main worry I came up with was, will I feel guilty being close by? 'Cause like a coupla times I, I do, like dad, you know, the same things as he's been saying all along, you know, he'll joke about "Oh yeah. You've brought your stuff over?" *(Laughs.)* Things like that. And, you know, because I'm, I don't know why I'm taking it different, but sometimes it strikes me as being, you know, like it's the first time he's ever said it.

T1: "You brought your stuff over," means what?

L: "Are you," well, "You've come over to move back in, huh?" Yeah. *(Laughs.)*

T1: More of that in the last three weeks?

L: No. It's a, wh, he always kids about it, but I feel it more now. Like it's just something new, and I, I'm wondering if I will feel more guilt, seeing as Nancy, how Nancy has left. Or if they'll feel bad if I don't move back in when she goes. *(Laughs.)*

T1: That's your worry. What else are you worried about?

L: Nothing, really. I can't think of anything else.

(Five-second pause.)

N: My worry is that *(laughs and says something unintelligible)*, that they won't have anything to do, um, dad will go to work, you know, and he'll come home and he'll just, I don't know, I, I, I can't picture those two back together as husband and wife without the little kids running around the house.

(Curiously, in view of the structural shifts in the family, Nancy quickly speaks up here and voices a typical concern of children leaving home, stating it directly and rather graphically.)

M: Oh, I think it's terrific.

(Mother immediately brushes aside Nancy's worries.)

F: *(Overlaps, speech is unintelligible.)*

N: *(Overlaps, speaking excitedly.)* No, see, we were talking about it in school, we were ta, reading *Future Shock* and comparing different families. And they say sometimes parents, after the kids leave, they have no communication. They've gone both their separate ways and it's very hard for them to get back together. And I can kinda see that with you and dad, trying to get back together.

(But Nancy is persistent.)

T1: What might happen?

N: Uh, I don't know, I just. . . .

F: (*Overlaps, speaking to mother.*) What is she talking about?

(*Here father attempts to collude with mother to deny any real basis for Nancy's concerns.*)

M: I know what she's talking about.

(*But now mother sides with Nancy.*)

L: Yeah, you two won't have, anything else to talk about. Well, okay, while we're living there, while we're at home, it's "Oh, the kids did this, the kids did that." When we're gone. . . .

(*And Laurie joins them. Here Nancy, mother, and Laurie are clearly in an alliance against father.*)

F: (*Overlaps, speech is unintelligible.*)

L: (*Continues.*) No, when we're gone, what do you talk about?

M: Right. (*Turns to look at father.*)

N: Are you going to say "How was work?" "Fine." Okay, so what, I mean, that's it. It's no. . . .

M: (*Overlaps.*) That's right.

F: (*Unintelligible.*)

T1: What might happen?

T2: Yeah?

N: (*Sighs and smiles.*) Well, I do, that they'll never get back together again, that they won't be able to communicate with each other.

T2: And what if they can't? Then what?

N: (*Puts head down into hand.*) I don't know.

F: What do you mean, we "won't be able to communicate"? I don't follow you.

(*Father persists in pushing aside his daughters' concerns.*)

L: Instead of saying "Well, Laurie called," or "Nancy called," or "Nancy's done this," or "Laurie's done that."

N: (*Overlaps.*) Yeah, talk about what you guys did and be able to sit down and talk about us.

L: (*Overlaps.*) What are you guys going to talk about when you don't have us to talk about?

M: (*Overlaps, speech is unintelligible.*)

(*Again the three women unite against father. Notice how they finish each other's sentences, speaking as if with one voice.*)

N: (*Overlaps.*) And not blowing up in people's faces if they're offering a point of view or something.

(*Now Nancy gets to the heart of the matter: How will mother and father manage their conflict without their daughters' help?*)

M: We'll get bored with (*unintelligible*). (*Laughs.*)

(*This time mother abandons Nancy and distracts from the talk of conflict by injecting humor.*)

N: No, it's not bored with one another, but I have always felt like sometimes that Laurie and I were the, ringmasters and made sure that you. . . . (*Mother laughs.*) Okay, okay (*to father*), sometimes when mom says something. . . .

(*But Nancy persists and begins to lay out the daughters' role in the couple's relationship.*)

L: (*Overlaps, speaking emphatically.*) Oh, yeah.

N: (*Continues.*) You get irritated with what she said and (*to mother*) if dad says something sometimes you feel hurt. So there's no one gonna be there to be able to say "Okay, break it up or whatever."

(*Here Nancy provides a vivid description of the job of the triangulated child in her family.*)

M: We'll have to handle it our. . . .

F: (*Unintelligible.*)

L: (*Speaks in exasperated tone of voice.*) Dad, we're trying to be serious.

F: Well, I am too. I'm quite serious.

N: (*To therapists.*) That's why I'm worried.

(*At this point, with conflict emerging in the process of the session as well as in its content, Nancy turns to involve the therapists.*)

T1: You thought he wasn't taking you seriously?

(*Therapist 1 is drawn into an exchange with Nancy.*)

N: No, not that, but, um, just now the way he, the expression on his face, it's like a big joke.

M: But don't you think that's, when couples start out it's the same thing?

(*Here the momentum of the family's interaction prevails and the process within the family continues. A structurally more elegant response to Nancy's bid would have been for therapist 1 to point back to the family and suggest that she discuss her worries with them instead of with him. With the focus on couple conflict now established, mother begins to challenge her daughters.*)

N: Yeah, it's the same thing, but this has been such a long time. . . .

(*Again Nancy and Laurie refuse to allow their concerns to be brushed aside.*)

L: (*Overlaps.*) Yeah, this has been for twenty-four years. . . .

M: (*Overlaps.*) I understand, and, it, that's the adjustment.

N: (*Softly.*) Actually, twenty-six.

F: Twenty-seven.

N: Twenty-seven.

L: (*To Nancy.*) But twenty-three years actually with us. The first few we weren't there.

M: So life's a, always adjustments. But it is an adjustment.

   (*Mother continues to minimize the problem.*)

T1: You know, in a lot of families I've worked with kids are worried enough about what's going to happen to their parents when they grow up and leave that they actually think about divorce.

   (*Therapist 1 now moves to up the ante by making the implicit explicit. By referring to "a lot of families" he normalizes the situation and takes Nancy and Laurie off the hook a bit.*)

N: I didn't want to say that (*laughs nervously*).

   (*Nancy validates therapist 1's statement and confirms the anxiety associated with the issue.*)

T1: I didn't think you did.

T2: But that was something on your mind?

N: I wanted to say it, but I can't see those two gettin' divorced. It's hard for me to even say (*turns to look at mother*).

   (*Notice the nonverbal exchange between mother and Nancy here and in what follows, suggesting that Nancy is speaking for mother.*)

M: (*Overlaps.*) To use the word.

N: Yeah.

T1: It's a scary word.

N: (*Nods agreement.*)

T2: Really.

M: And it does happen.

   (*Mother is now remarkably receptive.*)

N: A lot of time when the kids. . . .

M: (*Overlaps.*) That's the time when it happens.

N: That's when they say "You go this way, You go that way," and they can't get back together.

M: Right. (*Turns to look at therapists.*)

   (*Here mother makes a subtle attempt to involve the therapists but this time therapist 1 immediately turns it back to the family.*)

T1: What about that?

N: I know it won't happen, but it's, you know. . . . It's there, and you can't, you know, say it's not going to happen. Makes a lot of sense (*laughs nervously*).

M: It makes sense.

T2: (*To Nancy.*) It sounds like it's something you've given some thought to. (*Mother turns to look intently at Nancy.*)

N: Just recently, yeah. Since I've been reading, or I might not even know those kind of things happened, so. . . .

The discussion continued a bit longer and Laurie voiced the concern that her father's illness would complicate the parents' adjustment to being alone in the home, citing in particular the couple's inability to travel and do some of the other things they had planned to do when Mr. Miller retired. We then asked the parents about their reactions to their daughters' worries that they might divorce. The mother indicated that she was both surprised and pleased by their concern.

Mr. Miller responded with contradictory messages that had an overall binding impact. He first stated that he was hurt by his daughters' statements of concern about the couple's relationship. He explained that he had not wanted his children to suffer the same problem he had faced: As a young man, he was unable to get out on his own because he had to stay home and care for his folks. "I don't feel they owe anything to either one of us. . . . They have to lead their lives, get out on their own." The following exchange then occurred:

T2: Where does that (*the daughters' departure from the home*) leave your life?

F: It leaves a void in our life. There's no doubt about it. We'll have to find something to fill the void, temporarily, as it were. We know that. But right at the present time we can't fill the void, owing to the fact that I can't get out and do things like I want to right now, as a couple. We can't do the things we want to do as a couple. That's why (*unintelligible*).

(*Having earlier said that his daughters should lead their own lives, father now reverses himself by stating that the couple are unable to fill the void created by their daughters' departures.*)

T1: (*To daughters.*) Where does that leave you, or you?

(*Therapist 1 now presents Laurie and Nancy with the dilemma of father's binding statements. In what follows, notice the differential impact: Laurie is caught but Nancy is not.*)

N: Out.

L: (*Turns to Nancy.*) What do you mean, "Out"?

N: (*Gestures away from parents.*) Pushing us out. They don't want us.

L: I don't think so. I caught that "temporarily filling the void."

N: Well, a, I, I figure temporarily. . . .

F: (*Overlaps.*) What do you mean "temporarily"?

N: You said "temporarily fill the void."

L: Yeah, and I was, in my mind I, a question popped "Oh, until we come back?"

F: (*Overlaps.*) No, no. . . .

N: (*Overlaps.*) No, I was thinking until they got together. They, they do. . . .

L: (*Overlaps.*) It didn't strike me that way.

F: It's not (*unintelligible*) fill the void permanently. . . .

N: (*Overlaps.*) You said temp. . . .

F: (*Continues.*) 'Cause we're going to find some diversion, to fill that void.

T1: But I just heard you say, Mr. Miller, that it's going to be very difficult for you to do that, because of your health.

F: That's right. That's right. Exactly.

T2: And that's where the question came: "Where does that leave you two?"

(*The therapists now move to pin down the reality of father's message to the daughters: Right now, because of my ill health, we cannot get along without you.*)

(*Five-second pause.*)

N: (*Immediately looks at Laurie and then speaks softly.*) Standby.

(*Nancy now revises her position from "out" of the family to "standby" —an interesting choice of words.*)

T2: Standby?

T1: (*Overlaps, speaking simultaneously with therapist 2.*) Standby?

N: Yeah.

L: We can't, I don't know, Nancy and I both have different ways of thinking on this, from what I've heard her talk. . . .

N: (*Laughs.*)

L: But I don't feel we, you know, have to be right there to, you know, jump at any, you know, if anything goes wrong. Because if we do that, it's like, a, we never left. . . .

T1: (*Overlaps.*) I think we're right at the heart. . . .

L: (*Overlaps.*) I mean, right now, I, I want, I do want to be close, close by. Yeah, but not that (*emphasizes*) close.

(Laurie's last two statements reveal the contradictory feelings she experiences.)

T1: I think we're right at the heart of the family issue right now. And that is, whether or not, with your health, Mr. Miller, the two of you are going to be able to fill the void which your daughters' leaving will make. And, if not, will the two of them need to hang around, somehow, to fill it?

(Therapist 1 now labels the family's central developmental dilemma.)

F: (*Softly.*) No.

M: 'Cause that wouldn't be fair.

T1: No. But I think that's the bind that the family's in.

F: No, no, no. There's no. . . .

L: (*Overlaps.*) Yeah, but. . . .

F: (*Continues.*) Thought about that at all.

L: (*Continues.*) I'm, okay, it's like (*sighs, eight-second pause*), what's the words I want? Um, you say one thing but I feel another. 'Cause like, you know, you can say, well, you know, "You don't have to do this" but underneath I'm reading. . . .

(Laurie verbalizes the contradictory messages.)

N: (*Overlaps, speaking softly.*) Reading between the lines. . . .

(And she is supported by Nancy. The sibling subsystem is working well here to establish a coherent reality for themselves.)

L: (*Continues.*) "We'd sure like you if did stay." You know, "We'd sure like it if you did stay."

(Here Laurie appears to make a slip—"like you"—which she quickly corrects—"like it." This is significant in view of what happens later.)

T1: (*To Laurie.*) You're exactly in Nancy's position now.

(Therapist 1 frames Laurie as caught in the same bind as Nancy had been.)

N: That's the (*nods in vigorous agreement with therapist 1*).

T1: (*Overlaps.*) If we played the tape back and listened to what your father said, your reactions would be exactly like what happened about three or four weeks ago with Nancy in that position.

N: (*Nods emphatically.*) Uh-huh.

F: (*To Nancy.*) I think you're reading something in there. I never said. . . .

(Again father begins to defend himself against blame for the bind.)

L: (*Overlaps.*) I know. . . .

N: (*Interrupts, speaking to father.*) That's the same thing you told me.

(Nancy is so clearly on top of the previous pattern that she is able to label father's next statement as yet another part of the same process.)

L: *(Overlaps, speaking emphatically.)* But that's the way I'm feeling. Yeah.

F: But I don't mean it that way at all.

L: I know *(emphasizes)*, but that's, I don't know, it's the feeling I get. It's not your fault.

(And Laurie insists that her parents are not to blame.)

F: *(Overlaps.) (Unintelligible.)* What is that, a guilt complex?

(This is precisely the put-down maneuver father used on Nancy earlier when she was loyal to the family and accepted personal responsibility for what is clearly a family-wide process.)

L: *(Voice has edge.)* Yeah. I mean, maybe. . . .

M: *(Overlaps.)* But that's not our fault. . . .

L: *(Overlaps.)* I know, that's what I'm saying. I'm feeling it.

T1: No one's to blame for this.

L: *(Overlaps.)* It's, yeah, I. . . .

T1: *(Continues.)* It's where the family's stuck right now.

M: Right.

L: I mean, even the, the change in perception, you guys haven't caused it, you know. It's, it's been me.

T1: No, it's been Nancy. She's gotten better. . . .

(Therapist 1 emphasizes that the process involves the whole family, not just Laurie and her parents.)

L: *(Overlaps.)* Yeah. It's been all her fault. *(Laughs.)*

M: *(Laughs.)*

T1: *(To therapist 2, laughing.)* We've got to find someone to blame it on.

M: Right.

The Attempt to Extricate Laurie

By this time we had become quite alarmed by the extent to which Laurie had assumed the position in the family formerly occupied by Nancy. At the end of the session we pushed Laurie hard about the payoffs for taking on this job, but she resisted the notion that there were any advantages. Laurie stated, for example, that moving back home would mean living rent-free, but insisted that she would not like it because she would then feel like a kid again. Nancy, on the other hand, understood perfectly our talk about payoffs: "You wouldn't feel guilty . . . and you get love and attention."

At the end of session five we gave Laurie the following "riddle": "If you don't take a look at the advantages of taking over Nancy's role, then you are likely to fall into it." Laurie insisted that this did not make sense at all; rather, if she wished to avoid Nancy's job she should look at its *dis*advantages. We inscrutably urged her to consider the riddle just as we had posed it.

The sixth session began with a discussion of the riddle. Again Laurie balked at considering the advantages of taking over Nancy's old job. We noted that if she moved back home Laurie would become the "special daughter," the one who stays home to take care of things. Both Laurie and Nancy immediately denied that Nancy had ever been special, insisting that their parents had always treated them the same. This was stated so vehemently and unanimously that it immediately suggested that another family myth was being recited here, to ward off our advance into dangerous territory.

We then named one difference that the family had failed to mention: *Laurie had been adopted.* This brought another and even more adamant statement of the family myth, this time by the parents as well as the daughters: Laurie's adoption has always been handled openly by the family and has never been an issue.

Laurie, however, opened a chink in the family's armor when she gleefully recalled that as children, when she and Nancy got angry at each other they used to argue about her adoption, with Nancy taunting "You're adopted, you're adopted." The rest of the family instantly claimed amnesia for any such events.

Despite this opening, we did not get much further on this issue. The family focused on each daughter's "specialness." When we countered that one advantage of taking over Nancy's role was to take on her kind of specialness as well, the family again defended its handling of Laurie's adoption.

As with the earlier session discussed at the beginning of this chapter, we were working too strategically here, attempting to shift the frame for Laurie's behavior, but succeeding only in provoking massive family resistance. So we turned instead to the issue of the couple relationship and began to work more structurally again.

Working on the Couple Relationship

(*The sixth session. Family is seated as in previous interviews, Nancy, Laurie, mother, and father.*)

T1: I'd like to switch gears a little here. Last week we stirred up a whole lot of excitement and talk by initially asking you two (*indicates Nancy and Laurie*) what, what fears you have about leaving home, leaving the two of them alone. We talked some about fears about divorce and how you two (*to parents*) were going to fill the void in your life when your daughters leave. I'm wondering what thoughts all of you have had in the last week about all of that?

(*Five-second pause.*)

M: Well, a, I have thought about it and I think it will be rather wonderful, a, for John (*father*) and I to have, really a chance to be together and, a, we'll just have each other, you know (*turns to look at daughters*), it's always been children around, and, young ladies, and a, really when we're just together we can really pay a lot more attention to each other, and maybe listen a little better? (*To father.*) John, huh? (*Turns and again speaks to therapists.*) Because, a, when you're in a rush and hurry and this and that, you really don't have time to sit and, and really enjoy (*speaks wistfully*) like you should, conversations and thoughts and. . . .

(*Here mother states the positive side of getting rid of the kids, and gently puts father on notice that he should listen to her better than he now does.*)

T1: It sounded to me like you started to say something important to your husband. The trouble was, you were talking to me because I asked the question in the first place.

M: Um-hum.

T1: Talk with him a minute (*mother immediately turns her whole body to face father*) about what you were thinking about in the last week.

(*Therapist 1 picks up on mother's message to father and instructs her to talk directly to him.*)

M: (*To father.*) Well, we'll have more time, John, you know, and (*unintelligible*).

F: (*Softly.*) That's very true. (*Here, and throughout the following exchange, father avoids eye contact with mother, speaking with head bowed.*)

(*This brief exchange, together with what follows, demonstrates the distance between mother and father and the gap between mother's *dreams for their life together and the reality of her husband's withdrawal and avoidance.*)

M: It will be rather peaceful, don't you think?

F: Well, there hasn't been any chaos, but we won't have to worry about what they're doing (*unintelligible*).

M: Because "Out of sight, out of mind." (*Laughs.*)

F: (*Unintelligible.*)

M: I think it will be nice. (*Three-second pause during which mother continues to look at father. She then turns to therapists and continues speaking.*) It certainly will be a little bit lonely at times, after a busy, a busy (*turns to look momentarily toward daughters*) schedule. But a, I think it will be very (*glances at father*), very nice. A togetherness.

(*Mother finally gives up her attempts to make contact with father and turns to the therapists, commenting upon her "lonely" feelings and contrasting these with the "busy" life with her daughters.*)

F: (*Continues to avoid mother's gaze.*) Maybe we can take a, maybe we can retire and rest for a change.

M: Right. (*Seven-second pause.*) And do, just what we want to do. (*Mother continues to look directly at father, but he avoids eye contact.*)

(*The conversation grinds to a halt.*)

L: Something I was thinking about was that, um. . . .

(*And Laurie immediately involves herself.*)

(*Mother breaks her eye contact with father and turns 180 degrees to face Laurie. For the first time since the beginning of the couple's discussion, father lifts his head and looks attentive as he gazes toward Laurie. Nancy's hand jerks up to cover her mouth.*)

(*Father indicates interest only now that Laurie has joined the conversation.*)

T1: (*Softly.*) Wait.

(*Therapist 1 stops Laurie.*)

N: (*Laughs nervously.*)

T1: (*To Laurie.*) How did you get in there?

F: (*Unintelligible, laughing.*)

M: (*Laughs.*)

L: I stick my nose in it.

T1: (*Softly.*) How come?

L: 'Cause (*speaks in very defensive tone of voice, getting louder as she talks*) I just wanted to add something.

(Laurie becomes defensive in the face of therapist's implied criticism.)

T1: *(Softly.)* Um-hum.

(Three-second pause. Mother turns sharply to look directly at Laurie.)

L: *(Almost yelling.)* Because I wanted to say it.

T1: *(Bolts upright in chair, speaking unintelligibly.)*

F: *(Overlaps, talking unintelligibly to Laurie.)*

L: *(Harshly, to father.)* No. *(More softly.)* I just wanted, um, to comment on something my mom said in that last sentence.

T2: What was happening, as you were listening?

L: Well, she was saying one of the things I was thinking, kinda like, well, being able to do what they want when they want without, a, like Nancy has the car just now, and things like that. . . .

M: *(Overlaps.)* Or pick up, or. . . .

L: *(Overlaps.)* Yeah, take. . . .

M: *(Continues.)* Take Nancy, or, a. . . . *(To therapists.)* A lot of things.

(Notice how mother and Laurie finish each other's sentences here, suggesting how closely they are identified with each other at this point.)

T1: *(To Laurie.)* How come you thought you needed to add that rather than let that come from the two of them?

L: *(Speaks with edge to voice.)* I just wanted to say it.

T1: How come?

L: *(Speaks with some defiance.)* 'Cause I'm part of the family too.

(Nine-second pause as Laurie and therapist 1 glare at each other.)

(Therapist 1 and Laurie have reached a stand-off.)

T2: *(Softly.)* What else? *(Eight-second pause.)* I noticed you started to have a reaction when your mother first started talking to your father, and I'd wondered what was going on.

(Therapist 2 attempts to shift away from the impasse between therapist 1 and Laurie and onto the link between mother and Laurie.)

L: Well, just before he *(therapist 1)* said "Talk to dad," I wanted, you know, to add to that, so I couldn't at that point.

T1: You wanted to add to what?

(But therapist 1 refuses to let go and again hooks Laurie's defensiveness.)

L: *(Again speaks with some irritation.)* Well, I wanted to say what I said just now. Before mom turned to talk to dad.

(Fifteen-second pause.)

T1: You interrupted and started to talk just at the point where it seemed that the conversation between your parents was starting to wind down. Wasn't sure, I wasn't sure where it was going to go next.

L: I didn't know whether mom was finished. I didn't want to sit here, you know, for five minutes and let (*unintelligible*).

(*Therapist 1 labels what has happened structurally but again provokes a defensive reaction from Laurie, who reveals her fear that the discussion between her parents was dead.*)

T2: And I had the feeling that you felt a need to respond to your mother (*Laurie nods agreement*), particularly.

(*Seven-second pause.*)

(*Therapist 2 instead deftly joins Laurie, reframing her behavior as "responsive" to mother rather than "interruptive" as therapist 1 had labeled it.*)

L: Yeah, I guess. Plus, what we were talking about before. You asked us, Nancy and I, what we (*emphasizes*) thought about it. (*Shrugs shoulders as if to say "Well?"*)

(*Twenty-one second pause.*)

T1: What was it about responding to your mother that was important?

(*Therapist 1 attempts to join Laurie by acknowledging the "importance" of her response to mother.*)

L: I don't know. I just wanted to say it. (*Speaks emphatically, but with less irritation now.*) Because I had been thinking about it. (*Affect now seems sad.*) And before, it had been a group thing.

(*The softening in Laurie's tone suggests that therapist 1 has finally had some success in joining Laurie.*)

T2: My guess, my feeling is, that you weren't too sure how much support your mother was going to get back from your father. And you felt the need to give your mother some support.

L: I may have been. I wasn't thinking that consciously, no.

T1: It's clear to me that it was important that you say what you did. It was important to you. And that my jumping on you and cutting it off was frustrating you.

L: Um-hum.

T1: There was a push behind it.

L: Yeah. 'Cause you started out by making a group discussion. And then when I tried to add, it's like, you know, you're no longer part of the group.

This unproductive exchange between Laurie and me highlights a point made in Chapter 9 when discussing the Bach family: One can be structurally correct, yet fail with an intervention because a workable frame has not been created for the structural work. My observations about Laurie's involvement in the marital interaction when her parents reached an impasse were structurally sound and to the point. However, I had not made it clear that we were shifting from a family to a couple discussion and, when Laurie did speak up, I failed to create a frame she could join and instead left her feeling hurt and put-down. This made it impossible to accomplish the structural goal: Blocking Laurie's involvement so the couple's discussion could continue.

To reiterate, *all* therapy in whatever model has strategic elements and the therapist must choose a frame that allows the necessary (in this case, structural) work to occur.

Accordingly, we framed a new task for the therapy: Mr. and Mrs. Miller now needed to talk with each other in the session, with their daughters listening, in order to answer some of Laurie's and Nancy's questions and worries about their parents. This new frame did not work either, but instead provoked resistance when Mrs. Miller immediately insisted that she and her husband had no worries about being together. So we changed the emphasis a bit: Laurie and Nancy do have worries that are interfering with their getting on with their own lives, and maybe the couple's discussions will help *the daughters*. With this frame, we were able to define the generational boundary in the session and get Mr. and Mrs. Miller to talk with each other.

In their discussion, the couple attributed their emotional distance to Mr. Miller's illness. Both insisted that things would get better between them as Mr. Miller's health improved. We wondered if Mr. Miller anticipated that his wife would have more emotional needs of him when the daughters left. He first replied: "No, because she's not that type of person." But he then acknowledged that currently her need for "attention" was partially met by Nancy and Laurie. Mrs. Miller agreed that she likes "lots of attention" and was direct in stating that she would want more affection from her husband when her daughters left home. As the discussion continued, Mr. Miller brightened a bit, becoming more animated and involved.

We then moved to the other side of the generational boundary to hear the daughters' reactions to their parents' discussion.

T1: (*To parents.*) We've been spending some time now focused on the two of you and (*to daughters*) the two of you have been sitting there listening attentively.

T2: Quietly.

T1: Quietly.

F: (*Warmly.*) Grinning like chessy cats.

T1: Uh-huh. Now I'd like to (*gestures from parents to daughters*) shift over to this side of the room and find out what reactions and feelings you have to your parents' talking. (*Nancy and Laurie exchange glances and Nancy gestures for Laurie to speak first.*)

(*Again there is a moment of ambiguity as Nancy and Laurie each invite the other to comment upon the parents' interaction.*)

L: I'm always first. You go ahead.

N: Age before beauty (*laughs*).

L: No, you.

N: (*Gestures again for Laurie to begin, then laughs.*)

L: Uh-huh (*indicating "No"*).

N: I can't start 'cause I don't know what to say. You first. (*Draws sweater closed and holds arms across stomach, then flaps arms nervously at her sides.*) There's something that I know that I should say. . . . (*Loudly to Laurie.*) Go on. Go on, just do something. (*Nancy and Laurie stare at each other and then Nancy breaks eye contact and laughs.*)

L: I don't know what to say yet.

N: (*Overlaps.*) Me either.

L: (*Continues.*) If you've got something to say, then say it.

N: I don't have anything to say. Um. . . .

T1: (*To Nancy.*) You look a little embarrassed.

N: Yes.

(*This begins a long exchange with Nancy in which she is very uncomfortable as therapist 1 solicits her reaction to the parental discussion.*)

T1: I think in a way your embarrassment is because they're talking, they've been talking about something quite intimate that concerns their relationship, um. . . .

N: (*Interrupts.*) And I was thinking it was none of our business and we should not listen (*continues to fidget with sweater*).

T1: And to some extent you're right. I mean, that's really true, it is their business. The thing is, in my experience kids never quite get that through their heads and always worry about the parents' business anyway.

N: (*Laughs emphatically.*) Um-hum.

T1: And that's why I think we need to do a little talking about it here, before you go off and. . . . So granted that it's embarrassing and not quite your business, you still have some reactions to what was said.

(*Eleven-second pause.*)

N: (*Softly.*) They seem to have (*unintelligible*). (*Seventeen-second pause during which Nancy glances at Laurie who avoids eye contact. Nancy squirms in her chair and throws up her hands in a helpless gesture.*) I can't think of anything. When I get embarrassed or anything like that, and it's something people are talking about, I just kinda let it go in one ear and kinda float out the other. It doesn't stay there, 'cause it's just like none of my business, "Butt out." That's just the way I'm, I click, I guess. (*Again sits with arms drawn across stomach.*) I don't like butting into people's business, but I do it anyway.

T1: One thing I know about you is that you have a very sensitive body. At least, your stomach is very sensitive. And my guess is it doesn't just go in one ear and out the other (*Nancy gestures "in one ear, down through the stomach, and out the other ear"*) but it percolates inside in some way (*Nancy again crosses arms across stomach*). So we, where did it stick this time?

N: It didn't stick. I really don't know what to say. I mean, uh, what you want or whatever, so I can't, I don't know where to go.

T1: Look inside (*nods down toward Nancy's stomach*). That's where to go. That's where the answers are.

(*Eighteen-second pause. Nancy looks to Laurie and they exchange glances. Then Laurie initiates eye contact. Nancy laughs nervously.*)

L: One of my concerns about it, like I know mom, you know, talks to me and stuff. She needs more affection, physical affection, than dad does. (*To parents.*) It's just the way you guys were brought up. And, from two entirely different families. You know, one showed affection all the time and (*to father*) your family was, you know, not all that physical.

(*Given Nancy's by now clear refusal to become involved, Laurie speaks up, emphasizing her mother's need for affection.*)

M: Different personalities.

L: Yeah. Like. . . .

M: (*Interrupts.*) That's good.

L: Yeah, but, I'm kinda, afraid or worried or whatever, that with Nancy gone, like to school for the year except for the holidays, and me being able to visit every day, every couple of days or whatever. Yet, it will hurt, not having like, maybe, Nancy or I around all the time, to touch or pat or. . . .

F: (*Overlaps.*) It will take some getting used to, there's no doubt about that.

L: (*Interrupts, speaking to father.*) But I was wondering how well you will take over that?

(*This is the heart of Laurie's concern for her mother.*)

N: (*Overlaps.*) Well, I never did much of that while I was there, so. . . .

M: (*Overlaps.*) No, Nancy's not very demonstrative either.

(*But when she finally faces father with the issue Nancy and mother join to protect father.*)

L: I don't know. It's just like. . . .

T1: (*Overlaps.*) Laurie, they're going to talk you out of your question if you don't watch out. You struggled to get an important question out, which is really a question for you. And the Greek chorus comes in (*Laurie laughs loudly and is joined by mother*). Right.

T2: "Don't have that question. Don't worry about it."

(*The therapists now block mother and Nancy and support Laurie's attempt to air her concerns.*)

M: (*Nods.*) I see.

T1: (*To Laurie.*) Say the question again, because it was so important. And the question was directed toward your father. You looked at him (*nods for Laurie to continue*).

L: Well, are you. . . .

T1: (*Interrupts, gesturing toward father.*) Say it to him.

L: Are you going to be able to take over the physical affection that Nancy and I have supplied?

(*Laurie restates her question.*)

F: (*Softly.*) As much as I am able to.

L: 'Cause like there'll be two less people there to touch.

F: That's right.

L: I think that was, that's what mom was talking about.

(*Here Laurie indicates how much she has been speaking for mother. Whereas Nancy appears to have been triangulated to regulate the couple's conflict, Laurie's role seems more related to managing intimacy in the marital relationship.*)

F: There's no doubt about it, that we're going to miss you. We'll miss you very much. 'Cause we haven't got that physical contact every day. We'll have to face up to it. . . .

(Here father side-steps Laurie's concern by emphasizing that the parents will miss their daughters.)

L: *(Interrupts.)* No, but, I'm, I'm talking about for mom. . . . Like when we were there, a lot of times mom would want something from you, a hug or something, and she'd be the one. . . .

(But Laurie refocuses on her mother's need for affection.)

F: Yeah, I see.

L: And then we'd give her *(gestures to mother)* our share. And now that we're not there, she's always going to have to be the one to ask. . . . She shouldn't have to ask.

F: Right.

(Ten-second pause.)

T1: Mrs. Miller, you started to say something to Mr. Miller.

(It is not clear from the tape what therapist 1 was responding to here, i.e., some actual behavior by mother versus "creating" some behavior in an attempt to get mother to speak for herself.)

M: I did? What, to John?

T1: I think it was. . . .

M: Well, I, I don't know, I was just thinking, uh, we're, that, a, I mean, John and I are not as one, like some great loves of history or, one, we think the same, our hearts as one. And we're not like that, I, our, our love is terrific but we're individuals and we can think alone. And I think that's great.

(Here mother gallantly and somewhat poetically takes father off the hook.)

T1: And that's true, and it's also true that you need physical affection.

(But therapist 1 pushes her to not neglect her own needs.)

M: Yes. I think I admit that.

T1: Um-hum.

T2: And that Laurie's aware of that.

L: I think we're *(indicates mother)* more alike. . . .

(Laurie labels her identification with mother.)

M: *(Overlaps.)* I think so.

L: *(Continues.)* And Nancy and dad are alike in. . . .

(And Nancy's identification with father.)

M: (*Overlaps.*) This is true.

L: That's how it has always been. So I think I can understand mom's needs.

N: (*Unintelligible.*)

L: (*Overlaps.*) More than. . . . (*To Nancy.*) Yeah, more than you. Because mom and I are more alike.

M: And there's nothing wrong with being different.

L: But when you have a need, and you. . . .

M: (*Starts to interrupt.*)

L: (*Overrides, continuing.*) And you like to touch, and stuff.

M: That's true.

(*A few moments later the following exchange occurred and the meaning of the earlier interaction with Nancy became clearer.*)

T1: Nancy, you got off the hot seat because Laurie volunteered her concern and reaction.

N: (*Looks away, again embarrassed.*) I want to stay out.

(*Nancy very clearly says that she wishes to stay out of her parents' relationship.*)

T1: You want to stay out.

N: Uh-huh. I, uh, in a way, uh, don't want to be involved any more. I'll take my exit now, instead of (*shifts in chair, looking as though she is about to get up and leave*) in a few months.

T1: Really. That's what all this embarrassment was about. Not wanting to get re-involved.

(*Nancy has succeeded in reframing her behavior for therapist 1.*)

N: Yeah, 'cause I don't like being in the limelight, or right there. I like staying off to the side, or out of the picture.

T1: You're perfectly happy to have Laurie be the worrier right now.

N: (*Laughs.*) Uh-huh.

T1: Right?

N: Or someone, I mean.

T1: Just not you.

N: Yeah.

(*Seven-second pause. Nancy looks at Laurie, then mother turns to Laurie.*)

T1: (*To Laurie.*) Think you got her (Laurie's) job?

L: I don't think so. It's been more on my mind lately, about, what, you know, I might be taking it over. I don't think I could totally take over the job she had. Because. . . .

N: (*Overlaps.*) I think mom and dad will take part of it.

L: Yeah. . . .

N: (*Overlaps.*) Or whatever. . . .

L: But I, it's (*ten-second pause*). . . . I don't know, I, I've just been more selfish than Nancy, and now I just (*emphatically*) won't take over her whole job.

T1: Maybe you'll be more self-protective.

(*Therapist 1 reframes Laurie's behavior from "selfish" to "self-protective."*)

(*Ten-second pause.*)

L: I mean, it's like, it's a rotten job to have, to do that. But if you look at it, it seems like, "Oh, gee, you know, the good one of the family who's always watching out." (*Voice becomes soft, warm, and Laurie smiles broadly.*)

(*Laurie finally reveals the appeal of taking over Nancy's old job: Being the "good one" of the family.*)

T1: That's one of the advantages. . . .

L: (*Overlaps.*) Yeah, but, geez. . . .

T1: (*Continues.*) That I was telling you about.

L: Yeah. (*Laughs.*)

M: (*To therapist.*) Is that a guilt complex (*unintelligible*)?

(*Laurie kicks Nancy.*)

N: Owww!

L: (*To Nancy.*) Sorry. (*To mother.*) Yes.

M: That's the whole thing (*laughs*).

L: If I don't take it over, gee, I, I'm a skunk (*voice suggests eagerness and even pleasure rather than distress*).

(*Here Laurie reveals her ambivalent feelings about her new role in the family.*)

M: By, by your own. . . .

L: Yeah. Yeah.

M: Oh, I. That's the guilt complex.

L: Yeah. Yeah.

M: Oh, I see.

L: Because I'm selfish and I just don't want to do it.

T1: We need to talk some more about that.

M: Because you can't live with a guilt complex. And have a full life.

Tl: Weights you down.

M: Right. Makes you ill.

As the session ended, we asked Laurie to pay special attention during the week to her worries about her parents.

Nancy Is Out and Laurie Is In

Nancy began session seven by announcing that we could talk to the rest of the family, but she did not wish to be involved. I responded that we had made a big mistake the previous week when we had put her on the spot, pressing her so hard for her reaction to her parents' discussion: "You were telling me that you are on your way out of the family and I wasn't paying attention." To further emphasize her new position in the family, we turned Nancy into the camera operator for the rest of the session.

(I then continued to take a one-down position, this time with Laurie.)

Tl: And the second way I completely missed the boat last week was, we were talking with you, Laurie, about the danger that you might (*emphasizes*) slip into Nancy's role.

L: Um-hum.

Tl: What I realized after the session was that you already have.

(*Therapist 1 begins to reframe Laurie's behavior, here from "might take over Nancy's role" to "have taken it over."*)

L: Totally, or. . . .

Tl: I'm not sure yet. You smiled as I said it, so. . . .

L: (*Speaks decisively.*) I think I have taken over a lot, but not to the point that Nancy had it.

T2: But enough so that you really are in it.

L: Yeah.

Tl: And it's, it would be a mistake for us to pretend that you haven't. To continue to talk about the danger that you might. And we have to start dealing with the fact that you have. And so, what about it? Will you slip in further? Might you develop some symptoms yourself? (*Unintelligible.*)

(Implicit in this frame is the notion that Laurie's new position in the family is bad.)

L: Well, okay, right now, I feel good. You know, I don't, well, I used to get tension headaches and just, be all the way down. I haven't felt any tension, you know, in my body. Like muscle spasms or headaches. Um, I guess I know (*emphasizes*) I've assumed the role.

(Rather than be made sick by her new position in the family, Laurie makes it clear that she feels better.)

T1: What are you doing now that lets you know that?

L: I don't know. Nancy lets me know all the time. If I say something inadvertently or start talking and not really realize it's the way Nancy used to talk, she'll g, you know, she'll point it out to me.

T1: Like? For example.

L: I don't know. (*To Nancy who is standing behind the camera.*) Give me a hint.

T1: See, the reason that she's (*Nancy's*) back there is exactly so that she doesn't have to. . . .

(Therapist 1 blocks Laurie from turning to Nancy.)

L: (*Overlaps.*) Yeah. I can't remember. They're all little things. Like I'll say something, a, "How's dad doing at work?" This, that, start asking questions and she'll say "You're doing just what I did." Being more concerned. Um. I can't think of any big thing, any incident. Just little things that sometimes she'll point out to me. But I don't, I don't feel I'm constantly worried or worried too much. I feel good about it. Maybe because Nancy's not going to be here to take it away from me or whatever, now that I've assumed it.

(Here Laurie gives the reason for her satisfaction with her new place in the family: Nancy will not be around to displace me.)

T1: You won't have to fight with her over who gets to do it.

L: Yeah. I didn't before, because I just didn't have it. Nancy had it. She won't be here to take it away once I have it (*slight laugh*).

T1: What's that like for you now?

L: I get, I feel secure.

(This is the payoff for Laurie.)

What followed in a long discussion with Laurie was a remarkable glimpse inside her struggles to become emancipated from the family. Laurie stated that without Nancy around as "competition" she felt more relaxed in the family. She put her finger nicely on the polarization that had occurred within the family over the past months, contrasting the independence for which she was struggling with Nancy's dependent position. She also spoke of her failure to complete school as both a response to the stress of her father's illness and a way to assert her independence from her parents.

Laurie remarked that now that she was no longer struggling so hard to assert her independence, she felt freer to move closer to her parents and develop a better relationship with them ("I can call or go over rather than not call or go over, to assert that I am independent.") As we discussed the changes that had permitted this to happen, Laurie attributed them more to herself than to her parents (e.g., she now listens to her parents more). Mrs. Miller added that she now found herself less angry with her daughter. Laurie and her mother discussed how they had become much closer recently. Laurie remarked: "I have always felt that mom and I were very much alike, emotionally. . . . I sort of cut myself off from that. . . . I think I tried to say that I was different. And now that I'm not defensive anymore, I can go back again."

The change in Laurie's affect was striking. In recent sessions she had been angry, demanding, at times strident. Now she spoke softly, thoughtfully, and very warmly about her family and the things they all had gone through. During this discussion, Mr. Miller, who was for the first time sitting between Laurie and his wife, appeared very depressed, staring blankly at the floor.

The talk of the new closeness between Laurie and her mother expanded to include the father by focusing on Laurie's identification with her mother's emotional needs and her concern that Mr. Miller would not be able to meet them. Laurie described herself as a "bridge" between her parents, "until dad can take care of mom's emotional needs that Nancy used to fill."

We wondered whether Laurie would be able to give her father the chance to take care of her mother. Laurie acted hurt, insisting that her better relationship with her mother would not take away from the parents' relationship with each other. We agreed, emphasizing that we did not wish to take away Laurie's new closeness with her mother. Laurie reiterated her view of her new role in the family: "Maybe the relationship we (Laurie and mother) have now will just, I don't know, help mom over, while dad tries to take over part of Nancy's absence." Laurie then again expressed her worry that her father would not be able to make up emotionally for the loss of the daughters in the home.

As the session ended we invited Nancy back into the circle and discussed what had happened. Nancy remarked on her surprise at Laurie's talk about the competitiveness between them. Laurie added: "So was I. The last few sessions made me realize it."

This session had also reframed for me Laurie's new role in the family, which I discussed with them:

I also have a reaction to the session. I've been mulling over, for the last two weeks, especially after the last session, you (*to Laurie*), where you are in the family. And I, I must admit that I have not been able to figure out what I think about it. Part of me thinks that your new role in the family is awful and part of me thinks, I, I'm just not sure how I feel. This session was important for me because I saw where you are in a new way. And I want to tell you what I saw today. What I see, Laurie, is you taking a step back into the family so that you can now leave properly. Back in August you left improperly, impulsively to assert yourself and all kinds of stuff. Jumped out. What I see you doing now is stepping back in. Nancy's graciously created room for you by stepping aside. There's actually room for you to be back in the family now. And you've stepped back in, I think, so that you can now leave properly. I'm not as worried, after today I'm not as worried as I was that you would decide that it's so nice that you'd stay.

The interview ended with the parents' reactions to the session. Mrs. Miller said that she realized that her daughters are capable of being on their own. "And John and I have our own lives. And I can concentrate on myself. It will be fun, won't it, John?" Mr. Miller replied glumly, tapping his chair nervously: "A new adventure."

The final session of the eight-week treatment contract occurred a couple of weeks later. Nancy, preparing to leave shortly for her European trip, had experienced no further vomiting. The interview again focused on the marital relationship and on how Laurie could maintain her new closeness with her parents and still pursue her own life. Laurie's new job made it difficult for her to continue attending the family sessions, so we decided to begin meeting with Mr. and Mrs. Miller alone after Nancy left for Europe.

Follow-up

The next session with Mr. and Mrs. Miller proved to be disastrous. Long-buried marital conflict quickly surfaced. Mr. Miller revealed that he had deeply resented his mother-in-law's intrusions into their lives throughout the years of the couple's marriage. And

Mrs. Miller admitted that before the couple had adopted Laurie she had very seriously considered divorce because of her husband's violent temper. Once uncorked, the bitterness came pouring out, and the session ended with the couple greatly distressed.

Mr. Miller subsequently refused any further contact with us and Mrs. Miller declined our offer of a termination session for herself, apparently out of deference to her husband.

Approximately six months later, while Nancy was home from school for the holidays, she and her mother contacted us and the two of them came in for a follow-up visit. Nancy had indeed gone off to Europe as planned and had enjoyed her trip with only minor stomach difficulties, which she attributed to the foreign food. Since fall she had been away at school and was doing fairly well, but had begun to experience some intermittent vomiting. Moreover, Nancy described a pattern of overresponsibility at school that was strikingly similar to the one she had displayed in the family. For example, she was staying up until three in the morning typing term papers for dorm-mates. And she traveled an hour each way by bus every Saturday morning to tutor orphan children. In both cases, Nancy described her behavior as something she simply had to do. In the session, Mrs. Miller advised her daughter that the vomiting was something she was probably "going to have to learn to live with, just like my arthritis." We were distressed by Mrs. Miller's pessimism and urged Nancy to seek psychotherapy at school.

Laurie was busy with her new job and maintained sporadic contact with the family. Mr. Miller's health had remained stable, with no further signs of cancer. He continued to work a few hours a week. Mrs. Miller appeared depressed, but resigned to her situation. She admitted feeling disappointed and dissatisfied with her husband, but felt that she could do nothing about it.

Could a more satisfactory treatment outcome have been achieved in this case? I have often wondered about this, without coming to any firm conclusions. It is possible that a longer course of family therapy would have produced more permanent results. For example, Minuchin et al. (1975) report on 36 successful psychosomatic cases, describing family treatment ranging in length from 2 to 15 months, with an average of approximately 7½ months. The intensive (and productive) phase of our work with this family occurred in just eight sessions. Had Nancy been available for further work, we may well have continued the family sessions, perhaps with a better long-term outcome.

The failure of the couples therapy in this case left me with a nagging question. Although we made no particular effort to stir up the marital conflict in that final session (and really had no clear idea even what the specific issues were), what occurred may have simply been too much, too fast for the Millers to handle. Perhaps we could have managed the session differently and kept the couple in therapy? On the other hand, what happened in that interview may have been an inevitable consequence of the changes in the family with the daughters' emancipation. The couple's estrangement was certainly deep and pervasive, enough to have provided the context for Nancy's dramatic symptom in the first place.

12

Brief Strategic Treatment
of Post-Traumatic Stress Disorder

Post-traumatic stress disorder, an interesting and important clinical syndrome, has received little attention in the family therapy literature. A notable exception is Figley and Sprenkle's (1978) paper on family therapy indications in treating delayed combat stress disorders.

In this chapter, I outline the diagnostic criteria for post-traumatic stress disorder and then present a promising example of brief strategic treatment of a Vietnam combat veteran who had experienced classic post-traumatic symptoms throughout the ten years since his return from Vietnam. As the patient remembered Vietnam, his autonomic arousal was so intense that he literally felt as though he were back in combat. During six treatment sessions, the veteran learned to reduce this arousal using deep breathing and the post-traumatic symptoms ceased. The case material is discussed in terms of the *tasks* typically confronting the strategic therapist.

The concluding sections of this chapter review psychodynamic and behavioral approaches to post-traumatic disorder and develop a cybernetic model for the syndrome. In this model, which operates simultaneously on biological, psychological, and social levels, autonomic arousal and combat memories form a central deviation-amplifying cybernetic circuit; suppressing behaviors by the veteran and actions by others in the social environment that maintain this suppression serve as homeostatic, deviation-reducing influences. Treatment using deep breathing is a form of biofeedback that provides a more effective deviation-reducing mechanism. This cybernetic model is discussed in light of reports of successful treatment of post-traumatic disorder using the MAO-inhibiting antidepressant drug phenelzine. Additional applications of the model to anger management in post-traumatic disorder and to spouse abuse are presented.

Post-Traumatic Stress Disorder

HISTORY OF THE SYNDROME

Although post-traumatic stress disorder can certainly result from stresses other than military combat, psychiatry's attention to this syndrome is closely related to our twentieth-century wars. Over the years, combat stress disorders have been known by various names. Prior to World War I, the trauma of war was thought to give rise to specific central nervous system damage. The term *shell shock* then in use vividly describes the hypothesized results of exposure to battlefield explosions. During World War I, a functional explanation for combat stress began to predominate. Under the influence of the growing psychoanalytic movement, the term *traumatic war neurosis* became popular (Kardiner, 1959). During World War II, military psychiatry's approach to combat stress was essentially pragmatic: The idea was that every man has his breaking point, and the terms *combat exhaustion* and *battle fatigue* were used (Kormos, 1978). In his recent work (chiefly with patients suffering from noncombat-related disorders), Horowitz (1976) has used the term *stress response syndrome*. And finally, DSM-III (American Psychiatric Association, 1980) put psychiatry's official stamp of approval on the name *post-traumatic stress disorder*.

In the opening sentence of his chapter "Traumatic Neuroses of War" in the *American Handbook of Psychiatry*, Kardiner (1959) states: "The neuroses incidental to war alternate between being the urgent topic of the times and being completely and utterly neglected" (p. 245). As Kardiner suggests, we seem to forget about the syndrome from one war to the next.

VIETNAM POST-TRAUMATIC DISORDER

Nowhere is this amnesia more evident than following Vietnam. In our haste to put the war behind us, we managed, until the past few years, to ignore the continuing effects of combat trauma experienced by thousands of Vietnam veterans. The social and political aspects of the treatment of Vietnam veterans is well documented elsewhere and will not be emphasized here. See, for example, Figley (1978) for an overview. In this chapter, I concentrate on the clinical issues.

Veterans Administration studies indicate that post-traumatic disorder is underdiagnosed in Vietnam combat veterans. This is partially a result of the inadequacies of DSM-II (American Psychiatric Association, 1968), which had no category for the syndrome. Sarah Haley (1978), for example, reports that over 80 percent of the veterans in her study who manifested symptoms of post-traumatic disorder received diagnoses of anxiety or depressive neurosis. Van Putten and Emory (1973) emphasize that acute symptoms of post-traumatic disorder tend to be misdiagnosed as psychomotor epilepsy, LSD abuse, or schizophrenia, and that the diagnosis of schizophrenia may lead to inappropriate long-term treatment with phenothiazines.

My own interest in post-traumatic disorder developed incidentally, out of my ignorance of the syndrome. I was treating Mr. Jackson, a 32-year-old Vietnam combat veteran in couples treatment for depression, alcohol abuse, and marital conflict. The patient described himself as depressed and "different" ever since Vietnam. Although I made a brief attempt to focus on his Vietnam experience very early in the treatment (I was working in a VA setting and did have some exposure to combat-related problems), I soon settled into doing the familiar couples therapy with which I felt more comfortable and sure of myself. A couple of months into the treatment, I gave a homework assignment designed to interrupt the wife's depression-maintaining behavior [i.e., her attempts to cheer her husband up or encourage him to get more active, which resulted in still more of his depressive behavior; see Coyne (1976)]. What emerged was massive rage and anxiety in the patient, along with heavy drinking. I did not know what to make of it. Was he crazy and in need of Thorazine? Should I refer him to an alcohol treatment program after all? Fortunately, I had a consultant (my colleague Neil Scott) who helped me diagnose and treat post-traumatic disorder in this case.

The remainder of this section introduces a second case example and discusses the DSM-III criteria for post-traumatic stress disorder.

THE CASE OF MR. HAYES

Mr. Hayes was a white male in his early thirties, married, with one young daughter and a wife who was seven months pregnant at the time of referral. He worked at a trade and lived in a small town about an hour's drive from San Francisco. The patient had dropped out of school in the eleventh grade and joined the Army, serving combat duty as an infantryman in Vietnam during 1970–1971.

Mr. Hayes sought psychiatric help at the VA Hospital in the summer of 1979. Prior to that time he had received no psychological treatment. He did consult the medical clinic at the VA complaining of night sweats. When the medical work-up was negative, he was told that the clinic could be of further help to him only if he came into the emergency room in the middle of one of these episodes.

The patient was noted to be acutely anxious when screened in the admissions unit at the time he requested psychiatric treatment, as well as a week later when he was seen in the outpatient clinic by an intake worker.

It is important to note here that Mr. Hayes was seen as one of the best psychotherapy candidates among the Vietnam combat veterans referred to the psychiatry clinic during the previous year. Treatment of veterans showing symptoms of post-traumatic disorder is often complicated by pre-combat character problems and/or by heavy drug or alcohol abuse. Mr. Hayes did not present these complications and appears to represent a "pure" case of post-traumatic disorder. He is presented here not as a necessarily typical treatment case, but rather as illustrative of the core features of post-traumatic disorder.

THE DIAGNOSTIC CRITERIA

According to DSM-III (American Psychiatric Association, 1980), the essential feature of post-traumatic stress disorder is the development of characteristic symptoms after a trauma that is outside the range of ordinary human experience (e.g., rape, automobile accident, military combat).

Two central symptoms characterize the disorder: re-experiencing the trauma event (in recurrent and intrusive recollections, recurrent dreams, or suddenly acting or feeling as if the event were recurring) and numbing of responsiveness to or reduced involvement with the external world (through diminished interest in significant activities, feeling detached or estranged from others, or constricted affect).

A variety of additional symptoms are also typically seen, including exaggerated startle response, sleep disturbance, survival guilt, impairment in memory or concentration, and the avoidance of activities that activate memories of the traumatic event.

These diagnostic criteria (American Psychiatric Association, 1980, p. 238) are summarized as follows.

A. Existence of a recognizable stressor that would evoke significant symptoms of distress in almost everyone.
B. Reexperiencing of the trauma as evidenced by at least one of the following:
   1. recurrent and intrusive recollections of the event
   2. recurrent dreams of the event
   3. sudden acting or feeling as if the traumatic event were reoccurring, because of an association with an environmental or ideational stimulus
C. Numbing of responsiveness to or reduced involvement with the external world, beginning some time after the trauma, as shown by at least one of the following:
   1. markedly diminished interest in one or more significant activities
   2. feeling of detachment or estrangement from others
   3. constricted affect
D. At least two of the following symptoms that were not present before the trauma:
   1. hyperalertness or exaggerated startle response
   2. sleep disturbance
   3. guilt about surviving when others have not, or about behavior required for survival
   4. memory impairment or trouble concentrating
   5. avoidance of activities that arouse recollection of the traumatic event
   6. intensification of symptoms by exposure to events that symbolize or resemble the traumatic event

A number of associated symptoms (common, but not central to the diagnosis) are listed in DSM-III, including irritability and episodic outbursts of aggressive behavior, with little or no provocation, and impulsive behavior such as sudden trips and changes in life-style.

It is important to note that these symptoms may begin immediately or soon after the traumatic event or may instead be delayed for months or even years.

MR. HAYES' POST-TRAUMATIC SYMPTOMS

In my initial interview with Mr. Hayes, he described his intrusive recollections: "I'll just be thinkin, all of a sudden I'll think about Vietnam again. Things will just be there again. I'll try to think about something else, whatever. Just, they pop in real quick like, now." Mr. Hayes indicated that the experience of coming to these hospitals and talking about Vietnam had stirred up more of the troublesome recollections. This, as will be evident below, makes treatment difficult because the last thing these patients wish to do is to remember.

Mr. Hayes went on to say that at least for the first four or five years following Vietnam the intrusive recollections were so frequent and intense that he felt "almost like I was there again. I get that feeling. You stop thinking about something. You just think you're there, sort of."

In addition to the intrusive recollections, Mr. Hayes reported the other forms of re-experiencing the traumatic event listed in DSM-III. He described recurrent dreams about Vietnam and told of suddenly acting as if the combat trauma were recurring. For example, he would awaken from a nightmare about Vietnam, grab the gun he kept under his pillow, and point it toward the door of his bedroom until his wife managed to convince him he had had a dream and calm him down. Although he no longer slept with the gun under his pillow, at the time he sought psychiatric treatment (almost ten years after Vietnam), he still kept the loaded gun under his bed. He was unable to say why he had hung onto the gun, admitting that, although he grew up with guns and used to enjoy hunting, since Vietnam "I've never gone hunting or nothing. . . . Now I won't even step on an ant. . . . I can't shoot nothing."

The patient also reported numbing of responsiveness, the second characteristic post-traumatic symptom, describing a low-level depression and pervasive loss of interest in life. When asked about the main problem at the beginning of the evaluation interview Mr. Hayes said:

> Being depressed all the time, I guess. Not seeing anything in the future as substantial, or whatever you want to say, you know. Being able to plan something in the future. I just don't care. It doesn't matter anymore or nothing. I just get real depressed, I guess.

Among the other characteristic post-traumatic symptoms, Mr. Hayes described exaggerated startle response, guilt about behavior required for survival, avoidance of activities that arouse recollections of the traumatic experience, and an intensification of his post-traumatic symptoms upon exposure to events resembling the traumatic event.

He also reported various forms of self-destructive behavior that are often seen in veterans with post-traumatic disorder. He talked of working himself 16 hours a day, 7 days a week, so that he would fall into bed so exhausted that he could sleep. He admitted to abusing alcohol for several years, which he was able to stop without assistance. And he described riding his motorcycle so recklessly for the first six or seven years after Vietnam that during the interview he looked back and concluded that this behavior was suicidal. Mr. Hayes spontaneously associated his reckless motorcycle riding with his behavior in Vietnam, where he always took more chances with his life than did anyone else in his company. He described a feeling of invulnerability that he correctly saw as an extreme response to his fear in combat.

POST-TRAUMATIC DISORDER AND THE MARITAL RELATIONSHIP

Experiences with cases like that of Mr. Jackson, mentioned briefly above, had led me to anticipate a possible connection between the marital relationship and the veteran's methods for coping with his post-traumatic symptoms. Accordingly, I had arranged to see Mr. and Mrs. Hayes together for the evaluation interview. Near the end of that session I asked the marital quid pro quo question [Jackson (1965); see discussion in Chapter 7]. I learned that the patient had met his wife about one year after returning from Vietnam. The couple talked warmly to me about their meeting and Mr. Hayes' pursuit of his wife: He was serious about her, but she was young and not ready to get married yet, so she went out with other men, but managed to keep him hanging around; at one point they split up and a few weeks later decided to get married. At the end of the story, Mr. Hayes speculated that he might not have survived the reckless years following Vietnam were it not for his wife and wondered aloud about his reasons for marrying her. He concluded: "Well, I think that's why. 'Cause I found someone to, you know, talk to. Open and free enough. That she probably was the one. If I could be that way around her, then that's got to be the woman for me in my life." Still, it took Mr. Hayes six or seven years to begin to tell his wife about Vietnam.

It is not uncommon, in my experience, to see a connection between the post-traumatic patient's Vietnam experience and his choice of spouse. In the case described above, for example, Mr. Jackson told of coming home on leave between his two tours of duty in Vietnam and being very distressed to find that the straight, conservative town in which he grew up had been overrun by crazed hippies espousing drugs and free love (it was 1968). Mr. Jackson met his wife during that leave. He saw her on a bus and was immediately attracted to her because she was modestly and conservatively dressed and carefully made-up and groomed. "She looked like a lady. Someone you'd want to marry." Thirteen years later when I saw them in my office, Mrs. Jackson still had the "baby doll" look that must have initially attracted her husband that day on the bus.

The Treatment

As emphasized in Chapter 7, the strategic model is a problem-solving approach to treatment. The strategic therapist starts with the particular problem presented by the family and designs a solution unique to the case at hand. In describing Mr. Hayes' treatment in the remainder of this chapter, the clinical material is organized according to the various *tasks* typical in strategic treatment: Defining the treatment problem, framing the problem as solvable, dealing with the resistance to change, the strategic intervention, framing the success, grief, getting on with life, and ending treatment.

This is a post-hoc organization of the material of this particular case and represents neither the careful *a priori* plan of action by which I worked nor a general prescription for how to do strategic therapy. As emphasized in Chapter 7, there is no *method* for strategic treatment. However, the tasks described here typically confront strategic therapists. They follow roughly the order listed here, but should not be thought of as stages of therapy to be marched through in rigid, cookbook fashion. As will be evident below, the work of a single session generally spanned two or more of the tasks and it typically took more than one session to complete each of them.

DEFINING THE TREATMENT PROBLEM

At the end of the evaluation session, I contracted with Mr. Hayes for six sessions with a treatment goal defined as vaguely as "helping you deal with your leftover problems from Vietnam." It is certainly desirable when doing strategic treatment to have a more specific goal, if possible. However at that point, I had no clearer idea about what needed to be accomplished in the therapy. And I felt that, since Mr. Hayes had already had two prior intake interviews before seeing me, it would not be useful to prolong my own assessment. Rather, it was time to get on with treatment, wherever it would lead.

As the evaluation session ended, I was still not sure whether or not Mrs. Hayes should be involved in the therapy so I asked her to come along again to the next session.

In the first of those six treatment sessions, Mr. Hayes introduced the metaphor of "that little door" that controls access to his memories of Vietnam. Later in that session, the patient described what happens when he opens that door. This description led to a focus for the entire therapy. It began when I used Mr. Hayes' own metaphor:

> (*Here, and in the transcript segments that follow,* H *stands for husband, Mr. Hayes, and* T *for therapist.*)

T: That little door that we talked about that's somewhere inside that you can open and close. How far open is it now?

H: A quarter of the way? A little way.

T: A crack?

H: Yeah. (*Unintelligible.*)

T: Yeah.

H: I don't like what it does to my body when I open up that door.

> (*In retrospect, this sentence can be seen as the presenting problem the therapy must solve.*)

T: What happens?

H: I start getting all shaky and I s, I feel real funny and I can't hardly talk right. I don't like it.

(*Husband begins to describe the intense autonomic arousal he experiences when he opens the door.*)

T: Are you worried that that might happen in here as you open up the door?

H: I guess. It does every time I do. I don't know why it would be different here.

T: I think it will happen. That's one of the things that you've got to work through. Is what, thinking about that, talking about that, does to your body. Your body's telling you how important the experience is and how painful and all it is for you.

(*This is a weak beginning attempt to reframe husband's physiological arousal.*)

H: Do you think that it's worth doing that, to make it better in the long run?

(*Here husband asks a crucial question of the therapist.*)

T: I do. I think that it will be very painful in the short run. But that it really is something that you can work through and get rid of.

(*It is absolutely necessary that therapist answer husband's question simply, directly, and affirmatively. Otherwise, the patient would be foolish to go any further with the therapy.*)

H: Just by talking about it? (*Fourteen-second pause.*) What I'd like to be able to forget is the faces.

(*This statement demonstrates therapist's success so far in leading husband into a frame within which his problem can be solved. The first sentence expresses the old frame within which the patient's problem is unsolvable. The long pause suggests a change in frames, which is confirmed by the following sentence in which husband reveals more of his buried experience than he has done so far.*)

T: What faces do you see?

H: Dead people.

T: Tell me about that.

H: When I think about back there I just see that, those faces and stuff and they're just there (*voice begins to shake with anxiety*).

(*Husband opens the door and immediately becomes notably anxious. Visual imagery accompanying the memories is common in posttraumatic disorder.*)

T: Do you see them now?

H: Just flashing, you know. I don't want to see them. I'm tired of looking at 'em.

T: Trying to keep them away?

H: Yeah. (*Ten-second pause.*) Seeing myself touching them and stuff. (*Twenty-seven second pause.*)

T: What are you seeing now?

H: Nothing. I closed the door again. I don't like it.

(*Husband closes the door.*)

T: It's real important that you can close the door when you need to.

(*Therapist supports husband's ability to close the door.*)

H: Yeah (*emphatically*). If I felt like that and couldn't stop feeling like that I'd be real worried.

T: Yeah. Exactly. Exactly. We can take all the time you need to in here. We're going to basically have to work an hour, an hour at a time. But we can take a pace that works for you, that's comfortable for you. And when you need to close the door it's okay to do that. 'Cause it's real important for you to learn and be secure that you can close it down when you need to do that. (*Pause.*) What's happening inside your body now?

(*The therapist needs to be able to make friends with the patient's defenses in order to have a chance to slip in under them.*)

H: It's calming down. I feel like, I'm back to normal again.

T: Uh-huh. How charged up was it a couple of minutes ago?

(*Therapist accepts husband's shutting down of his memories and uses this as an opportunity to learn more about what happens when the patient opens the door. This discussion also helps husband get some distance from his experience, which assists his defenses and reassures him.*)

H: Real charged up.

T: What was happening?

H: I was just rushing all over. Feel like I was going to take off.

T: Tell me more about that.

H: It's just, a, real high feeling, just heart beat really fast and you feel like you just ran a mile or something. You could run another mile. Just getting started.

T: Your body was all, getting revved up?

H: Yeah. Like when something'd happen over there (*Vietnam*). Instantly you'd get that feeling.

(*Here husband spontaneously connects his autonomic arousal upon remembering Vietnam with what his body felt like in combat.*)

T: It's like what happens to your body when there's a sudden danger.

(*Here therapist begins what is to become the main frame for working on the patient's arousal while remembering: Your body reacts to your memories of Vietnam just like it did to the actual combat situation.*)

H: Uh-hum.

T: The adrenalin starts flowing.

H: I guess so.

T: Your heart rate goes up. Do you breathe faster?

H: Yeah.

T: What else happens?

H: I just feel hot. I just start feeling tingly all over. Sort a, it's like my hair gets alive.

T: (*Unintelligible*) that happen?

H: Just tingly, sort of.

T: Do you get images, visual images?

H: Um-hum.

T: You can see the, the faces?

H: Um-hum.

T: See yourself touching the bodies?

H: Yeah. That's when I start, feeling like that. All the things come back. Rockets and things like that.

(*The experience is so intense that as he remembers he sees and hears all over again what he experienced in Vietnam.*)

T: Do the sounds come back?

H: Yeah. The sound of those rockets really, really gets to me sometimes. I don't think I'll ever forget that sound.

T: Really. What reaction do you have to that? To that sound?

H: When I hear it I want to duck somewhere. Get on the ground. I got really close to a couple of rockets one time. They got really close to me (*laughs*).

At this point the vague treatment goal of doing something about the left-over effects of Vietnam can be made much more specific. Mr. Hayes complains that when he opens the door to his memories he experiences profound distress in his body. This becomes the treatment problem. And a frame for this problem has also begun to emerge. My first attempt to frame his body's arousal as a signal of the importance of his memories was unconvincing (but the only thing I could think of at the moment). Mr. Hayes' comment on the similarity between his autonomic arousal in the session and his experience in combat gave me the data I needed to (eventually) frame the arousal as *the same.*

Two comments on my own reactions during the above segment. First, I felt very much on the spot when Mr. Hayes directly asked me whether it would be worth it in the long run for him to open that door. In my very affirmative response, I was borrowing the words of my colleague Neil Scott. At that point I did not have enough personal experience in working with such cases that *I* knew it would be worth it. But I trusted Neil, and *he* knew, and this enabled me to reassure Mr. Hayes. Had I not been able to convey this faith to the patient, I doubt that he would (or should) have continued in treatment with me.

Second, in this session, it was not easy for me to support the patient's resistance to opening the door to his Vietnam memories. At this point I feared that I was doing something wrong: He had been very anxious when seen by the two previous interviewers, yet with me he managed to cover it over quite well; I must be an inept therapist (I thought). However, had I pushed too hard on that little door, I would likely have gotten only more resistance to opening it and Mr. Hayes might even have bolted from treatment.

Near the end of the session, I explored whether Mr. Hayes found his wife's presence comforting at those times when he remembered Vietnam and experienced intense physiological arousal. He indicated that only once in his wife's presence had he allowed himself to remember to the point of intense arousal, and that at other times he had always closed the door on his memories to protect her from having to listen. (So maybe I was not just a bad therapist who helped shut the patient's memories down: The other two evaluation interviews had been conducted without the wife's presence.) I had already decided that Mrs. Hayes was not significantly involved in maintaining her husband's post-traumatic symptoms (as Mrs. Jackson had been). This additional information convinced me that the patient was avoiding recollections during the sessions partly to protect his wife and that it was not productive or appropriate to continue her involvement in treatment at the present time. We agreed that Mrs. Hayes would continue to accompany her husband to the clinic, but until some unspecified time in the future, would not attend the sessions themselves.

FRAMING THE PROBLEM AS SOLVABLE

According to the strategic approach as discussed in Chapter 7, it is not sufficient simply to *define* a treatment problem (in this case, the autonomic arousal associated with remembering Vietnam). The therapist must also create a frame for that problem within which the problem is solvable and entice the patient into joining him in this new frame. Here I present two excerpts from the second treatment session that demonstrate this reframing.

When Mr. Hayes arrived alone for his second treatment session he looked very depressed. The date was July 5 and he explained that the Fourth of July fireworks "made me feel like I was back in Vietnam." He described intense anxiety and sleeplessness the previous night.

H: Is there some sort of trick or something for forgetting this stuff? Do I have to go through all this to accomplish the end goal or whatever?

(*The patient implicitly defines Vietnam as something to be forgotten and solicits the therapist's help in forgetting.*)

T: Do you have to talk about it? Is that what you mean?

H: Yeah. It's been so much a part of my life for the last ten years I just don't want, I want to forget it. I don't want to talk about it no more. I don't even want to think about it.

T: That really hasn't worked for ten years.

(*Therapist challenges the effectiveness of forgetting as a solution to the problem of Vietnam.*)

H: Um-hum.

T: To try to put it out of your mind hasn't worked.

H: No.

T: And I don't think it's going to work.

H: Well, is what we're going to be doing will be working?

(*Husband again asks for therapist's reassurance that the treatment will work.*)

T: Yeah.

H: Definitely going to be different than what it's been like?

(*Husband pushes hard, testing therapist's faith in the therapy.*)

T: Yeah.

H: I guess it will be worth it then.

(*When therapist stands firm, husband accepts the treatment.*)

T: I think it will be worth it for you to go through it. It is something you can work through and put behind you. It's hard to do that. It's hard to work through. It's hard to let the pain back.

(*Therapist summarizes the frame of the problem as* solvable: *"Something you can work through and put behind you."*)

In the next segment the treatment problem is made more explicit: Instead of *forgetting* about Vietnam, the patient can *unlearn his body's reaction* to his memories.

H: It seems like no one scares me or bothers me but myself.

T: Um-hum. And that's a hell of a way to live.

H: Yeah. If I'm not afraid of anything else, anybody else, or any, doing anything or going anywhere, how can I be so afraid of my own mind (*affect here is deep weariness and sadness*)?

T: And that's what you need to get over.

H: (*Softly.*) Being afraid of my mind?

T: And all the things inside it. That you try and shut the door on.

H: Those things that are there. I don't understand how they're going to change. It doesn't seem possible. Maybe it will be different, but I can see (*unintelligible*) all them years are gone.

T: That's right. You can never get those years back. And you'll always feel some anger and regret about that. And you'll never forget what happened.

H: You just learn to live with it, huh?

T: What will happen is the upsetness that you feel in your body, especially attached to those memories of what happened, the upsetness will go away.

(*Therapist makes explicit for the first time that husband can get rid of the arousal in his body.*)

H: You mean I won't feel like, when I talk I won't feel that way?

T: (*Indicates agreement.*)

H: What is that? I, I don't understand that at all. I feel like I know my body good enough to not feel like that.

T: A lot of the things that you feel in your body, the sense of, that something's about to happen, the readiness that you feel, your body's all charged up. Those are adaptive responses in, in Vietnam, in war. You were in danger there. And your whole physiological system was aroused and ready. And that was necessary if you, if you were to survive. That state of readiness, the reflexes. That actually contributed to your survival.

(*The autonomic arousal is framed as a normal response to the real danger of combat.*)

H: But how come it's still that way now?

T: Well, because it, in some way you haven't, you haven't learned that you're not there. Your, in other words, your body hasn't learned that. And that memories, um, fireworks, these things all automatically make your body react as though you were there. And that, that was a kind of learned response that happened while you were there. It had survival value. And you haven't unlearned it yet. And that's something you can unlearn.

(*And therapist indicates that the patient's body must and can unlearn this reaction.*)

H: It's all from being that scared over there, in Vietnam. I haven't changed or anything.

(*This response suggests that husband is very much with therapist in this new frame for his problem: He connects the current arousal in his body with the fear he experienced in combat.*)

T: Um-hum. There was a damn good reason to be scared while you were there. And your body hasn't learned yet that there's not that same reason to be scared here.

H: That's why, when things happen, I (*unintelligible*).

T: (*Overlaps.*) That's right.

DEALING WITH THE RESISTANCE TO CHANGE

It is a truism in therapy that at times the patient resists the therapist's attempts at change. In cybernetic terms, the organism has negative feedback loops that cancel out the effects of therapy-induced deviations from homeostatic conditions. This is perhaps more profoundly true in the case of post-traumatic disorder because the resistance to treatment in the form of an attempt to *avoid* re-experiencing the traumatic event is a central part of the syndrome itself (i.e., numbing of responsiveness). Here I illustrate, with segments from the second and third treatment sessions, the delicate job of side-stepping the resistance to treatment.

T: What's happening to that door inside as I talk?

(*The patient's metaphor of the door provides a useful way to talk about the resistance.*)

H: It's opened up a little bit.

T: How much is it opened now?

H: Just a little bit.

T: A small crack? What would happen if you opened it a little further? (*Therapist pushes gently on the door.*)

H: I'd start getting all funny and weird and I wouldn't like it. I'd find it hard to talk.

T: Um-hum.

H: It scares me, I guess.

T: Um-hum. You get scared all over again?

H: I guess so. It's like it was yesterday. I can still see (*unintelligible*) in full color.
(*Husband opens the door a bit further.*)

T: You can see it in full color now?

H: A little bit.

T: What do you see?

H: Vietnam. (*Unintelligible.*)

T: What do you see now?

H: Just the jungle.

T: Describe it to me.
(*Therapist pushes harder.*)

H: Just real thick. (*Unintelligible.*) (*Thirty-four second pause.*) I just shut that door.
(*And husband shuts the door again.*)

T: You shut it?

H: It happened automatically, I think. I don't want to think about it.

T: What might happen in here if you let it open?

H: I might start hating myself again.

T: You might start hating yourself again?

H: Not caring.

Along with my shoving against the door and the patient pushing back, I also explored Mr. Hayes' fears about what might happen were he to open the door. When I had approached this issue in an earlier session, Mr. Hayes stated that the worst thing that could happen was that no change would occur and he would continue to have his symptoms. This time he admitted to a fear of becoming upset enough to again take chances with his life. I acknowledged that it could happen and assured him that I could hospitalize him briefly, if necessary, for his own protection.

It is not uncommon, in working with cases of post-traumatic disorder, that brief hospitalization is necessary at some point in the treatment, and it is crucial that the therapist know what resources are available and be able to reassure the patient that such controls will be provided if needed. The therapist's *own* frame for a possible hospitalization is important. Some therapists see hospitalization only as a sign of therapeutic failure. This is generally more true of nonpsychiatric therapists with little experience in a hospital setting. It is necessary for the therapist to instead frame an indicated hospitalization as a temporary measure, which is often part of the normal course of treatment of post-traumatic disorder.

So far it had not really been productive for me to push at the door—Mr. Hayes held it closed as forcefully as I attempted to shove it open. At the beginning of treatment session three, I reframed the battle in terms of *his own choice*.

T: How's your week been?

H: Alright. I wasn't depressed or nothing.

T: Really.

H: A fair week, I guess. Thought more about coming down here again (*laughs nervously*).

T: I figured you would. What have you thought about it?

H: I don't know. Just, gets me worried.
    (*This is a replay of discussions in earlier sessions.*)

T: About?

H: Coming down here.

T: Um-hum. And what are you worried about?

H: Just, that feeling afterwards. That attitude again.

T: The attitude is what?

H: Just, I don't care.

T: Not caring.

H: Getting mad and angry.

T: Yeah.

H: I get nervous.

T: Um-hum. All those things that you've been experiencing for ten years. (*Pause.*) I think all those things will happen.

H: I know. That's what you told me last time. They've been happening.

T: They've been happening.

H: I find it real hard to bring myself down here.

T: Um-hum. But you keep coming. That means to me that you really do want to work on things.

(*Here therapist uses positive reframing. He ignores husband's resistance to treatment and focuses instead on the commitment to therapy demonstrated by the fact that the patient keeps coming week after week.*)

H: I guess once I started it I decided I'd better go through with it no matter what.

(*It works.*)

T: I think you did decide that. Even though it's hard to get going once you get here, I think you did decide that you're going to go through with this and get it behind you.

H: That's what I said the first day I come down here. I said I wasn't going to stop until I got some satisfaction.

T: I believe you.

H: It sure has been tough though.

T: Um-hum. It will get even tougher. But you'll survive.

H: I'm not afraid of surviving. I just don't like myself when I'm that way.

(*Fifty-second pause.*)

T: Are you ready to open that door?

(*Therapist introduces the notion that the patient has a* choice *about opening the door.*)

H: I don't know. (*Fourteen-second pause.*) I like to think to myself that it's gone. No such thing. (*Eleven-second pause.*) I guess it's still there.

The notion that Mr. Hayes can choose whether or not to open the door to his memories of Vietnam is elaborated in the next segment, which follows the last excerpt after a pause of 64 seconds. The length of this pause suggests that it is a crucial moment. The patient's quick and automatic ways of shutting the door are not operating as smoothly, making change possible.

T: So what about it? Are you ready to open the door?

(*Therapist repeats the question.*)

H: I don't know. I don't know how to open it.

(*Husband pleads inability: "I don't have a choice, I can't."*)

T: Sure you do.

(*Therapist does not buy it and instead insists on the frame of husband's choice.*)

H: I don't like to open it (*anxious laugh*).

(*Husband accepts therapist's frame.*)

T: Huh?

H: I don't like to open it.

T: Yeah. I think that's, that's the truth. You know how to open it.

H: How do I get around that? I mean, every time I do open it I get, it's, you know. It stays with me and I don't like it, the feeling. It seems like since I've been opening it it just closes more tighter each time I close it again. (*Unintelligible.*) (*Eleven-second pause.*) It's just all this time I've been fighting it away and now you want me to bring it up again (*voice becomes intense and anxious*). I don't know where to begin.

T: It really doesn't matter where you begin.

H: Just start talking.

T: Yeah.

H: I see them, I see them faces still. I feel that feeling like being there.
(*Husband opens the door.*)

T: (*Unintelligible.*)

H: (*Speaks intensely.*) I feel that feeling of being there.
(*And he immediately experiences the autonomic arousal.*)

T: Uh-huh.

H: Inside of my body.

T: You feel if you start talking?

H: Yeah.

T: Right.
(*Twenty-six second pause.*)

H: You know most everything. There isn't much more.
(*Husband closes the door, once again pushing therapist and himself away from his experience.*)

T: It's, it's not important. It's not so important telling me what happened, and the words and all that. Not so important what I know. It's important that you learn to talk about it and remember without feeling like you're there.
(*Therapist re-emphasizes the frame for the treatment: What is important is to be able to remember without the arousal.*)

H: Is that what it is?
(*Husband's response here is very interesting, implying that he just had the all-or-none change in his perception of treatment that constitutes reframing.*)

T: So that you don't have to keep pushing it all away. That's what's important that you learn.

H: I thought it was that you were looking for something in my mind.

(*Husband has grasped the notion that therapy is something other than an attempt to exhume some long-buried content.*

T: Like what?

H: The rest of the story or whatever. Me, or whatever. I don't know. What's behind that door or whatever.

T: Yeah. It's, it's less important what's behind the door than you, you learn that you're really not there. In other words, that you can recall and remember what happened like you're there, without your body getting aroused and alert and all the stuff that you've been experiencing. It's important that that go away, and it can only go, it can't go away if you keep pushing it down. It just stays there.

(*Working in the new frame, therapist emphasizes the therapeutic process of relearning a new response to the memories rather than focusing on the content of the memories themselves.*)

H: Ohh (*emphatically*). I thought, I had in my head that, there'd be, it just needed, like if I wrote down everything that's in my mind I (*anxious laugh*) wouldn't have to talk about it.

T: There's, there's no magic to it. And there's no way of getting rid of the pain of going through it. Because it's the going through it in here that's important.

H: I see. (*Pause.*) It doesn't seem as bad if you look at it that way.

(*This statement demonstrates Watzlawick et al.'s 1974 definition of reframing as an affective as well as a cognitive change.*)

T: How so?

H: It doesn't seem like, well now I have to sit down and give you all the gory details, which I don't. 'Cause what you just said, it's just talking about it. But I guess that's part of it too, huh?

T: What's part of it?

H: Talking about the gory details.

(*This is a nice example of how elusive and fragile new frames really are. By the end of his statement husband is back in the old content-oriented frame, focused on "all the gory details."*)

T: I think it is. 'Cause it's the gory details, my guess is, that get you most upset.

H: (*Emphatically.*) Yeah. I guess so. I've seen people mutilated.

T: Yeah.

H: But I don't see how talking about it that's going to make me any better.

(*Husband restates his resistance to treatment and it looks like a set-up for another struggle with the therapist.*)

T: I guess you just have to kinda take a risk and a, a leap of faith there. You have to trust me that it will and that it's something you can work through and get it behind you. There's no way I can convince you that it will ahead of time 'cause you really have to go through it yourself and find out.

(*Therapist does a one-down and refuses to fight. Instead, he gambles with the "leap of faith" frame.*)

H: I know. That's why I'm here. 'Cause I've tried everything else.

(*And it appears to pay off as husband reaffirms his commitment to treatment.*)

T: You have. For ten years.

THE STRATEGIC INTERVENTION

The following segment demonstrates the successful results of telling the patient that he would simply have to take a "leap of faith." It should be evident from the information presented above that the timing of such a frame is crucial. I had, in previous sessions, worked very hard to establish a relationship with Mr. Hayes and to frame the therapy in a way that made it possible for him to join me in the treatment frame. To have attempted the "leap of faith" frame much earlier would have been premature. On the other hand, to have simply repeated once again my earlier efforts aimed at the patient's resistance would have (eventually, at least) entangled me in the process of helping him avoid the work that needed to occur.

What happens in the next excerpt turns out, in retrospect, to be the turning point of the therapy, although at the time I did not realize how crucial this single intervention was.

(*Follows previous segment after seven-second pause.*)

H: I see the same face and stuff. I feel myself touching it.

(*Husband opens the door and again his body gets revved up.*)

T: Touching what?

H: Touching the dead bodies.

T: Tell me about the face.

H: I feel like somebody else is doing it, not me. I just, see (*emphatically*) it. I see myself doing it.

(*The anxiety is so intense that husband experiences a dissociated state.*)

T: (*Overlaps.*) What do you see? Describe it.

H: (*Overlaps.*) I see this dead pile of bodies (*voice becomes louder*) layin' there and I was pushing them and looking through their clothes and doing that stuff (*voice begins to crack with emotion*).

T: Do you see it now?

H: Yeah (*emphatically, breathing now noticeably rapid*).

(*At this point husband's breathing is much more out of control than in previous sessions.*)

T: Tell me what you see.

H: I see a, body with half a head on it (*breathing very rapid and loud*).

T: What's happening in your body now?

(*Therapist now focuses husband's attention away from the memories themselves and onto his body's arousal.*)

H: (*Almost gasping for breath.*) I feel all funny inside.

T: Tell me what you're feeling inside.

H: (*Emphatically.*) Baaad.

T: Tell me about that. What's happening to your body?

H: It feels like someone's punishing me for what I did.

(*It is very tempting to embark on a* psychological *exploration of this statement.*)

T: What do you feel in your body that feels like punishment?

(*Instead, therapist continues to focus husband on the experience in his body.*)

H: Real hot and tingly and I feel like I can't breathe too well.

T: Feel pressure on your chest?

H: I get this funny feeling in my head.

T: You're breathing faster?

H: Yeah. My heart starts going real fast.

T: It's pounding now?

H: Yeah.

T: And you feel the pressure on your chest?

H: It's starting to go away now.

T: I want you to take a minute and take a few slow deep breaths and let your body relax after each breath. Pay attention to your breathing. Let yourself breathe in (*speaks slowly*) slowly and exhale slowly. (*Pause.*) Let your breathing slow down.

(*Therapist instructs husband to reduce his autonomic arousal by focusing attention on his breathing and slowing it down.*)

H: Yeah. Now I feel better.

(*Husband reports feeling more comfortable.*)

T: It's slowing down?

H: I feel hot now, that's all.

T: You feel hot but your breathing is not as fast?

H: No. My heart's still going a little fast.

T: Okay. It's important that you learn to pay attention to your breathing.

H: Well, how did it, I should be able to control it before that happens.

T: No, I think it's important that you learn to do something about it after it happens. That as your body starts getting revved up, that you learn to pay attention to your breathing, take deeper, slower breaths, let your breathing slow back down.

(*This is an extremely important reframing in work with many anxiety symptoms. Most patients wish to eliminate the symptoms and often their anticipatory anxiety exacerbates the problem. The frame of "nipping the symptom in the bud" before it reaches out-of-control proportions is generally much more workable than is the attempt to prevent the symptom from occurring in the first place.*)

H: That's why I come down here.

(*Husband accepts the frame.*)

T: Why?

H: 'Cause that happens to me when I talk about it.

(*Husband confirms the appropriateness of making the autonomic arousal itself the treatment problem.*)

T: Right. I know, I know. You can learn here to talk about it without your body getting that revved up. I can teach you to do that.

H: (*Whispers.*) Okay.

T: You can retrain your body so that it reacts more normally and more comfortably to the memories that you have. We can start with your breathing, 'cause that's the thing that seemed to get revved up the fastest.

H: It sure happened fast, huh?

T: Yeah. It happened real fast.

H: Sometimes I get real, where I feel like I'm gonna pass out or something.

T: How's your breathing now?

H: It's alright now.

T: Your body's feeling more comfortable?

H: A calmer feeling.

Instructing the patient to regulate his breathing as I did here is a very simple form of biofeedback. It would have been possible to use complex monitoring machinery to provide information about a number of indices of autonomic arousal. I chose breathing because it is easy for the patient to monitor without using an expensive device and especially because, once attended to, it is easy for the patient to control his breathing rate voluntarily.

My goal at this point was to teach Mr. Hayes that he could control his autonomic response to the memories of Vietnam *rather than* to explore those memories or his reactions to them. I deliberately chose to ignore Mr. Hayes's reference to feeling as if he were being punished and instead continued to focus on his body's reaction. And I moved in rather quickly to help him get more comfortable. Psychotherapists working with combat veterans frequently permit (and encourage) the anxiety to get to intolerable levels in order to have time to explore things psychologically. What they fail to realize is how very quickly the patient's anxiety mounts to extraordinary heights. The danger—and this happens frequently —is that the patient becomes so alarmed that he bolts from treatment and leaves even more convinced that he cannot be helped. This point is emphasized by Horowitz and Solomon (1978), who note that most psychodynamic techniques are designed to counteract defenses rather than to increase the patient's capacity for control.

A further word about timing here. Just before I instructed Mr. Hayes to slow his breathing, he indicated that his level of arousal was already beginning to subside. Although I was not aware at the time of using this information, his statement undoubtedly cued me. In fact, it could be argued that the decrease in his arousal really had nothing to do with my intervention. Even if this were so (I think it is not), it does not matter. The seeds were sown for the patient's *belief* that he can control his body's reaction to the Vietnam memories.

I next moved to capitalize on this experience and to further reinforce the frame of control.

(Immediately after last segment.)

T: Okay, when you're ready I want you to let your mind drift back to the images you were describing. Okay? When you're ready I want you to let your mind drift back to those images. And as your body, and I want you to start talking about the images. And as your body gets revved up again I want you to start paying attention to your breathing and to start breathing deeper and more slowly, to let your body slow back down.

(Eighteen-second pause.)

(Therapist instructs husband to repeat this experience, but again makes him responsible for the timing—"when you're ready.")

H: I don't think I'm ready to think about them again.

(Husband makes it clear that he is not ready now.)

T: When you're ready.

(Therapist accepts patient's hesitance.)

The last segment was followed by several minutes of talk *about* the memories (rather than the patient's further re-experience of them), including discussion of how tough the patient was. ("Looking through a pile of bodies for souvenirs to see who was the toughest guy in the company.") Physiological arousal was absent during this talk. After a 30-second pause, the following occurred:

T: When the image comes of you going through the bodies, what do you see yourself doing?

(Therapist uses the word "see," which is likely to stimulate a visual image and lead to arousal.)

H: *(Voice cracks with emotion.)* Movin' 'em and kickin' 'em and, you know, just lookin', diggin' through the pockets *(gasps loudly for breath).*

(Husband opens the door and is immediately very aroused.)

T: Your breathing's getting faster?

(Therapist focuses husband on his breathing.)

H: Just pushing other guys out of the way getting to 'em *(sighs loudly).*

T: As you started talking your breathing speeded up, right? Could you pay attention to that?

H: Yeah. But it didn't help until after I said it.

(Husband tells therapist that his breathing has slowed back down, but he frames the experience negatively.)

T: So you said it, and you paid attention to your breathing, and you let your breathing slow back down, so you're a little more comfortable now?

(Therapist starts to reframe what has just happened in a positive light, first by mentioning husband's increased comfort.)

H: Yeah, but I'm starting to feel funny, making my body do that. It makes me feel hot and cold all over and I just start feeling faint.

T: You're feeling faint now?

H: Sorta, not, I ain't going to pass out or nothin', but I just, I don't like that feeling. I feel closed in or somethin'.

T: It looks to me like this time, by paying attention to your breathing and letting it slow down, you were able to prevent it from going as high as it did the first time. Is that right?

(*This is a positive frame for what has happened: It did not get as high as the first time.*)

H: Um-hum.

T: Yeah. That's good. So this time you were able to talk about the images that you have. Kicking the bodies, going through the bodies. Your breathing started getting revved up and you were able to turn it back down, slow down, feel a little more comfortable. That's important. You can open the door and prevent your body from getting out of control.

(*Therapist summarizes the frame for the entire treatment: You can open the door and still prevent your body from getting out of control.*)

H: It felt like it was out of control to me.

(*Husband disputes therapist's frame.*)

T: From the outside it didn't look like it was as out of control as the first time.

(*Therapist sticks to his view, invoking his power as "outside observer."*)

H: Yeah, it wasn't that much.

(*Husband accepts therapist's frame.*)

FRAMING THE SUCCESS

So far it is like the proverbial glass of water which Watzlawick et al. (1974) used to illustrate reframing. Husband plays the pessimist (it was out of control) and I the optimist (but it was not as out of control this time as it was the first time). At the end of this session, husband gave the first solid indication that something really had begun to change.

T: W, when you were in Vietnam, were there times you felt your body getting revved up like this?

(*Therapist moves to connect husband's arousal in the session with his Vietnam experiences.*)

H: Yeah.

T: W, what were those times like. What was happening at that time?

H: I was getting shot at. Rockets were coming in. Things were happening like that. Walking through the jungle and startin' gettin' shot at, and stuff, and startin' shootin' my gun and stuff. I'd start gettin' that way. I didn't notice at the time that I was that way.

(*Husband associates the arousal with extreme danger in combat.*)

T: Right.

H: I was just, doing (*emphasizes*) it, I wasn't thinkin' about anything, what was happenin'.

T: You don't have to think about that. Getting that revved up, that's your body's natural response to danger. So you were, your body was reacting in a way that, was natural. . . .

H: (*Overlaps.*) It should. . . .

T: (*Overlaps.*) It should have reacted, and if it didn't react like that you probably wouldn't have survived.

(*Therapist frames the physiological arousal in combat as the body's natural response to real danger, a response that contributed to his survival in Vietnam.*)

H: That's what I was thinking. 'Cause I r, I was always right with it. If everything ever happened I was the first one there.

T: Exactly.

H: I didn't sleep at all, hardly. The most I ever slept was an hour at a time.

T: Really.

H: Yeah. All of the rest of the time I was awake, waiting for someone else to fall alseep.

T: You were pretty charged up, a lot of the time.

H: All the time.

T: All the time. Especially when you were actually under attack.

H: Yeah. I, I had enough energy to take them all on.

T: Um-hum. A, and all that contributed to your survival.

H: I'm sure of that now. 'Cause if I would have just laid around like the other guys did I wouldn't have made it.

T: That's right. And what's happening now is when you let yourself remember, especially the images you have, that that same arousal in your body is now connected with those memories.

(*Therapist frames the current arousal as the same as the arousal in Vietnam.*)

H: And that's what they come out like that? That's why my body does that?

(*The frame makes sense to husband.*)

T: (*Overlaps.*) Yeah, yeah.

H: That's the reason?

T: Um-hum. But that's not contributing to your survival anymore. It's getting in the way.

(*Therapist labels husband's physical response as no longer aiding his survival.*)

H: Yeah.

T: So much that you have to push it all down.

H: Yeah. It takes so much of my mind to hold it all back.

(*In this statement and those that follow, husband simply but eloquently describes the profound impact of attempting to cope with post-traumatic disorder by pushing the memories away.*)

T: It does. It really does.

H: And all this time I could have studied or, I could have done anything with my life. Instead I've just been hidin' it all those ten years.

(*Husband begins to grieve for his lost years.*)

T: That's right.

H: Now I look back at age twenty to thirty and I don't see anything.

T: Yeah. What you need to do in here is unlearn that connection between the memories that you have and your body's arousal, getting all revved up. And you started it today. 'Cause the second time you let the memories come, you paid attention to your breathing, let your breathing slow back down, and it didn't get quite as revved up as it did the first time.

(*Therapist sticks to framing today's session as a success and a "start."*)

H: It didn't. But the first time seemed like, it was more of an image, it was like I was really there, it got so, you know, that kind of. The second time I just, more or less thought about it, instead of being there. Thought about seeing myself being there instead of being there like the first time.

(*Husband accepts the frame of success and then goes on to provide additional data that can be used to strengthen the frame: The first time I really was back there but the second time I only thought about being there.*)

T: I think that's also a sign of progress.

(*Therapist assimilates this new information to the frame of success.*)

H: Seein' myself, away from there, instead of. . . .

T: (*Overlaps.*) Yeah.

H: (*Continues.*) Being there?

T: Yeah.

H: (*Continues.*) Being part of it again?

T: Yeah. Because the goal is to be able to remember without feeling like you're right back there. And for these ten years when you let yourself remember you were immediately back there and your body was so revved up.

H: 'Cause I wouldn't talk about it. It's just in my head it was that way.

T: Right.

H: So I wouldn't have never known how to deal with it and how to breathe anyway (*unintelligible*) to somebody.

T: That's right.

H: So all the talking in the world to other people wouldn't have helped anyway, unless they knew, like friends and stuff. They tell you "Well, don't go to a psychiatrist. Just talk to your friend. It's just the same."

(*Here husband begins to attribute knowledge and power to the therapist.*)

T: It's not.

H: No. I never believed that. I always believed there's a reason for something even if there's a reason for something. You went to school for it, there must be a reason for it. You must know something that I don't know. And what other people don't know too, or you wouldn't be here as a psychiatrist. What I think what it is is that most people are afraid of psychiatrists 'cause other people'll think they're crazy or something.

T: That's right.

H: I've always known that I'm not crazy.

(*Although the fear of being—thought—crazy or going crazy is common in combat stress disorders, it is only after he has begun to change that husband is able to verbalize this fear.*)

T: You're not crazy, that's right.

H: Pretty smart guy. Just got tangled up in somethin' I didn't need to, or somethin'.

T: But yet the experiences you had, your body getting revved up and all, that's scary enough to make you worry about what's going on.

H: Yeah. See, nobody else would understand anything like that. "Just forget. Just forget things. Forget about Vietnam." This and that.

T: It doesn't work.

H: Sure doesn't. You can't forget something that's got your head (*unintelligible*).

T: And your body.

(*Here again therapist focuses on the body's reaction.*)

H: And my body too. That's what I could never explain before, it's, you know, what it, what i, how, how it affected my body, just talking about it.

(*It is clear that his body's reaction is very important to husband.*)

T: That's right.

H: I just never told 'em about it.

(*Nine-second pause.*)

T: Is your wife here today?

H: Um-hum.

T: Would it be useful for you to have her come up and for me to talk with her about the session today, what you've learned?

(*Therapist is still looking for ways to underscore the importance of what happened in the session and suggests bringing wife in for a few minutes.*)

H: Well, we used to talk all the way home.

(*Husband makes it clear that he does not wish to involve her now.*)

T: Fine. (*Seven-second pause.*) Do you, do you have any questions about what we did today, about what happened?

(*So therapist tries husband, again looking for additional ways to frame the success.*)

H: It feels different than last time.

(*Husband frames things as "different."*)

T: How?

H: I feel, I feel like I, you know, learned a little somethin', or, it feels like I got something out of it, you know, instead of come here and give.

(*This is the first solid indication from the patient that an important change has occurred. His last remark is also interesting in another light. Mr. Hayes and his wife were initially asked to participate in a study of the outcome of family therapy being conducted at the time they were seen. Of the 25 families invited, only this patient refused. Discussion with husband subsequent to the present session revealed that he saw himself as being "experimented" upon by the VA. Only in this session did he begin to feel that he would get something instead of having to continue to give.*)

T: Really.

H: Yeah. Just that second feeling, you know, being able to shut it down so fast.

(*Here it is clear that husband accepts the frame of success.*)

T: Um-hum. I think you did get something from today. I think we've got a lot more work like that to do. Same type of stuff. There's a lot more learning there to do. But you, you've made a start and you've got the basic thing that you need to learn. From here on it will get better.

(*Therapist confidently predicts that "from here on it will get better."*)

H: That's what it feels like. I feel like I've made some sort of headway as far as knowing what, what it's all about, that I was going through, that I've been going through.

(*Husband believes it.*)

T: Um-hum.

H: Without having to stop myself from thinking about it.

(*This remark is important. Husband's old way of dealing with his Vietnam memories was to try to stop thinking. He very clearly indicates that he has now learned a new way.*)

The work of framing the patient's success at controlling his body's reaction to his Vietnam memories continues in the next session.

(*Near the beginning of treatment session four, Mr. Hayes reports feeling very depressed about the ten lost years of his life.*)

H: I used to work all the time to hel, to help me. I was working sixteen and eighteen hours a day, seven days a week. I worked real hard, as hard as I could. Just so I wouldn't think about it.

T: Um-hum.

(*Thirty-five-second pause.*)

H: I think some of the reality, what happened last week, it felt like some of the reality (*of Vietnam*) left me. It did, you know. I felt sort of relieved, like, you know, that there was another option, that I, you know, like I was looking at myself as being there and not being there all the time. (*Husband now sounds less depressed as he speaks.*)

(*A remarkable statement of the powerful impact of the previous session.*)

T: Um-hum.

H: It felt good. I feel like I was before I even went in the army. Then I realized how messed up I've been all these years (*once again sounds more depressed*). Realized that (*begins to cry*) I didn't get anywhere. I might as well be nineteen years old again.

(*Again husband begins to grieve for his lost years.*)

T: And that makes you feel sad.

H: (*Voice breaks.*) Sad 'cause I'm thirty and I didn't get anything in between but a bad time (*continues to cry*).

T: How about angry?

H: Thirty-two. There's nothing you can do about it (*sobs*). Nobody can give me my life back.

T: Only you.

H: I guess that's my consolation, is to look forward to the future (*sobs*), 'cause I sure don't got no past.

Buoyed by statements like these, I commented that I thought a turning point had been passed. Mr. Hayes accurately perceived my new confidence in his improvement: When I remarked "After the session last week (treatment session three) I knew that I could help you," he responded "Maybe that's why I felt better."

The reality of his improvement was demonstrated again later in that session: While discussing a particularly gory and distressing memory, the patient was able to turn down his intense physiological reaction without shutting off the thoughts of Vietnam. He remarked: "That's controlling your body."

GRIEF

Although I knew at the time that something very important had happened in treatment session three, I see only in retrospect that Mr. Hayes was cured in that session. What I outline here is the psychological work that occurred in subsequent interviews.

From the case of Mrs. Green presented in Chapter 7, I knew that the natural and normal response to successfully changing a major unproductive frame is the patient's grief over the lost years. As discussed there, it is crucial that the therapist be prepared for this grief and be able to frame it appropriately. This is especially true when the presenting complaint includes depression. Here the danger is that the depression and sadness associated with the grief will be experienced as the same as the old depression, canceling out real improvement. This phase of strategic treatment is illustrated in this case as I framed Mr. Hayes' new depression as part of the necessary grief work.

(*The beginning of treatment session four, prior to the last excerpt given above.*)

T: So how are you today?

H: I don't know. A little bit depressed, I think.

T: Really. What's been happening?

H: I've been feeling real bad, really down.

T: Down? Since when?

H: Couple days ago. I felt real good when I left here last week.

T: Did you?

H: Felt like I was getting somewhere or somethin'.

T: Uh-huh.

H: Then I guess I let it get to me (*unintelligible*) about the last ten years of my life.

(*Husband clearly connects his current depression with the loss of ten years of his life.*)

T: Um-hum. And then you got down? (*Ten-second pause.*) I think it's pretty appropriate that you get down about that. I think that you, you've really got some, some mourning and grieving to do about that. 'Cause you have lost ten years of your life, in a way. It's pretty impor, pretty important and pretty appropriate to be sad about that. And angry and whatever else you're feeling.

(*Therapist builds the frame for grief work.*)

H: Real bad.

T: Real bad.

H: I feel like crying.

T: Really. You've got a lot to cry about.

(*Eight-second pause. Therapist's empathic response is an attempt to keep husband in the frame of the grief.*)

H: It sure was a hard ten years.

T: It was. (*Thirteen-second pause.*) You've been through a hell of a lot.

H: It's important I keep coming back (*to the sessions*), huh?

T: Um-hum.

H: Even though it hurts, huh?

T: Even though it hurts. (*Ten-second pause.*)

H: I feel so helpless.

T: Yeah. (*Ten-second pause.*) Why don't you tell me about that?

H: Just, all them years are gone, now, and I don't even know, didn't even know what I was doin'. (*Thirteen-second pause. Patient begins to cry.*)

T: It's okay to let the tears come.

H: (*Cries.*) Every day was living in a nightmare. (*Pause. Therapist hands husband some Kleenex.*) I guess I've gotten to trust you.

(*When therapist comforts husband by giving him some Kleenex he also indicates that it is alright to cry in the session. Husband responds by commenting on his trust in therapist.*)

T: Um-hum. Even enough to cry in here.

H: I've never done this before, with anybody else. Except for my wife.

T: I know that.

H: I'm (*unintelligible*) glad you're helping me.

T: You've got a lot of pain and tears inside.

It is common following a successful strategic intervention for the patient to report memories and other experiences related in an obvious way to the central treatment issues. This illustrates a basic tenet of strategic therapy (and family systems therapy, in general; see Chapter 3): The goal of treatment is change and that understanding, when it occurs at all, comes *after* change has occurred. It is also consistent with the view that mourning follows successful reframing: One of the tasks of grieving is to rework the past.

Mr. Hayes remarked that after treatment session three he had felt better than any time since Vietnam. I commented on the real loss of the intervening ten years and he spontaneously stated: "I didn't have much of a childhood either," and began to sob. He told of having an undiagnosed kidney problem from ages seven through eleven, which caused him to wet the bed:

> I feel like my mother used to beat me all the time when I was a kid 'cause I used to pee the bed 'cause I couldn't control it 'cause of my kidneys and stuff. Every morning when I'd wake up she'd beat me with a wire coat hanger or wood coat hanger or something. And when I got older (*sobs*) and got drafted I just wanted everybody to be proud of me instead of being (*sobs*) ashamed of me and stuff. And I went in the army and thought everybody'd be proud of me and stuff. But it didn't end up to be that kind of a war. (*Unintelligible*) if anyone cared, anyway.

Traditional, psychodynamically oriented therapists might finally recognize the above as "real" therapy, in contrast to what I have presented so far. It is certainly very interesting material and just the kind of mental archeology that has fascinated therapists since Freud. But it is clearly a by-product here of a change that has already occurred.

This material suggests at least two psychological issues that may predispose an individual to develop post-traumatic disorder when faced with extraordinary, life-threatening circumstances. First, a concern with being able to maintain control over the body's reactions, particularly the reactions to danger. And second, a related concern about behaving heroically rather than being a coward when facing danger. This second theme was present at several points in the material provided by Mr. Hayes (e.g., he told of his fearlessness, to the point of reckless behavior, which led his sergeant to take him out of the field). The issue of valor versus cowardice was also prominent in the case of Mr. Jackson. He described in vivid detail his memories of landing in Vietnam for the first time and told with shame how he was so scared that he left his gun in the helicopter. He talked of going to Vietnam to prove he was not a coward and of being terrified during the last months and weeks of his tour that he would not survive. Ironically, having survived his first tour of duty in Vietnam, Mr. Jackson was still not convinced of his courage, so he re-upped for another tour.

In the next session, the grief work continued as Mr. Hayes's depression "turned to anger," to use his own words. Although it might seem that he had read Freud, this is unlikely in view of his limited education. It appears instead that Mr. Hayes was simply describing his experience in a way that made sense to him.

GETTING ON WITH LIFE

Later, in treatment session five, Mr. Hayes introduced a topic that I used to turn the focus of treatment to the future. He described having seen some hang-gliders the previous Sunday and as he talked about them he became very excited. This excitement distressed him for two reasons. First, he felt out of place sitting there talking to me and feeling so excited. And second, he associated the excitement he now felt with the arousal he used to feel in his body while remembering Vietnam. I introduced instead a positive frame for his excitement, contrasting this new aliveness with the deadness he had felt for most of the last ten years. Mr. Hayes accepted this frame and spontaneously associated his new excitement with being a kid, before Vietnam: "And, like, here I am, a 30-year-old, 19-year-old kid." To reinforce a positive view of this new experience, I introduced the frame of "making friends with his excitement."

The work on making friends with the new excitement continued into treatment session six. The patient stated that in the past he had shut off all excited feelings because they were so closely related to the feelings he experienced whenever he thought about Vietnam. At one point Mr. Hayes said "When I get so excited I feel like a fool, like a 10-year-old kid." I responded: "Your excitement is appealing to me. That's one of the things we like about kids." I talked with him about how, as we grow up, we often learn to shut down that excitement, adding that after Vietnam he had learned this lesson so well that he was able to deaden almost everything. I told him that I hoped that he would not let the worry that he was being silly interfere with feeling excited and allowing others to see those feelings. Mr. Hayes replied: "I don't think I will, now that I've heard how *you* feel about it. That's what I needed to hear, somebody else's opinion, how they felt about me getting excited. And if it is like that, I guess I ain't afraid to show my feelings."

When strategic treatment is conducted using individual therapy sessions, the task of helping the patient get on with life includes helping him bridge the gap between the private experience of therapy and the social context of his life. In the case of Mr. Hayes, the issue of his excitement offered an opportunity to begin this work. Near the end of treatment session five, as we discussed the new excitement with life that he now felt, Mr. Hayes admitted that he had not yet talked with his wife about the changes he had experienced. In fact, he was not sure that she or anyone else had noticed these changes. This issue came up again in treatment session six, when he reported that no one including his wife had yet mentioned any changes they had seen in him, and he had not asked. With some prodding from me, Mr. Hayes agreed to have his wife join the session. When he finally got around to asking if she had noticed a change in him, Mrs. Hayes responded affirmatively, explaining: "Just being happier, I've noticed it. And just, I don't know, I just noticed a change in him completely."

Later in this session, the discussion again returned to the topic of Mr. Hayes's new-found excitement with his life. Mrs. Hayes again admitted noticing it, but reacted very uncertainly and in a manner that suggested to me that she was less than thrilled. Mr. Hayes responded: "*This* is the way I was before I went into the army." I turned to Mrs. Hayes and said "So now *you've* got the big adjustment to make. You've got a new husband." I went on to predict that there would be moments in the months to come when she would wish she had her old husband back. This was met with humor and denial by both husband and wife.

As it turned out, I had to wait only until the end of the session for my prediction to come true. Mr. Hayes began playfully teasing his wife, asking her again about whether she had noticed his improvement and if she liked it. To the latter question she replied "I don't know" and he responded "Too bad, because I didn't like me the other way." Mrs. Hayes then told her husband that his teasing had become worse lately, which I promptly framed as an example of the big adjustment ahead for her and her understandable momentary desire to have her old, familiar husband back.

ENDING TREATMENT

At the beginning of the last (sixth) scheduled treatment session (before Mrs. Hayes was invited to join us), Mr. Hayes and I reviewed his progress in the therapy by discussing the "highlights" of our work together (see Chapter 10). The patient's first highlight was when I had confirmed that he really did have a problem. He also emphasized how important it was that I thought he had a problem that could be solved: "Like you get a cut and have stitches and it will be better. Something like that. If I went and told someone all my problems and they said 'Well, that's tough. You're just going to have to live with them.'"

Mr. Hayes's second highlight was the times he had cried in the sessions: "I always thought of myself as strong. I didn't cry in any of the worst situations I was in. I never thought about crying now."

He summarized the changes he had experienced since treatment began: Feeling more at ease with himself; not feeling as angry about Vietnam as he had felt; and "there isn't all that confusion in my head like there was—every half hour or so popping into Vietnam."

Mr. Hayes also rather nicely described *change without understanding*: "I feel like you didn't really do anything for me but something or other happened and I, it seems like, that was awful quick, awful easy, compared to what I thought I was going to go through."

My own highlight, which I discussed with Mr. Hayes during our review, was in the third treatment session when the patient had learned that he could control his breathing while remembering Vietnam and I had learned that I could help him. Mr. Hayes agreed that this experience had been crucial.

At this point I was quite prepared to end Mr. Hayes's individual treatment for his post-traumatic symptoms. I framed Vietnam as over with and I predicted that any future psychological trouble would be normal distress, unrelated to Vietnam. The patient replied:

Okay. I feel now that, you know, I don't see it in my future at all anymore. The way it was, you know, how horrible it was, you know. I mean, all the horrible part of it now is over. I mean, it really feels dead now. So I genuinely don't think that it's ever going to happen to me again. The way it did, you know. But I just, you know, had to sort of confirm it, to see what you would think. But that's the way I've been feeling lately, is it really is dead. That horrible feeling I'd get. And even if I do start thinking about Vietnam real bad again, you know, thinking about everything, it won't affect me like it did. It'd just be thoughts.

This last is a wonderful statement of the goal of treatment for post-traumatic disorder: To turn his reexperience of the traumatic event into "just thoughts."

I did have some reservations about Mrs. Hayes's adjustment to her husband's improvement and would have preferred to see the couple together for a few more weeks. However, they were eagerly preparing for their new baby and looking forward to ending therapy, so I agreed to terminate.

FOLLOW-UP

Six months following the end of the six-week treatment, I requested a follow-up interview with Mr. and Mrs. Hayes to re-evaluate therapy outcome and the couple's adjustment. Mr. Hayes reported that he continued to be free of post-traumatic symptoms and that Vietnam really was dead, just as we had predicted at the end of treatment. His wife confirmed this picture. There continued to be signs that Mrs. Hayes was less than happy with her new husband, but the couple felt they were doing okay and I did not press the issue of their readjustment.

Approximately one year after treatment, I received a phone call from Mrs. Hayes who stated that her husband was depressed and requested an appointment. When I saw them I again found that the post-traumatic symptoms continued to be absent. Instead, Mr. Hayes complained of feeling depressed over not being able to find a direction in his life. As the couple talked about the problem, it became clear that they had been unable to adjust satisfactorily to the cure of his post-traumatic disorder. Mr. Hayes stated that he now wants to have more fun and do things with his wife, but she never seems interested. Mrs. Hayes complained that he is sometimes too energetic and excited, teasing and bothering her, and that she does not have time to do all the things her husband wishes to do with her because she has two young children to care for. Mr. Hayes admitted that, at times, he feels resentful of the attention she gives the new baby. His wife reported that sometimes she feels as if she has two new babies to raise—her infant son and her husband.

I framed the couple's problem as one of adjustment to the cure of Mr. Hayes's Vietnam problems and recommended couples therapy, emphasizing that this time the two of them both had some changing to do. As I said this, I saw Mrs. Hayes become very uncomfortable and wondered if I had moved too quickly to re-define the problem as a couples issue. They agreed to consider my recommendation and call for an appointment, but never did. A month or two later, when I left the VA, I wrote to them explaining that I was leaving and restating my advice to seek couples therapy. I sometimes wonder if they might have returned to see me had I not left the hospital, but have no further follow-up information.

My recent work with a case of (noncombat) post-traumatic stress disorder has convinced me that the task of couple (re)integra-tion following successful treatment of the identified patient is often more difficult than I had believed when working with Mr. and Mrs. Hayes. In retrospect, I should have insisted on the need for couples work.

Previous Theoretical Approaches to Post-Traumatic Disorder

Over the years as post-traumatic disorder has attracted consider-able interest in its various guises (e.g., shell shock, war neurosis, battle fatigue), the major psychological theories, particularly psychodynamic and behavioral, have taken a crack at understand-ing the syndrome.

THE PSYCHODYNAMIC APPROACH

During and after World War I, Freud and his followers became very interested in traumatic neurosis, in general, and in combat neurosis, in particular. Kardiner (1959) writes that "these neuroses contain a syndrome of the highest importance for psychodynamics, particularly for psychoanalytic psychodynamics" (p. 245).

Kardiner traces the change in Freud's view of traumatic neu-rosis. At first, following libido theory, early trauma was seen as causing developmental arrest. Later in life, then, a traumatic event could rekindle the original trauma and trigger a regression to the point of arrest in development. By the early 1920s Freud's view had changed. Traumatic events came to be seen as those that overload the individual's defensive capacities designed to protect the organism against external stimuli, resulting in the experience of anxiety. In an effort to be free of this anxiety, the patient was seen to be involuntarily repeating the traumatic event—the intrusive recollections and other forms of re-experiencing the traumatic event, one of the essential symptoms in the modern diagnosis of post-traumatic disorder. In fact, according to Kardiner, it was in this tendency to repeat that Freud discovered a new basic principle, the repetition compulsion.

Horowitz's (1976) important work modernizes and extends the basic analytic approach. He stresses the centrality of the major post-traumatic symptoms: The compulsive repetition of the traumatic event, on the one hand, and the defense against such repetition using ideational denial and emotional numbing, on the other. Horowitz substitutes the more current idea of information overload for Freud's energy overload metaphor. He (Horowitz, 1974) suggests that the overload of information must be processed by the organism and that "this information is both repressed and compulsively repeated until processing is relatively complete" (p. 769). Horowitz (1974) goes on to describe this information processing by noting that, in order to adapt appropriately to the traumatic event, the individual must

> perceive the event correctly; translate these perceptions into clear meanings; relate these meanings to his enduring attitudes; decide on appropriate actions; and revise his memory, attitude, and belief systems to fit this new development in his life. (p. 770)

Despite the prominence of physiological symptoms in most clinical descriptions of post-traumatic disorder, psychodynamic theorists tend to ignore or minimize their role. Kardiner (1959), for example, correctly sees the traumatic neurosis as "created by the stress situation, that is, by the self-preservative crisis due to the danger of destruction" (p. 246), but he emphasizes the psychological aspects of this crisis over the physiological. In particular, Kardiner describes the life of the soldier as a constant state of resentment (about having to serve at all, about authority, etc.) and then goes on to dismiss the physiological stress of war as only an extra, added irritant (pp. 247–248).

BEHAVIOR THEORY AND POST-TRAUMATIC DISORDER

The physiological aspects of combat stress have received much more attention from the behaviorists who became interested in post-traumatic disorder following World War II. A 1960 study by Dobbs and Wilson, conducted at the Durham VA Hospital, is representative of this approach.

The behavioral model for post-traumatic disorder is essentially that of the conditioned "experimental neurosis." In the classical paradigm, an animal is trained to respond discriminatively to a conditioned stimulus. The experimental neurosis is then produced, for example, by forcing the animal to make discriminations beyond its capacity. Typically, the animal responds with behavioral signs of neurosis along with accompanying autonomic changes in cardiac, respiratory, and other systems.

Dobbs and Wilson see combat experience as having all the elements needed to produce such a conditioned response. These authors argue that the sights and sounds of war itself serve as conditioned stimuli. (It seems that these might be better described as unconditioned stimuli. See below.) The unconditioned responses are those related to self-preservation—autonomic arousal and fight or flight behaviors. They go on to suggest that war neurosis develops in those individuals whose capacity to respond discriminatively and appropriately is exceeded under battlefield conditions.

Dobbs and Wilson investigated the psychophysiological conditioning of combat experience in an experiment in which subjects listened to an eight-minute recording of combat sounds while brain waves and pulse and respiration rates were monitored. Subjects in a control group with no combat experience responded to the combat sounds with an initial "orienting response" (an increase in attention, pulse, and respiration, etc.) followed by habituation and inattention. Of a second group of "compensated" combat veterans (those without symptoms of post-traumatic disorder), several manifested mild to moderate physiological and behavioral responses in the experimental situation, including anxiety, startle response, and the wish to "take cover." Finally, a third group of "decompensated" combat veterans showed a much more pronounced reaction to the combat sounds: Over one-half the group were unable to tolerate the sounds for more than a few seconds to a few minutes; all appeared extremely anxious after the experimental situation, with tremulousness and tearfulness. The behavioral responses of this group were, in fact, so extreme (restlessness and even thrashing around in an apparent attempt to escape from the situation) that it was not possible to monitor their physiological responses.

These investigators see their results as demonstrating dramatically that humans can develop conditioned responses to combat that persist long after the original battlefield experiences.

Interestingly, behavior theory does a better job of accounting for the original development of such response patterns than it does of explaining their persistence. Dobbs and Wilson, in the concluding sentence of their paper, have recourse to the notion proposed by Pavlov (1941) and Gantt (1944) in the 1940s that a genetic factor must be invoked to account for the fact that these conditioned responses persist for varying lengths of time in different individuals. Eysenck (1963) explained the persistence of such conditioned responses by complicating a pure classical conditioning scheme with respondent conditioning. He argued that, in the original conditioning situation, the conditioned motor response is always accompanied by a conditioned autonomic arousal, as well. Upon subsequent encounters with the conditioned stimulus, if the subject withdraws from the stimulus, then arousal and anxiety are lowered, which reinforces the avoidant behavior.

A Cybernetic Model

THE MODEL

Building upon the psychodynamic and behavioral approaches, and the case of Mr. Hayes presented earlier in this chapter, I now outline a new cybernetic model for post-traumatic disorder.

Figure 16 summarizes the original battlefield learning situation. Real life-threatening danger (the unconditioned stimulus) leads to physiological arousal (the unconditioned response), as well as to fight or flight behavior (at least some of which is conditioned through military training). Memories of combat (including visual and aural re-experiences) are paired with the actual events of combat and themselves become capable of evoking the autonomic arousal and associated behavioral responses (i.e., the memories become conditioned stimuli).

So far this is conventional behavior theory. Figure 17A turns this classical conditioning paradigm into a cybernetic model. Memories of combat lead to increased physiological arousal *and*

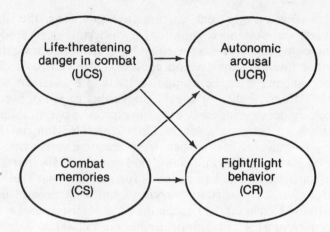

Figure 16. The original battlefield learning situation. UCS = unconditioned stimulus; UCR = unconditioned response; CR = conditioned response; CS = conditioned stimulus.

the physiological arousal leads, in turn, to more memories. The result is a deviation-amplifying cybernetic circuit. The "combat memories" are the intrusive-recollections half of the post-traumatic symptomatology.

Following the cybernetic principles discussed in Chapter 3, the amplification in this circuit will continue until either (1) the system breaks down in some way (i.e., the organism's capacity to remember or to become aroused reaches a limit or the feedback loop is disrupted) or (2) a higher-order control mechanism comes into play to limit the activity in the circuit.

The "suppressing behaviors" that constitute the second half of the post-traumatic syndrome (avoidance, denial, emotional numbing, depression) can be seen as such a higher-order control mechanism, as shown in Figure 17B. Here a deviation-reducing circuit has been added to the system as depicted in Figure 17A, regulating the activity of the deviation-amplifying loop.

This deviation-reducing circuit has been emphasized by the psychoanalytic approach to post-traumatic disorder, which focuses on the repressive maneuvers by which the individual defends against the painful traumatic memories. In fact, Figure 17B suggests that the behavioral and psychoanalytic models for post-traumatic disorder have each focused on a particular portion of what is actually a complex process that occurs at both psychological and physiological levels. The deviation-reducing element of Figure 17B also corresponds to the conservation-withdrawal factors identified by the psychosomatic theorists Engel and Schmale (1972) as playing a part in the organism's homeostatic regulation.

To complete the cybernetic picture, it is necessary to extend the complexity one more step, to include the social level as well. In the case of Mr. Jackson, which I discussed only briefly at the beginning of this chapter, the patient's intrusive recollections erupted in the therapy at precisely the point where the therapist got Mrs. Jackson to stop her behaviors that were maintaining his depression. This suggests the cybernetic model shown in Figure 17C. Here, the suppression-maintaining behavior by others in the social environment serves as yet another deviation-reducing mechanism, which ultimately functions to limit the activity in the original deviation-amplifying circuit. Interrupt this regulation by the social environment and the post-traumatic symptoms escalate out of control unless the patient himself is quickly able to recalibrate and maintain the necessary level of suppressing behaviors.

So far, this cybernetic model for post-traumatic disorder describes the syndrome's core symptoms and accounts for their maintenance. Finally, it is possible to cast the treatment of Mr. Hayes, as outlined above, into cybernetic terms by adding one more cybernetic loop (Figure 17D). Here, voluntary control of breathing becomes the deviation-reducing element that regulates the level of activity in the basic arousal-memories circuit. This new form of self-regulation is more effective then and replaces the old type of self-regulation (suppressing behaviors) and the social regulation of the post-traumatic symptoms.

ABOUT BIOFEEDBACK

It is useful to take a closer cybernetic look at what is called "voluntary control of breathing" in Figure 17D. Figure 18 dissects this element into its cybernetic components: receptor, analyzer, and effector (see Chapter 3). The receptor consists of attention to kinesthetic and visual information about the rate (and depth) of breathing. Such *attention* to this information is the most crucial part of teaching patients these self-regulation skills. The information about our rate of breathing is always potentially available to us, but in the normal course of events, we rarely pay attention to it, relying upon automatic regulation by various psychobiological

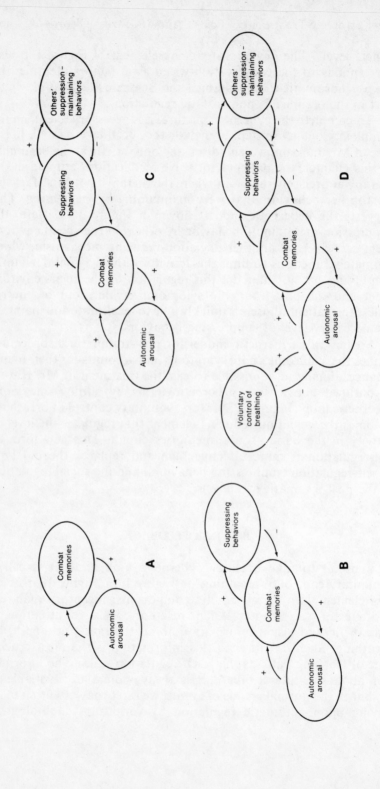

mechanisms (including, but not limited to those diagrammed in Figure 17C). Given this information about breathing, the analyzer, consisting of the mind's conscious decision-making faculties, makes a binary decision of the form: "Breathing too fast? Yes/No." If the answer is "Yes" the effector (consisting of the muscles controlling respiration) is instructed to slow the rate of breathing.

The parallel between Figure 18 and the perhaps more familiar forms of biofeedback should be clear. After all, "biofeedback" literally refers to feeding back (in the cybernetic sense) information about the body's state, which can then be used by the mind for self-regulation. In its usual application with various biofeedback machines, the receptor is some physical instrument measuring temperature, electrical activity of the muscles, etc. This is displayed in either digital or analogic form (numerical readout, dial, auditory tone) and the patient attends to this transformed information. The analyzer still consists of some kind of decision about whether or not the desired body state has been achieved and the effector involves an "action" of some sort (muscle relaxation, mental imagery, etc.).

MORE BIOLOGY

A recent paper by Hogben and Cornfield (1981) suggests some intriguing but frankly speculative notions about the biological mechanisms that may underlie the cybernetic model for post-traumatic disorder proposed here. These investigators report

Figure 17. A cybernetic model for post-traumatic disorder. (A) The heart of the model. Autonomic arousal and combat memories form a deviation-amplifying cybernetic circuit. (B) Self-regulation in post-traumatic disorder. Suppressing behaviors (avoidance, denial, emotional numbing, depression) limit the level of combat memories and thus regulate the activity in the basic arousal/memory circuit of Part A. (C) Social regulation of post-traumatic symptoms. Suppression-maintaining behaviors by others in the social environment regulate the level of suppressing behaviors by the post-traumatic patient and thus limit the activity of the basic arousal/memories circuit of Part A. (D) Therapeutic self-regulation of post-traumatic symptoms. By teaching the post-traumatic patient to control his respiratory rate voluntarily, a new self-regulating cybernetic circuit is established. This higher-order control mechanism utilizes feedback directly from the autonomic arousal itself and replaces the need for self- and social regulation by the circuits of Parts B and C.

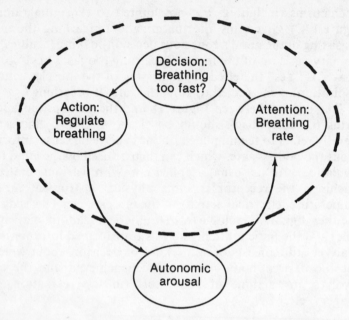

Figure 18. Cybernetic components for voluntary control of autonomic arousal. Here the mechanism for voluntary control of breathing shown in Figure 17D is broken down into its cybernetic components (enclosed within the large oval): Receptor = attention to rate of breathing; analyzer = decision whether rate is too fast; effector = muscular regulation of respiratory rate.

dramatic improvement in five cases of post-traumatic disorder upon treatment with phenelzine, an MAO-inhibiting antidepressant drug. All five patients had severe and disabling post-traumatic symptoms, ranging from five to thirty years duration, and all had previously failed to respond to antipsychotics and tricyclic anti-depressants as well as to psychotherapy. Furthermore, the course of these patients' response to drug treatment showed striking parallels to the psychotherapeutic treatment of Mr. Hayes, discussed above. Each patient felt calmer almost immediately after phenelzine treatment was begun. As treatment progressed, panic attacks and generalized anxiety decreased. Intrusive recollections in the form of nightmares or flashbacks ceased. Startle reactions stopped and general irritability lessened. And psychotherapy (Hogben and Cornfield, 1981) became possible:

Phenelzine actually seemed to enhance psychotherapy with these patients by stimulating an intense abreaction that had not been achieved in earlier therapies with or without psychotropic medication. Each patient had a period of emotional outpouring that began approximately four days after starting phenelzine treatment and lasted for three to four weeks. Rage was the primary emotion expressed during this period. It was followed by depression and, finally, by a short period of elation. The patients associated many old memories and attitudes during the periods of intense feelings. These memories arose from all time periods of the patients' lives. Service memories consisted of traumatic war scenes and scenes of conflict with authority. The recollections of traumatic war scenes and associated affect seemed much more integrated with phenelzine than without phenelzine. Before treatment, the patients mentioned war scenes rarely and without affect, except for intense anxiety. With phenelzine, the patients expressed intense and appropriate affect and much less anxiety. (p. 444)

Earlier sections of this chapter describe Mr. Hayes's recounting of both traumatic war scenes as well as thematically related memories from earlier periods of his life, his ability to recollect these events with appropriate affect, but without the intense anxiety he had previously displayed when remembering Vietnam, and periods of depression, anger, and then elation.

These observations on phenelzine treatment, together with the cybernetic model for post-traumatic disorder presented in this chapter, suggest that MAO-inhibitors may act *directly as antianxiety agents* and only *indirectly as antidepressants*. The cybernetic model suggests that the depressive withdrawal of the post-traumatic disorder is a solution to the problem of run-away somatic anxiety. As the anxiety is reduced (e.g., using phenelzine or biofeedback-type interventions), the need for depressive withdrawal decreases and the patient's mood improves. A number of studies (e.g., Klein, 1964; Robinson et al., 1973) have demonstrated the utility of MAO-inhibitor treatment of patients showing a mixture of depressive and anxiety symptoms. On the other hand, depressed patients without significant anxiety and those with more endogenous symptoms appear to respond better to tricyclic antidepressants (Greenblatt et al., 1964; Robinson et al., 1978). Tyrer et al. (1973) found, in a controlled trial of phenelzine treatment of agoraphobia and social phobias, "that phenelzine is anxiolytic but acts in a quite different way from other anxiolytic drugs which are sedative in large doses and exert a rapid effect" (p. 123). It may be, again following the cybernetic model presented here, that the effect of MAO-inhibitors is mediated, at least in part, by the autonomic nervous system, perhaps through regulation of the balance between sympathetic and parasympathetic activity.

THE PERSISTENCE OF POST-TRAUMATIC SYMPTOMS

As described above, both psychodynamic and behavioral theorists have grappled with the question of why post-traumatic symptoms often persist long after the original trauma. The cybernetic model developed here sheds some additional light on this interesting issue. From this new perspective, post-traumatic symptoms continue as diagrammed in Figure 17B simply because, once the cybernetic circuit is established, it grinds along until one of the components breaks down or a feedback loop is disrupted or until a higher-order control circuit intervenes.

This answer is deceptively simple because it involves a paradigm shift. An analogous shift occurred in the history of physics. Philosophers from at least the time of Aristotle struggled with the question "What keeps a moving body in motion?" Galileo came along and realized that the early natural scientists had been asking the wrong question. He saw that, unless acted upon by certain forces (e.g., friction), a moving body will remain in uniform motion forever. The crucial question becomes instead: "What prevents a moving body from maintaining its uniform motion?" Galileo's revolution in thought ushered in a new age in physics by focusing scientific attention on an ideal world (in which, for example, there is no friction), wherein physical laws can be stated simply and elegantly.

Cybernetics, with its emphasis on circular rather than linear causality (see Chapter 3), represents a paradigm shift of the same magnitude. Behaviorist thinking, in contrast, is essentially linear, cause–effect thinking. To explain a continuing effect, a behaviorist must look for a continuing linear cause. Hence the recourse to "genetic factors" or respondent conditioning, as noted above. Psychodynamic theorists, also constrained by the linear model, made the "repetition compulsion" into the continuing cause of the post-traumatic symptoms. Viewed in cybernetic terms, the repetition compulsion is simply a metaphor for describing the basic circular nature of cybernetic processes.

Additional Applications of the Cybernetic Model

The cybernetic model described here has considerable generality and can be applied to other problems of self-regulation besides the management of anxiety in post-traumatic disorder.

ANGER IN POST-TRAUMATIC DISORDER

In many cases of combat stress disorder, anger and violent behavior threaten to get out of control rather than (or in addition to) anxiety. This is not surprising, given the nature of the learning situation provided by the original traumatic event (see Figure 16). Real life-threatening danger automatically triggers the autonomic arousal necessary to support *either* fight or flight behavior. If fight behavior ensues, we say that the predominant emotion is anger. If flight occurs instead, we call it fear or anxiety. The point here is that, in both cases, the physiological state is the same (or similar), but the situation is interpreted (framed) in very different ways and thus leads to very different behavioral responses. Military training is carefully designed to maximize the likelihood that life-threatening danger will provoke aggressive behavior rather than fearful flight. Unfortunately, the military provides little retraining for its veterans following combat. This was particularly true in the case of Vietnam, when soldiers found themselves in the jungle fighting to survive one day and on the streets of this country the next. Some veterans have had difficulty relearning that danger and threat need not automatically be met by aggressive violence.

A brief clinical vignette illustrates the application of this approach to such a case. Mr. Bond, a 33-year-old Vietnam combat veteran, sought treatment following his arrest for an assault in which he lost control over a minor traffic incident and began beating the man who threatened and angered him. One such episode had occurred previously, about a year before, when he became enraged when a dog attacked and killed a little kitten. In that case, Mr. Bond had attacked the dog's owner. Mr. Bond saw such violent outbursts as uncharacteristic of him, and he related their intense and uncontrollable nature to his combat experiences. He denied having had difficulty controlling his anger prior to Vietnam. Careful history-taking revealed that the patient had experienced the symptoms of post-traumatic disorder during the years following discharge from the military, although the syndrome was by no means as clear-cut and severe as that of Mr. Hayes. He also displayed the difficulty in dealing with the aggressiveness of his two-year-old son described in Vietnam combat veterans by Sarah Haley (1978).

In working with Mr. Bond, it became clear that he experienced his angry outbursts as (1) under the control of events in the social environment and (2) happening very quickly: Something would anger him and BAM! he would be fighting mad and sometimes fighting. As with most individuals who experience their behavior as tightly linked to what is happening in their social environment, Mr. Bond was unaware of the arousal in his body that accompanies angry feelings. I instructed him to pay attention to this arousal and taught him to regulate his breathing to control the arousal, just as I had done with Mr. Hayes. He soon learned that the connection between angry feelings and violent behavior is neither as quick (the arousal builds up gradually over a period of time) nor as automatic (by regulating his breathing he could limit the level of arousal and prevent the angry outbursts) as he had thought.

In addition to increasing his capacity for self-control in everyday social interactions in general, these interventions allowed Mr. Bond to respond differently to his normally active, normally aggressive two-year-old son. Previously, the patient had been so worried that his anger would get out of control that he avoided disciplining or in any way setting limits for his son, leaving the matter to his wife, who was unable to handle the boy effectively by herself. As the son's behavior got more out of control and he pushed the limits more and more, Mr. Bond became increasingly worried about his mounting anger and withdrew further from parenting his son. Once he learned that he was capable of monitoring and regulating his angry feelings, Mr. Bond was able to become involved in his son's discipline and work with his wife to set limits appropriate for a two-year-old.

SPOUSE ABUSE

To take the cybernetic model of Figure 17D one step further from post-traumatic disorder, its application to the problem of spouse abuse will be discussed briefly. Take the typical case of the violent husband who beats his wife. Such men are traditionally seen as character-disordered individuals who lack the self-control necessary to modulate their aggressive impulses. Their behavior is tightly linked, in a cybernetic sense, to events in their social environments and their violent behavior is socially regulated, and not, to any significant degree, self-regulated (see discussion of immature-level functioning in Chapter 9). A systemic view of spouse abuse (Goodstein and Page, 1981; Hanks and Rosenbaum, 1977) recognizes, in addition, the role of the wife's behavior in perpetuating the abusive cycle and triggering the attacks. In this case, the cybernetic effects of the behavior of others in the social environment can have deviation-amplifying results, as well the deviation-reducing effects shown in Figure 17D.

Systems-oriented therapists may focus on the importance of the wife's behavior in the abusive process and seek to change the entire sequence of interactional events, of which the physical attacks are but one link. The trap in this approach, however, lies in blaming the victim. Family therapists sometimes find it easier and more comfortable to focus on the wife and attempt to get her to change. The danger here is in reinforcing the frame that the husband's behavior lies totally outside his control, and he, therefore, is in no way responsible for his actions.

Serious spouse abuse is among those life-threatening clinical problems (e.g., suicide, homicide, starvation in anorexia nervosa) that require immediate and vigorous intervention aimed directly at stopping the life-threatening behavior. For example, when beginning treatment of an anorexic girl in immediate danger of death from starvation, the initial strategic focus must be on her eating behavior, and hospitalization and a behavior modification regimen are often used.

Analogously, the self-regulation techniques described here can be applied in the initial phase of work with wife-abusers and their families. This is framed as a way for the husband to gain better control over his anger so the whole family can then have a chance to work out their problems. Using the breathing-regulation technique described above (often combined with muscle relaxation), the husband begins to experience a sense of mastery over his physiological arousal and angry behavior. As this occurs, the level of tension throughout the family system decreases. It then becomes safer to work on the couple interaction patterns that perpetuate the abusive behavior. Working from a social-learning perspective, Margolin (1979) describes a similar approach for intervening in cases of spouse abuse and elaborates on ways to identify preliminary anger cues.

13

Final Comments: Systemic Change and Systemic Psychology

Since I began thinking about this book several years ago, its basic organization has remained essentially unchanged. For a long time I considered ending with an "epilogue," but hesitated to commit myself to writing one since I was not sure what, if any, concluding remarks I had to make. I suppose it is entirely appropriate that one not know what to put in an epilogue until the writing approaches an end. Regardless, it was certain recent developments within family therapy that led me to undertake this concluding chapter. In this chapter, I attempt to place this book within the context of issues currently being debated in the field and to sketch some directions for future work.

I have chosen to present these observations in this concluding chapter rather than to disperse them among earlier chapters, where relevant, for two reasons. First, the book's structure highlights the changes in my own thinking as well as in the field as a whole, changes that are of interest in their own right. I am reminded here of Bateson's attempt in the epilogue of *Naven* (1936) to present his ideas and to examine his process of arriving at those ideas.

The second reason is pedagogical. As I suggested in the Preface of this book, learning family systems thinking recapitulates the field's historical development. I hope that my struggles to differentiate and finally to integrate family systems approaches, as reflected in the progression of the chapters of this book, will prove useful to others who embark on a similar project.

Systemic Change

Three articles appearing in the first 1982 issue of *Family Process* have generated lively and heated debate: Keeney and Sprenkle's (1982) "Ecosystemic Epistemology: Critical Implications for the Aesthetics and Pragmatics of Family Therapy"; Allman's (1982a) "The Aesthetic Preference: Overcoming the Pragmatic Error"; and Dell's (1982a) "Beyond Homeostasis: Toward a Concept of Coherence." The first two take the field to task for ignoring "aesthetic" issues in systems thinking to focus instead on mechanical, "pragmatic" techniques for symptom cure. The last and perhaps most ambitious article, by Dell, lambasts the field for its emphasis on homeostasis, an "epistemologically flawed concept" (p. 21), which must now be replaced, he asserts, by the concept of "coherence," "perhaps, a *perfectly* [italics are Dell's] defined explanatory notion" (p. 38).

What is the family systems thinker and therapist to make of all this? Certainly *my* first reaction was annoyance at having the security of my family systems world view challenged by these upstarts. This was followed by several months of ignoring the controversy: I simply failed to finish reading the articles and hoped the whole thing would go away.

But it has not. In fact, these three articles generated such critical response that almost one-half of *Family Process'* final 1982 issue was devoted to their discussion, with critiques by Coyne et al. (1982), Wilder (1982), Watzlawick (1982), and Whitaker (1982) and replies by Dell (1982b), Allman (1982b), and Keeney (1982).

In his rejoinder, Dell (1982b) admits that "a couple of friends have compared my 'Beyond Homeostasis' article to Martin Luther nailing his proclamation to the castle door" (p. 407). Although Dell is certainly not guilty of the sin of excessive modesty, it may just be true that he has launched a "reformation" of the family therapy field. It is at best hazardous to make such a prediction without the historian's luxury of hindsight. Yet what is now happening in the field seems to be sufficiently interesting and important to warrant serious scrutiny.

What convinced me to take the whole matter this seriously was Donald Bloch's (1982) "Thirteen Years: An Editor's Valedictory" appearing in the same issue of *Family Process* as the printed debate on the original three papers. Here Bloch, retiring as the journal's second editor (succeeding Jay Haley), put the current controversy in a developmental perspective.

Why, he wondered, did these three articles, along with the accompanying turmoil, appear now? Bloch's answer "lies in the waning influence of the founding fathers in the field and the beginning senescence of their first-line interpreters" (p. 386). He notes, in particular, the recent deaths of Gregory Bateson and Al Scheflen. To this list, the name of Milton Erickson could certainly be added. Bloch also notes that Dell, Keeney, Sprenkle, and Allman are younger men and concludes his discussion of the current upheaval in the field by observing that "the generational transfer of power must somehow be managed" (p. 387).

Inspired by Bloch's observation, in the remainder of this section I use Prigogine's notions about systemic transformation (see Chapter 3) to examine the changes that now appear to be underway in the family therapy field.

Systems thinking notwithstanding, I often have seen "my" ideas as something I create (quite heroically) apart from any context. Implicit here is the traditional view of mind as "intrapsychic." Although I have long recognized my debt to the families I see as a crucial source of ideas, it was only in struggling with this chapter that I have become keenly aware of the *system of family systems thinking*, of which the ideas in this book are a part. As a subsystem of this larger system, the notions presented in the preceding chapters have been influenced by the entire system of ideas and, in turn, feed back upon and influence this system. It is both distressing and exciting to sense that a system important in one's life is undergoing some unpredictable transformation.

Following Prigogine (1976), Dell's paper can be seen as *a large "fluctuation" in the system of family systems thinking*. Several implications follow from this point of view.

First, it is impossible to say at this point whether the fluctuation introduced by Dell (i.e., that the concept of homeostasis must be abandoned) is *large enough* to catalyze a genuine transformation in the system of systems thinking.

Second, the critiques of Dell and the others by Coyne et al., Watzlawick, and Wilder can be seen as "entropic effects" (those homeostatic forces so thoroughly disliked by Dell), which have the effect of damping out fluctuations like Dell's.

Third, following the suggestion of Bloch, as generational change occurs and people leave and enter the family therapy arena, the threshold for systemic change is lowered. Here Prigogine's notion of the "nucleon" around which transformations are catalyzed appears relevant (see Chapter 3).

And finally, the system of family therapy ideas may undergo transformation even if Dell's critique is not "right." In Prigogine's terms, the fluctuation around which systemic change occurs does not contain the new organization of the system. Rather, the new structure is already implicit in the old system.

So, I am suggesting, not only is Prigogine's work part of the new ideas in family systems thinking, it also provides a way to examine the very process of transformation in systems thinking itself. To put it another way, the current controversy in the field is a natural experiment for studying the process of systemic change.

I next examine some of the critical issues currently under discussion.

On Dualisms

Dell (1982a) decries the "dualistic" as well as "animistic" and "vitalistic" (p. 21) thinking that he finds prevalent if not rampant in the family field today. Keeney and Sprenkle (1982) lament that

> owing to the structure of occidental language, there is no way of avoiding slicing the world into namable pieces. The naming of "parts" consequently leads one to engage in some form of dualism, even when one is attempting not to be dualistic. (p. 6)

There is, however, another frame for this matter: Rather than being seen as sin or sickness, dualisms can instead be the source of healthy tensions to be harnessed for growth. This is, after all, the essence of dialectic thinking: Synthesis arises from the juxtaposition of thesis and antithesis.

It is fashionable these days to cite Bateson (e.g., 1977) on the "immorality" of dualistic thinking and the evils of "chopping up the ecology" (e.g., Hoffman, 1981, p. 342). Yet the real sin, to continue the ecclesiastical metaphor embraced by Dell, is not in chopping up the world, but rather in being unable to put it back together again *and* then mistaking one's fragmented map of the world for the real thing [Dell refers to the latter as Whitehead's (1925) "fallacy of misplaced concreteness"].

Following Werner (1948), the point of view on development outlined in Chapter 9 suggests that the creation of dualisms be seen as the differentiation of parts from an undifferentiated whole and, thus, as the cornerstone of subsequent growth and development. From this Wernerian perspective, Dell's and Keeney and Sprenkle's target should not be dualism itself, but rather the subsequent failure to transcend dualism by putting the parts back together in an integrated, more complex whole.

This point can be illustrated with the example from the history of physics introduced in Chapter 7. There it was noted that the traditional view of light as "rays" or beams of particles, although perfectly adequate, for example, for designing very precise lenses, was unable to account for so-called anomalous diffraction. To explain the latter, it was necessary to reconceptualize light as "waves" of electromagnetic radiation. This classical theory of electromagnetic fields turned out to be entirely sufficient to account for the observed behavior of light until the early part of this century when certain new data (e.g., the emission of radiation by atoms, the photoelectric effect) required that light be again seen as "particles," newly christened "photons."

Here was a profound dualism: Is light really waves or is it really particles? Sometimes it seemed to act like one, at other times the other. So it was expedient to conclude that light was really *both* waves and particles. This conceptually unsatisfactory state of affairs was finally remedied around 1925 by the invention of quantum mechanics, according to which light is *neither* waves nor particles. Rather, it behaves in ways that can be rigorously described by the equations of quantum mechanics. Under certain conditions, its behavior is consistent with the classical notion of a wave and under others fits what is ordinarily meant by particle. So in the atomic and subatomic realms, where classical physics gives way to quantum physics, *both* classical concepts, wave and particle, are no longer viable.

It is silly, though, to blame pre-quantum mechanics notions of the behavior of light on dualistic thinking. Rather than impeding the progress of scientific thought, as Dell and the others would have us believe is generally the case, (1) the wave and particle concepts themselves served physics well within certain realms and (2) the tension between these two notions contributed to their ultimate transcendence in quantum mechanics. Thus, as Werner suggests, differentiation necessarily precedes integration.

Three particular dualisms in the field will now be examined. Each was important in differentiating family therapy from previous views of human problems and, thus, helped launch the field. Each is indicted by Dell (1982a), Allman (1982a), or Keeney and Sprenkle (1982) as a source of current trouble in the field. And all three shape the ideas presented in this book.

PSYCHE VERSUS SYSTEM

This first dualism was inherent in my insistence, following Minuchin (see Chapter 3), that from the point of view of systems thinking (versus that of individual psychology), the individual is a "part," not a "whole." Family therapy successfully differentiated itself from the view of human problems dominant in the 1940s and 1950s by emphasizing the larger whole, particularly the family, and de-emphasizing the individual person. This is implicit in, for example, the title of Neill and Kniskern's (1982) collection of Carl Whitaker's collected papers: *From Psyche to System*.

I still believe that to learn systems thinking one must initially set aside the old way of explaining focused on what goes on "inside" the individual and look instead to the larger context to understand behavior. Yet in struggling in this book with the task of integrating family systems thinking, I have been led, somewhat against my will (after all, what will those "systems purists" think and say), to reconsider the place of the individual person and of the mind within the systemic point of view. My clinical work, particularly with neurotics, has been especially important in pushing me in this direction.

Most persuasive was the case of a 69-year-old woman who had suffered from headaches for the past 26 years. Mrs. Tate had had every medical test available, and none revealed an organic cause for her distress. She had been treated with every conceivable physical intervention, including various pain medications, electroconvulsive shock, chiropractic manipulation, and surgery to sever some nerves in her head. Typically, her headaches would become progressively worse, requiring more pain medication and eventually more and more frequent trips to her doctor's office and to emergency rooms for injections. Finally, every nine months or so, she would be hospitalized for two weeks, the head pain would gradually subside, and the cycle would begin again.

When I saw Mrs. Tate she told me that she had fallen from a

horse at age 10 or so, landing on her head. I began to think that I could use neuropsychological testing to find an organic cause for her head pain where all the medical technology had so far failed. As I was explaining the testing to Mrs. Tate, she abruptly stopped me, saying "I never told this to any of my other doctors, but I had an abortion forty years ago." As it turned out, the patient, a good Catholic woman, had had an abortion at a time when she was already overwhelmed with the care of three children, two of them bedridden for many months with rheumatic fever. Despite having confessed her sin to a priest, Mrs. Tate was unable to forgive herself for what she had done. The headaches apparently began at the time of the patient's menopause, when she could no longer conceive a child to replace the one she had aborted.

I framed the headaches as the patient's own punishment for her sin and suggested that she continue to have them until she herself was convinced that she had suffered enough and was able to forgive herself. Within a few weeks, the headaches decreased and Mrs. Tate began recalling events related to the abortion that she had repressed for 40 years. Following this, she went through a brief period of mourning for the lost child. Treatment terminated after eight sessions, with the patient free of head pain.

A little more than a year after those sessions ended, Mrs. Tate again began having headaches. A couple of months later she came to see me, handing me a slip of paper upon which she had copied notations from her calendar. The first entry was the statement "My brother died two months ago," followed by the subsequent dates on which she had experienced severe headaches. After I had read the note, Mrs. Tate said: "And I suppose you are going to tell me that I haven't grieved for my brother."

This is precisely what had happened. The brother had died a horrible death of cancer, with much suffering and pain for several months. Mrs. Tate reported that she had been unable to feel sorry for her brother at all and had not cried when he died. She soon related this to the fact that, for 26 years, she had blamed him for the headaches: He was leading the horse from which she had fallen at age 10. When the headaches began some 35 years later, Mrs. Tate blamed her brother. A week or two after this discussion in therapy, the patient forgave her brother, mourned his death (e.g., was able for the first time to have a Mass offered for him), and the headaches again stopped.

Although it is likely that the headaches may have initially served the interpersonal function of keeping her husband from

demanding sex, thus eliminating the worry of yet another un-
wanted pregnancy, it was hardly the case that the symptom was
needed for this job at age 69. Rather, the head pain appeared to
regulate the patient's feelings of guilt over the abortion (and later,
about her ill feelings toward her brother): If she began feeling
guilty she developed a severe headache, which promptly reduced
the feelings of guilt as she took to her bed to suffer with her
physical pain.

Of course, this is a bit like re-inventing the wheel: Analysts
from Freud on have encountered cases like this. However, apart
from the early days of analysis when Freud and others reported
brief cures (see Malan, 1963), psychoanalytic treatment of such
cases generally takes much longer than the fewer than 20 sessions
with Mrs. Tate. And Freud notwithstanding, there was nothing like
seeing it for myself to convince me of the necessity of including the
mind in a conceptual scheme for understanding neurosis.

If family therapy started with the shift "from psyche to system,"
then my recent struggles as reflected in this book might be labeled
"from system back to psyche." And indeed, Dell (1982b) uses the
same metaphor when he independently states: "Thus, I have moved
(apologies to Carl Whitaker, John Neill, and David Kniskern)
from system to psyche. And my therapy is improving" (p. 413).

Basing his re-emphasis of the place of the individual within
family therapy partly on the work of the Chilean biologist Hum-
berto Maturana (1978, 1980), Dell (1982a) suggests that "the behavioral coherence of each individual member is primary, whereas
the higher-order coherence of the interactional system . . . is
secondary" (p. 35). Dell calls for a new "clinical epistemology"
(p. 37), which, among other things, should reflect the special place
of the individual among the various systemic levels.

Chapter 9 on systemic psychopathology represents my own
attempt to reclaim what family therapy threw out in the 1950s, that
is, individual psychopathology, and integrate it with systems
thinking.

CHANGE VERSUS STABILITY

In Chapter 3, I introduced another duality by juxtaposing deviation-
amplifying feedback describing continuous change in systems with
deviation-reducing feedback, which refers to processes through
which systems maintain their stability. The issue of stability versus

change in systems has a venerable history in the field, beginning at least with Bateson's *Naven*, first published in 1936 (see Chapter 2), and continuing to the present time with Dell's recent attack on the concept of homeostasis.

From his work among the Iatmul, Bateson arrived at a concept —schismogenesis—that describes escalating *change*, and he next wondered how systems in which schismogenic processes occurred could maintain their stability. Then cybernetics came along in the 1940s and 1950s and emphasized *stability* by focusing on the homeostatic processes through which systems are regulated. Jackson (1957a) called family therapists' attention to such processes, observable in clinical work with patients and their families, and began what Dell rightly sees as an overemphasis on the family's stabilizing processes at the expense of processes leading to change.

Dell (1982a) does note that, since Jackson's original paper, there has been a trend within the field (e.g., Speer, 1970) to recognize that families, as well as other living systems, display both morphostatic *and* morphogenic processes, but he promptly dismisses such attempts as "indulge[nce] in dualisms" and "paradigm-protecting patchwork" (p. 31).

Within the frame suggested here, such dualistic thinking need not simply be rejected out of hand, but rather the tension between the two poles should be utilized creatively to transcend the dualism and achieve an integration of the opposing processes. Prigogine's work (see Chapter 3), including as it does both entropic, system-maintaining processes and processes that act catalytically to transform the system, appears to be a major contribution to such an integration. Dell himself offers his notion of "coherence" as a solution to the problem of stability and change. In the final section of this chapter, I add my own speculations on the issue, in light of the systemic psychology discussed there.

PRAGMATICS VERSUS AESTHETICS

Of the three, this is the most difficult dualism to discuss. On one hand, the critics of Allman (1982a) and Keeney and Sprenkle (1982) attack these authors' "vague, metaphorical notions" (Coyne et al., 1982) and muddled thinking (Wilder, 1982). Yet I suspect that the obscure quality of this discussion reflects *the family therapy field's* muddle as well. On this issue, whatever it turns out to be, development has not yet reached the stage at which differentiation has occurred, much less integration. At least this is true of my own thinking on the matter.

In an effort to further the differentiation of my own thinking on this issue, I speculate here on what pragmatics versus aesthetics might mean, without attempting to review the *Family Process* articles in detail or belabor their limitations.

Whatever else it involves, this dualism was reflected concretely in the *problem-solving versus growth* dimension used in Chapter 1 to organize the map of the field of family therapy.

At one level, the pragmatic versus aesthetic issue reflects my complaint in Chapter 1 that the field is too technique-oriented. Keeney and Sprenkle (1982) make a similar argument in their section on "Art and Technique in Therapy" (p. 11). In Chapter 1, I emphasized a major theme of this book, that (even) pragmatic, problem-solving therapy needs techniques that are securely imbedded in systemic thinking about families and how they change.

But what additional questions are involved here? The following come to mind: What is growth? And whose growth are we talking about? The family's? That of individual family members? The therapist's? How does individual or family growth and change affect the larger ecology? How can we think about the issue of adapting therapeutic approaches to the therapist's personality? Most of these questions are beyond the scope of this concluding chapter, but I return to this issue again in the following section.

Systemic Psychology

In this final section, I outline a new *systemic psychology* that builds upon and generalizes the systemic psychopathology of Chapter 9. The task of systemic psychology is to understand and explain the *behavior of the individual* from a systemic point of view. The cybernetics of systemic psychology is diagrammed in Figure 19. Here the system is composed of four elements: (1) the person's behavior; (2) the mind (thoughts plus feelings) of that individual; (3) that person's biological systems; and (4) that person's social context. These four elements are arranged as the vertices of a pyramidal polyhedron having a triangular base and sides. Each system element is linked to all others by circular feedback loops.

Figure 19 is a generalization of the cybernetics of systemic psychopathology as presented in Chapter 9. Loops 2 and 3, con-

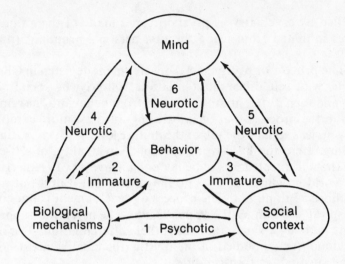

Figure 19. The cybernetics of systemic psychology. The biopsychosocial system is composed of four elements: behavior, mind (thoughts plus feelings), the biological system, and the social context. Each system element is linked to all others by circular feedback loops. Loops are labeled according to their associated level of psychosocial functioning. The functioning of the mature level encompasses all six loops.

necting the individual's behavior with biology and social context, correspond to the cybernetics of the immature level (see Figure 14B), whereas loops 4, 5, and 6 form the cybernetics of the neurotic level (Figure 14C).

The interpretation of loop 1 is more complex. On the one hand, it has to do with the self/other differentiation that occurs at the moment of birth as the biological organism is separated from the social context. In this sense, loop 1 is related to the cybernetics of the psychotic level (Figure 14A) in which self/other differentiation, in a psychological rather than a biosocial sense, is incomplete.

But loop 1 is about more than psychosis. For example, mystical belief systems typically emphasize a merger of self with other, ultimately linking biology with social context. Bateson (1972) appears to be referring to such phenomena when he writes about Learning III as "a world in which personal identity merges into all the processes of relationship in some vast ecology or aesthetics of cosmic interaction" (p. 306). He notes that the journey to Level III "can be dangerous, and some fall by the wayside. These are often labelled by psychiatry as psychotic, and many of them find themselves inhibited from using the first personal pronoun" (pp. 305–306).

The process of psychosocial development depicted in Chapter 9 begins with self/other differentiation, followed by social integration and then differentiation of mind from behavior. The remaining step in the process, that of integrating this now more complex organism, was seen as the job of the mature level of psychosocial functioning. Here the hard-won sense of individuality, of self-control and the self-directedness of behavior, can give way to a merger with the world in which "self" is no longer relevant. But is not this just psychosis? I think not. The process of development is not circular, but spiral (see Langer, 1969, pp. 95–96). The psychotic is a prisoner of an inability to maintain self/other differentiation. The mature individual (as embodied in the mystic, the creative artist, and the lover) succeeds in transcending it.

The edge between madness and genius (reflected in the nature of loop 1 in Figure 19) is both very thin and crucial. The difference between psychosis and creative genius or mystical experience lies, I think, in the state of development of the other loops of Figure 19 as well, particularly those involving mind. That is, the nature of the biosocial interaction depicted in loop 1 depends upon its context—by itself, it describes psychosis, but linked with the other cybernetic processes of Figure 19, it is a feature of mature functioning.

Regarding the dualism of psyche and system, systemic psychology embeds the individual's mind and behavior firmly within both biology and social context (see Figure 19). Traditional mechanistic understanding of the individual's behavior corresponds to loops 2 (biological psychology) and 6 (psychodynamic psychology), whereas the systemic thinking introduced in Chapter 3 focuses on loop 3. Within systemic psychology, soma, psyche, and social system are seen as a complex, articulated, and integrated whole. The cybernetic model presented in Chapter 12 (see Figure 17) maps the relevant parts of Figure 19 in the case of post-traumatic stress disorder.

To further understand the relationship between the systemic psychology of Figure 19 and the systemic psychopathology depicted in Figure 14, it is useful to introduce the concept of the *strength of a cybernetic coupling*: Two system elements are strongly coupled when there is a high probability that a change in one element will lead to a change in the other. In a cybernetic system consisting of just two elements, this concept is of little importance. However, when many links between multiple elements are involved, it is important to know whether a given element is more strongly linked to some system components than to others.

Given this definition, we can say, for example, that at the immature level of psychosocial functioning the cybernetic couplings with the individual's mind are weak compared to the other links and Figure 19 reduces to Figure 14B.

The notion of the strength of a cybernetic coupling also helps put the concept of *self-control* in perspective. In Chapter 9, I argued that at the neurotic level of psychosocial functioning "self-control" is the regulation of an individual's behavior via feedback from his own behavior, body, or mind rather than from the social context. Critics like Dell (1982a), however, insist that concepts such as "self-control" are nonsense:

> The problem . . . is that *self-regulation is itself an epistemologically flawed notion* [italics are Dell's]. If the self (or part of the self) regulates the self, then what regulates the aspect of the self that is doing the regulating? (p. 25)

To conclude, therefore, that concepts such as self-control are so untenable that they must be junked is about as useful as insisting that, according to systems thinking, everything is linked to everything else and it is an epistemological error to attempt to understand anything without considering its place in the cosmos.

The issue in both cases is: What are the strengths of the couplings between the system element under scrutiny and other system components? When the couplings between the person's behavior and his mind, body, and his own behavior itself (loops feeding back from each system element to itself should really be added to Figure 19) outweigh the couplings with the social context, then it makes sense, I think, to speak of self-control of behavior.

As far as the dualism of stability versus change is concerned, Figure 19 emphasizes the need to simultaneously consider more than one cybernetic circuit. The apparent opposition of deviation-reducing versus deviation-amplifying feedback is, in fact, an artifact of looking at just one loop at a time. This can be seen by referring to Figure 20. Here the typical representations of deviation-reducing (20A) and deviation-amplifying (20B) feedback are translated into new diagrams, in which circular arrows are shown moving in opposing directions for deviation reduction (20C) and in the same direction for deviation amplification (20D). These new representa-

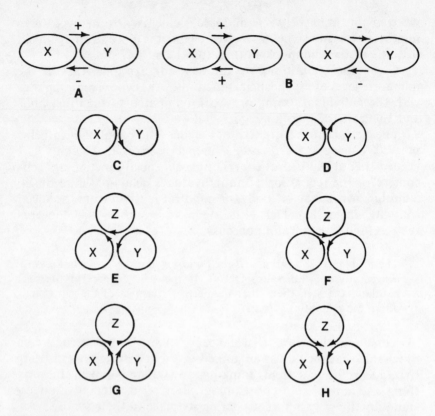

Figure 20. The cybernetics of two- and three-element systems. System components are X, Y, and Z. **(A,B)** Typical representations of deviation reduction **(A)** and deviation amplification **(B)** in a two-element system. **(C,D)** Alternate representation of deviation-reduction **(C)** and deviation amplification **(D)** in a two-element system. **(E,F)** Alternate representation of two "coherent" three-element systems. **(G,H)** Two "incoherent" three-element systems.

tions make it easier to grasp the more complex relationships discussed next.

With just two system components (X and Y), Figures 20C and 20D are the only possible configurations. What happens when a third component (Z) is added? The results are shown in 20E through 20H. Only two feedback arrangements are possible: In Figure 20E, two of the links are deviation amplifying, whereas the third is deviation reducing; in 20F, all three links are deviation reducing. The configurations shown in Figures 20G and 20H are in some sense internally inconsistent and will not be considered further here (although it appears possible to interpret them as transformations representing transitions between the stable states depicted in 20E and 20F).

Figure 20 helps make concrete Dell's (1982a) abstract and rather vague term *coherence*: "Coherence simply implies a congruent interdependence in functioning whereby all the aspects of the system fit together" (p. 31). Figures 20E and 20F "fit together," whereas Figures 20G and 20H do not.

When only two system components are considered, deviation amplification and deviation reduction appear dualistic. When a third is added, the dualism is transcended and two coherent solutions are possible. Both have an odd number of deviation-reducing links, a condition on overall system stability noted by Maruyama (1963).

Dell (1982b) complains that the notion of feedback is slippery because "If you looked at it *this* way it was positive; if you looked at it *that* way it was negative" (p. 408). Figure 20E is especially interesting, since it combines both types of feedback and helps make sense of this ambiguity: The relationship between X and Y is deviation reducing, whereas that of X with Z is deviation amplifying. This diagram makes it clear how a symptom, for example, may be both stabilizing in its relationship with one part of the system, while contributing to a process of change vis-à-vis another part of the system.

It appears that the way to transcend a dualism is not to retreat to a monistic, undifferentiated state of affairs, but rather to add a third element to the two and take into account the interrelationships within this still more complex system. Another way of saying this is that a system comprised of two elements is an artificially closed system, a fragment of an open system consisting of at least three elements.

This has implications for the elementary systems paradigm introduced in Chapter 3. There, we focused on the feedback loop between the two elements *subsystem* and *system*, although lip service was paid to the system's links to a third element, the *environment*. It now appears to me that this is a fundamental error: The basic configuration is *always* subsystem–system–environment. Although we can sometimes get away with temporarily narrowing our focus to the subsystem–system interface, sooner or later this gets us into one conceptual (or pragmatic?) muddle or another.

Finally, Figures 20E and 20F make graphic the relationships among system elements with which Bateson struggled in his 1930s investigations of the Iatmul and Balinese cultures (see Chapter 2). If we let X and Z each stand for "aggressive behavior by males" and Y indicate "submissive behavior by females," then Figure 20E depicts what Bateson found among the Iatmul in New Guinea, whereas 20F depicts that found in Bali.

In Figure 20E, the deviation amplification between X and Z represents the symmetrical schismogenesis of the males' continual warlike behavior with each other; the deviation amplification between Y and Z corresponds to the complementary schismogenesis of the extreme differentiation between the sexes among the Iatmul. The deviation reduction shown between X and Y, on the other hand, represents *naven* behavior, in which male aggression leads to decreased female submission (or increased female aggression), which, in turn, leads to decreased male aggression (or increased male submission). So Figure 20E in a precise way depicts Bateson's hunch: Counterbalancing schismogenic processes can produce system stability.

In Figure 20F, all the links are deviation reducing. Male aggression does not escalate symmetrically and exaggerated differentiation between the sexes (in terms of aggression/submission) does not occur, consistent with Bateson's observations in Bali.

Finally, systemic psychology offers a schema for transcending a pragmatic family therapy aimed at fixing a problem by focusing on just one or two loops in Figure 19 (e.g., loops 2 and 3, in the case of the immature-level problems discussed in Chapters 4, 5, and 9). If "growth" is to move beyond the status of an important but vague and muddled concept, then the multiple links depicted in Figure 19 need to be clearly specified and their complex interactions traced.

But such a systemic psychology will have to remain a project for the future.

Annotated Suggested Readings

Chapter 1

Beal, E. (1976). Current trends in the training of family therapists. *American Journal of Psychiatry* 133:137–141.
  Identifies a theoretical dimension ranging from an experiential orientation, at one end, to a structural orientation, at the other.
Bell, J.E. (1975). *Family Therapy*. New York: Aronson.
  A survey of the family therapy field by one of its pioneers.
Erickson, G.D. and Hogan, T.P. (1980). *Family Therapy: An Introduction to Theory and Technique*. 2nd ed. Monterey, CA: Brooks/Cole.
  Another good overview of the entire family therapy field.
Gurman, A.S. and Kniskern, D.P. (eds.) (1981). *Handbook of Family Therapy*. New York: Brunner/Mazel.
  This monumental volume is already being called the "Physician's Desk Reference (PDR)" of family therapy. It contains good articles written by practitioners of the leading schools of family therapy as well as papers on the history of the field and on family therapy outcome and process research.
Haley, J. (1975). Why a mental health clinic should avoid family therapy. *Journal of Marital and Family Counseling* 1:3–13.
  Should be read by anyone learning family systems therapy. Emphasizes the conceptual differences between systems thinking and traditional mental health approaches, as well as the practical problems that arise in clinical settings when these differences are not fully appreciated.

Madanes, C. and Haley, J. (1977). Dimensions of family therapy. *Journal of Nervous and Mental Disease* 165:88–98.
A good overview of the various schools of family therapy and the underlying dimensions along which the schools differ. The first chapter of Madanes (1981) contains an expanded version of this paper.

Chapter 2

Ackerman, N.W. (1954). Interpersonal disturbances in the family. *Psychiatry* 17:359–368.
Written for a psychiatric audience, this paper reflects the state of the mental health field at the time family therapy emerged as well as Ackerman's own early family thinking.

Bateson, G., Jackson, D., Haley, J., and Weakland, J. (1956). Toward a theory of schizophrenia. *Behavioral Science* 1:251–264.
The classic double-bind paper.

Bowen, M. (1978). Treatment of family groups with a schizophrenic member. In *Family Therapy in Clinical Practice*. New York: Aronson. (Presented at the Annual Meeting of the American Orthopsychiatric Association, Chicago, March, 1957.) Here Bowen describes the early observations on schizophrenic young women and their mothers that led him to reconceptualize schizophrenia in family terms and launched his subsequent research in the field.

Fromm-Reichmann, F. (1948). Notes on the development of treatment of schizophrenics by psychoanalytic psychotherapy. *Psychiatry* 11:263–273.
In this paper, Fromm-Reichmann introduced the famous (or infamous) term *schizophrenogenic mother*. In this and other articles written during the 1940s she raised the hope that psychotherapeutic technique could be modified to treat schizophrenics.

Lidz, T., Cornelison, A.R., Fleck, S., and Terry, D. (1957). The intrafamilial environment of the schizophrenic patient: II. Marital schism and marital skew. *American Journal of Psychiatry* 114:241–248.
Another classic article and the best known of the series of reports on Lidz's schizophrenia studies.

Wynne, L.C., Ryckoff, I.M., Day, J., and Hirsch, S.I. (1958). Pseudomutuality in the family relations of schizophrenics. *Psychiatry* 21:205–220.
This paper, important in the field's early development, also marked the beginning of Wynne and Singer's productive program of research on the families of schizophrenics.

Chapter 3

Bertalanffy, L. von. (1974). General system theory and psychiatry. In *American Handbook of Psychiatry*, ed. S. Arieti. 2nd ed. New York: Basic Books.
One of the originators of general systems theory discusses its application to psychiatry.

Hoffman, L. (1971). Deviation-amplifying processes in natural groups. In *Changing Families*, ed. J. Haley, pp. 285–311. New York: Grune & Stratton.
A good theoretical overview. Argues that family therapy has focused on deviation-reduction processes to the neglect of equally important deviation amplification. Includes sociological points of view.

—— (1981). *Foundations of Family Therapy: A Conceptual Framework for Systems Change.* New York: Basic Books.
One of the most important recent books in the field, likely to become a classic theoretical statement. Discusses many of the topics of Chapter 3, this volume.

Wender, P.H. (1968). Vicious and virtuous circles: The role of deviation amplifying feedback in the origin and perpetuation of behavior. *Psychiatry* 31:309–324.
Useful discussion of cybernetics. Includes many examples from the behavioral sciences.

Chapters 4 and 5

Kaplan, S.L. (1977). Structural family therapy for children of divorce. *Family Process* 16:75–83.
Applies the structural model to the case of divorce.

Malcolm, J. (1978). A reporter at large: The one-way mirror. *The New Yorker*, May 15, pp. 39 ff.
A journalist's account of Minuchin's work at the Philadelphia Child Guidance Clinic. Besides giving the reader the best picture of Minuchin's therapeutic style, short of seeing him live or on videotape, the article begins with a sophisticated discussion of some of the philosophical issues in the field.

McGoldrick, M. et al. (eds.) (1982). *Ethnicity and Family Therapy.* New York: Guilford.
A good resource book covering a very wide range of socioeconomic and cultural family variations.

Minuchin, S. (1974). *Families and Family Therapy.* Cambridge, MA: Harvard University Press.

The basic theoretical description of structural family therapy. Chapters 3 and 5 are particularly important and a good place to start.

Minuchin, S. and Fishman, H.C. (1981). *Family Therapy Techniques.* Cambridge, MA: Harvard University Press.

In this latest book, Minuchin and Fishman concentrate on the technical aspects of structural family therapy. Up-to-date and practical.

Minuchin, S. et al. (1967). *Families of the Slums: An Exploration of Their Structure and Treatment.* New York: Basic Books.

Describes the beginnings of structural family therapy in Minuchin's work with delinquent children and their families in New York.

Minuchin, S., Baker, L., Rosman, B.L., Liebman, R., Milman, L., and Todd, T.C. (1975). A conceptual model of psychosomatic illness in children: Family organization and family therapy. *Archives of General Psychiatry* 32:1031–1038.

A good short introduction to Minuchin's recent psychosomatic work. If you wish more after reading this, see Minuchin's 1978 book (with Rosman and Baker) *Psychosomatic Families.*

Minuchin, S., Rosman, B.L., and Baker, L. (1978). *Psychosomatic Families: Anorexia Nervosa in Context.* Cambridge, MA: Harvard University Press.

Here Minuchin has moved from New York and juvenile delinquents to Philadelphia and psychosomatic children. A central contribution to family therapy.

Stanton, M.D., Todd, T.C., Heard, D.B., Kirschner, S., Kleiman, J.I., Mowatt, D.T., Riley, P., Scott, S.M., and Van Deusen, J.M. (1978). Heroin addiction as a family phenomenon: A new conceptual model. *American Journal of Drug and Alcohol Abuse* 5:125–150.

Outlines a promising new model for understanding and treating young adult drug abusers based upon the structural and strategic models. Calls attention to the failure of approaches that do not include the family of origin and suggests a link between unresolved family grief over premature deaths in the family and subsequent drug addiction in the young adult.

Stanton, M.D., Todd, T. C., and Associates (1982). *The Family Therapy of Drug Abuse and Addiction.* New York: Guilford Press.

An important new book that details this team's structural–strategic treatment of drug abuse.

Walker, K.N. and Messinger, L. (1979). Remarriage after divorce: Dissolution and reconstruction of family boundaries. *Family Process* 18: 185–192.

Discusses the application of the structural model to "blended" families.

Weltern, J.S. (1982). A structural approach to the single-parent family. *Family Process* 21:203–210.

A practical discussion of this important topic.

Chapter 6

Carter, E.A. and McGoldrick, M. (1980). *The Family Life Cycle: A Framework for Family Therapy*. New York: Gardner Press.
The most comprehensive description of the developmental model. Contains good discussions of important life cycle variations, including premature death, separation and divorce, remarriage, and cultural influences.

Coleman, S.B. and Stanton, M.D. (1978). The role of death in the addict family. *Journal of Marriage and Family Counseling* 4:79–91.
Develops the thesis that the unusual incidence of premature deaths and unresolved grief in the families of young adult heroin abusers results in the addict undergoing a slow death through heroin as a substitute for the deceased family member.

Haley, J. (1973). *Uncommon Therapy: The Psychiatric Techniques of Milton H. Erickson, M.D.* New York: Norton.
Here, in delightfully readable form, Haley introduces the reader to Erickson's wizardry. Chapter 2 is especially useful for the developmental framework Haley describes using the concept of the family life cycle.

Lindemann, E. (1944). Symptomatology and management of acute grief. *American Journal of Psychiatry* 101:141–148.
A classic paper that some consider to be the beginnings of crisis intervention. Lindemann discusses the care of patients experiencing acute grief, including victims of the famous Coconut Grove fire. He describes both normal and pathological grief reactions and outlines approaches to treatment.

Paul, N.L. and Grosser, G.H. (1965). Operational mourning and its role in conjoint family therapy. *Community Mental Health Journal* 1: 339–345.
An early article that alerts family therapists to the role of unresolved grief in compromising family development by making it difficult for the family to deal with subsequent losses.

Chapter 7

Fisch, R., Weakland, J.H., and Segal, L. (1982). *The Tactics of Change: Doing Therapy Briefly*. San Francisco: Jossey-Bass.
The most recent volume on the MRI brief therapy approach.

Haley, J. (1963). *Strategies of Psychotherapy*. New York: Grune & Stratton.
A basic work. Haley's analysis of psychotherapy here foreshadows his later "strategic" therapy.

———— (1973). *Uncommon Therapy: The Psychiatric Techniques of Milton H. Erickson, M.D.* New York: Norton.
If Haley is appropriately called the father of strategic therapy, then Milton Erickson is undoubtably the field's grandfather. Here Haley introduces the reader to Erickson's important work.

———— (1976). *Problem-Solving Therapy*. San Francisco: Jossey-Bass.
A good "how-to-do-it" guide to strategic therapy by one of its originators. Chapter 1, "Conducting the First Interview," is especially useful.

———— (1980). *Leaving Home*. New York: McGraw-Hill.
Haley's most recent discussion of his approach.

———— (ed.) (1967). *Advanced Techniques of Hypnosis and Therapy: Selected Papers of Milton Erickson, M.D.* New York: Grune & Stratton.
A collection of early materials. This is an advanced work. Read after *Uncommon Therapy* if you become interested in Erickson.

Madanes, C. (1981). *Strategic Family Therapy*. San Francisco: Jossey-Bass.
An important new book by a clinician intimately involved in the development of strategic therapy.

Rabkin, R. (1977). *Strategic Psychotherapy*. New York: Basic Books.
A highly readable introduction to strategic therapy.

Watzlawick, P., Beavin, J.H., and Jackson, D. (1967). *Pragmatics of Human Communication*. New York: Norton.
A classic work. Basic for understanding the communication analysis of individual and family therapy. The discussion of paradox is especially important.

Watzlawick, P., Weakland, J., and Fisch, R. (1974). *Change: Principles of Problem Resolution*. New York: Norton.
An important book detailing the MRI brief therapy approach. The discussion of *reframing* is central to strategic therapy and no one describes it better than do Watzlawick and his colleagues.

Weakland, J.H., Fisch, R., Watzlawick, P., and Bodin, A.M. (1974). Brief therapy: Focused problem resolution. *Family Process* 13:141–168.
The briefest description of the important Mental Research Institute (MRI) model for brief strategic therapy.

Weeks, G.R. and L'Abate, L. (1982). *Paradoxical Psychotherapy: Theory and Practice with Individuals, Couples, and Families*. New York: Brunner/Mazel.
A comprehensive discussion of paradox.

Chapter 8

Singer and Wynne's prolific writings over the past 25 years are scattered through many journals and the authors have never summarized their work in book form, making it difficult for a new reader to become familiar with it. The articles listed below, in chronological order, are among Singer and Wynne's most important and provide a good starting point for readers wanting more on the transactional model.

Wynne, L.C., Ryckoff, I.M., Day, J., and Hirsch, S.I. (1958). Pseudo-mutuality in the family relations of schizophrenics. *Psychiatry* 21: 505–220.
One of the early classic papers in the field. Provides the context for subsequent research work.

Singer, M.T. and Wynne, L.C. (1965). Thought disorder and family relations of schizophrenics: III. Methodology using projective techniques. *Archives of General Psychiatry* 12:187–200.
The third of a series of four papers. Describes Singer and Wynne's first study in which they predicted the diagnosis of young adult offspring from their parents' transactional behavior. This paper is particularly useful for its discussion of one of Singer's most important contributions: The use of the Rorschach technique to sample transactional behavior. The second paper in the series (Wynne and Singer, 1963) introduces the "amorphous" versus "fragmented" classification of disordered thinking.

—— (1966). Principles for scoring communication defects and deviances in parents of schizophrenics: Rorschach and TAT scoring manuals. *Psychiatry* 29:260–288.
Here the authors described, for the first time, the communication deviance codes they used to move beyond the global predictive study of their 1963–1965 series of papers to generate quantitative data on disturbed transactions in the families of schizophrenics.

Singer, M.T. (1977). The Rorschach as a transaction. In *Rorschach Psychology*, ed. M.A. Rickers-Ovsiankina, pp. 455–485. Melbourne, FL: Robert E. Krieger.
A good recent overview of the Singer–Wynne research methods. Contains the most current reorganization of the communication deviance codes, used as a basis for the classification scheme of Chapter 8, this volume.

Wynne, L.C. (1977). Schizophrenics and their families: Research on parental communication. In *Developments in Psychiatric Research*, ed. J.M. Tanner, pp. 254–286. London: Hodder & Stroughton.
Summarizes the family studies of schizophrenia from both biological and psychosocial perspectives and suggests a schema for integrating

these two lines of inquiry. Presents the Singer–Wynne research findings on communication deviance in the families of young adult schizophrenics.

Chapter 9

Lewis, J.M. (1980). The family matrix in health and disease. In *The Family: Evaluation and Treatment*, eds. C.K. Hofling & J.M. Lewis, pp. 5–44. New York: Brunner/Mazel.
A brief introduction to the ambitious program of family research mentioned in Chapter 9, this volume. If you are interested in reading more, see Lewis et al. (1976).

Vaillant, G.E. (1977). *Adaptation to Life*. Boston: Little, Brown.
Here Vaillant uses the notion of a continuum of defensive/adaptive strategies to organize the data from a major longitudinal study of human development. Highly readable, with many case examples.

Chapter 10

Haley, J. (1975). Why a mental health clinic should avoid family therapy. *Journal of Marriage and Family Counseling* 1:3–13.
Reread this paper as a reminder that it is not easy or even possible to practice family systems thinking and therapy in certain treatment contexts.

——— (1976). *Problem-Solving Therapy*. San Francisco: Jossey-Bass.
Chapter 1, "Conducting the First Interview," is a good cookbook guide to the strategic-style initial session with the family.

Minuchin, S. (1974). *Families and Family Therapy*. Cambridge, MA: Harvard University Press.
For a discussion of the initial interview conducted in the structural style, see, in particular, Chapter 7, "Forming the Therapeutic System."

Chapter 11

Hill, O.W. (1968). Psychogenic vomiting. *Gut* 9:348–352.
One of the few articles to look at psychogenic vomiting outside of anorexia nervosa, in young children, or a mentally retarded population.

Chapter 12

American Psychiatric Association (1980). *Diagnostic and Statistical Manual of Mental Disorders*, 3rd ed. Washington, D.C.: American Psychiatric Association.
Pages 236–238 concisely review the post-traumatic stress disorder syndrome.

Figley, C.R. and Sprenkle, D.H. (1978). Delayed stress response syndrome: Family therapy indications. *Journal of Marriage and Family Counseling* 4(3):53–60.
One of the few articles in the family therapy literature to discuss post-traumatic disorder.

Haley, S. (1978). Treatment implications of post-combat stress response syndromes for mental health professionals. In *Stress Disorders among Vietnam Veterans*, ed. C.R. Figley. New York: Brunner/Mazel.
Discusses the under-diagnosis of post-traumatic disorder in Vietnam combat veterans (particularly due to the inadequacies of DSM-II). Describes the issues involved in treating these veterans, including the relationship between the patient's symptoms and the marital and family contexts.

Horowitz, M. (1974). Stress response syndromes: Character style and dynamic psychotherapy. *Archives of General Psychiatry* 31:768–781.
A brief presentation of Horowitz's important modern psychodynamic approach to post-traumatic disorder. See Horowitz (1976) for a more detailed discussion.

References

Ackerman, N.W. (1937). The family as a social and emotional unit. *Bulletin of the Kansas Mental Hygiene Society* 12(2).

—— (1954a). Interpersonal disturbances in the family: Some unresolved problems in psychotherapy. *Psychiatry* 17:359–368.

—— (1954b). The diagnosis of neurotic marital interaction. *Social Casework* 35:139–143.

—— (1956). Interlocking pathology in family relationships. In *The Strength of Family Therapy*, eds. D. Bloch and R. Simon. New York: Brunner/Mazel, 1982.

—— (1958). Toward an integrative therapy of the family. *American Journal of Psychiatry* 114:727–733.

—— (1959). The psychoanalytic approach to the family. In *Individual and Familial Dynamics*, ed. J.H. Masserman. New York: Grune & Stratton.

—— (1960). Theory of family dynamics. *Psychoanalysis and the Psychoanalytic Review* 46(4):33–49.

—— (1962). Family psychotherapy and psychoanalysis: The implications of difference. *Family Process* 1:30–43.

—— (1964). Prejudicial scapegoating and neutralizing forces in the family group. *International Journal of Social Psychiatry, Congress Issue* 2:90.

—— (1968). The role of the family in the emergence of child disorders. In *Foundations of child psychiatry*, ed. E. Miller. Oxford: Pergamon Press.

Ackerman, N.W. and Behrens, M.L. (1956). A study of family diagnosis. *American Journal of Orthopsychiatry* 26:66–78.

Ackerman, N.W. and Sobel, R. (1950). Family diagnosis: An approach to the preschool child. *American Journal of Orthopsychiatry* 20:744–752.

Alexander, F. (1950). *Psychosomatic Medicine*. New York: Norton.

Allman, L.R. (1982a). The aesthetic preference: Overcoming the pragmatic error. *Family Process* 21:43–56.

———— (1982b). The poetic mind: Further thoughts on an "aesthetic preference." *Family Process* 21:415–428.

American Psychiatric Association (1968). *Diagnostic and Statistical Manual of Mental Disorders*, 2nd ed. Washington, D.C.: American Psychiatric Association.

———— (1980). *Diagnostic and Statistical Manual of Mental Disorders*, 3rd ed. Washington, D.C.: American Psychiatric Association.

Anon. (1972). Toward a differentiation of self in one's own family. In *Family Interaction: A Dialogue Etc.*, ed. J.L. Framo. New York: Springer.

Aponte, H. (1976a). The family-school interview: An eco-structural approach. *Family Process* 15:303–311.

———— (1976b). Under-organization in the poor family. In *Family Therapy: Theory and Practice*, ed. P. Guerin. New York: Gardner Press.

Aronovich, J. (1982). *Life Cycle: Stability and Evolution in Families*. Workshop presented at the meeting of the American Orthopsychiatric Association, San Francisco, April.

Ashby, W.R. (1945). Effect of controls on stability. *Nature 155*, No. 3930: 242–243.

Auerswald, E.H. (1968). Interdisciplinary versus ecological approach. *Family Process* 7:202–215.

Bandler, R. and Grinder, J. (1975). *Patterns of the Hypnotic Techniques of Milton H. Erickson, M.D.*, vol. 1. Cupertino, CA: Meta Publications.

Bateson, G. (1936). *Naven*. Cambridge: Cambridge University Press.

———— (1941). Experiments in thinking about observed ethnological material (1972). In *Steps to an Ecology of Mind*. New York: Ballantine.

———— (1949). Bali: The value system of a steady state. In *Social Structure: Studies Presented to A.R. Radcliffe-Brown*, ed. M. Fortes. New York: Russell & Russell.

———— (1958). *Naven*, rev. ed. Stanford, CA: Stanford University Press.

———— (1969). *Double bind, 1969*. Annual Meeting of the American Psychological Association, August.

———— (1971). The cybernetics of self: A theory of alcoholism. *Psychiatry* 34:1–18.

———— (1972). *Steps to an Ecology of Mind*. New York: Ballantine.

———— (1977). The birth of a matrix or double bind and epistemology. In *Beyond the Double Bind*, ed. M. Berger. New York: Brunner/Mazel.

Bateson, G., Jackson, D.D., Haley, J., and Weakland, J.H. (1956). Toward a theory of schizophrenia. *Behavioral Science* 1:251–264.

Behan, R.C. and Hirschfeld, A.H. (1963). The accident process: II. Toward a more rational treatment of industrial injuries. *Journal of the American Medical Association* 186(4):84–90.

Bell, J.E. (1970). A theoretical position for family group therapy. In *Family Process*, ed. N.W. Ackerman. New York: Basic Books.

——— (1975). *Family Therapy*. New York: Aronson.

Bertalanffy, L. von (1968). *General System Theory: Foundations, Development, Applications*. New York: George Braziller.

——— (1974). General system theory and psychiatry. In *American Handbook of Psychiatry*, 2nd ed., ed. S. Arieti. New York: Basic Books.

Bloch, D.A. (1982). Thirteen years: An editor's valedictory. *Family Process* 21:383–389.

Bloch, D. and Simon, R. (eds.) (1982). *The Strength of Family Therapy: Selected Papers of Nathan W. Ackerman*. New York: Brunner/Mazel.

Bogdonoff, M.D. and Nichols, C.R. (1964). Psychogenic effect on lipid mobilization. *Psychosomatic Medicine* 26:710.

Boscolo, L. and Cecchin, G. (1981). *Systemic Therapy*. Workshop presented at Stanford University, Palo Alto, CA, November.

Bowen, M. (1960). A family concept of schizophrenia. In *The Etiology of Schizophrenia*, ed. D.D. Jackson. New York: Basic Books.

——— (1961). The family as the unit of study and treatment: Family psychotherapy. *American Journal of Orthopsychiatry* 31:40–60.

——— (1966). The use of family theory in clinical practice. *Comprehensive Psychiatry* 7:345–374.

——— (1978a). *Family Therapy in Clinical Practice*. New York: Aronson.

——— (1978b). Treatment of family groups with a schizophrenic member. In M. Bowen, *Family Therapy in Clinical Practice*. New York: Aronson.

——— (1979). *Reflections on Family Therapy*. Lecture presented at Don Jackson Memorial Conference, San Francisco, August.

Broderick, C.B. and Schrader, S.S. (1981). The history of professional marriage and family therapy. In *Handbook of Family Therapy*, eds. A.S. Gurman and D.P. Kniskern. New York: Brunner/Mazel.

Burke, J.D., White, H.S., and Havens, L.L. (1979). Which short-term therapy?: Matching patient and method. *Archives of General Psychiatry* 36:177–186.

Burns, R.C. and Kaufman, S.H. (1970). *Kinetic Family Drawings*. New York: Brunner/Mazel.

Carter, E.A. and McGoldrick, M. (eds.) (1980). *The Family Life Cycle: A Framework for Family Therapy*. New York: Gardner Press.

Chalk, M. (1979). *Long-Term Hospital Treatment of Schizophrenic and Borderline Adolescents and Young Adults*. Lecture presented at VA Medical Center, San Francisco, March.

Chance, M.R.A. (1962). An interpretation of some agonistic postures: The role of 'cut-off' acts and postures. *Symposium of the Zoological Society of London* 8:71–89.

Chance, P. (1974). After you hit a child you can't just get up and leave him; you are hooked to that child. *Psychology Today* 7(8):76–84.

Coleman, S.B. and Stanton, M.D. (1978). The role of death in the addict family. *Journal of Marriage and Family Counseling* 4:79–91.

Colon, F. (1980). The family life cycle of the multiproblem poor family. In *The Family Life Cycle: A Framework for Family Therapy*, eds. E.A. Carter and M. McGoldrick. New York: Gardner Press.

Cowan, P.A. (1978). *Piaget: With Feeling.* New York: Holt, Rinehart, & Winston.

Coyne, J.C. (1976). Depression and the response of others. *Journal of Abnormal Psychology* 85:186–193.

Coyne, J.C., Denner, B., and Ransom, D.C. (1982). Undressing the fashionable mind. *Family Process* 21:391–396.

Cronen, V.E., Johnson, K.M., and Lannamann, J.W. (1982). Paradoxes, double binds, and reflexive loops: An alternative theoretical perspective. *Family Process* 21:91–112.

de Monteflores, C. and Schultz, S.J. (1978). Coming out: Similarities and differences for lesbians and gay men. *Journal of Social Issues* 34(3):59–72.

Dell, P.F. (1981). Some irreverent thoughts about paradox. *Family Process* 20:37–42.

——— (1982a). Beyond homeostasis: Toward a concept of coherence. *Family Process* 21:21–41.

——— (1982b). In search of truth: On the way to clinical epistemology. *Family Process* 21:407–414.

Deutsch, F. (1959). *On the Mysterious Leap from the Mind to the Body.* New York: International Universities Press.

Doane, J.A., Jones, J.E., Fisher, L., Ritzler, B., Singer, M.T., and Wynne, L.C. (1982). Parental communication deviance as a predictor of competence in children at risk for adult psychiatric disorder. *Family Process* 21:211–223.

Dobbs, D. and Wilson, W.P. (1960). Observations on the persistence of war neurosis. *Diseases of the Nervous System* 21:686–691.

Drye, R.C., Goulding, R.L., and Goulding, M.E. (1973). No-suicide decisions: Patient monitoring of suicide risk. *American Journal of Psychiatry* 130:171–174.

Duncan, S. (1972). Some signals and rules for taking speaking turns in conversations. *Journal of Personality and Social Psychology* 23:283–292.

Engel, G.L. and Schmale, A.H. (1972). Conservation-withdrawal: A primary regulatory process for organic homeostasis. In *Physiology, Emotion, and Psychosomatic Illness.* Amsterdam: CIBA Foundation Symposium 8 (New Series).

Erickson, E.H. (1963). *Childhood and Society*, 2nd ed. New York: Norton.

Erickson, G.D. and Hogan, T.P. (1980). *Family Therapy: An Introduction to Theory and Technique*, 2nd ed. Monterey, CA: Brooks/Cole.

Eysenck, H.J. (1963). Behaviour therapy, extinction, and relapse in neurotics. *British Journal of Psychiatry* 109:12–18.

Falicov, C.J. and Karrer, B.M. (1980). Cultural variations in the family life cycle: The Mexican–American family. In *The Family Life Cycle: A Framework for Family Therapy*, eds. E.A. Carter and M. McGoldrick. New York: Gardner Press.

Ferreira, A.J. (1963). Family myth and homeostasis. *Archives of General Psychiatry* 9:457–463.

Festinger, L. (1957). *A Theory of Cognitive Dissonance*. Stanford, CA: Stanford University Press.

Feynman, R.P., Leighton, R.B., and Sands, M. (1963). *The Feynman Lectures on Physics*. Reading, MA: Addison-Wesley.

Figley, C.R. (ed.) (1978). *Stress Disorders among Vietnam Veterans*. New York: Brunner/Mazel.

Figley, C.R. and Sprenkle, D.H. (1978). Delayed stress response syndrome: Family therapy indications. *Journal of Marriage and Family Counseling* 4:53–60.

Fisher, L., Anderson, A., and Jones, J.E. (1981). Types of paradoxical intervention and indications/contraindications for use in clinical practice. *Family Process* 20:25–35.

Framo, J.L. (1981). The integration of marital therapy with sessions with family of origin. In *Handbook of Family Therapy*, eds. A.S. Gurman and D.P. Kniskern. New York: Brunner/Mazel.

Freud, S. (1904). On psychotherapy. In *Collected Papers*, vol. I. London: Hogarth Press, 1924.

——— (1914). On narcissism. In *Collected Papers*, vol. IV. London: Hogarth Press, 1925.

——— (1920). *A General Introduction to Psychoanalysis*. Garden City, NY: Garden City Publishing Co., 1943.

——— (1926). Inhibitions, symptoms, and anxiety. In *Collected Papers*, vol. XX. London: Hogarth Press, 1959.

——— (1930). *Three Contributions to the Theory of Sex*. New York: Nervous and Mental Disease Publishing Company.

——— (1933). New introductory lectures on psycho-analysis. In *Collected Papers*, vol. XXII. London: Hogarth Press, 1964.

Friedman, M. and Rosenman, R.H. (1974). *Type-A Behavior and Your Heart*. New York: Knopf.

Fromm-Reichmann, F. (1941). Recent advances in psychoanalytic therapy. *Psychiatry* 4:161–164.

——— (1943). Psychoanalytic psychotherapy with psychotics. *Psychiatry* 6:277–279.

——— (1946). Remarks on the philosophy of mental disorder. *Psychiatry* 9:293–308.

—— (1948). Notes on the development of treatment of schizophrenics by psychoanalytic psychotherapy. *Psychiatry* 11:263–273.

Gantt, W.H. (1944). *Experimental Basis for Neurotic Behavior.* New York: Hoeber.

Golden, C.J. (1981). *Diagnosis and Rehabilitation in Clinical Neuropsychology,* 2nd ed. Springfield, IL: Charles C Thomas.

Goodstein, R.K. and Page, A.W. (1981). Battered wife syndrome: Overview of dynamics and treatment. *American Journal of Psychiatry* 138:1036–1044.

Greenberg, G.S. (1977). The family interactional perspective: A study and examination of the work of Don D. Jackson. *Family Process* 16: 385–412.

Greenblatt, M., Grosser, G.H., and Wechsler, H. (1964). Differential response of hospitalized depressed patients to somatic therapy. *American Journal of Psychiatry* 120:935–943.

Gurman, A.S. and Kniskern, D.P. (1978a). Research on marital and famliy therapy: Progress, perspective, and prospect. In *Handbook of Psychotherapy and Behavior Change*, eds. S. Garfield and A. Bergin, 2nd ed. New York: Wiley.

—— (1978b). Deterioration in marital and family therapy: Empirical, clinical, and conceptual issues. *Family Process* 17:3–20.

Haley, J. (1959). An interactional description of schizophrenia. *Psychiatry* 22:321–332.

—— (1962). Whither family therapy. *Family Process* 1:69–100.

—— (1963). *Strategies of Psychotherapy.* New York: Grune & Stratton.

—— (1968). Editorial. *Family Process* 7:1–6.

—— (1973a). *Uncommon Therapy: The Psychiatric Techniques of Milton H. Erickson, M.D.* New York: Norton.

—— (1973b). Strategic therapy when a child is presented as the problem. *Journal of the American Academy of Child Psychiatry* 12: 641–659.

—— (1975). Why a mental health clinic should avoid family therapy. *Journal of Marriage and Family Counseling* 1:3–13.

—— (1976). *Problem-Solving Therapy.* San Francisco: Jossey-Bass.

—— (1979). *Reflections on Family Therapy.* Lecture presented at Don Jackson Memorial Conference, San Francisco, August.

—— (1981). On the right to choose one's own grandchildren. *Family Process* 20:367–368.

—— (ed.) (1967). *Advanced Techniques of Hypnosis and Therapy: Selected Papers of Milton Erickson, M.D.* New York: Grune & Stratton.

Haley, S. (1978). Treatment implications of post-combat stress response syndromes for mental health professionals. In *Stress Disorders among Vietnam Veterans*, ed. C.R. Figley. New York: Brunner/Mazel.

Hanks, S.E. and Rosenbaum, P.C. (1977). Battered women: A study of women who live with violent alcohol-abusing men. *American Journal of Orthopsychiatry* 47:291-306.

Hart, J.T. and Tomlinson, T.M. (eds.) (1970). *New Directions in Client-Centered Therapy*. Boston: Houghton Mifflin.

Herz, F. (1980). The impact of death and serious illness on the family life cycle. In *The Family Life Cycle: A Framework for Family Therapy*, eds. E.A. Carter and M. McGoldrick. New York: Gardner Press.

Hill, L. (1955). *Psychotherapeutic Intervention in Schizophrenia*. Chicago: University of Chicago Press.

Hill, O.W. (1968). Psychogenic vomiting. *Gut* 9:348-352.

Hill, R. (1964). The developmental approach to the family field of study. In *Handbook of Marriage and the Family*, ed. H.T. Christensen. Chicago: Rand McNally.

Hill, R. et al. (1953). *Eddyville's Families*. Chapel Hill, NC: Institute for Research in Social Science.

Hirschfeld, A.H. and Behan, R.C. (1963). The accident process: I. Etiological considerations of industrial injuries. *Journal of the American Medical Association* 186(3):113-119.

Hoffman, L. (1971). Deviation-amplifying processes in natural groups. In *Changing Families*, ed. J. Haley. New York: Grune & Stratton.

—— (1981). *Foundations of Family Therapy: A Conceptual Framework for Systems Change*. New York: Basic Books.

Hogben, G.L. and Cornfield, R.B. (1981). Treatment of traumatic war neurosis with phenelzine. *Archives of General Psychiatry* 38:440-445.

Hope, R. (trans.) (1961). *Aristotle's Physics*. Lincoln, NE: University of Nebraska Press.

Horowitz, M.J. (1974). Stress response syndromes: Character style and dynamic psychotherapy. *Archives of General Psychiatry* 31:768-781.

—— (1976). *Stress-Response Syndromes*. New York: Aronson.

Horowitz, M.J. and Solomon, G.F. (1978). Delayed stress response syndromes in Vietnam veterans. In *Stress Disorders among Vietnam Veterans*, ed. C.R. Figley. New York: Brunner/Mazel.

How human life begins. (1982). *Newsweek*, Jan. 11, pp. 38-43.

Inhelder, B. and Piaget, J. (1958). *The Growth of Logical Thinking from Childhood to Adolescence*. New York: Basic Books.

Jackson, D.D. (1954). Some factors influencing the Oedipus complex. *Psychoanalytic Quarterly* 23:566-581.

—— (1957a). The question of family homeostasis. *The Psychiatric Quarterly Suppl.* 31:79-90.

—— (1957b). A note on the importance of trauma in the genesis of schizophrenia. *Psychiatry* 20:181-184.

—— (1965). Family rules: The marital quid pro quo. *Archives of General Psychiatry* 12:589-594.

—— (ed.) (1960). Introduction. In *The Etiology of Schizophrenia*. New York: Basic Books.

—————— (ed.) (1968). *Communication, Family, and Marriage: Human Communication*, vol. I. Palo Alto, CA: Science and Behavior Books.

Jackson, D.D. and Weakland, J. (1959). Schizophrenic symptoms and family interaction. *Archives of General Psychiatry* 1:618–621.

Jantsch, E. (1975). *Design for Evolution: Self-organization and Planning in the Life of Human Systems*. New York: Braziller.

Johnson, A.M. (1956). Studies in schizophrenia at the Mayo Clinic: II. Observations on ego functions in schizophrenia. *Psychiatry* 19: 143–148.

Kaplan, H.S. (1974). *The New Sex Therapy: Active Treatment of Sexual Dysfunction*. New York: Brunner/Mazel.

—————— (1979). *Disorders of Sexual Desire and Other New Concepts and Techniques in Sex Therapy*. New York: Brunner/Mazel.

Kaplan, S.L. (1977). Structural family therapy for children of divorce. *Family Process* 16:75–83.

Kardiner, A. (1959). Traumatic neuroses of war. In *American Handbook of Psychiatry*, vol. I, ed. S. Arieti. New York: Basic Books.

Kasanin, J. (ed.) (1944). *Language and Thought in Schizophrenia*. Berkeley, CA: University of California Press.

Keeney, B. (1982). Not pragmatics, not aesthetics. *Family Process* 21: 429–434.

Keeney, B.P. and Sprenkle, D.H. (1982). Ecosystemic epistemology: Critical implications for the aesthetics and pragmatics of family therapy. *Family Process* 21:1–19.

Kelley, J.B. and Wallerstein, J.S. (1976). The effects of parental divorce: Experiences of the child in early latency. *American Journal of Orthopsychiatry* 46:20–42.

Kernberg, O. (1975). *Borderline Conditions and Pathological Narcissism*. New York: Aronson.

Kerr, M.E. (1981). Family systems theory and therapy. In *Handbook of Family Therapy*, eds. A.S. Gurman and D.P. Kniskern. New York: Brunner/Mazel.

Kintsch, W. (1970). *Learning, Memory, and Conceptual Processes*. New York: Wiley.

Klein, D.F. (1964). Delineation of two drug-responsive anxiety syndromes. *Psychopharmacologia* 5:397–408.

Kohler, W. (1929). *Gestalt Psychology*. New York: Horace Liveright.

Kohut, H. (1966). Forms and transformation of narcissism. *American Journal of the Psychoanalytic Association* 14:243–272.

Kormos, H.R. (1978). The nature of combat stress. In *Stress Disorders among Vietnam Veterans*, ed. C.R. Figley. New York: Brunner/Mazel.

Krystal, H. (1979). Alexithymia and psychotherapy. *American Journal of Psychotherapy* 33:17–31.

Langer, J. (1969). *Theories of Development*. New York: Holt, Rinehart, & Winston.

Levitan, H.L. (1978). The significance of certain dreams reported by psychosomatic patients. *Psychotherapy and Psychosomatics* 30:137–149.

Lewin, K. (1935). *A Dynamic Theory of Personality: Selected Papers.* New York: McGraw-Hill.

Lewis, J.M. (1980). The family matrix in health and disease. In *The Family: Evaluation and Treatment*, eds. C.K. Hofling and J.M. Lewis. New York: Brunner/Mazel.

Lewis, J.M., Beavers, W.R., Gossett, J.T., and Phillips, V.A. (1976). *No Single Thread: Psychological Health in Family Systems.* New York: Brunner/Mazel.

Lidz, R.W. and Lidz, T. (1949). The family environment of schizophrenic patients. *American Journal of Psychiatry* 106:332–345.

Lidz, T., Cornelison, A.R., Fleck, S., and Terry, D. (1957a). The intrafamilial environment of the schizophrenic patient: I. The father. *Psychiatry* 20:329–342.

——— (1957b). The intrafamilial environment of the schizophrenic patient: II. Marital schism and marital skew. *American Journal of Psychiatry* 114:241–248.

——— (1958a). The intrafamilial environment of the schizophrenic patient: IV. Parental personalities and family interaction. *American Journal of Orthopsychiatry* 28:764–776.

——— (1958b). The intrafamilial environment of the schizophrenic patient: VI. The transmission of irrationality. *Archives of Neurology and Psychiatry* 79:305–316.

Lindemann, E. (1944). Symptomatology and management of acute grief. *American Journal of Psychiatry* 101:141–148.

Madanes, C. (1981). *Strategic Family Therapy.* San Francisco: Jossey-Bass.

Madanes, C. and Haley J. (1977). Dimensions of family therapy. *Journal of Nervous and Mental Disease* 165:88–98.

Malan, D.H. (1963). *A Study of Brief Psychotherapy.* London: Tavistock Publications.

Malcolm, J. (1978). A reporter at large: The one-way mirror. *The New Yorker*, May 15, pp. 39 ff.

Mann, J. (1973). *Time-Limited Psychotherapy.* Cambridge, MA: Harvard University Press.

Margolin, G. (1979). Conjoint marital therapy to enhance anger management and reduce spouse abuse. *American Journal of Family Therapy* 7:13–23.

Marty, P. and de M'Uzan, M. (1963). La Pensee operatoire. *Revue Francaise Psychoanalyse* 27 (Suppl):1345–1346.

Maruyama, M. (1963). The second cybernetics: Deviation-amplifying mutual causal processes. *American Scientist* 51:164–179.

——— (1968). The second cybernetics: Deviation-amplifying mutual causal processes. In *Modern Systems Research for the Behavioral Scientist*, ed. W. Buckley. Chicago: Aldine.

Maturana, H. (1978). Biology of language: The epistemology of reality. In *Psychology and Biology of Language and Thought*, eds. G.A. Miller and E. Lenneberg. New York: Academic Press.

—— (1980). Autopoiesis and evolution. In *Autopoiesis, Dissipative Structures, and Spontaneous Social Orders*, ed. M. Zeleny. Boulder, CO: Westview Press.

McDougall, J. (1974). The psychosoma and the psychoanalytic process. *International Review of Psychoanalysis* 1:437.

McGoldrick, M., Pearce, J.K., and Giordano, J. (eds.) (1982). *Ethnicity and Family Therapy*. New York: Guilford.

Meyerstein, I. (1974). *Promise Her Anything but Send a Postcard: An Adventure in Structural Family Therapy*. Galveston, TX: University of Texas Medical Branch. [Videotape reviewed in Schultz, S.J. (1981). *Family Process* 20:127–128.]

Minuchin, S. (1974). *Families and Family Therapy*. Cambridge, MA: Harvard University Press.

—— (1979). Constructing a therapeutic reality. In *Family Therapy of Drug and Alcohol Abuse*, eds. E. Kaufman and P.N. Kaufman. New York: Gardner Press.

—— (1980). *Structural Family Therapy*. Workshop presented at the Family Institute, Berkeley, CA, February.

—— (1982). Reflections on boundaries. *American Journal of Orthopsychiatry* 52:655–663.

Minuchin, S. and Fishman, H.C. (1981). *Family Therapy Techniques*. Cambridge, MA: Harvard University Press.

Minuchin, S. et al. (1967). *Families of the Slums: An Exploration of Their Structure and Treatment*. New York: Basic Books.

Minuchin, S., Baker, L., Rosman, B.L., Liebman, R., Milman, L., and Todd, T.C. (1975). A conceptual model of psychosomatic illness in children: Family organization and family therapy. *Archives of General Psychiatry* 32:1031–1038.

Minuchin, S., Rosman, B.L., and Baker, L. (1978). *Psychosomatic Families: Anorexia Nervosa in Context*. Cambridge, MA: Harvard University Press.

Morin, S.F. and Schultz, S.J. (1978). The gay movement and the rights of children. *Journal of Social Issues* 34(2):137–148.

Mosher, L.R. and Wynne, L.C. (1970). Methodological issues in research with groups at high risk for the development of schizophrenia. *Schizophrenia Bulletin* 1(2):4–7.

Neill, J.R. and Kniskern, D.P. (1982). *From Psyche to System: The Evolving Therapy of Carl Whitaker*. New York: Guilford Press.

Nemiah, J.C. (1977). Alexithymia: Theoretical considerations. *Psychotherapy and Psychosomatics* 28:199–206.

Olson, D.H. (1972). Empirically unbinding the double bind. *Family Process* 11:69–74.

Omer, H. (1981). Paradoxical treatments: A unified concept. *Psychotherapy: Theory, Research, and Practice* 18:320–324.

Parsons, T. and Bales, R.F. (1955). *The Family*. Glencoe, IL: Free Press.

Paul, N.L. and Grosser, G.H. (1965). Operational mourning and its role in conjoint family therapy. *Community Mental Health Journal* 1: 339–345.

Pavlov, I.P. (1941). *Lectures on Conditioned Reflexes*, vol. II, trans. and ed. by W.H. Gantt. New York: International Universities Press.

Physicians' Desk Reference (1982). *Physician's Desk Reference*, 36th ed. Oradell, NJ: Medical Economics Company.

Piaget, J. (1950). *The Psychology of Intelligence*. New York: Harcourt, Brace & World.

—— (1951). *Play, Dreams, and Imitation in Childhood*. New York: Norton.

—— (1954). *The Construction of Reality in the Child*. New York: Basic Books.

—— (1971). *Genetic Epistemology*. New York: Norton.

Prigogine, I. (1976). Order through fluctuation: Self-organization and social system. In *Evolution and Consciousness: Human Systems in Transition*, eds. E. Jantsch and C.H. Waddington. Reading, MA: Addison-Wesley.

Rabkin, R. (1977). *Strategic Psychotherapy*. New York: Basic Books.

Richardson, L.F. (1939). Generalized foreign politics. *British Journal of Psychology Monog. Suppl.* 23:1–48.

Riskin, J.M. and Faunce, E.E. (1972). An evaluative review of family interaction research. *Family Process* 11:365–455.

Robinson, D.S., Nies, A., Ravaris, C.L., Ives, J.O., and Bartlett, D. (1978). Clinical pharmacology of phenelzine. *Archives of General Psychiatry* 35:629–635.

Robinson, D.S., Nies, A., Ravaris, C.L., and Lamborn, K.R. (1973). The monoamine oxidase inhibitor, phenelzine, in the treatment of depressive-anxiety states. *Archives of General Psychiatry* 29:407–413.

Rose, R.M., Bernstein, I.S., and Gordon, T.P. (1975). Consequences of social conflict on plasma testosterone levels in rhesus monkeys. *Psychosomatic Medicine* 37:50–61.

Ruesch, J. and Bateson, G. (1949). Structure and process in social relations. *Psychiatry* 12:105–125.

Ryckoff, I., Day, J. and Wynne, L.D. (1959). Maintenance of stereotyped roles in the families of schizophrenics. *AMA Archives of General Psychiatry* 1:93–98.

Satir, V. (1964). *Conjoint Family Therapy*. Palo Alto, CA: Science and Behavior Books.

—— (1979). *Reflections on Family Therapy*. Lecture presented at Don Jackson Memorial Conference, San Francisco, August.

Schachtel, E.G. (1954). The development of focal attention and the emergence of reality. *Psychiatry* 17:309–324.

Schachter, S. (1971). *Emotion, obesity, and crime.* New York: Academic Press.

Scott, N.R. (1979). *Basic Contributions of Gregory Bateson and the Mental Research Institute.* Lecture presented at VA Medical Center, San Francisco, September.

Selvini Palazzoli, M. (1979). *Reflections on Family Therapy.* Lecture presented at Don Jackson Memorial Conference, San Francisco, August.

——— (1981). Comments on Dell's paper. *Family Process* 20:44–45.

Selvini Palazzoli, M., Cecchin, G., Prata, G., and Boscolo, L. (1978). *Paradox and Counterparadox: A New Model in the Therapy of the Family in Schizophrenic Transaction.* New York: Aronson.

Selvini Palazzoli, M., Boscolo, L., Cecchin, G., and Prata, G. (1980). Hypothesizing—circularity—neutrality: Three guidelines for the conductor of the session. *Family Process* 19:3–12.

Shon, S.P. and Ja, D.Y. (1982). Asian families. In *Ethnicity and Family Therapy*, eds. M. McGoldrick, et al. New York: Guilford Press.

Sifneos, P. (1967). Clinical observations on some patients suffering from a variety of psychosomatic diseases. In *Proceedings of the 7th European Conference on Psychosomatic Research.* Basel: Karger.

Simon, R. (1982a). "Mara Selvini Palazzoli." *The Family Therapy Networker* 6(3):29–32.

Simon, R. (1982b). Behind the one-way mirror: An interview with Jay Haley. *The Family Therapy Networker* 6(5):18ff.

Singer, M.T. (1967). Family transactions and schizophrenia: I. Recent research findings. In *The Origins of Schizophrenia*, ed. J. Romano. Amsterdam: Excerpta Medica Foundation.

——— (1974). *Impact versus Diagnosis: A New Approach to Assessment Techniques in Family Research and Therapy.* Paper presented at the Nathan W. Ackerman Memorial Conference, Cumana, Venezuela, February.

——— (1977). The Rorschach as a transaction. In *Rorschach Psychology*, ed. M.A. Rickers-Ovsiankina. Melbourne, FL: Robert E. Krieger.

——— (1979). *The Origins of the Singer and Wynne Family Studies.* Lecture presented at VA Medical Center, San Francisco, October.

Singer, M.T. and Wynne, L.C. (1966). Principles for scoring communication defects and deviances in parents of schizophrenics: Rorschach and TAT scoring manuals. *Psychiatry* 29:260–288.

Speck, R. and Attneave, C. (1974). *Family Networks.* New York: Basic Books.

Speer, D.C. (1970). Family systems: Morphostasis and morphogenesis, or, is homeostasis enough? *Family Process* 9:259–278.

Spiegel, J.P. (1957). The resolution of role conflict within the family. *Psychiatry* 20:1–16.

Stanton, M.D., Todd, T.C., and Associates (1982). *The Family Therapy of Drug Abuse and Addition.* New York: Guilford Press.

Stern, P.N. (1978). Stepfather families: Integration around child discipline. *Issues in Mental Health Nursing* 1(2):50–56.

Sullivan, H.S. (1947). *Conceptions of Modern Psychiatry.* Washington, D.C.: William Alanson White Foundation.

––––––– (1953). *The Interpersonal Theory of Schizophrenia.* New York: Norton.

Tyrer, P., Candy, J., and Kelly, D. (1973). Phenelzine in phobic anxiety: A controlled trial. *Psychological Medicine* 3:120–124.

Vaillant, G.E. (1977). *Adaptation of Life.* Boston: Little, Brown.

Van Putten, T. and Emory, W.H. (1973). Traumatic neuroses in Vietnam returnees: A forgotten diagnosis? *Archives of General Psychiatry* 29:695–698.

Visher, E.B. and Visher, J.S. (1979). *Stepfamilies: A Guide to Working with Stepparents and Stepchildren.* New York: Brunner/Mazel.

von Neumann, J. and Morgenstern, O. (1953). *Theory of Games and Economic Behavior,* 3rd ed. New York: Wiley.

Walker, K.N. and Messinger, L. (1979). Remarriage after divorce: Dissolution and reconstruction of family boundaries. *Family Process* 18: 185–192.

Wallerstein, J.S. and Kelley, J.B. (1976). The effects of parental divorce: Experiences of the child in later latency. *American Journal of Orthopsychiatry* 46:256–269.

Watzlawick, P. (1981). Comments on Dell's paper. *Family Process* 20: 45–47.

––––––– (1982). Hermetic pragmaesthetics or unkept thoughts about an issue of *Family Process. Family Process* 21:401–403.

Watzlawick, P. and Coyne, J.C. (1980). Depression following stroke: Brief, problem-focused treatment. *Family Process* 19:13–18.

Watzlawick, P., Beavin, J.H., and Jackson, D. (1967). *Pragmatics of Human Communication.* New York: Norton.

Watzlawick, P., Weakland, J., and Fisch, R. (1974). *Change: Principles of Problem Resolution.* New York: Norton.

Weakland, J. (1974). "The double-bind theory" by self-reflexive hindsight. *Family Process* 13:269–277.

Weakland, J.H., Fisch, R., Watzlawick, P., and Bodin, A.M. (1974). Brief therapy: Focused problem resolution. *Family Process* 13:141–168.

Webster's Seventh New Collegiate Dictionary (1963). Springfield, MA: G. & C. Merriam.

Weeks, G.R. and L'Abate, L. (1982). *Paradoxical Psychotherapy: Theory and Practice with Individuals, Couples, and Families.* New York: Brunner/Mazel.

Weiner, N. (1948). *Cybernetics.* New York: Wiley.

Weltner, J.S. (1982). A structural approach to the single-parent family. *Family Process* 21:203–210.

Werner, H. (1948). *Comparative Psychology of Mental Development.* New York: International Universities Press.

Whitaker, C.A. (1976). A family is a four-dimensional relationship. In *Family Therapy: Theory and Practice*, ed. P.J. Guerin. New York: Gardner Press.

——— (1977). Process techniques of family therapy. *Interaction* 1(1):4–19.

——— (1979). *Reflections on Family Therapy.* Lecture presented at Don Jackson Memorial Conference, San Francisco, August.

——— (1982). Comments on Keeney and Sprenkle's paper. *Family Process* 21:405–406.

Whitaker, C.A. and Miller, M.H. (1969). A re-evaluation of psychiatric help when divorce impends. *American Journal of Psychiatry* 126:57–64.

Whitaker, C.A., Rose, J.W., Geiser, F.N., and Johnson, N. (1982). The role of silence in brief psychotherapy. In *From Psyche to System*, eds. J.R. Neill & D.P. Kniskern. New York: Guilford Press.

Whitehead, A.N. (1925). *Science and the Modern World.* New York: Macmillan.

Whitehead, A.N. and Russell, B. (1910). *Principia Mathematica.* Cambridge: Cambridge University Press.

Wilder, C. (1982). Muddles and metaphors: A response to Keeney and Sprenkle. *Family Process* 21:387–400.

Wynne, L.C. (1977). Schizophrenics and their families: Research on parental communication. In *Developments in Psychiatric Research*, ed. J.M. Tanner. London: Hodder & Stroughton.

Wynne, L.C., Rycoff, I.M., Day, J., and Hirsch, S.I. (1958). Pseudomutuality in the family relations of schizophrenics. *Psychiatry* 21: 205–220.

Wynne, L.C. and Singer, M.T. (1963). Thought disorder and family relations of schizophrenics: II. A classification of forms of thinking. *Archives of General Psychiatry* 9:199–206.

Yalom, I. (1975). *The Theory and Practice of Group Psychotherapy*, 2nd ed. New York: Basic Books.

Zeig, J.K. (ed.) (1982). *Ericksonian Approaches to Hypnosis and Psychotherapy.* New York: Brunner/Mazel.

Credits

The author is grateful for permission of the publishers to reprint material from the following sources:

American Psychiatric Association. *Diagnostic and Statistical Manual of Mental Disorders*, 3rd ed. Washington, D.C.: American Psychiatric Association, 1980.

Bateson, G. *Naven*, rev. ed. Stanford, CA: Stanford University Press, 1958.

Bateson, G. The cybernetics of self: A theory of alcoholism. *Psychiatry*, 1971, 34:1–18.

Bowen, M. A family concept of schizophrenia. In *The Etiology of Schizophrenia*, ed. D.D. Jackson. New York: Basic Books, 1960. Copyright 1960, Basic Books.

Bowen, M. *Family Therapy in Clinical Practice*. New York: Aronson, 1978.

Chance, P. After you hit a child you can't just get up and leave him; you are hooked to that kid. *Psychology Today*, 1974, 7(8):76–84. Copyright 1974, American Psychological Association.

Dell, P.F. Beyond homeostasis: Toward a concept of coherence. *Family Process*, 1982, 21:21–41.

Fromm-Reichmann, F. Notes on the development of treatment of schizophrenics by psychoanalytic psychotherapy. *Psychiatry*, 1948, 11:263–273.

Haley, J. Whither family therapy. *Family Process*, 1962, 1:69–100.

Haley, J. Editorial. *Family Process*, 1968, 7:1–6.

Haley, J. *Uncommon Therapy: The Psychiatric Techniques of Milton H. Erickson, M.D.* New York: Norton, 1973.

Hill, O.W. Psychogenic vomiting. *Gut*, 1968, 9:348–352. Reprinted by permission of the author and publisher.

Hogben, G.L. and Cornfield, R.B. Treatment of traumatic war neurosis with phenelzine. *Archives of General Psychiatry*, 1981, 38:440–445. Copyright 1981, American Medical Association.

Horowitz, M.J. Stress response syndromes: Character style and dynamic psychotherapy. *Archives of General Psychiatry*, 1974, 31:768–781. Copyright 1974, American Medical Association.

Jackson, D.D. (ed.). *Communication, Family, and Marriage: Human Communication*, vol. I. Palo Alto, CA: Science and Behavior Books, 1968. Reprinted by permission of the author and publisher.

Jackson, D.D. and Weakland, J. Schizophrenic symptoms and family interaction. *Archives of General Psychiatry*, 1959, 1:618–621. Copyright 1959, American Medical Association.

Keeney, B.P. and Sprenkle, D.H. Ecosystemic epistemology: Critical implications for the aesthetics and pragmatics of family therapy. *Family Process*, 1982, 21:1–19.

Lewis, J.M. The family matrix in health and disease. In *The Family: Evaluation and Treatment*, eds. C.K. Hofling and J.M. Lewis. New York: Brunner/Mazel, 1980.

Lidz, R.W. and Lidz, T. The family environment of schizophrenic patients. *American Journal of Psychiatry*, 1949, 106:332–345.

Lidz, T., Cornelison, A.R., Terry, D., and Fleck, S. The intrafamilial environment of the schizophrenic patient: VI. The transmission of irrationality. *Archives of Neurology and Psychiatry*, 1958, 79:305–316. Copyright 1958, American Medical Association.

Minuchin, S. and Fishman, H.C. *Family Therapy Techniques.* Cambridge, MA: Harvard University Press, 1981.

Minuchin, S., Rosman, B.L., and Baker, L. *Psychosomatic Families: Anorexia Nervosa in Context.* Cambridge, MA: Harvard University Press, 1978.

Rose, R.M., Bernstein, I.S., and Gordon, T.P. Consequences of social conflict on plasma testosterone levels in rhesus monkeys. *Psychosomatic Medicine*, 1975, 37:50–61. Copyright 1975, Elsevier Science Publishing Company. Reprinted by permission of the authors and publisher.

Schachter, S. *Emotion, Obesity, and Crime.* New York: Academic Press, 1971. Reprinted by permission of the author and publisher.

Singer, M.T. Family transactions and schizophrenia: I. Recent research findings. In *The Origins of Schizophrenia*, ed. J. Romano. Amsterdam: Excerpta Medica Foundation, 1967. Reprinted by permission of the author and publisher.

Singer, M.T. The Rorschach as a transaction. In *Rorschach Psychology*, ed. M.A. Rickers-Ovsiankina. Melbourne, FL: Robert E. Krieger, 1977.

Watzlawick, P., Weakland, J. and Fisch, R. *Change: Principles of Problem Resolution*. New York: Norton, 1974.

Weakland, J. "The double-bind theory" by self-reflexive hindsight. *Family Process*, 1974, 13:269–277.

Wynne, L.C., Rycoff, I.M., Day, J., and Hirsch, S.I. Pseudomutuality in the family relations of schizophrenics. *Psychiatry*, 1958, 21:205–220.

Index